Designing for Networked Communications:
Strategies and Development

Simon B. Heilesen
Roskilde University, Denmark

Sisse Siggaard Jensen
Roskilde University, Denmark

IDEA GROUP PUBLISHING

Hershey • London • Melbourne • Singapore

Acquisitions Editor:	Kristin Klinger
Development Editor:	Kristin Roth
Senior Managing Editor:	Jennifer Neidig
Managing Editor:	Sara Reed
Assistant Managing Editor:	Sharon Berger
Copy Editor:	Amanda Appicello
Typesetter:	Amanda Appicello
Cover Design:	Lisa Tosheff
Printed at:	Integrated Book Technology

Published in the United States of America by
Idea Group Publishing (an imprint of Idea Group Inc.)
701 E. Chocolate Avenue, Suite 200
Hershey PA 17033-1240
Tel: 717-533-8845
Fax: 717-533-8661
E-mail: cust@idea-group.com
Web site: http://www.idea-group.com

and in the United Kingdom by
Idea Group Publishing (an imprint of Idea Group Inc.)
3 Henrietta Street
Covent Garden
London WC2E 8LU
Tel: 44 20 7240 0856
Fax: 44 20 7379 0609
Web site: http://www.eurospanonline.com

Library of Congress Cataloging-in-Publication Data

Designing for networked communications : strategies and development / Simon B. Heilesen and Sisse Siggaard Jensen, editors.
    p. cm.
  Summary: "This book explains how to plan, use, and understand the products and dynamic social processes and tasks some of the most vital innovations in the knowledge society depend upon- social as well as technological. It Focuses on various forms of design, implementation and integration of computer mediated communication, bridging the academic fields of computer science and communication studies"--Provided by publisher.
  Includes bibliographical references and index.
  ISBN 1-59904-069-7 (hardcover) -- ISBN 1-59904-070-0 (softcover) -- ISBN 1-59904-071-9 (ebook)
  1. Local area networks (Computer networks) I. Heilesen, Simon B. II. Jensen, Sisse Siggaard, 1951-
TK5105.7.D49 2007
004.6'8--dc22
                                        2006033747
British Cataloguing in Publication Data
A Cataloguing in Publication record for this book is available from the British Library.

All work contributed to this book is new, previously-unpublished material. The views expressed in this book are those of the authors, but not necessarily of the publisher.

Designing for Networked Communications:
Strategies and Development

Table of Contents

Preface

Designing for Networked Communications: Strategies and Development is a book about how we plan, use, and understand the products, dynamic social processes, and tasks upon which depend some of the most vital innovations in the knowledge society—social as well as technological ones. Focusing on various forms of design, implementation, and integration of computer-mediated communication (CMC), the book bridges the academic fields of computer science and communication studies. In this way, an interdisciplinary approach allows us to substantiate the overall argument of this book: The successful designing, integration, and adaptation of networked communications must involve users and actors at all stages of the development process, from the first outline of a strategy for the designing of systems and artefacts to the manner in which they are finally integrated and merged with existing practices, technologies, and media.

Managing complex processes such as these requires the development of strategies that will take into account some of the problems and processes, which can be anticipated. As will be demonstrated repeatedly in the chapters to follow, it is essential to further our understanding of such processes by identifying strategies employed by both developers and users in the dynamic processes of creating and using artefacts and systems. This book contributes substantially to answering some of the questions that arise from such *challenges*, as it presents the findings from well-documented research projects and in-depth studies of organizational work practices and learning environments.

The Challenges

Networked communications are proliferating. Today, not only are existing mediated forms of communication being remediated in electronic form (Bolter & Grusin, 1999), but also hitherto direct forms of communication in complicated social settings are being supplemented or even replaced by computer-mediated communication (CMC). We have come to depend on CMC products. As a result, the way they function and the way we use them inevitably influence or even determine how we communicate and how we think about communication. Thus, the continuous designing, integration, and adaptation of systems and artefacts in support of networked communications has already brought about profound changes in the everyday life of communities and organizations. This is particularly pronounced if the organized activities of such units depend on knowledge intensive work and learning.

In the present volume, several chapters present research results that substantiate the notion that such changes in our ways of communicating often bring about various difficulties and barriers. This is especially so, if the introduction of new communication systems is technology-centered and conceived of as an end in itself—meaning that users and actors are not involved in the process, even if they are required to put the systems into practice. If no urgent demand for technological innovation is experienced, and if the benefits of rearranging existing work practices are not evident, then such changes may make no sense to the users and actors. Even worse, if the early phases of introducing new artefacts and systems make existing work practices more difficult, then strain is added to a workday that often is already stressful. At the time of writing, a number of these problems have been identified (Kyng & Mathiassen, 1997), and they are becoming well documented through research that is conducted partly in parallel to research in the area of general technology studies (Czarniawska & Hernes, 2005; Engeström, 2005).

Although similarities between production technology and networked communication systems are evident, so too are differences. Very often, technologies and systems, brought into practice in support of human communications, are treated in much the same ways as production technologies (Moran & Dourish, 2001). However, the difference is striking although surprisingly unnoticed. According to the still-prevailing sender-receiver conception of communication, networked communications are said to rationalize and inform work practices; virtual organizing and virtual teams may replace existing collaborative practices and traditions; information and communication practices are modelled as if they were infrastructures; communication and information flows are charted and depicted in terms of input/output systems; and signals are being "sent"—almost like information package deliveries (Dervin & Foreman-Wernet, 2003).

If one accepts such understandings, it may well come as a surprise when human communication actually works quite differently from what was anticipated. It seems that production does have the capacity to rationalize, replace, and reproduce.

Communication technologies, on the other hand, are apt to produce even more communication. Networked communications systems and technologies produce rather than replace communication, increase rather than rationalize, and reorganize and transform rather than reproduce. If one is strategizing without taking into consideration such differences, then it will come as a surprise that virtual universities, distributed virtual organizations, globally "located" enterprises and businesses face serious problems due to the confining "production-technology" conceptions of human communication practices (Dourish, Grinter, Dalal, Delgado de la Flor, & Joseph, 2003).

New technologies and new media generally attract attention, in both popular *litany* and in reflected *systemic* understanding of technological and social development (Inayatullah, 2002, 2003); they almost invariably are assumed to represent improvements. Thus, when brought into practice with a one-sided focus on what is new, they tend to overshadow "old" ways of communicating. Thorough studies of organizational work practices, however, show us that the use of new technologies and media is best understood and integrated into work practices if regarded as a complexity of interplays or *assemblages* (Latour, 2005) merging new and older media. In this process of merging, they are both remodeled and rearranged while being adapted to the practices and activities that they were designed for. The interplay between old and new technologies and media is, therefore, an important aspect to be taken into consideration by designing strategies.

In line with this notion of assemblage in the implementation and integration of tools for networked communications, the actual *designing* of such products may be understood as a cycle, where tasks require the creation of systems and artefacts, and where these in turn condition modifications of tasks (Carroll, Kellogg, & Rosson, 1991). The contributors to the present volume share the basic premise that the processes of designing and adapting must involve the active participation of the eventual users of communication systems.

To illustrate the breadth and complexity of the subject, we have chosen to understand the concept of *designing* in a broad sense covering both development and strategies, namely as: (1) the underlying scheme for the planning, functioning, and development of an artefact; (2) the actual arrangement and functionality of various elements of the artefact; (3) the development of strategies and adaptations required for performing tasks by means of the artefact in the given social context and subject to certain basic conditions; and (4) the development of creative strategies for social innovation and the identification of new tasks to be performed by means of a redesign of existing artefacts or with new artefacts.

Similarly, the complementary components of designing, for example, tasks and artefacts, are to be understood in an inclusive sense. The *tasks* discussed in the chapters of this book can either be interactive processes of communication between individuals by means of computer or telenetworks (within and across organizations) or the dissemination of information from a sender to a target group. The *artefacts* range from a macro- to a micro-level, including networks, software, instantiations of systems, organizational frameworks, files, and even actual symbols being manipulated in the act of communicating.

On these pages, as in some of our earlier writings (Heilesen & Jensen, 2006), we may have introduced a slightly pessimistic view of the current state of designing for networked communications. Too often, it seems, the challenges of developing networked communications are underestimated or even misunderstood. But, of course, it should be recognized that this is a very recent and rapidly developing field in which the all-embracing and conclusive answers have yet to be devised. There are, however, a great many good beginnings, and we are happy to be able to present a fine sample of them in the present volume.

Organization of the Book

The book chapters are organized on the basis of three underlying themes:

- Organizational aspects and practices;
- Designing methods and principles; and
- Development of social conventions and interactions.

In 12 chapters, the authors of the book explore different instantiations of these themes, reflecting on the two complementary aspects, namely *strategies* and *development*. Although the importance and focus attached to these two aspects and three main themes do vary from chapter to chapter, we have decided not to organize the book into two, three or even six sections. Although you will certainly notice a progression from the first to the third theme as you read the book, we find it most natural not to impose too strict boundaries on the various themes and aspects. If we were to do so, we would obscure the fact that in most of the chapters more than one theme and aspect are in fact developed. This "overlapping" of themes and aspects only goes to illustrate the dynamic interrelations between organizing practices, methods of designing, and the influence of networked communications on human communication, conventions, and social interactions.

Below follows a brief description of each of the chapters:

Hanne Westh Nicolajsen and Jørgen P. Bansler, in Chapter I, *Evolving Information Ecologies: The Appropriation of New Media in Organizations*, examine how people in organizations appropriate new computer-based media, that is, how they adopt, reconfigure, and integrate advanced communication technologies such as groupware or desktop conferencing systems into their work practice. Prior empirical studies of the introduction of new computer-based media in organizations have shown that appropriation and sustained use is often difficult to achieve. The chapter presents and analyzes findings from an in-depth field study of the adoption and use of a Web-based groupware application—a "virtual workspace"—in a large multinational firm. This study focuses on the fact that people in modern organizations have plenty of media at their disposal and often combine old and new media to accomplish their work tasks by adapting current genres and creating working configurations or assemblages of media with complementary affordances. Thus, the crucial role of organizational communication genres in shaping how people adopt and use new media is highlighted. The authors argue that understanding and facilitating the process of appropriation is the key to successful introduction of new media in organizations. The users of technology must play an essential role in this process because they have an intimate knowledge of the local needs and circumstances, and they are the ones who are required to change their behaviour and adjust to new technology. However, the enrollment of users and their active participation requires the necessary time to take part; users must be allowed to "play around" and experiment; and they must be provided with ongoing support and resources. This can, be organized, for instance, by creating a new position as *gardener* or *mediator*.

In Chapter II, *Incompleteness and Unpredictability of Networked Communications in Use*, Dixi Louise Strand explores the use practices of a Web-based information system in large, distributed pharmaceutical development projects. This study highlights the process in which the system in question is held together, extended, and transformed into a working system for pharmaceutical projects. Assemblage is proposed as a productive concept in making visible the particularities of networked communications, their malleability, and the way in which they evolve in use through extensions, interferences, and unpredictable circumstances. The author presents an understanding of networked communications in use and consequently draws implications for further development strategies for such technologies. Thinking about the evolving use of Web-based information systems as a practiced assembly can thus turn our focus to the practices in which skills, demands, resistances and problems, and benefits emerge and how they may differ from one place and time to the next. The author argues that the concept and themes proposed provide an antidote to existing studies and a tendency toward being overly concerned with explaining use patterns through structures or depicting use as a matter of human resistance to fixed technological characteristics embedded by designers. The examples presented in this chapter emphasize the importance of continual user support and training and suggest that existing experiences and experimentation might be incorporated in multiple cycles of professional redesign.

Chapter III, *Strategies for Organizational Implementation of Networked Communication in Distributed Organizations*, written by Keld Bødker, Jens Kaaber Pors, and Jesper Simonsen, presents the results from a longitudinal case study of the use and implementation of a virtual workspace product used to support communication in a large distributed organization. The authors observe how implementation contexts are quite diverse, and they identify six factors important for understanding the implementation of CMC technologies: management position and role, administration, membership, evaluation and redesign, work practice integration, and dependency. Combining two recent models for change management, the authors identify three types of typical changes—anticipated, emergent, and opportunity-based—at an organization/infrastructure level and a work group level. Relating change management models to the findings from the empirical study, the authors synthesize implementation strategies on the premise that the levels identified are mutually interdependent. The authors conclude that the particular characteristics of technologies for networked communication cause successive changes, including configuration and re-configuration of the technology used in local organizational contexts. In this light, the options for organizational implementation are further operationalized by identifying challenges, immediate expectations, and aims, as well as strategies to stimulate change beyond the immediate effects of implementing CMC technology.

In Chapter IV, *Participatory Design and Creativity in Development of Information and Communication Technologies*, Nette Schultz, Lene Sørensen, and Dan Saugstrup present a new framework for user-centered designing of ICT products. The basic idea is to involve users at an early stage in the process of developing ICT products. The methods developed for this purpose combine principles for participatory design, focusing on human values and team work, with creativity techniques such as brainstorming, picture simulation, and the setting-up of a creative environment. Creating scenarios to serve as the basis for communication between system designers and users, the authors implement such creative environments in the form of a sequence of design workshops, conducted for creative users and experts, respectively. Both kinds of workshops are observed to be helpful in generating ideas and in stimulating the creation of a shared design language, bridging the gap between the user focus and the technical focus typically to be found in development projects. In addition, the framework of expert workshops also helps to create the team atmosphere that is highly important to large ICT projects. The framework is applied and discussed using the case of the MAGNET mobile communication development project (My personal Adaptive Global Net).

In Chapter V, *Information and Function Chunks as Building Blocks in the Control Room of Life*, Georg Strøm proposes a new way of ordering and presenting information on the computer. His premise is that we continue to organize information on the Internet in much the same way as we did when information was distributed only on paper. As a one-time specialist in designing control systems for telecommunications networks, he notes that the situation of the Internet user, running several applications simultaneously on a complex and highly-dynamic network where changes occur constantly, is not that different from that of the control room operator who has to supervise several pieces of equipment and react instantly to changes. Both types of users need to organize information in a flexible way so as to reduce both the cognitive load and the effort required for dealing with information. As a possible way to reach such a goal, Strøm proposes five design principles that are likely to help facilitate user interaction with net-based systems: (1) informing the user of all changes that may affect him or her; (2) dividing information and functions into chunks representing the smallest possible units of meaning; (3) automatic synchronization of navigation and parameters in the different chunks; (4) using views to give users access to chunks that are relevant to a particular task or in a particular situation; and (5) facilitating the pushing or pulling of a view from one terminal to another where it is needed. Strøm concludes that, while it is technically feasible to implement these principles, the heterogeneity of the existing networks, considerations of compatibility, and market forces offer practical obstacles.

Simon B. Heilesen, in Chapter VI, *A Short History of Designing for Communication on the Web*, establishes that Web design is important for how we communicate on the Internet, and also how it has an effect on computer interface design in general. In this chapter, the author examines the development and history of Web design as a prerequisite for understanding what it has become today. The history of Web design is outlined in terms of the complex interplay of various social, cultural, economic, technological, and communicative factors, and the outline concludes with the presentation of a framework for Web design. The author suggests that Web design may be facing major changes as the requirements of users and the technologies employed to meet them are changing. The chapter concludes by offering some reflections on the future of Web design. As the Web has become all-embracing, some conventions—and genres—have emerged, on one hand, making it possible for the trained user to recognize quickly the look and feel of common types of Web sites such as the corporate Web site, the news site, the fashion site, the e-commerce site, and so forth. On the other hand, the advent of Web logs, wikis, and similar social software are blurring the distinction traditionally made between Web publishing and computer-mediated communication, thus challenging the notion that Web design is something unique. Furthermore, the author concludes that we are just witnessing the early stages of pervasive, wireless networked computing, where Internet access will be integrated in all kinds of electronic devices. This development seriously challenges the conventions of Web design that have been developed in the first decade or two of the WWW era.

In Chapter VII, *Fostering Innovation in Networked Communication: Test and Experimentation Platforms for Broadband Systems*, Pieter Ballon, Jo Pierson, and Simon Delaere pose the question of how to foster innovation in networked communications by setting up broadband environments for joint testing and experimenting. The authors identify six types of test and experimentation platforms (TEPs): testbeds, field trials, prototyping platforms, living labs, market pilots, and societal pilots. The typology of TEPs is matched with the characteristics of real-life TEPs in three European benchmark countries, that is, Finland, The Netherlands, and the United Kingdom. By constructing this conceptual framework, the authors suggest that the creation of open platforms should further the interplay between business actors, helping to tackle the systemic failures associated with broadband innovation. The authors argue that the strategic relevance of TEPs lies in the extent that networked communications are made possible between various public and private stakeholders—including users; in the establishment of a trusted setting that resembles real-life situations; and in supporting non-linear, mutual shaping innovation processes with semi-mature technology. The notion of networked communications is closely linked to many of the characteristics for differentiating TEPs. This refers to: the openness in results and partnerships, the objective of open innovation activities, the stakeholder involvement (technology producers, service providers, professional users, and/or private users), the real-life organizational setting, and the involvement of "medium immature" technology.

Based on their work at Coventry University in implementing a university-wide strategy of rolling out a learning environment, Frances Deepwell and Kathy Courtney in Chapter VIII, *Envisioning Potential: Stories of Networked Learning Designs from a UK University*, explore the ways in which new understandings of the potential of technologies in higher education may be developed and shared within communities within an organization. As well as emphasizing the importance of community-building and the creation of communities of practice in a networked learning implementation, a particular focus of the chapter is the way in which the design of artefacts and processes can enable these shared understandings of new technologies to spread within a complex, organizational context. The authors draw on their experiences of the managed introduction of the Web-based virtual learning environment, WebCT®, and apply techniques of narrative inquiry to aid their understanding. Deepwell and Courtney have explored the narrative accounts in terms of an overarching theme of "building shared understandings" which they have organized around three areas of their experience, namely designing for a community, developing a discourse, and developing artefacts. They argue that design decisions in these three areas have been highly significant in terms of the levels of acceptance and future direction of an online learning implementation.

In Chapter IX, *Reflective Designing for Actors and Avatars in Virtual Worlds*, Sisse Siggaard Jensen proposes a *virtual 3D exploratories* designing strategy by which to facilitate knowledge sharing and social innovation in organizations and work groups. The strategy will allow users to build virtual worlds aimed at exploration, and to interact and communicate with one another by means of avatars. To substantiate the designing strategy, the chapter discusses virtual phenomena such as avatar-based interaction and communication, and scenarios designed for reflective practices. As an empirical background, this chapter presents narratives and video-based self-observations from 12 experiential sessions undertaken as part of the international EQUEL research project involving the construction of a *Virtual 3D Agora-world*. The findings from the Agora-world sessions indicate that problems seem to arise in a process of remediation. With reference to her findings and a comparison with some of the general features of multi-user online role-playing games, the author observes that, first, a reflective designing strategy should emphasize the differences between virtual and real-world framings to challenge existing ideas, notions, practices, expectations, and strategies. Second, that in communicating and interacting with avatars, actors also need a well-known framing in support of their activity. To address these challenges, and inspired by Brenda Dervin's "sense-making triangle", Jensen introduces a "designing triangle of exploratories" meant to serve as a thinking tool for the designing of virtual worlds for organizational knowledge sharing and social innovation.

Torkil Clemmensen, in Chapter X, *The Psychology of Online Sociability: Theory and Examples*, reviews current approaches to online sociability and presents the psychological *social reality theory* of online sociability while focusing implicitly on cultural models. The social reality theory is exemplified by analyzing sociability in a university-level, virtual world course. The author examines the question of how to understand the students' design of conditions for sociability as a communication of cultural symbols, such as avatars and virtual landscapes, and the social reality of perceived groups of people. The results from the analysis illustrate different kinds of online sociability: superficial, convivial, and negative sociability. The author concludes that the experience of sociability is an outcome of complex and culture-specific structures and processes. In practice, this means that planning the sociability of both products and dynamic social processes in a knowledge-creating context, such as a university course, only constitutes half of the design for networked communications; the other half involves understanding how people with different cultural backgrounds actually use the processes and products. Finally, the chapter provides solutions and recommendations to designers and researchers emphasizing that we need to understand different cultural practices in terms of cultural models for classroom performance, romance or flirt, collective movements, and so forth, both offline and online to design and support human forms of online sociability.

Jørgen Skågeby, in Chapter XI, *Designing Control of Computer-Mediated Gifting in Sharing Networks*, addresses the number of domains where sharing technology increasingly has come into use: open source software development, health care, self-fulfilling leisure activities, social networking, teaching, and research. It is argued that not only conversation-driven communication is of importance to end users, as the networked gifting of digital material indicates. The pro-social provision, or gifting, of goods in multiple user sharing networks is largely determined by the relationship that an individual has to the larger group(s) of which he or she is a member. This relationship can be both a conflict of interest and a pattern of cooperation reflecting a predicament of acting in self interest versus in the interest of the collective. The author outlines the relationship model to be used as a relatively stable determinant of types of gifting acts, and five dimensions of control are also introduced. Modeled in this way, the dynamics of sharing networks make gifting a continuous re-negotiation between reactive actions and overall tactics. The author claims that the benefits of studying and designing for gifting are several: it can help managers in supporting and sustaining communities; it provides designers and developers of services with a well-researched foundation for the design of digital gifting; it creates transferable design conclusions to be used within domains with commercial or utility-based interests; and it makes service providers able to distinguish and evolve their services.

Finally, extending networked communication to include telecommunications (which are rapidly converging with computer-mediated communication), Louise Barkhuus, in Chapter XII, *Mobile Networked Text Communication: The Case of SMS and Its Influence on Social Interaction*, presents a qualitative study of the use among young adults of mobile text messaging (SMS). Based on a case study and drawing on the available literature on the social impact of mobile telephony, she discusses what effects the SMS technology has on social interaction. Focusing on how this new communication technology helps overcome shyness, how it is used for micro-grooming, and how it can be controlled by the user, the author illustrates how SMS helps maintain social relations and assists users in their activities. The author argues that SMS facilitates users in their everyday life through the ways it supports awareness and accountability, characteristics that make the technology socially translucent in much the same way as is the case with richer media. She concludes that simple information and communication technologies such as SMS may provide powerful tools in new designs of information and communication technologies.

Simon B. Heilesen & Sisse Siggaard Jensen

References

Bolter, J. D., & Grusin, R. A. (1999). *Remediation: Understanding new media.* Cambridge, MA: MIT Press.

Carroll, J. M., Kellogg, W. A., & Rosson, M. B. (1991). The task-artefact cycle. In J. M. Carroll (Ed.), *Designing interaction: Psychology at the human-computer interface* (pp. 74-102). Cambridge, UK: Cambridge University Press.

Czarniawska, B., & Hernes, T. (2005). *Actor-network theory and organizing.* Copenhagen: Copenhagen Business School Press.

Dervin, B., & Foreman-Wernet, L. (2003). *Sense-making methodology reader.* New Jersey: Hampton Press, Inc.

Dourish, P., Grinter, R., Dalal, B., Delgado de la Flor, J., & Joseph, M. (2003). *Security day-to-day: User strategies for managing security as a practical, everyday problem.* Technical Report UCI-ISR-03-5, UCI Institute for Software Research, Irvine, CA.

Engeström, Y. (2005). *Developmental work research. Expanding activity theory in practice.* Berlin: Lehmanns Media.

Heilesen, S. B., & Jensen, S. S. (2006). Making sense of technologically enhanced learning in context – A research agenda. In E. Sorensen, & D. Ó. Murchú (Eds.), *Enhancing technologically enhanced learning* (pp. 269-291). Hershey, PA: Information Science Publishing.

Inayatullah, S. (2002). Layered methodology: Meanings, epistemes and the politics of knowledge. *Futures, 34*(6), 479-491.

Inayatullah, S. (2003). Causal layered analysis: Unveiling and transforming the future. In J. C. Glenn (Ed.), *Futures research methodology* (CD-ROM). Washington D.C.: The American Council for the United Nations University.

Kyng, M., & Mathiassen, L. (Eds.) (1997). *Computers and design in context*. Cambridge, MA: MIT Press.

Latour, B. (2005). *Reassembling the social. An introduction to actor-network theory*. Oxford: Oxford University Press.

Moran, T., & Dourish, P. (2001). Introduction to the special issue on context-aware computing. *Human Computer Interaction, 16*(2-3), 87-95.

Acknowledgments

The editors would like to acknowledge the many people who have made this book possible. For us, and hopefully for all those involved, this has been an intense, rewarding, and highly successful practical experience in networked communications across countries and continents. First and foremost, we would like to thank the authors of the individual chapters for sharing their valuable insights in the important field of networked communications and for their disciplined and dedicated work throughout the many stages of planning, writing, and editing the book. Most of the authors of the chapters included in this volume also have served as referees for articles written by other authors. In addition, some of our colleagues at Roskilde University have served as referees. Thanks go to all those who have provided highly competent, constructive, and comprehensive reviews.

A special note of thanks goes to Ms. Kristin Roth of Idea Group Inc., whose timely and encouraging contributions throughout the whole work process have been extremely valuable. Also, special thanks to Mr. Andrew Somerville for correcting the language of a number of the chapters. Our gratitude also goes to the head of the Roskilde University Department of Communication, Professor Kim Christian Schrøder, for providing extra funds for proof reading.

Finally, we would like to thank our spouses, Lise and Søren, for their patience, support, and love throughout the long and sometimes stressful process of moving our project forward from initial idea to printed book.

Simon B. Heilesen and Sisse Siggaard Jensen,
Roskilde, Denmark
June 2006

Chapter I

Evolving Information Ecologies:
The Appropriation of New Media in Organizations

Hanne Westh Nicolajsen
Technical University of Denmark, Denmark

Jørgen P. Bansler
Technical University of Denmark, Denmark

Abstract

This chapter examines how people in organizations appropriate new computer-based media, that is, how they adopt, reconfigure, and integrate advanced communication technologies such as groupware or desktop conferencing systems into their work practice. The chapter presents and analyzes findings from an in-depth field study of the adoption and use of a Web-based groupware application—a "virtual workspace"—in a large multinational firm. The analysis focuses, in particular, on the fact that people in modern organizations have plenty of media at their disposal and often combine old and new media to accomplish their work tasks. Furthermore, it highlights the crucial role of organizational communication genres in shaping how people adopt and use new media. The authors argue that understanding and facilitating the process of appropriation is the key to the successful introduction of new media in organizations.

Introduction

This chapter provides an account of how people in organizations adopt new computer-mediated communication (CMC) technologies and incorporate them into their working practices. It focuses specifically on how people fit the new media together with their existing communication technologies, creating a configuration of media that matches their communication needs. The current proliferation of new computer-based media such as chat, SMS, instant messaging, desktop conferencing, virtual workspaces, and MOO-based meeting technologies (see, e.g., Yoshioka, Yates, & Orlikowski, 2002) exacerbates the challenges associated with establishing and maintaining appropriate configurations of media in the workplace. Although the potential for developing very effective patterns of media use is high, given the large number of diverse technologies to choose from, there is also a significant risk that the outcome will be messy and inefficient.

It is well documented that established organizational communication genres influence how individuals and groups adopt and use new CMC technologies (Crowston & Williams, 2000; Orlikowski & Yates, 1994; Yates, Orlikowski, & Okamura, 1999). Genres, as conventions for social interaction, both shape and are shaped by organizational members' communicative practices. When new communication media are introduced in the organization, existing genres provide people with a resource that they can draw on in their efforts to incorporate the new technology into their daily work practice. In doing so, they not only reproduce but also redefine their existing repertoire of genres.

We address these issues based on an analysis of a longitudinal field study of the adoption and use of a Web-based groupware application in a large multinational company. The analysis employs insights and concepts from two strands of research on electronic communication in organizations. The first strand is concerned with understanding the "affordances" (i.e., the distinctive communicative properties, see the next section) of different communication technologies and how these affordances affect the process, content, or outcome of communication (see, e.g., Whittaker, 2003, for an overview). The second strand comprises an emergent body of work on organizational communication genres (e.g., Grimshaw, 2003; Yates & Orlikowski, 1992; Yates et al., 1999). This research explores the complex interrelations between media and genres and sheds light on how genres evolve over time as new technologies are introduced.

Theoretical Background

Technology appropriation is the process by which people in organizations adopt, reconfigure, and integrate new technologies into their work practice (Dourish, 2003).

This involves not only adapting or "customizing" the technology to suit local needs and requirements, but also devising appropriate ways of using the technology for one's own, particular purposes. As Dourish (2003) points out, understanding how people appropriate new CMC technologies is a "key problem" for both researchers and practitioners, "since it is critical to the success of technology deployment" (p. 465).

Attempts to introduce new CMC technologies in organizations often fail because managers and technologists underestimate the time and effort it takes successfully to appropriate and incorporate a new communication medium into the existing "information ecology," that is, the system of people, practices, genres, and information and communication technologies in the local environment. Appropriation is difficult to achieve because information ecologies are diverse, continually evolving, and "marked by strong interrelationships and dependencies among [the] different parts" (Nardi & O'Day, 1999, p. 51). For instance, communication media, genre repertoires (that is, the set of genres in use within a community [Orlikowski & Yates, 1994]), and local work practices are interrelated and fit together in complex and subtle ways.

Change in an ecology is systemic and difficult to predict (Nardi & O'Day, 1999). Changing one element sometimes can have self-reinforcing effects that can be felt throughout the whole system, but in other instances, if the changes are incompatible with the rest of the system, they may disappear without a trace. For instance, studies have shown that, when a new electronic medium is introduced in an organization, it sometimes transforms the entire organization and the ways in which work is conducted (see, e.g., Sproull & Kiesler, 1991), whereas in other cases it may have only marginal impact or fail completely, because people stick to their old familiar media and habitual modes of communication (see, e.g., Ciborra, 1996; Mark, 2002).

The ecology metaphor draws attention to the fact that no communication medium exists in the workplace in isolation. When introduced in an organization, a new communication medium must "compete" with existing media, either displacing one or more existing technologies (such as telephone and fax have done to the telegraph) or fitting into a niche that can ensure its "survival" alongside the existing media. In other words, potential users must perceive the new technology as reliable and useful, and they must be both willing and able to adjust their work practices and communication patterns to exploit the new opportunities afforded by the technology.

Despite its practical importance, there has not been much research into how new media are appropriated in organizations and the process is not yet well understood. The fundamental goal of research in computer-mediated communication "has been to explain the relationship between the affordances of different mediated technologies and the communication that results from using those technologies" (Whittaker, 2003, p. 244), rather than to understand how people in real work settings combine different media and use them in complementary ways to accomplish their tasks. Although CMC research has used a variety of methods (e.g., interviews, surveys, and ethnographic studies), the bulk of the available data on the use of electronic media comes from "laboratory studies where users are given predefined technologies, tasks, and instructions" (Whittaker, 2003, p. 248). These studies leave out important aspects of "real life" media use in organizations—for instance, how people use different media in combination with each other or how communication genres and conventions of use develop when the technology is used by a community for extended periods of time.

In the following, we expand upon the concepts of *affordances* and *organizational communication genres* and use them to explain important aspects of technology appropriation.

Technology Affordances

Most advanced CMC technologies are flexible, generic media, which can support a wide variety of possible communication patterns. However, despite their inherent flexibility and open-endedness, these electronic media have a constraining as well as enabling materiality. For example, e-mail and chat convey only text (linguistic information), whereas videoconferencing provides a combination of speech (linguistic information) and images (visual information).

In other words, different CMC technologies possess different affordances[1] (Hutchby, 2001a), that is, they offer different possibilities for action, and these affordances "constrain both the possible meanings and the possible uses of the technologies" (p. 447):

> ... *affordances are functional and relational aspects which frame, while not determining, the possibilities for agentic action in relation to an object. In this way technologies can be understood as artefacts which may be both shaped by and shaping of the practices of human use in interaction with, around and through them.* (Hutchby, 2001a, p. 444)

As Hutchby points out, the affordances of a technological artifact are not just functional but also relational aspects of its materiality. Affordances are *functional* in the sense that they facilitate certain actions: for instance, using a calculator to compute a number or using a fax to communicate across distance. However, affordances may differ from person to person and from context to context, and in that sense they are *relational*. For instance, a PC with a compiler has the affordance of programmability, but only if you are a skilled programmer and know the appropriate programming language (and only if you have access to appropriate input-output devices, a stable power supply, and so on). Similarly, an advanced, digital camera has different affordances for a novice and a professional photographer.

The full range of affordances of any technology cannot be perceived immediately, for two reasons. First, as just mentioned, the affordances depend on the user and the context. The possibilities that a technology affords, therefore, will only be revealed through actual use and, in many cases, only after extended periods of time in which people gain hands-on experience with the technology and learn how to utilize it. Second, the affordances may change over time as the context evolves and users develop their competence and skills. The technology's affordances exist regardless of whether people exploit them or not, but they only become manifest when people act in terms of them.

Although—in their effort to accommodate certain imagined communicative purposes and use patterns—designers deliberately design specific features into the technology, they are unable to control, or even fully grasp, the entire range of the technology's communicative affordances (Hutchby, 2001b). The result is that designers are often taken aback by the way people "tamper with" their designs and make use of them for quite novel and unintended purposes.

Conventions and Genres

Social conventions are essential for governing communication and guiding the use of communication media. There are, for instance, widespread social conventions about the use of one medium rather than another for specific purposes (e.g., you do not send your condolences to a bereaved person by e-mail or SMS).

When a new communication medium is introduced in an organization, people need to develop appropriate conventions for when and how to use it. As Mark (2002) recently has pointed out, people cannot just be given a new CMC technology (e.g., a groupware system) and "be expected to optimally use it without some common agreements on the means of operation" (p. 351). Rather, conventions must evolve to regulate behavior so as to provide a "*modus vivendi* for making interactions proceed smoothly" (p. 351)—and if such conventions fail to develop, the technology will fail too.

In the context of computer-mediated communication, *genres* constitute a particularly important type of conventions. Organizational communication genres—such as the business letter, meeting minutes, or project plan—are social conventions that both structure and are structured by people's communicative practices. Genres are important because they help people make sense of interactions and guide them both in how to communicate and how to interpret the communicative actions of others.

Orlikowski and Yates (1994) have defined genres as "distinctive type[s] of communicative action, characterized by a socially recognized communicative purpose and common aspects of form" (p. 543). Genres—like technology affordances—both enable and constrain action without determining it:

A genre established within a particular community serves as an institutionalized template for social interaction—an organizing structure—that influences the on-going communicative action of members through their use of it within and across their community. Genres as organizing structures shape, but do not determine, how community members engage in everyday interaction. (Yates & Orlikowski, 2002, p. 15)

Genres are produced, reproduced, or changed through the everyday communicative practices of people. That is, even though genres structure the communicative actions, they are not fixed, unchangeable. On the contrary, when engaging in communication and enacting established genres, people sometimes advertently or inadvertently challenge and modify elements of existing genre rules (Yates & Orlikowski, 1992). These modifications may be triggered by social or technological changes in the organizational context, for instance, by the introduction of a new electronic communication medium, which possesses new affordances and thus offers new opportunities for action. For example, Crowston and Williams (2000) have shown that the World Wide Web has led to the emergence of new genres that exploit the features of hypermedia linking provided by the Web technology.

What typically happens when a new communication medium is introduced in an organization is that people draw on existing genres in their efforts to make sense of the medium and to figure out how to use it (Orlikowski & Yates, 1994; Yates & Orlikowski, 1992; Yates et al., 1999). In many instances, and especially in the beginning, they simply reproduce familiar genres in the new medium, adapting them slightly to fit the technology, but without substantially departing from the existing genre rules. However, over time, as people learn more about the new technology's affordances and introduce more significant changes and modifications to the established genre rules, new genres may emerge.

Yates et al. (1999) suggest that these "processes of genre structuring are ongoing, and do not just occur at the initial implementation of the new medium" (p. 96). They distinguish between implicit and explicit genre structuring. *Implicit structuring* comprises the unreflective and unintentional shaping of genres and communicative practices, which take place through people's mundane, day-to-day interactions, for example, when familiar genres inadvertently spread from one medium or community to another. Two types of implicit structuring can be identified, namely migration and variation (see Table 1). Migration is the transfer of established genres from one medium or community to another, while variation denotes a change in existing genres that emerges tacitly from use of the technology over time. *Explicit structuring* applies when individuals or groups deliberately try to either reinforce or change established patterns of communication, for example, by adapting existing genres to the new medium. Explicit structuring includes planned replication, planned modification, and opportunistic modification (see Table 1). Planned replication aims to reproduce existing genres within a new medium with minimal changes. In contrast,

Table 1. Processes of genres structuring (based on Yates et al., 1999)

	Implicit structuring	**Explicit structuring**
Reproduction of genre rules	Migration	Planned replication
Change of genre rules	Variation	Planned modification Opportunistic modification

planned modification aims to alter the genres rules, for instance, by changing the purpose and the intended audience or readership. The last type, opportunistic modification, "involves purposeful changes introduced in response to some unexpected occurrence, condition, or request" (p. 98), for instance as a result of prior actions intended to either replicate or modify existing genres.

It is, however, important to stress that communication genres are social conventions and that they therefore cannot be designed like technologies can. One may attempt to influence the communicative practices of a community in various ways, for example, by codifying genre rules or by sanctioning "inappropriate" behavior, but one can never control the outcome.

Field Study

Organizational Setting

In the field study, we examined how people in a large multinational corporation appropriated a novel CMC application intended to support the company's globally dispersed product development groups. Medica (a pseudonym) is a highly successful pharmaceutical company, which manufactures a range of pharmaceutical products and provides a host of services. Medica's headquarters are situated in Northern Europe, but the corporation has production facilities, research centers, and sales offices in more than 60 countries around the world.

Product development projects in Medica are complex, large-scale, long-term endeavors. A typical project lasts 9-10 years and involves up to 500 people from many different functional areas within the company. Most of the activities take place at sites in Northern Europe, but clinical trials are conducted in the U.S., Singapore, Japan, and a number of other countries worldwide. The fact that a growing number of Medica's new medicinal drugs are developed in close collaboration with external partners in other parts of the world adds to the distributed and complex nature of these projects. The development process itself is highly structured and regulated by the health authorities in various countries, particularly the U.S. Food and Drug Administration (FDA). Getting a new drug approved by the health authorities entails

standardized deliverables, following strict procedures, and detailed documentation, which involves high levels of confidentiality (see, e.g., the Hoffman LaRoche
pharmaceutical case in Ciborra, 1996).

The development projects in Medica are organized in the following way: Work is
carried out by a number of interdependent teams responsible for different parts of
the development process such as clinical testing, registration, manufacturing, and
marketing. Together, the managers of these teams form the so-called "core group"
of the project. A full-time project director, responsible for meeting pre-established
goals of cost, schedule, and functionality imposed by senior management, heads the
core group. Each project director has a project assistant who acts as his or her "right
hand". The project director (and his or her assistant) usually follows a project from
beginning to end, while most other participants only work on the project for shorter
periods of time and, in most cases, they work on several projects simultaneously.
All project directors and project assistants are located at company headquarters,
in the Project Management Unit (PMU). Most project members hold a university
degree at master or PhD level, but their knowledge about IT and their experience
with electronic media varies significantly.

Although formal as well as informal face-to-face meetings are central to communication within the projects, the dispersed nature of the organization means that
project members also rely heavily on a variety of communication technologies to
facilitate various modes of collaborative work. These include familiar technologies
such as mail, telephone, and fax, as well as more advanced technologies like FTP,
shared LAN (local area network) drives, e-mail, videoconferencing, and electronic
calendars.

The CMC technology, *ProjectWeb*, which we studied, is a Web-based application
of the virtual workspace type (similar to BSCW from GMD in Germany, see bscw.
fit.fraunhofer.de, or Lotus® Quickplace® from IBM, see www.lotus.com), offering
facilities for sharing documents, exchanging files, publishing information, event
notifications, group management, and so forth. The purpose of the system was to
improve communication and collaboration among participants in the drug development projects across organizational boundaries and geographical distance.

We followed the introduction and use of ProjectWeb in three projects, of which two
were joint ventures that involved close collaboration with external partners in the
U.S. and Europe. The three projects were chosen because they were considered to
be examples of "successful implementation" by the head of the project management
unit (PMU), and not because they were considered to be typical in some sense or
representative of ProjectWeb use in Medica.

Data Collection and Analysis

Our investigation of Medica's use of ProjectWeb was part of a larger longitudinal field study of computer-mediated communication in the company (see, e.g., Bansler & Havn 2006; Strand 2006). Data collection started in 1999 and continued until the end of 2002.

Consistent with the focus of our research, we followed an interpretive case study approach of the constructivist type (Guba & Lincoln, 1994; Walsham, 1993). This implies that "the investigator and the object of investigation are assumed to be interactively linked so that the 'findings' are *literally created* as the investigation proceeds" (Guba & Lincoln, 1994, p. 111). The interpretive-constructivist approach is particularly appropriate for understanding human thought and action in natural organizational settings (Klein & Myers, 1999), and it allowed us to gain detailed insights into the processes related to the introduction, appropriation, and use of the technology. Moreover, this approach is also useful for discovering new insights when little is known about a phenomenon. It allows for casting a new light on complex processes whose structure, dimensions, and character are yet to be completely understood (Myers, 1997).

Data were collected in four phases, separated by periods in which we analyzed the data and interpreted our findings in the light of relevant literature. This iterative process of investigation, analysis, and interpretation, which allowed insights from one phase to inform data collection in the next, helped us focus our fieldwork, and improve the overall quality of our findings (Klein & Myers, 1999).

We have used several data sources and modes of inquiry (for triangulation). The primary data source was semi-structured and open-ended interviews, but we also examined archival data and participated in a number of formal and informal meetings with developers and users of the technology. We conducted more than 30 interviews with managers and employees in Medica. Interviewees included project directors, project assistants, members of the core management group, members of the various working groups (e.g., medical writers, production engineers, lawyers, and marketing people), as well as the designers and programmers of ProjectWeb. The interviews lasted between ½ hour and 2 hours, and all interviews were recorded and transcribed.

We analyzed the interviews, our field notes, and the archival data in an iterative manner; a process "not unlike putting the pieces of a puzzle together, except that the pieces are not all given but have to be partially fashioned and adjusted to each other" (Klein & Myers, 1999, p. 79). As already mentioned, we sought to place our findings in the context of relevant literature, and, in interpreting our data, we continually referred to relevant bodies of research on technology appropriation, genres, and computer-mediated communication.

Findings

In the following, we will provide some examples that illustrate how people in Medica's product development projects have appropriated ProjectWeb and incorporated the new medium in their work practices. First, however, we will briefly describe communication practices in the development projects prior to the introduction of ProjectWeb.

As mentioned earlier, the development projects are very complex work arrangements involving people from many different parts of the organization and with work teams spread across different countries. Already before the advent of ProjectWeb, project members had for some time employed a wide range of communication technologies to coordinate work and communicate with co-workers at a distance. *Face-to-face meetings* played a prominent role and regularly took place both within and across working groups. As the geographic distribution of project members increased, face-to-face meetings became less frequent but were still given high priority. Face-to-face meetings were often supplemented with periodic *videoconferences* to reduce travel costs. *Shared LAN (local area network) drives* were commonly used for sharing documents and large data files in co-located work teams, and were typically configured to meet the specific local requirements. *E-mail* was widely used for disseminating information and distributing documents (as attachments), both within small, local groups as well as in vast international networks of people connected by *list servers*. E-mail was, of course, also used extensively for person-to-person communication, not only between distant co-workers, but also between co-located project members, for instance, when people were not available for synchronous communication. *FTP (file transfer protocol)* were often used for long distance exchange of large data files, for example, between engineering teams in headquarters and production units in China or Japan, because it was considered the simplest and most secure way to exchange files over the Internet.

In other words, project members used a whole array of different communication media, depending on the communicative purpose and content as well as the number and location of the communicating partners. They took advantage of the fact that different technologies possess different communicative affordances, and they often used several technologies in combination (e.g., e-mail and LAN drives or face-to-face meetings and videoconferences).

When ProjectWeb was introduced into this "information ecology", it triggered people to reconsider their old technologies and prompted them to experiment with new ways of communicating. Over time, this brought about significant changes in established genres and communication patterns. In the following, we present four examples that shed light on different aspects of this development.

Example 1: Distributing Documents

The first example illustrates the *planned replication* of genres to take advantage of the affordances of the new medium, that is, the deliberate and predetermined reproduction of well-established genres with minimal modifications of purpose and form.

The earliest and most widespread use of ProjectWeb in Medica was for disseminating documents of all kinds to relatively large, distributed groups of people. People found it particularly well suited for this purpose because it combined global geographical and organizational reach with a "user friendly" graphical interface and a central document repository or archive. One project assistant simply described it as the "ideal communication tool":

ProjectWeb is the greatest revolution since the e-mail. You can communicate in a much better way. It's more graphical, and you have a kind of library that includes all the information. It is possible that the exact same information already has been sent as an attachment to a mail—a monthly report etc.—but it's a lot easier to find, when it's all in one spot, instead of one having to search through old mails.[2] (Project Assistant, Project #1)

When it comes to disseminating many documents to many people in many different locations, the affordances of ProjectWeb were superior to both e-mail and shared LAN drives. The geographical scope of LAN drives is, per definition, very limited; and the drawback of distributing documents by means of e-mail (as attachments) is that the burden of organizing and storing the documents for (potential) future use is placed on the individual receiver.

The so-called "Project Development Plan" (PDP) provides a good example of an important document that was much easier to distribute and manage with the use of ProjectWeb. The PDP is an overall project plan that includes milestones and decision points, and it is a document for managing, planning, and coordinating work across the different groups in the project. This document must be available to all project members throughout a project's lifetime, and the company requires that it be updated regularly (at least once or twice a year). Thus, the PDP is a very voluminous document, and before ProjectWeb, it was printed in hard copies, assembled in binders, and distributed by mail.

Of course, this was extremely time-consuming, expensive and cumbersome, so it is not surprising that the PDP was one of the first documents to be transferred to ProjectWeb and distributed over the net:

As one of the first things, I have chosen to upload our PDP, which we compile once a year, on ProjectWeb. There are a lot of appendices, which are updated continually. When we had to send out paper copies... We would have just sent out a copy and then we'd get a new update. It was so irritating. But now it is on ProjectWeb, and everyone can find the latest version of the PDP, with all the necessary appendices. (Project Assistant, Project #3)

Using ProjectWeb to disseminate the document was not just much easier, faster, and cheaper, it also had the additional advantage that people could be absolutely sure that they always had access to the latest version of the document. This was not the case with the old paper-based procedure.

The transfer, or remediation (Bolter & Grusin, 1996), of the PDP from paper to ProjectWeb neither changed the document's purpose, content, nor its intended readership.

Example 2: Distributing Meeting Minutes

This is an example of *planned modification* of genres, that is, the deliberate and pre-planned effort to modify genres rules. It shows that initiatives to transfer existing, communication genres to a new medium may lead to rethinking certain aspects of the genres such as the communicative purpose, the content, and the target group. Furthermore, it illustrates how two communication technologies (ProjectWeb and e-mail) can be combined to solve a specific task.

In two of the projects (#1 and #2), the project director decided to start publishing the minutes from core group meetings on ProjectWeb instead of distributing them as e-mail attachments. This apparently quite straightforward and inconsequential move prompted a fundamental reconsideration of the purpose of the minutes. Before ProjectWeb, the minutes were only distributed to the participants in the meeting (and possibly a few others, typically project members with a particular interest in the topics discussed). However, when the minutes were published on ProjectWeb, they immediately became available to all project members.[3]

In the first project, the project director chose to publish all core group meeting minutes on ProjectWeb without any limitations or restrictions. This marked a fundamental break with the former practice of keeping these minutes confidential. The change was motivated by a desire to keep project members better informed and more up to date:

I would rather risk disclosing proprietary knowledge than have people being unable to maneuver. (Project Director, Project #1)

The underlying assumption was that a higher level of communication and information sharing throughout the project would motivate people to do their best and provide a better foundation for coordination and decision making in the project:

It is a question of people management rather than project management, because once you get people on board, you can motivate them, and get them all to pull in the same direction, well, ya, then work becomes the least of it. (Project Assistant, Project #1)

Interestingly, not all project members agreed with management. They did not embrace the idea of totally open communication but found that it was in the company's interest to impose some limits on the flow of information. In particular, they were unwilling to share freely information with employees outside the company's headquarters in Northern Europe:

Maybe it's best that not all employees know everything, particularly in the subsidiaries where mobility is greater. It's not sensible that an employee that perhaps has worked for a competitor is given access to our ProjectWeb only, then, ironically to return to his or her former employer. (Scientific Manager, Core Group Member, Project #1)

In Project #2, the project director opted for a more cautious approach than the director of Project #1. She decided to publish the core group minutes on ProjectWeb and thus make them publicly available, but at the same time, she decided to change the content of the minutes so that they did not contain information perceived as too confidential or sensitive:

At a core group meeting we can discuss things that are strictly internal, but then we don't record it in the minutes. If there are instances, and there have been a few, where we need some kind of minutes, then we ask the project assistant to send it out as a separate mail. (Working Group Leader, Packaging, Project #2)

In other words, the project director and her assistant created a new "sanitized" version of the minutes suitable for open publication and continued to circulate confidential information within the core group by e-mail.

In both projects, the new practice of putting the minutes from core group meetings on ProjectWeb and, in that way, making them "public" altered, or maybe rather augmented, their communicative purpose. The original purpose was to coordinate work in the core group by keeping track of key decisions, tasks, and responsibilities. In addition to this, the purpose of publishing the minutes on ProjectWeb was to keep all project members well informed and raise their general awareness of project priorities.

Many project members found the open publication of meeting minutes—not only from the core group, but also from various other working groups—to be extremely useful because it improved communication and coordination within the project as a whole. A person responsible for the development of packaging for new products told us, for instance, that she regularly checked the minutes from the logistics group, because its decisions might have an impact on her own work.

I often look at the minutes from the logistic group's meetings to see if there is any-thing new in them, because it is important to packaging. (Working Group Leader, Packaging, Project #2)

While a new communication technology like ProjectWeb creates new opportunities for improving communication, it may also create new problems or difficulties to be dealt with. For instance, a general drawback associated with using ProjectWeb to disseminate minutes and other types of documents was that people had to "pull down" the files themselves, instead of receiving an e-mail in their inbox with the file attached. As a consequence, if people did not regularly check ProjectWeb, then they might be quite unaware of recent developments in the core group. To counter this and ensure that people actually received important documents, the project assistants sometimes used e-mail to prompt others that a new document had been added to ProjectWeb:

I wouldn't say that ProjectWeb in itself works perfectly, not if we don't combine it with e-mails. E-mail is something that everyone has at hand all the time. People just have to be prompted with an e-mail. (Project Assistant, Project #1)

When to send out e-mail notifications and to whom was, however, a difficult question. If e-mails were sent too often or addressed to the wrong group of people, then they would be considered a nuisance—a kind of spam—rather than helpful reminders. People in Medica already thought that they received way too much e-mail, so they were not very tolerant of e-mail found to be irrelevant or trivial:

I don't know if you have a feel for the way things work here; what a typical workday is like. But if I'm gone for a day, there'll be more than 50 e-mails in my in-box, and the work of just reading them, copying them, deleting them—because they can't stay there forever—is enormous. It takes me half a day, if I've been away for just one day. There's been an explosion [of e-mails]. (Medical Writer, Project #3)

When uploading minutes from core group meetings, the project assistant in Project #1 tried to find a workable solution to this dilemma by sending e-mail notifications to core group members only, although the minutes might also be relevant to others (as discussed earlier).

Example 3: Publishing News, Personal Stories, and Background Information

The third example also illustrates the *planned modification* of genres. In this case, however, the purposeful adaptation of genres is associated with elements of *migration* and *variation,* that is, the unreflective and emergent reproduction/adaptation of genres that arise tacitly from the situated use of technology over time.

After having used ProjectWeb for some time, the management team in two of the projects (#1 and #2) began to rethink their whole approach to communication and information sharing. They realized that ProjectWeb could be used not only to disseminate "hard facts" and other work-related information (such as the PDP or meeting minutes). It could also be used to create a common identity or sense of belonging among project members by publishing background information, personal stories, pictures from important social events, and so forth.

The project assistant from Project #1, for instance, explained that she wanted ProjectWeb to be a living forum that inspired people and encouraged them to work hard to make the project a success:

We really want it to be a living forum, so people know that we regularly update the site and that it's worthwhile visiting it. They should have it as a "favorite" [bookmark], which they check every day to see if "there is something new." (...) News, it could be case stories. They're very good. A case is when a doctor contacts Medica and says, "we've used this product and it really helped." We send it out in the organization, and everyone cheers. (Project Assistant, Project #1)

First, she simply took existing documents, photos, PowerPoint slides, and so forth, and put them on the Web, but later she started asking people to write news items, case stories, background papers, and personal histories specifically for ProjectWeb. She became fascinated by the notion of "organizational storytelling", and how stories can be used to motivate people and create shared feelings of identity:

I recently got a hold of this book. It's called "Organizational Storytelling." Exactly. How one goes about building the employees' sense of identity. (Project Assistant, Project #1)

As an example, she referred to the story about the Gamma product (a pseudonym): how a single, heroic researcher—despite the skepticism of her colleagues and the reluctance of her superiors—believed so much in her idea that she succeeded in overcoming all obstacles and creating a new miraculous drug, which turned out to be a very lucrative business:

Because there is a story behind this gamma-product, and it is actually a researcher that has fought it through. (...) Because it was actually her, her alone—that is the interesting part, when you have a product that can be associated with one person. One thing is, you have a company that develops and introduces a product, but when there is only one person behind it all. It's such a unique story that isn't, so that ya, we shouldn't miss a chance at... at focusing on it. (Project Assistant, Project #1)

Many project members told us that they valued these more personal news, stories, and pictures, and that they helped create team spirit and a sense of belonging within the project:

It can also be announcements that so-and-so has just had a baby or things like that. It's neat. I think that Peter [project director] and Laura [project assistant] are good at it [striking a balance]. I mean you get the human dimension without letting it overshadow everything. At the moment, there's a picture of John [a colleague] in a kilt, from an event in Scotland, and I think it's funny to upload pictures like that. It is not something you spend lots of time on, you look at the pictures, laugh a little, and then you go on [with your work]. (Working Group Leader, Project #2)

What these examples show is that ProjectWeb, over time, triggered the gradual development of a variety of new organizational communication genres such as the *case story,* the *private news item,* the *humorous picture,* and the *historical background article.* Although all of these context-specific, local genres resemble more general and familiar communication genres known from, for example, corporate newsletters, business magazines, and the press, they exploited many of the unique affordances of ProjectWeb as a medium of communication, for example, the broad scope and the ability to publish not only text but also graphics and pictures in a nice and inviting way.

Example 4: Co-Authoring Documents

The last example has been included to demonstrate that people often find new uses for a technology, which its designers had not originally intended or thought of. It is an example of *opportunistic modification,* that is, the purposeful, but not predefined adaptation of existing genres in response to some unexpected problem or opportunity. Moreover, it provides another illustration of how different technologies with complementary affordances (ProjectWeb, LAN drives, and e-mail) can be used in concert.

Although ProjectWeb was not designed to support close collaboration, such as the co-authoring of documents (it did not, for instance, include facilities for version control or for locking documents), after a while people were using it for exactly this purpose—despite its shortcomings.

It happened in Projects #2 and #3, which were carried out as joint ventures together with external partners in the U.S. and Europe. In these projects, the usual ways of distributing and sharing documents—via shared LAN drives or as e-mail attachments—within the working groups for various reasons did not work very well. The geographical distance made the use of common LAN drives impossible; limits to the size of e-mails (including attachments) were often imposed by the different e-mail systems; and company policy with regard to the protection of business information made using e-mail attachments cumbersome because Medica required that all outgoing e-mails had to be encrypted, if they contained confidential information.

It turned out that ProjectWeb provided a workable solution to the problem of co-authoring documents across distance and organizational boundaries. It had global reach, and it was perceived as much easier to use than encrypted e-mail:

But it is also because we at Medica have had it hammered into our heads how dangerous it is to send documents by e-mail. It [the project Web site] is a much safer place to exchange documents than is throwing them in a fax or sending them around by e-mail. And we don't fill our mailboxes either, or get the nasty messages about taking up too much space, because we've put it on the Web instead. We're very happy with it. I think it is really well suited. And we don't have to cryptograph and pack it and send passwords all over the place, so it works really well. (Project Assistant, Project #2)

It was, however, still far from a perfect solution, and in some respects, it was actually inferior to LAN drives and e-mail. For instance, people had to keep track of different document versions themselves, and they had to take care not to work simultaneously on the same document so as to avoid accidentally overwriting each other's work.

Furthermore, some project members found ProjectWeb rather awkward to work with compared to the shared LAN drives because it was not possible to work directly "on" the documents in the workspace. To work on a document in ProjectWeb, it had to be downloaded to a PC first, and when completed, it had to be uploaded again.

This procedure also precluded using common multi-user services in the Windows®
environment, such as locking documents, which were available when working on
a shared LAN drive:

*It's difficult working in ProjectWeb, I think, in the sense that you have to download
it [the document], work with it and, then, you have to save it under a different name
and upload it again. And then it is not very user-friendly. I think it should be like
a file-server that is just there and you work on it, and when you say save, then it's
saved up there. And if others go in and work on it at the same time, then there should
be some standard rules so that it is read only. That's how it should be.* (Working
Group Leader, Marketing, Project #2)

When using ProjectWeb to support co-authoring, people often used e-mail to coordinate work, for example, by notifying others that a new version of a document
had been uploaded, soliciting comments to a draft, giving feedback to the author,
or negotiating the next step in the preparation of the document:

*It's a place where documents are uploaded. You use e-mails to notify others that
it's on ProjectWeb and where it's located. Bring it home, look at it, upload it again
and give a comment, and, then, we'll take it down again. It's a replacement for the
working directory [on the shared LAN drive].* (Working Group Leader, Engineering, Project #2)

In some cases, people also combined ProjectWeb with shared LAN drives to exploit
the unique advantages of each technology. Typically, people in the same office or
department used their shared LAN drive in the beginning of the writing process,
when producing the first drafts or versions of a document. But as soon as the document reached a more final state, ready to be shared with others, it was uploaded to
ProjectWeb and made broadly available to project members. In one of the projects,
for instance, minutes from local working group meetings were first discussed internally via the LAN drive and later published on ProjectWeb:

*Typically, I take our minutes, once they have been approved, and put them out on
ProjectWeb. In some way, we have a mirror of these folders [on the LAN drive] on
ProjectWeb.* (Working Group Leader, Engineering, Project #2)

Taken together, these four examples illustrate how people often mix and match different communication technologies to meet their needs. The examples also show
that the introduction of a new communication technology does not mean that people

stop using their old tools. Instead, they seek to integrate the new medium in their work practices, combining it with the existing technologies and taking advantage of the unique affordances of each technology. In this process, they redefine not only the role and meaning of existing technologies, but also of communication patterns, genres, and work practices.

Discussion

The primary concern of this chapter is to explore the appropriation process for new media in organizations—the processes by which new communication technologies are adopted and incorporated in people's work practice. Our study is premised on the assumption that introducing a new communication medium in an organization involves a mutual adaptation of the technology and work practice, a co-evolution of social and technical aspects of work within a specific locality. This is what we metaphorically refer to as an *information ecology.* The ecology metaphor draws attention to several key aspects of technology use in organizations: (1) there are strong interrelationships and dependencies among different technologies and work practices; (2) there are different kinds of technological resources and people with different kinds of skills and knowledge, which work together in complementary ways; (3) work practices and technologies constantly (co-)evolve; and (4) these practices and technologies are grounded in local settings and evolve in response to specific material and social circumstances (Nardi & O'Day, 1999).

The analysis of the case confirms that the use of communication technologies in organizations has a strong systemic quality and is highly situated. We found that people in Medica had a wide variety of different communication technologies at their disposal and that they—as part of their everyday work—routinely used many different kinds of media for a host of purposes. They took advantage of the different affordances, which the different media possess, and used the media in complementary ways, dependent on their objective and the specific circumstances of the tasks at hand.

The introduction of the virtual workspace technology, ProjectWeb, led to complex and often unexpected changes in the established patterns of media use and communicative behavior. The introduction of ProjectWeb did not simply result in the substitution of the old (e.g., e-mail) with the new. On the contrary, people continued to use all of their "old" media, but they found a niche for the new technology, combining it with their existing communication technologies. This usually entailed a redefinition of the existing technologies and their role in the organization's communication. In some projects, for instance, the role of e-mail changed substantially. Prior to the introduction of ProjectWeb, project members used e-mail attachments to distribute all sorts of documents, but with ProjectWeb, people uploaded the documents to a virtual workspace and used e-mail to notify others that the documents were available for downloading.

These changes in the prevailing media use and organizational communication patterns did not happen overnight. Rather, they emerged slowly over time, as people became more familiar with the new technology and learned about its affordances. Thus, our findings confirm Nardi and O'Day's (1999) proposition that organizations are "filled with people who learn and adapt and create" and that information ecologies continually evolve "as new ideas, tools, activities, and forms of expertise arise in them" (p. 52):

Even when tools remain fixed for a time, the craft of using tools with expertise and creativity continues to evolve. The social and technical aspects of an environment coevolve. People's activities and tools adjust and are adjusted in relation to each other, always attempting and never quite achieving a perfect fit. (Nardi & O'Day, 1999, p. 53)

In many cases, and especially in the beginning, the use of the virtual workspace was based on remediation of existing organizational communication genres, that is, on transferring and adapting familiar genres to the new medium. This is a relatively straightforward and very common way to begin using a new communication technology (see, e.g., Crowston & Williams, 2000; Hutchby, 2001b; Yates et al., 1999). However, along with the apparent recreation of the familiar genres, users gained experience with the communicative affordances of the new medium and novel patterns of communicative behavior evolved. This, in turn, set the stage for further evolution of genres and practices.

As Hutchby (2001b) points out, the appropriation and use of new media "both rely upon and transform basic communicative patterns" (p. 3). That is, while the technology itself may be fixed (at least for some time), it is difficult to control or even predict how the actual use of the medium will evolve in a given organizational context. This is, according to Hutchby (2001b), because "in an important sense, the affordances of an artefact are 'found' by its users in the course of their attempts to use it for various ends" (p. 123). The emerging use of ProjectWeb to facilitate co-authoring provides a good example. Although ProjectWeb was never designed with this purpose in mind, users soon figured out that they could support co-authoring and other collaborative work processes by combining ProjectWeb with the use of LAN drives and e-mail notifications.

The reproduction and adaptation of communication genres in Medica was always the result of a complex interplay of planned, improvised, and tacit structuring processes; and we found that, in general, it was very difficult to distinguish clearly between the different forms of structuring, that is, migration, variation, planned replication, planned modification, and opportunistic modification. Although these concepts have great analytical and theoretical value, they are difficult to separate from one another empirically. They overlap with gradual transition from one course of action to another.

Implications for Research and Practice

People in contemporary organizations have a multitude of communication media at their disposal and routinely pick and choose among them to achieve their tasks. Consequently, we have argued that understanding the appropriation of new media in today's organizations must include an understanding of how people mix and match different communication technologies and adapt existing communication genres to accommodate their communication needs.

Prior empirical studies of the introduction of new computer-based media in organizations have shown that appropriation and sustained use of these technologies is often difficult to achieve for a number of reasons. Ciborra (1996) found that groupware systems often fail because they are rejected or bypassed by users who prefer more familiar technologies, which are considered to be more reliable and easy to use. In a study of videoconferencing, Mark, Grudin, and Poltrock (1999) found that people had difficulties with setting up and operating the technology, and that their inexperience with the technology resulted in communication failures and interaction problems. Ngwenyama (1998), in a study of groupware implementation, discovered that the new technology had numerous unintended organizational consequences, which complicated the adoption process. A study of the introduction of video telephony by Kraut, Rice, Cool, and Fish (1998) demonstrated that social norms influence adoption and are just as important in determining success or failure as the objective utility of the technology. Finally, Mark (2002) has emphasized that new media may fall through because people fail to develop appropriate conventions of use (i.e., agreements on how to use the technology and for what purposes).

While these studies have demonstrated that the introduction of new media in organizations is a highly complex, contested, and uncertain process, they have not examined the interaction among different communication technologies and genres—that is, how people incorporate new media into their communicative practices by adapting current genres and creating working configurations or assemblages of media with complementary affordances. The present study of ProjectWeb suggests that this interaction is an important aspect of computer-mediated communication in contemporary organizational life, and that people are both willing and able to use a range of different media to accomplish their tasks. Therefore, as researchers we need to concentrate on the—often novel and ingenious—ways in which people *combine* several media to meet their communication needs, rather than focus on how the affordances of *individual* media affect communication behaviors. A better understanding of this process requires longitudinal field studies of how people, in practice, appropriate new media and mix them to form practical and useful configurations.

The complex, dynamic, and often highly problematic nature of the appropriation process raises an important practical question: How can we facilitate the introduction and appropriation of new media in organizations? There are no simple, straightforward, and general strategies for how to do so, but one obvious starting point would be to acknowledge that the appropriation of new media requires substantial time and effort. Too often, managers and technologists seriously underestimate the attention, support, and resources it takes to successfully introduce new communication technologies in an organization.

The appropriation of a new medium involves a mutual adaptation of technology and organization. Advanced computer-based communication technologies, such as groupware or desktop conferencing systems, are generic, general-purpose media that must be customized to the local context of use. And local work practices, communication patterns, conventions, and genres must be adapted to take advantage of the new technological opportunities. The users of the technology must necessarily play a key role in this process because they have an intimate knowledge of the local needs and circumstances, and they are the ones who are required to change their behavior and adjust to the new technology.

However, the enrollment of users and their active participation in the mutual adaptation of technology and organization requires three things. First, they must be given the necessary time to take part in the process. Second, they must be allowed to "play around" and experiment with the new technology to explore its affordances and discover its potential uses. Third, they must be provided with ongoing support and resources, for example, in terms of training and access to technical expertise. This can be organized, for instance, by creating a new position as gardener (Nardi & O'Day, 1999) or mediator (Orlikowski, Yates, Okamura, & Fujimoto, 1995), responsible for customizing the technology and helping users. Several studies have indicated that such gardeners or mediators can have an important function by assisting users and enabling them to integrate the new technology in their work practice (Bansler & Havn, 2006; Gantt & Nardi, 1992; Henriksen, Nicolajsen, & Pors, 2002; Orlikowski et al., 1995).

Acknowledgments

We are grateful to the employees of Medica who participated in this research. We also thank Erling Havn, Dixi L. Strand (earlier Henriksen) and Jens K. Pors for their assistance in the fieldwork. This study was supported in part by a grant from the Danish Research Councils (grant no. 99-00-092).

References

Bansler, J., & Havn, E. (2006). Sensemaking in technology-use mediation: Adapting groupware technology in organizations. *Computer Supported Cooperative Work, 15*, 55-91.

Bolter, J. D., & Grusin, R. (1996). Remediation. *Configurations, 3*, 311-358.

Ciborra, C. U. (1996). What does groupware mean for the organizations hosting it? In C. U. Ciborra (Ed.), *Groupware & teamwork* (pp. 1-19). New York: Wiley.

Crowston, K., & Williams, M. (2000). Reproduced and emergent genres of communication on the World Wide Web. *Information Society, 16*(3), 201-215.

Dourish, P. (2003). The appropriation of interactive technologies: Some lessons from placeless documents. *Computer Supported Cooperative Work, 12*, 465-490.

Gantt, M., & Nardi, B. A. (1992). Gardeners and gurus: Patterns of cooperation among CAD users. In *Proceedings of CHI'92*, Monterey, CA, June 3-7 (pp. 107-117). New York: ACM Press.

Gibson, J. J. (1977). The theory of affordances. In R. E. Shaw, & J. Bransford (Eds.), *Perceiving, acting, and knowing* (pp. 67-82). Hillsdale, NJ: Lawrence Erlbaum Associates.

Gibson, J. J. (1979). *The ecological approach to perception.* London: Houghton Mifflin.

Grimshaw, A. D. (2003). Genres, registers, and contexts of discourse. In A. C. Graesser, M. A. Gernsbacher, & S. R. Goldman (Eds.), *Handbook of discourse processes* (pp. 25-82). Mahwah, NJ: Lawrence Erlbaum.

Guba, E. G., & Lincoln, Y. S. (1994). Competing paradigms in qualitative research. In N. K. Denzin, & Y. S. Lincoln (Eds.), *Handbook of qualitative research* (pp. 105-116). Thousand Oaks, CA: Sage Publications.

Henriksen, D., Nicolajsen, H. W., & Pors, J. K. (2002). Towards variation or uniformity? Comparing technology-use mediations of Web-based groupware. In S. Wrycza (Ed.), *Proceedings of the 10th European Conference on Information Systems,* Gdansk, Poland, June 6-8 (pp. 1174-1184). Poland: University of Gdansk.

Hutchby, I. (2001a). Technologies, texts and affordances, *Sociology, 35*(2), 441-456.

Hutchby, I. (2001b). *Conversation and technology.* Cambridge: Polity Press.

Klein, H. K., & Myers, M. D. (1999). A set of principles for conducting and evaluating interpretive field studies in information systems. *MIS Quarterly, 23*(1), 67-94.

Kraut, R. E., Rice, R. E., Cool, C., & Fish, R. S. (1998). Varieties of social influence: The role of utility and norms in the success of a new communication medium. *Organization Science, 9*(4), 437-453.

Mark, G. (2002). Conventions and commitments in distributed CSCW groups. *Computer Supported Cooperative Work,* 11, 349-387.

Mark, G., Grudin, J., & Poltrock, S. E. (1999). Meeting at the desktop: An empirical study of virtually collocated teams. In S. Bødker, M. Kyng, & K. Schmidt (Eds.), *Proceedings of the 6th European Conference on Computer Supported Cooperative Work,* Copenhagen, Denmark, September 12-16 (pp. 159-178). Dordrecht: Kluwer Academic Publishers.

Myers, M. D. (1997). Qualitative research in information systems. *MISQ Discovery.* Retrieved March 2, 2006, from http://www.qual.auckland.ac.nz/

Nardi, B. A., & O'Day, V. L. (1999). *Information ecologies.* Cambridge, MA: MIT Press.

Ngwenyama, O. K. (1998). Groupware, social action, and organizational emergence: On the process dynamics of computer mediated distributed work. *Accounting, Management and Information Technologies,* 8, 127-146.

Nicolajsen, H. W., & Scheepers, R. (2002). Configuring Web-based support for dispersed project groups. In T. Terano, & M. D. Myers (Eds.), *Proceedings of the 6th Pacific Asia Conference on Information Systems,* Tokyo, Japan, September 2-4 (pp. 81-95). Tokyo: Japan Society for Management Information.

Norman, D. (1988). *The psychology of everyday things.* New York: Basic Books.

Norman, D. (2005). *Affordances and design.* Retrieved November 23, 2005, from http://www.jnd.org/dn.mss/affordances_and_desi.html

Orlikowski, W. J., & Yates, J. (1994). Genre repertoire: The structuring of communicative practices in organizations. *Administrative Science Quarterly,* 39, 541-574.

Orlikowski, W. J., Yates, J., Okamura, K., & Fujimoto, M. (1995). Shaping electronic communication: The metastructuring of technology in the context of use. *Organization Science, 6*(4), 423-444.

Sproull, L., & Kiesler, S. (1991). *Connections – New ways of working in the networked organization.* Cambridge, MA: MIT Press.

Strand, D. L. (2007). Incompleteness and unpredictability of networked communications in use. In S. B. Heilesen, & S. S. Jensen (Eds.), *Designing for networked communications: Strategies and development* (pp. 26-51). Hershey: Idea Group Publishing.

Walsham, G. (1993). Interpretive case studies in IS research: Nature and method. *European Journal of Information Systems, 4*(2), 74-81.

Whittaker, S. (2003). Theories and methods in mediated communication. In A. C. Graesser, M. A. Gernsbacher, & S. R. Goldman (Eds.), *Handbook of discourse processes* (pp. 243-286). Mahwah, NJ: Lawrence Erlbaum.

Yates, J., & Orlikowski, W. J. (1992). Genres of organizational communication: A structurational approach to studying communication and media. *The Academy of Management Review, 17*(2), 299-326.

Yates, J., & Orlikowski, W. J. (2002). Genre systems: Structuring interaction through communicative norms. *The Journal of Business Communication, 39*(1), 13-35.

Yates, J., Orlikowski, W. J., & Okamura, K. (1999). Explicit and implicit structuring of genres in electronic communication: Reinforcement and change of social interaction. *Organization Science, 10*(1), 83-103.

Yoshioka, T., Yates, J.-A., & Orlikowski, W. (2002). Community-based interpretive schemes: Exploring the use of cyber meetings within a global organization. In *35th Annual Hawaii International Conference on System Sciences, (HICSS'02) – Volume 8,* Hawaii, January 7-10 (pp. 271-280). IEEE Computer Society Press.

Endnotes

[1] The term affordance is widely used within the fields of computer-mediated communication, industrial design, human-computer interaction, and CSCW and "has taken on a life far beyond the original meaning" (Norman, 2005). However, our use of the term is based on the work of the British sociologist Ian Hutchby (2001a, 2001b) and differs from the common use in HCI and CSCW in that it is much closer to the original definition. The American psychologist James J. Gibson (1977, 1979) invented the concept of affordance to refer to the possibilities for action, which objects in the world offer to different species (humans or animals). "The affordances of the environment are what it offers the animal, what it provides or furnishes, either for good or ill" (Gibson, 1979, p. 127). According to Gibson, these affordances are objectively measurable and exist independently of the individual's ability to recognize them. Within HCI and other design-oriented fields, the term has taken on a new meaning and denotes *perceived* affordance as opposed to real or objective affordance. For instance, Donald Norman (1988), in his influential book *The Psychology of Everyday Things,* uses the term to describe the properties of a designed object (e.g., a door handle) that indicate how that object can be used.

[2] All quotes have been translated into English by the authors.

[3] In principle, it was possible to restrict access to selected documents in ProjectWeb, but the management team, in this case, decided against making use of this option. For more information, see Nicolajsen and Scheepers (2002).

Chapter II

Incompleteness and Unpredictability of Networked Communications in Use

Dixi Louise Strand
IT University of Copenhagen, Denmark

Abstract

This chapter explores the use practices of networked communications, or more specifically, the use practices of a Web-based information system in large distributed pharmaceutical development projects. The analysis highlights the process in which the system in question is held together, extended and transformed into a working system for pharmaceutical projects. Assemblage is proposed as a productive concept in making visible the particularities of networked communications, their malleability, and the way in which they evolve in use through extensions, interferences, and unpredictable circumstances. The views presented here enhance an understanding of networked communications in use and consequently draw implications to further development strategies for such technologies.

Introduction

Web-based information systems are most often defined technically as a basic platform based on Internet protocols and standards (such as HTTP, HTML, CGI) that may tie together and integrate different applications in new ways and thereby support diverse aspects of communication, coordination, cooperative work, and distributed knowledge sharing, inside an organization as well as between organizations. Web-based information systems are also discussed as intranets and extranets, and have also sometimes been referred to as middleware that tie other systems together across operating systems, in a common portal or user interface. This category of networked technology has been described as being relatively simple and inexpensive to design and redesign compared to conventional computational technologies, and various authors have suggested that this type of technology tends to evolve through use and as the result of unplanned and uncoordinated activities (CACM, 1998; Lyytinen, Rose, & Welke, 1998; Lamb & Davidson, 2000; Williams, Stewart, & Slack, 2005).

In this way, existing studies of Web-based information systems (and other networked technologies) tend to revitalize and make pertinent a longer line of research, placing *use* and *the user* onto the research agenda for understanding, managing, and designing information technologies. Focusing on use has been prominent in the branch of systems development known as participatory design (e.g., Kensing & Blomberg, 1998) and in efforts to make designs that better "fit" with real-life settings such as in the computer supported cooperative work (CSCW) workplace studies (e.g., Luff, Hindmarsh, & Heath, 2000). In addition, evolving use has been examined in order to better understand the evolutional and unpredictable character of information technologies in organizations (e.g., Ciborra, 2000; Orlikowski, 2000). Another line of research in human computer interaction is likewise dedicated to use (and to design-in-use) by focusing on the design of interactive interface features that can facilitate users' own customization, tailoring or reprogramming of technical artefacts (e.g., Nardi & O'Day, 1999; Trigg & Bødker, 1994).

A wide range of literature affiliated with information systems has established use as an important topic to study, yet little work explores use and evolving use theoretically. A recent issue of the journal of CSCW notes this gap and brings forth possible theoretical frameworks that might form a foundation for understanding the evolving use of groupware in particular (Andriessen, Hettinga, & Wulf, 2003; Dourish, 2003). In this issue, structuration theory is highlighted as the most well-developed framework for such purposes. This chapter extends these contributions, although not by adding or testing another grand theory of evolving use or of the interplay between technology and practice. Instead, it challenges some of the presumptions of structuration theory and implies that importing (and adjusting) a grand sociological theoretical framework might not be what we need in order to better grasp the phenomenon of evolving use as an important research topic. Empirical work and empirically-based sensitizing concepts (Blumer, 1954; Fujimura, 1991) offer another fruitful route in adding to our understanding of use and evolving use. Through detailed analysis, this chapter presents empirical insights into the intricate dynamics through which a Web-based information system comes to play a role as a successful technology on one use occasion, and then presents problems and obstacles in the next. Based on this analysis, the chapter argues for the concept of *assemblage* as a productive analytical tool for exploring the everyday dynamics of evolving use of networked communications in new ways.

Besides information systems research, the adjacent and partly overlapping area of research known as science and technology studies also offers a range of sociologically inspired ways of thinking about information technology use and users. Fleck's (1988) notion of innofusion, along with a line of studies on processes of technology domestication (Lie & Sørensen, 1996; Silverstone, Hirsch, & Morley, 1992), have underscored how users incorporate technologies into their particular contexts and purposes, a process that may involve uses not anticipated by designers as well as continued innovation and redesign. In this line of research, users are conceptualized as active co-constructors of technology that may resist, circumvent, or rewrite the technological scripts embodying particular views of the user and user preferences through design (Akrich, 1992; Oudshoorn & Pinch, 2003). The views in this chapter are likewise inspired by this line of thinking (as well as attending to use as an important subject matter to study), but refrain from taking a fixed representation of user/use as starting point for analysis—to which the user as actor complies or refutes. As will be apparent, the chapter suggests that design should not be thought of as a one-shot process (embedded in a particular preconceived representation of a user), but as a much more iterative series of activities whereby design and use evolve (Mulcahy, 1998; Oudshoorn & Pinch, 2003; Stewart & Williams, 2005). This chapter seeks to unpack such a process and provide a resource for strengthening a continual interplay of use and design in practice.

The chapter is organized as follows. First, I review some related strands of literature devoted to analyzing enabling and constraining structures and to a conceptualization of the user actor. Thereafter, the notion of assemblage is depicted as a concept that may sensitize research to the particularities of networked communications in use, for example, the extensions, interferences, and indispensability found in a case study of a Web-based information system. Then, I introduce the case and the particular system in question: an internally developed Web-based information system aiming to provide a shared virtual workspace for large geographically distributed projects developing new pharmaceutical products. The main body of the chapter comprises a detailed analysis of three empirical situations where a Web-based situation is used *and* evolves. These empirical excerpts concern the everyday work of three different project assistants working in a project management department and serve to exemplify and illustrate a number of thematic interests that the notion of assemblage helps to foreground. The chapter closes with a summary and a conceptual discussion.

Background

Complying with or Resisting to Structures

To grasp use as practice, there is a tendency to adopt sociological ways of thinking about structures, rules, and resources. For example, reworkings of Giddens' structuration theory seek to understand technology's capability to embody relatively stable structures that over time shape social practices of use (DeSanctis & Poole, 1994; Giddens, 1984). Later, elaborations of this theory have pointed to how technology as a fixed and stable entity does not align with empirical studies (Orlikowski, 2000). Examples displayed in the literature include misunderstandings of designer intentions, inadequacy of user skills and competencies, or users deliberately resist in altering or working around the technological design, perhaps by adding, modifying, or substituting procedures or elements. By studying practice or enactments, rather than starting with inherent characteristics of a technology, we are better equipped to acknowledge and account for the processes through which technologies are used—both in line with the designer's expectations, and in new and different ways that may contradict or exceed the intended use foreseen by designers. Structuration theory and a focus on enactment allows us to think about technologies-in-use as being continually enacted, and long spirals of repetitive enactments come to look like sameness and stability, at least provisionally. According to Orlikowski (2000), what we can and should study is thus such practices and processes. "Rather than starting with technology and examining actors' appropriation of its embedded structures, this view starts with human action and examines how it enacts emergent structures through recurrent interaction with the technology at hand" (p. 407).

Structuration theory is thus a productive starting point for exploring the ongoing enactment of social and technological structures and their interplay: how technologies are modified, continually evolve in use, and do all sorts of things neither anticipated nor planned by designers. Studying the phenomenon of user practices shifts focus away from the interior stable properties of technologies to that which emerges or is enacted.

Yet, studies building on structuration theory tend to view use as a matter of complying with or resisting built-in technological structures and (continually reproduced) social structures. In the study discussed here, I have found it necessary to move beyond the notion of structures and open up for further scrutiny the range of technologies, people, and resources involved in "use" and how these may differ from one situation to the next. A recurring theme of contingency characterized the use situations studied in the case, and this aspect of use is not well grasped by a search for enabling and constraining structures. This point will be explicated in the analyses.

Users as Active Co-Constructors

Besides structurational orientations in research literature for studying users and user practices, existing work also offers another route: that of reconceptualizing users as active co-constructors or informal designers-in-use (Hales, 1994; Lie & Sørensen, 1996) and users as gardeners or cultivators (Mackay, 1990; Nardi & O'Day, 1999). In a study of spreadsheet packages for budgeting and financial computation, and CAD software for engineering and architectural drawing, Nardi and O'Day (1999), for example, stress that these particular skills are an evolutionary outcome of intensive use and experience in the particular work domain, and that closer examination of such practices can provide new perspectives from which to view IT artefacts. This notion of users as actors is thus another way to approach use and a way of understanding how both artefacts and practice evolve together over time. This line of thought often carries with it a concern about empowering the user in relation to the designer, in part a reaction to the field's emphasis on design as the privileged site of action (Suchman, 2002). But in attending to the user as actor, as the locus of agency, this view tends to tone down the specific situational resources that make certain kinds of use possible, difficult, and desirable, as well as overemphasizing the extent to which designers really base their designs on comprehensive representations of intended users. On the contrary, Stewart and Williams (2005) argue that the actual objectives and presumptions underpinning design are often difficult to discern. These are often justified in technical or pragmatic terms and emerge through a multiplicity of actors with varying concerns and agendas (finance, technical constraints, interoperability, market changes, deadlines, personal preferences, etc.) rendering design presumptions about the user less than straightforward or merely there to be read out by the analyst (p. 201). This kind of analysis tends to dissolve the distinction between users' reacting or resisting and leaves open the question of use.

Assemblage as an Additional Analytical Resource

This chapter presents the use practices of a Web-based information system as characterized by themes of extension, interference, and indispensability. These are aspects of use not well grasped by existing literature, which tends to focus on either structures, or on the user as actor. Here, the notion of assemblage has proven useful as an additional sensitizing concept allowing us to better understand how use is highly contingent upon specific situations, resources, and events. As mentioned earlier, I present the notion of assembly not as a grand theory as such, but as a productive concept for translating field observations and experiences in a way that can illuminate both the case material presented as well as issues of wider relevance to future studies of Web-based information systems and their evolving use.

Assemblage denotes the coming together of various technological features, applications, platforms, infrastructures, people and competencies, routines and paths of action, visions, desires—in short heterogeneous and disparate elements that are brought into relations, or assemblages.

Derrida (1978) applies the term assemblage to understand the production of meaning (of texts) as a neverending combination of elements and practices that are continually reshuffled to produce new effects. The term assemblage here is an endless weaving together, an interlacing of many different elements (of texts, but also of people, objects, resources) that form different temporary collage constellations of meaning.

The notion of assemblage has also been used analytically in exploring the relationship between technology and practice, as in the work of Suchman, Trigg, and Blomberg (2002). These authors explore how a new information system (for an engineering bridge project work) is designed through ongoing practices of assembly, demonstration, and performance. Assembly refers to the continual linking up of a working prototype to local circumstances such as the particular users, the industrial product developers involved, and to their own contexts of research. "Like any technology, the prototype does not work on its own, but as a part of a dynamic assemblage of interests, fantasies and practical actions, out of which new socio-material arrangements evolve" (p. 175).

Lastly, the concept is often used in studies inspired by actor-network theory as a conception that better designates a continual flow of translations than networks (Deleuze & Guattari, 1987; Latour, 2005; Law, 2005). The concept conveys the impossibility of making a clear distinction between signs and objects, the discursive and the material. Assemblage is a way of looking at sociotechnical phenomena such as practiced networked communications, as a collage collection, a jumbling together of technological parts and pieces, artefacts, people, ideas, visions, and so forth. The concept works to describe how the bringing together of such heterogeneous elements produces differing effects and may change the very elements involved. The connections created in assemblages may create subtle translations of meanings, concerns, interests, and identities involved. The following examples illustrate such transformations: how the use situations of a Web-based information system entail subtle changes for the user (their experiences, expectations, skills, and position in relation to other users, for example), and to the Web-based system's content (functionality and versioning), as well as changes to aspects of project work, shared responsibilities and tasks undertaken. The aim of the analysis (and the construct of assemblage) is to trace these changes and to highlight these as potential resources for further development and for the future work of professional designers and IT managers. To serve this purpose, the notion of assemblage is deliberately kept open and scalable so that any collection of elements can constitute an assemblage or multiple assemblages upon scrutiny and may enter into relation with new elements as well as form new extended and transformed assemblages.

This chapter thus explores the question: How can the analytical concept "assemblage" assist in exploring use as a productive aspect of networked communications? The answer to this question is provided through an empirical example that highlights situation specific extensions, interferences, and indispensability, aspects of use practices that a line of study focusing on enabling structures or users as actors tends to overlook. The analyses illustrate how characteristics of use, what is or is not a problem, are emergent effects produced through a process of assemblage where people, technology, and resources are brought together at particular times and places. Furthermore, assemblage assists in understanding how these very characteristics of the Web-based information system in question evolve as an assemblage that may transform, expand, or fall apart. Characteristics of experimentation, interference, and indispensability are thereby at the centre of analysis in order to better understand the critical role of use situations in networked communications today.

Case and Methodology

The specific case study concerns the application ProjectWeb, which was developed in-house for pharmaceutical project work in the company Medica (a pseudonym). Medica is a large pharmaceutical company based in Northern Europe and spanning subsidiary offices for research, production, and marketing in more than 60 countries distributed across the globe. Empirical data was gathered during 2000-2002 through methods of interviewing, participant observation, and document analysis. The case was approached methodologically and analytically through a multi-sited methodological framework of "following actors through multiple sites" (Latour, 1987; Marcus, 1995; Mol, 2002), studying the ways in which ProjectWeb was practiced at different locations such as the IT development department, a library research section, a project management department, and distributed sites of development project work. The study was carried out as part of a larger collaborative research project entitled *Design and Use of Interactive Web Applications (DIWA)* running from 1999-2004 (see Henriksen, 2003).

The material applied in this chapter is based on a focus study exploring in particular "intermediary use situations", various events and moments that might elucidate the circumstances and conditions under which the activity of design-in-use can take place. Design-in-use was approached as an activity to be explored openly rather than as a definitive analytical entity (where intermediary use is predefined). The examples presented are drawn from a series of short-term shadow observations of three different project assistants in the project management department one to two days a week during the months of June, October, November, and December 2001. Detailed notes were taken during observation and then written up the same day or the day after. The material was continuously coded openly (Emerson, Fretz,

& Shaw, 1995), and based on this, a number of broad themes and story lines were developed. Subsequently, a number of situations were analyzed in more detail in relation to these themes. These were selected according to the findings and the data available, as situations displaying themes relevant to the academic discussions on use referred to earlier and as somewhat typical or characteristic to the wider study. However, the aim here is not to generalize empirically. Rather, the chapter aims to bring forth via analysis and the notion of assemblage, situations that are under-recognized in the literature on user practice. The sensitizing concept of assemblage serves this purpose.

Analysis: Extensions, Interferences, and Indispensability

The situations considered next illustrate how the notion of assemblage can be productive in foregrounding three themes concerning networked communications in use. First, these are briefly summarized together with an introduction to the system and setting in question.

The information system, ProjectWeb, can be described by way of three main features as: (1) a project home page displaying project news and events to project members distributed across many departments, subsidiaries, and partner firms that collaborate to develop, produce, and market new pharmaceutical products; (2) a project archive where project members can store, organize, and retrieve relevant document files and meeting summaries; and (3) a Web tool that is customizable and easy-to-use, in the sense that it allows users to alter the graphic interface and document structure, create news articles, upload documents, and maintain user groups and access rights in a self-explanatory manner and without having to learn HTML programming.

The setting is a project management department at the firm's headquarters where project managers and project assistants are located. Project assistants work as the right hand of a project manager, and among other responsibilities, they maintain a ProjectWeb for each of the large distributed pharmaceutical projects in which they are involved. ProjectWeb is employed to assist the management by bringing together a core group of middle managers and geographically distributed working groups specializing in areas such as clinical research, quality assurance, marketing, regulatory affairs, as well as partner firms and collaborating research institutions abroad. Very few formal guidelines exist, and the way in which ProjectWeb is set-up, maintained, and used by project members differs remarkably, thus confirming the presumed flexibility of Web-based information systems as discussed at the introduction to this chapter. Furthermore, ProjectWeb is used in integration with other technologies such as e-mail, telephone, fax, ftp, shared LAN drives, video-conferencing, and electronic calendars as analyzed in further detail in Chapter I (Nicolajsen & Bansler, 2007).

Focus in the analysis of the present chapter is on the project assistant as user and on three examples of daily user practices.

Extending a Web-based information system: A project assistant attempts to publish project news to ProjectWeb. The project assistant does not just turn on and use ProjectWeb as a tool for fulfilling a task, but rather assembles it as a shared project space in the process. This example underscores the way in which a Web-based information system is assembled in order to be used as well as in order for other project members to engage in further use.

Interferences: The assemblage falls apart: A project assistant writing a meeting summary attempts to publish the summary to the Web-based information system. A number of interferences play into the decision whether or not to publish the summary or send it by e-mail. The example specifies the first example: a wider assembly holds a Web-based information system together in use and produces an up-to-date workspace as effect. The analysis reveals a wider assemblage that does not merely sit there as background or context for ProjectWeb, but can be seen as taking active part in making it what it is at specific moments. What is easy or troublesome, what is confidential or shared, what ProjectWeb is/can be used for is an outcome of the situation.

An indispensable link in the assemblage: A system administrator assists and trains the other project assistants and acts as a link back to the IT department and further development of ProjectWeb. This work forms an important link in the assembly, both in holding together the system for everyday use situations and in relating these situations to wider assemblages of formal development practices.

Isabelle's Use: Extending a Web-Based Information System

As a first example, I will discuss a selected situation: the project assistant Isabelle's activities of publishing project news. The project is developing a pulmonary insulin device, Aox (a pseudonym), and Isabelle has been working on the Aox project for two years. She has set up ProjectWeb colours and graphics in line with the project image and logo to "give the feeling of our own shared project space" and to ensure that people working on several projects will always be able to see that this is the Aox project's ProjectWeb. She has, for example, also added a section with successful case stories from patient trials and added small digital video clips with these patients.

She keeps the Aox project's ProjectWeb up-to-date by always posting upcoming events, the most recent results from clinical trials, and by adjusting the project plan and the *Objective and Goals* section (a menu category she has created in the "system administration section"). The Aox project comprises about 200 members dispersed globally across company subsidiaries, partner firms, and research institutions.

In the following section, I will describe how Isabelle adds pictures to the news page from a recent project celebration. Through Isabelle's activities, diverse elements are brought together and negotiated into place in order to use ProjectWeb and to make it work for others as a shared project space. I look at this situation of publishing project news as a sequence of events, presented in three parts, starting with her receiving digital pictures about an important project event, which she then proceeds to post on the news page of ProjectWeb.

Isabelle opens the e-mail program Outlook® and clicks on one of the newly received e-mails entitled "CPoC pictures". It is from Jesper, the project director who sits two doors down the hall. The e-mail opens up to 15 pictures of people drinking champagne. In the pictures there are green banners and bright balloons with the words "CPoC Celebration! CPoC – We made it!" printed on them, hanging down above the people and the cake-covered buffet tables. As Isabelle looks through the pictures on the screen by clicking the mouse and enlarging and minimizing the pictures, she laughs at some of her colleagues and explains to me who the people are. Through Internet Explorer® she opens ProjectWeb to post the pictures of the CPoC celebration to the news page of her project's ProjectWeb. (Office observation, Isabelle, Project Assistant)

CPoC is pharmaceutical project-speak for Clinical Proof of Concept. CPoC is about passing a "project milestone" that distinguishes one project phase from another. The product under development has now been approved for further development by a management reference board, thus moving project work into a third phase of clinical trials. The next time project members elsewhere open and log onto ProjectWeb, news of CPoC and these pictures will be visible. The party pictures marking this event will appear alongside news about a recent conference in Athens, the latest information on the development of a competing product, and a link to a world map showing where the new product will be marketed. Isabelle explains to me how important it is to publish visuals, pictures, and graphics in ProjectWeb, as a way of increasing awareness about what is going on in distant places and for getting to know one another.

In posting these pictures, ProjectWeb participates in the staging of the event as an important turning point. This is a moment in which ProjectWeb participates in connecting people in distant places and rendering present and visible events taking place elsewhere (Callon & Law, 1995). So, in this respect, ProjectWeb is somehow more than a technical entity, in the sense that it is inseparable from the project activities and events that form its content. It is also inseparable from the notions of virtual communities or digital spaces in which people may meet, get to know one another (or laugh at one another), that seem to induce Isabelle to post these pictures to ProjectWeb instead of, for example, sending them out by e-mail.

To upload the pictures, Isabelle clicks her way through the administration menu to the page "add news article". Here a template presents a series of boxes and buttons for selecting keywords, filling in date, title, and abstract sections, and adding a picture with the "add image" button and a browse function. Isabelle moves quickly through this sequence and knows from previous experience to upload the image file to the "library images" page, another similar page and template. Shifting back and forth between the two pages, she clicks the button "upload new image here", saves, and previews the article. A news page appears where the picture fills up half the screen. "Oh, it's too big" Isabelle remarks, and to adjust the size she opens another program, PhotoShop®, that offers menus and functionalities for adjusting the size of the digital image. She then proceeds through the steps of uploading the image and then goes through upload, save, and preview on this template again. When preview appears, the picture still fills half the screen, "oh, it's because I forgot to save it (the PhotoShop® image file) before I previewed". Isabelle shifts over to PhotoShop®, saves the files, and repeats the template steps above a third time. (Office observation, Isabelle, Project Assistant)

In this sequence, ProjectWeb begins to act more like an application or program as we commonly think of it. The administration section of ProjectWeb presents a template and various possibilities and paths that are available in order to publish a picture and text on the news page of ProjectWeb. On each page, certain boxes must be filled out or clicked on in specific ways and sequences. The abstract section, for example, cannot be empty nor exceed 2,048 characters. To choose more than one keyword, the Ctrl-key must be pushed while clicking with the mouse. Before clicking the upload image button, the image must be uploaded in "library image pages". Isabelle fills in the template as an experienced user.

ProjectWeb prescribes (Akrich, 1992) both Isabelle's activities at the keyboard and the particular way in which the CPoC event can be broadcasted from the project management department to project members around the world. For example, the page only allows for one picture and posts this in parallel with other project events and information, creating a quick overview of "what is going on" in the project when members log on to ProjectWeb.

At the same time, the template and pages of ProjectWeb offer resistance if the precise prescriptions are not followed or if, for example, the format of the picture is different from that required by ProjectWeb. Thus, Isabelle not only adjusts her work to follow the options offered by ProjectWeb pages, but she also engages in the creative work of re-negotiating the possibilities and functions provided. Redoing the sequence three times is a sort of tinkering work, where the incompatibility between a specific ProjectWeb functionality and the file format of the digital images is negotiated into alignment. A gap between the pictures and ProjectWeb is filled in by a detour into the PhotoShop® application and the adjustments made here.

What follows in this particular use event is an *extension* of the functionality and possibilities provided by the ProjectWeb news section. Isabelle attempts to create a hyperlink from the news page to an additional Web page that she creates in Front-Page® (Web-publishing application). The "add news article" page only permits one picture per article, but by making a page extension, Isabelle makes it possible for project members to click on a Web link and see more party pictures on a different page. Using ProjectWeb as a tool for publishing project news entails following templates and specific instructions, as well as extending these.

Isabelle struggles as the pictures on the linked page keep coming up blank. She goes through several attempts and strategies to locate the problem and to get these pictures and the additional Web page to connect with ProjectWeb. She moves back and forth between different desktop applications, incompatible file types, does a lot of redoing and rechecking of the hyperlink paths and the folder placement of files. She looks back at a page she has made earlier in an attempt to find out what it is that is not working. At one point she walks down the hall to ask Mia, another project assistant, who recognizes the problem: "yeah, that happens to me sometimes as well - just try uploading both the html-page and all the pictures again". After this Isabelle starts again, repeats the routine, yet a new set of contingencies arises when ProjectWeb replies that the page cannot be uploaded when a user page with the same name already exists. Isabelle renames the files and uploads them again one at a time. And still the pages refuse to link up. She remarks that if only Marge were here today, she could ask her. She then leaves the CPoC pictures and Pro-jectWeb until the next day, when Marge is present and shows her how to find and insert the precise link numbers necessary to make the two pages connect. Marge shows Isabelle how to insert <a href="images/projects/XXX/CpoP1.gif"> where XXX is the particular ProjectWeb identification number: 5578. (Office observation, Isabelle, Project Assistant)

To the IT designer, this may seem like a banal situation, perhaps indicating the need for redesigns and adjustments to the application and interface, or the need for further user training. Yet, the point suggested here is that this assembling and extending will continue to characterize use practices no matter how the system is improved upon in further design. This is what use of networked communications looks like and this is how use evolves.

Making ProjectWeb work for the task at hand involves tying together a range of other programs, people, and practices. This situation can be described as the work to make it work (Bowers, 1994) or as an artful integration of heterogeneous elements (Suchman, 2002), and as a key feature of well-working networked communications. The assembly that emerges includes: the event and the pictures taken (events in the project and the digital pictures provide content for the news page), notions of ProjectWeb's potential as a meeting point for distributed projects, inscribed templates, and functionalities, Isabelle's experiences with the new page template and the sequence of uploading pictures in ProjectWeb (routines of dealing with resistances, redoing it again and again when something does not work, negotiating incompatibilities of file formats, extending the page), other desk top applications such as e-mail, PhotoShop®, FrontPage®, and resources such as the manual and other people down the hall. Lastly, Isabelle's sense of urgency to get the news of this important event out to all project members and her curiosity and persistence in redoing and trying out different options to solve the problem likewise form part of the assembly through which ProjectWeb becomes a working tool, or shared space, for the Aox development project.

With this example of ProjectWeb in use, I point to a way in which we might think about technology in a different light, not as an isolated entity, but as something that is inseparable from previous, present and future use. In the example with Isabelle, the technology offers possibilities and resistances (what we normally would think of as fixed characteristics) as an *effect* of the particular resources available in the situation. If Isabelle remembered precisely how to write down the sequence of link numbers (which she might next time, since she took notes), or if Marge had been present the first day, ProjectWeb would at that moment have been less problematic and had less of a breakdown character. ProjectWeb offers specific pages and functionalities, but the way in which these features work in a seamless manner or are problematic and resistant is dependent upon other specific elements such as those listed earlier.

In the situation, links and connections to an assemblage of elements are what shape ProjectWeb as a useful and working technology for publishing a project news event. Through this activity, ProjectWeb gains its characteristics and properties; for example, as an appropriate tool for publishing important news events to distributed project members, as having silly quirks one has to redo and play around with. This empirical exploration of an everyday use situation brings forward the continual assembling of networked communications in use and illustrates the way in which the very elements involved undergo subtle transformations in the course of such assemblage.

Anne's Use: Interferences—The Assemblage Falls Apart

To develop the notion of assemblage, the following section analyzes another example from the office of another project assistant further down the hall. I examine various elements that go into writing a meeting summary to be published on ProjectWeb and a number of interferences that play into a decision on whether or not to publish this summary on ProjectWeb or to e-mail it to the relevant parties. The example specifies the previous example: a wider assembly holds ProjectWeb together, and ProjectWeb emerges as a working technology for pharmaceutical development projects through this assembly.

Anne, a project assistant, is working her way through a to-do list of various tasks in preparation for the launch of a new insulin device at an upcoming conference of the American Diabetes Association (ADA). The project has been underway for two years, and the product launch will take place at a conference in Philadelphia in two weeks time. About 75 people are officially involved in developing, producing, and marketing this new device. A third of these project members are employed in Medica headquarters and subsidiaries abroad, a third at the partner firm in California, while the rest are dispersed among the partner firm's subcontractors located in Scotland and Portugal. These subcontractors have produced the moulds and plastic materials for the device, whereas Medica and the main partner firm in cooperation are coordinating technical design specifications, testing, and quality assurance work, as well as packaging and marketing materials. ProjectWeb has been important to these collaborations, both for conveying news and events across the project as a whole and for collaboration in smaller working groups within the project. This includes a series of restricted workspaces for member groups that have been defined and set-up by the project assistant in the administration section of ProjectWeb (in collaboration with the manager and based on requests from the working groups).

The project assistant Anne is planning the product launch in Philadelphia, where the Medica group will meet with core group members from the partner firms to celebrate the launch and lay out future plans for marketing and production. She works on a meeting summary where the core group had discussed the trip, plans, and project delays two days earlier.

Anne finds the document from the core group meeting held the day before yesterday. This was the last meeting before the trip and where arrangements for the trip and launch were made. She explains the tension at the meeting due to the upcoming launch, time-pressures, and general impatience since quality assurance papers, marketing material, and the crucial approvals of the device from the Federal Drug Administration (FDA) are not yet in place. The meeting included a lot of complaints about the way the partner firm was working. Anne needs to tone these down in the summary. She shifts around sentences and sections and adds details to clarify the text. She opens an e-mail application, attaches the file, and sends it out to all the Medica core group members who were present at the meeting. A summary is always circulated first so the core group can check it and add comments before it is uploaded to ProjectWeb. Usually if there are confidential comments or topics that they do not want the partner firm to see, she sends these out on a separate e-mail to the Medica core group members. She shows me the menu category "meeting minutes" where all previous meetings can be found as a list named as REF#date, making the particular summary easy to locate on the screen. (Office observation, Anne, Project Assistant)

This situation illustrates some of the mundane activities and technologies that are involved in adding a new meeting summary to ProjectWeb. The meeting discussions are condensed into notes so that members who were not present can see what happened and who will do what next. We thus catch a glimpse of some of the work that goes into making a summary, the path it moves through from being talk in a meeting, notes in a template on a laptop, a file transferred to a desktop via the local network, a draft passed around for comment and modification, sections deleted, re-written, and adjusted by core group members, to a final version to be fixed and inscribed in ProjectWeb. The summary is thus transformed into one trace or clickable item in ProjectWeb, collapsed into a long list of other meeting summaries in a template format whereby project members elsewhere may stay informed or perhaps later backtrack what was decided at this last meeting before the launch—thus activating the inscription. This long line of activities (with different people and technologies involved) gets packaged into this summary, and once uploaded it is there as a list on a page of this project's ProjectWeb.

In cross-organizational collaborations such as this project, there are continuous discussions and negotiations about what kind of project information should or should not be shared with partner firms, who are both allies and, at the same time, possible future competitors. These discussions tend to surface in tense situations such as the one previously mentioned, where Medica project members are dissatisfied with the partner firm's handling of the upcoming launch. Summaries are almost always sent out and checked to ensure that the tentative results and decisions do not slip out in a final summary before they have been confirmed. And, the closed member groups in ProjectWeb have been specifically established for the sharing of confidential information or of unfinished materials and results. In several interviews, both project assistants and others express the benefits of sharing documents safely and securely in ProjectWeb and how this also alleviates the previous hassles of encryption and decryption when sending documents out of Medica via e-mail.

As in the previous example of Isabelle's work, many elements and continuous activities are brought together to create ProjectWeb as a project archive. The core group section to which Anne moves to upload the summary is such a "safe place" where top-level management in the three partner firms can share documents and meeting summaries. E-mail and ProjectWeb work in sync to provide this discretionary space and thereby balance what goes into or out of the formal archive (Brown & Lightfoot, 2002).

Effects are, however, open-ended and dependent not only upon ongoing use (as assembly work) and wider project practices but also on other elements that occasionally surface and interfere, as the next excerpt illustrates. Paul, the project manager, telephones Anne the next day, while she is incorporating into the meeting summary a few comments and corrections she has received by e-mail.

Anne and Paul discuss a number of things she needs to do in preparation for the trip; "Yes, I have booked the room for Sunday... No, I'll order the gifts for the partner firm people next." Anne says she is working on the summary. "Does he want to check it? Does he want to her to publish it to ProjectWeb or send it around by e-mail for commenting first? ok...oh ok, well then I'll do that." Paul, the project manager, is at home and has a very slow modem connection and therefore wants the summary by mail, because it is much easier than going into ProjectWeb. She conveys that there are a lot of sensitive comments concerning problems with the partner firm, and he also thought it would be better if they did not see it. She finishes the summary, mails the core group, and explains again why she is sending it by e-mail instead of publishing to ProjectWeb: things are sensitive toward the end of the launch, a lot of people are dissatisfied with the partner firm's collaboration, and they blame the firm's ways of working for the delays. (Office observation, Anne, Project Assistant)

The phone call, issues of confidentiality, and Paul's Internet connection are elements that enter into the use situation and interfere. Several elements enter into a relation in this situation: the timing of the meeting (the last one before launch), recent disagreements between the Medica people and the people at the partner firm, Paul's location working from home, his modem connection, and wider infrastructures. The example illustrates some of the contingent factors that go into the "decision" on whether to publish or not to publish, whether Web or e-mail is the relevant medium. And the picture is much more complex than that of an individual user resisting or complying with a fixed or finished system. The situation opens up the social and technical particularities of use situations that do not merely sit there as background or context for ProjectWeb, but can be seen as taking an active part in making it what it is at specific moments: what is easy or troublesome, what is confidential or shared, and what ProjectWeb is/can be used for is an outcome of the situation.

The analysis examines how ProjectWeb is brought into being through a continual engagement of elements that are fragile and may fall apart. Success, obstacles, and outcomes of these situations seem to be a very local matter of particular people, resources, technological links and infrastructures available here and now. The notion of assemblage underlines this here and now bringing together of heterogeneous elements into a working collage or montage. The analysis thus suggests an alternative way of thinking about use as the ongoing effect of social and material practices. Next, I will temporally elaborate on these practices, noting how these situations over time accumulate or layer into ProjectWeb in particular ways.

Emergent Effects

In the first example of publishing the party pictures, Isabelle's activities are based on prior experiences with ProjectWeb's template pages and the FrontPage® publishing application as well as on discussions within the project management department that this is a good way to broadcast project news as opposed to e-mail. Likewise, the sense of urgency in publishing the pictures on ProjectWeb is shaped by earlier experiences showing that project members actually use the pages she regularly maintains. Isabelle has, for example, created an e-mail survey to get a feel for how her users (as she calls them) like ProjectWeb and how it might be improved. She was pleased to find her case stories, video clips, and news items were in high demand. And she says: "They now expect news and summaries to be out immediately and available there 24 hours a day" (Isabelle, Interview). ProjectWeb is transformed into *the* place where project members can follow and backtrack project events, discussions, and decisions. Isabelle's use, and that of her project co-members, has co-evolved and layered into one another.

Similarly, the situation in which a meeting summary is not published may shift the identity of ProjectWeb and future use elsewhere. In interviews, I recorded enthusiastic comments on the advantages of ProjectWeb for rapidly obtaining documents and for backtracking action points, as well as extreme frustration from a project member because she just recently could not locate the meeting minutes she needed right then and there. In several cases, project members (or working groups) maintained additional parallel archives on the local area networks to make sure they had the documents available when they needed them.

The two assemblages I describe earlier thus leave particular material traces in ProjectWeb and participate in transforming ProjectWeb into a certain kind of system relevant and attachable to specific future use situations. The assemblages shift Isabelle and Anne's skills (as these become embodied and emerge with use) and the ways in which ProjectWeb can attach to other users (in that ProjectWeb becomes the place to find specific material, contact persons, or share working documents). Each situation extends and strengthens the use assemblage or weakens its connectedness. I suggest that by looking at ProjectWeb as enmeshed in continuous use events, circumstantial project concerns, and contests, we gain a different picture of how use evolves over time. Daily activities of the project assistants contribute in the form of news and pictures as described previously or as meeting minutes documents that keep track of project discussions and decisions. The project assistants also put together and upload monthly status reports and various formal documents and charts describing the particular project and work organization. They regularly maintain an overall plan where one can find upcoming deadlines and follow recent project accomplishments. Project assistants also ensure that all project members are entered as "users" and continually maintain yellow pages information and user groups by adjusting members and delegating appropriate access rights, such as read only, upload to some sections and not others, and so forth. They adjust menu categories and subdirectories and suggest conventions for file naming and the use of restricted areas.

In turn, a wider assemblage affords this work of keeping ProjectWeb "up-to-date", as they call it. Previously, I have discussed how these activities are carried out in mutual interaction with the activated templates and functionalities. The project assistants also exchange experiences with each another. They frequently receive requests and suggestions by phone and e-mail from their project members and managers. And as one project assistant notes, the more documents the more categories you need to get an overview. As use evolves, ProjectWeb makes demands on the use practices of these project assistants. In the offices of the project management department, as well as at other Medica sites, mundane practices like these are ongoing, and it is difficult to pin down one location as the locus of action. I suggest an alternative view of these small and almost invisible practices that continually keep ProjectWeb together as a working technology.

Marge's Use: An Indispensable Link in the Assembly

In the final analysis section, I move another three doors down the hall to the office of Marge. Among many other tasks, Marge offers technical support to project assistants and managers in the project management department. Marge is the head system administrator of ProjectWeb and has been actively involved in the development of earlier versions. She has a background in product engineering and is responsible for maintaining the department intranet Web pages. She herself emphasizes that her computer skills are largely self-taught and developed during her six years of employment at Medica. I will give some examples of how Marge forms an indispensable link in the ProjectWeb assembly. First, by returning to the first example of Isabelle's attempt to publish party pictures at the start of this chapter:

Isabelle is having trouble saving and linking an additional html page made in FrontPage® in ProjectWeb's library section: ... still the pages refuse to link up. Isabelle remarks that if only Marge were here today, she could ask her. She then leaves the CPoC pictures and ProjectWeb until the next day, when Marge is present and shows her how to find and insert the precise link numbers necessary to make the two pages connect... Marge also instructs Isabelle that it is a good idea to create a link back to ProjectWeb from the new Web page extension. (Office observation, Isabelle, Project Assistant)

In this situation, Marge is the link that enables CPoC pictures to become part of ProjectWeb. Marge instructs Isabelle in the sequence of actions necessary to make ProjectWeb work, and, in addition, she recommends that Isabelle also remembers to make a link back to ProjectWeb. The functioning of ProjectWeb's (for this particular task) is thus dependent upon Marge's presence.

In addition to assisting with such problem solving in everyday use, Marge surveys all ProjectWebs and occasionally provides individual project assistants with suggestions on how to reorganize menu categories or adjust the layout on a page. She sends out general e-mails now and then, with suggestions such as how to put in a background picture on the front news page to ProjectWeb, or how to create fancy Web page details in FrontPage® for pages linked to ProjectWeb. Marge also created her own extensions to ProjectWeb such as asp pages and a calendar functionality incorporated in ProjectWeb. The calendar page was made upon request from the project assistants to satisfy the need for the coordination of the numerous meetings and events that take place within the large development projects. Marge built the calendar system by tying Excel® spreadsheets together with an automatic generation of HTML pages in ProjectWeb.

For some changes in ProjectWeb, such as turning modules on and off or adjusting the top-level menu categories, project assistants need to go through Marge as the main system administrator. She sets up ProjectWebs for new projects and also withholds some parts of ProjectWeb by turning them off at set-up (for example, an "entire reporting module" is non-existent for most project assistants). As she remarked one day to the project assistant, Joan, who asked her if she could add other article types to her ProjectWeb.

"Well, actually you can do that yourself, I just haven't told you because I thought it would get too complicated with all the options and you would come running constantly." (Office observation, Marge)

So Marge holds the assembly together by also limiting some possible configurations.

Linking Use to Professional Development

Marge is also the main contact to professional developers in the development department of Medica and has been involved in the design of previous versions. Marge was, for example, in frequent contact with Neal, the programmer, for minor changes to beta versions of ProjectWeb. Marge gathers up problems and new demands as these arise through use in the project management department:

Marge has received an e-mail from the project assistant Jens down the hall. She explains to me that he is upset about the recurring uploading glitches in ProjectWeb experienced by their partner firm in Australia. Marge saves the e-mail in a folder "ProjectWeb improvements". In this folder she collects requests that come in by e-mail about ProjectWeb together with her own notes on reoccurring problems that she herself or the project assistants experience or complain about. E-mails and notes may also be on requests for additional features or changes to the existing interface or functionalities. (Office observation, Marge, Support Project Assistant)

Marge thus collects experiences and now and then sums these up into lists and requirements. In doing so, Marge labels certain properties as problematic in a document list. She translates use situations (such as those I have described earlier) into a language of requirements that professional developers can incorporate into their work.

Marge's ongoing assistance, her archive of requests, and the improvement list are elements that link use practices to formal development. Again, the notion of assemblage is relevant, since these practices (through selection, condensation, negotiation, and translations into a language developers understand) link up to the IT department of Medica. These improvement suggestions form one element in a conglomerate of other concerns that play into development. Earlier versions, though, have been rebuilt with more and more features for customization and more advanced document database functionalities specifically requested by project assistants (as they have become more and more familiar with possibilities and desire more). A log file statistics section that allows the project assistants to survey "their users" has, for instance, grown out of the project assistants' desire to see how the ProjectWebs they maintain are used by project members. Marge and her work thus comprise an important link in the ProjectWeb assembly—both in holding together ProjectWeb for everyday use situations in the project management department and in relating these situations to distant practices of formal development.

Incompleteness and Unpredictability of Networked Communications in Use

This chapter argues that assemblage is a productive concept for grasping ongoing use practices of Web-based information systems—as pinned out in the analysis earlier. The analyses have illustrated a starting point for thinking about how characteristics of use situations (e.g., what is or is not a user problem) as well as outcomes and effects of use (e.g., a successful or failed technology) are produced through an assemblage process where people, technology, and resources are brought together at particular times and places. Thinking about the evolving use of Web-based information systems as a practiced assembly can thus turn our focus to the practices in which skills, demands, resistances and problems, and benefits emerge and how they may differ from one place and time to the next. The notion of assemblage thus provides a new perspective from which to study and comprehend the ongoing process through which information systems come to be successes or failures, or both.

The concept is suggested as a descriptive tool and can be seen as a sensitizing mechanism in contrast to definitive concepts (Blumer, 1954). A definitive concept refers precisely to the commonalities of a class of objects, through a clear definition that identifies the individual instance of the class and the make-up of the instances covered by the concept. A sensitizing concept, on the other hand, does not have a precise specification and does not allow us to move directly to and from an instance and its relevant content. Instead, as Blumer (1954) notes, sensitizing concepts provide us with a general sense of reference and guidance in approaching empirical situations: "Whereas definitive concepts provide prescriptions of what to see, sensitizing concepts merely suggest directions along which to look…they rest on a general sense of what is relevant" (p. 7). The concept of assemblage seeks to sensitize the task of understanding networked communications in use, providing clues and suggestions as well as a path for understanding other similar situations that in turn may be tested, improved, and refined. The concept of assemblage is thus not the only proper way to approach networked communications, but it is suggested as a means of seeing and approaching use practices in a way that highlights incompleteness and unpredictability. This way of describing use situations taking place in three different offices in a pharmaceutical firm, thereby sensitizes us to a number of more general themes concerning the use and evolving use of networked communications:

Extensions: Networked communications are continuously being assembled and extended for particular use as well as in order for others to engage in further use.

Interferences: Network communications in use are highly contingent upon a wider assemblage of heterogeneous elements that must be brought together and aligned. What is easy or troublesome, working or not working, success or failure is an effect of ongoing user practices.

Indispensability: The success of networked communications is fragile, and some links in the assemblages (that make possible and sustain use) are indispensable at particular points in time and in relation to others' use.

To complement explanatory theories such as structurational approaches and existing conceptualizations of the user as actor, the notion of assemblage illuminates empirical actualities and offers new perspectives from which to explore use practices. The concept and themes proposed provide an antidote to existing studies and a tendency toward being overly concerned with explaining use patterns through structures or depicting use as a matter of human resistance to fixed technological characteristics embedded by designers. Thinking about the ongoing use of Web-based information systems as a practiced assemblage can turn our focus to the ways in which networked communications become entangled with and layered into a range of previous, present, and future use activities. Also, intermediary use can be conceived of not as an intentional mode of action, but instead as an event where possibilities for use and redesign activities are offered by particular circumstances and ways in which practices and technologies are brought into relation. The notion of assemblage helps to open up and scrutinize this intermediary space of design/use.

I suggest here that highlighting such emergent effects of use is particularly pertinent in dealing with open-ended and evolving aspects of networked communications as is evident in this case of Web-based information systems. Developers, designers, and IT managers would benefit from acknowledging and appreciating such unpredictability and incompleteness of networked communications as well as engaging more actively with such user practices and effects. The examples emphasize the importance of continual user support and training and suggest that existing experiences and experimentation might be incorporated in multiple cycles of professional redesign (rather than one-shot design of new versions). Furthermore, developers and IT managers might benefit from a broader view of design where preconditioning infrastructures, organizational particularities and application integration and experimentation are approached as interlinked and equally decisive for a new system's success or failure.

Acknowledgments

I am grateful to the study participants at Medica and to co-researchers Jørgen Bansler, Erling Havn, Hanne Nicolajsen, and Jens Kaaber Pors. The study was supported in part by a grant from the Danish Research Councils (grant no. 99-00-092).

References

Akrich, M. (1992). The de-scription of technical objects. In W. Bijker, & J. Law (Eds.), *Shaping technology, building society: Studies in sociotechnical change* (pp. 205-224). Cambridge, MA: MIT Press.

Andriessen, J. H., Hettinga, M., & Wulf, V. (2003). Introduction to special issue on evolving use of groupware. *Computer Supported Cooperative Work: The Journal of Collaborative Computing, 12,* 367-380.

Blumer, H. (1954). What is wrong with social theory. *American Sociological Review, 18,* 3-10.

Bowers, J. (1994). The work to make a network work; Studying CSCW in action. In R. Furura, & C. Neuwirth (Eds.), *Proceedings of the Conference on Computer-Supported Cooperative Work,* Chapel Hill, North Carolina, USA, October 22-26 (pp. 287-298). New York: ACM Press.

Brown, S. D., & Lightfoot, G. (2002). Presence, absence, and accountability: E-mail and the mediation of organizational memory. In S. Woolgar (Ed.), *Virtual society? Get real! The social science of electronic technologies* (pp. 209-229). Oxford: Oxford University Press.

CACM (Communications of the ACM) (1998). *Special Issue on Web-Based Information Systems, 41*(7).

Callon, M., & Law, J. (1995). Agency and the hybrid collectif. *South Atlantic Quarterly, 94,* 481-507.

Ciborra, C. U. (2000). From alignment to loose coupling: From MedNet to www. roche.com. In C. U. Ciborra (Ed.), *From control to drift: The dynamics of corporate information infrastructures* (pp. 193-211). Oxford: Oxford University Press.

Deleuze, G., & Guattari, F. (1987). *A thousand plateaus: Capitalism and schizophrenia.* Minneapolis: University of Minnesota Press.

Derrida, J. (1978). *Writing and difference.* London: Routledge.

DeSanctis, G., & Poole, M. S. (1994). Capturing the complexity in advanced technology use: Adaptive structuration theory. *Organization Science, 5*(2), 121-147.

Dourish, P. (2003). The appropriation of interactive technologies: Some lessons from placeless documents. *Computer Supported Cooperative Work: The Journal of Collaborative Computing, 12*, 465-490.

Emerson, R. M., Fretz, R. I., & Shaw, L. L. (1995). *Writing ethnographic fieldnotes*. Chicago: University of Chicago Press.

Fleck, J. (1988). *Innofusion or diffusation? The nature of technological development in robotics*. Edinburgh Programme on Information and Communication Technologies (PICT). Working Paper No. 7. Edinburgh University.

Fujimura, J. (1991). On methods, ontologies and representation in the sociology of science: Where do we stand? In D. Maines (Ed.), *Social organization and social process: Festschrift in honor of Anselm L. Strauss* (pp. 207-248). Hawthorne: Aldine de Gruyter.

Giddens, A. (1984). *The constitution of society: Outline of the theory of structure*. Cambridge: Polity Press.

Hales, M. (1994). Where are designers? Styles of design practice, objects of design and views of users in CSCW. In D. Rosenberg, & C. Hutchinson (Eds.), *Design issues in CSCW* (pp. 151-177). London; New York: Springer-Verlag.

Henriksen, D. L. (2003). *ProjectWeb as practice: On the relevance of radical localism for information systems development research*. Ph.D. dissertation, Roskilde University, Datalogiske Skrifter, 96.

Kensing, F., & Blomberg, J. (1998). Participatory design: Issues and concerns. *Journal of Computer Supported Cooperative Work: The Journal of Collaborative Computing, 7*(3-4), 167-185.

Lamb, R., & Davidson, E. (2000). The new computing archipelago: Intranet islands of practice. In R. Baskerville, J. Stage, & J. DeGross (Eds.), *Proceedings of the IFIP WG 8.2 Conference on Organizational and Social Perspectives on Information Technology*, Ålborg, Denmark, June 9-11 (pp. 255-276). Dordrecht: Kluwer Academic Publishers.

Latour, B. (1987). *Science in action: How to follow scientists and engineers through society*. Cambridge: Harvard University Press.

Latour, B. (2005). *Reassembling the social. An introduction to actor-network theory*. New York: Oxford University Press.

Law, J. (2005). *After method: Mess in social science research*. New York: Routledge.

Lie, M., & Sørensen, K. H. (Eds.) (1996). *Making technology our own? Domesticating technology into everyday life.* Oslo: Scandinavian University Press.

Luff, P., Hindmarsh, J., & Heath, C. C. (2000). *Workplace studies: Recovering work practice and informing system design.* Cambridge: Cambridge University Press.

Lyytinen, K., Rose, G., & Welke, R. (1998). The brave new world of development in the Internetwork computing architecture (InterNCA): Or how distributed computing platforms will change systems development. *Information Systems Journal, 8,* 241-253.

Mackay, W. E. (1990). Patterns of sharing customizable software. *Proceedings of the Conference of Computer Supported Cooperative Work,* Los Angeles, CA, October 7-10 (pp. 209-221). New York: ACM Press.

Marcus, G. (1995). Ethnography in/of the world system: The emergence of multi-sited ethnography. In G. Marcus (Ed.), *Ethnography through thick and thin* (pp. 79-104). New Jersey: Princeton University Press.

Mol, A. (2002). *The body multiple. Ontology in medical practice.* Durham: Duke University Press.

Mulcahy, M. D. (1998). Designing the user/using the design. *Social Studies of Science, 28*(1), 5-37.

Nardi, B. A., & O'Day, V. (1999). *Information ecologies: Using technologies with heart.* Cambridge: MIT Press.

Nicolajsen, H. W., & Bansler, J. (2007). Evolving information ecologies: The appropriation of new media in organizations. In S. B. Heilesen, & S. S. Jensen (Eds.), *Designing for networked communications: Strategies and development* (pp. 1-25). Hershey: Idea Group Publishing.

Orlikowski, W. J. (2000). Using technology and constituting structures: A practice lens for studying technology in organizations. *Organization Science, 11*(4), 404-428.

Oudshoorn, N., & Pinch, T. (2003). *How users matter: The co-construction of users and technology.* Cambridge; London: MIT Press.

Silverstone, R., Hirsch, E., & Morley, D. (1992). Information and communication technologies and the moral economy of the household. In R. Silverstone, & E. Hirsch (Eds.), *Consuming technologies: Media and information in domestic spaces* (pp. 15-31). London: Routledge.

Stewart, J., & Williams, R. (2005). The wrong trousers? Beyond the design fallacy: Social learning and the user. In D. Howcroft, & E. M. Trauth (Eds.), *Handbook of critical information systems research: Theory and application* (pp. 195-223). Cheltenham: Edward Elgar.

Suchman, L. (2002). Located accountabilities in technology production. *Scandinavian Journal of Information Systems, 14*(2), 91-105.

Suchman, L., Trigg, R., & Blomberg, J. (2002). Working artifacts: Ethnomethods of the prototype. *British Journal of Sociology, 53*(2), 163-179.

Trigg, R., & Bødker, S. (1994). From implementation to design: Tailoring and the emergence of systematization in CSCW. *Proceedings of the Conference of Computer Supported Work,* Chapel Hill, North Carolina, USA, October 22-26 (pp. 45-55). New York: ACM Press.

Williams, R., Stewart, J., & Slack, R. (2005). *Social learning in technological innovation; Experimenting with information and communication technologies.* Cheltenham: Edward Elgar.

Chapter III

Strategies for Organizational Implementation of Networked Communication in Distributed Organizations

Keld Bødker
Roskilde University, Denmark

Jens Kaaber Pors
Niels Steensens Gymnasium, Denmark

Jesper Simonsen
Roskilde University, Denmark

Abstract

This chapter presents results elicited from empirical studies of the implementation and use of an open-ended, configurable, and context specific information technology supporting networked communication in a large distributed organization. Our findings are based on a longitudinal case study of the implementation and use of the technology that spread rapidly throughout the organization. We demonstrate the kind of expectations and conditions for change, that management face, when implementing such technologies for computer-mediated communication. Our synthesis from the empirical findings is related to two recent models, the improvisational change management model suggested by Orlikowski and Hofman (1997), and Gallivan's model for organizational adoption and assimilation (Gallivan, 2001). We operationalize the change management models by identifying and characterizing four different and general implementation contexts and propose strategies for the organizational implementation of such technologies.

Introduction

This chapter deals with strategies employed by management and users in large distributed organizations in relation to networked communication. More specifically, we have studied the implementation and use of a particular technology for computer-mediated communication (CMC) that has spread rapidly throughout a distributed organization. We describe the implementation and use of this open-ended and flexible product from an information systems perspective by using theories and models related to implementation of information technology as well as to change management.

Introducing information technology in organizations has been researched under different labels such as: diffusion (e.g., Rogers, 2003); infusion (e.g., Massetti & Zmud, 1996); adoption (e.g., Davis, 1989); assimilation (e.g., Fichman, 2000); and change management (e.g., Kwon & Zmud, 1987). Also researchers within computer supported cooperative work (CSCW) like Bullen and Bennet (1990), Grudin (1994), and Orlikowski (1993, 2000) have early identified technological as well as organizational and social factors influencing the implementation of information technologies to support communication and coordination in groups.

CMC technologies are often used in distributed organizations to support communication. Managers direct resources and set up goals for the implementation of CMC technologies, but it is difficult to foresee the effects of the implementation. Our studies show that the outcome is definitely more complex than the apparent intended goals, and that ambitious goals are difficult to obtain. Generic, open-ended, configurable, and context-specific CMC technologies mediate interactions among multiple distributed actors, who are not only users (in the traditional sense) but also contributors to the system's evolving structure and content. Organizational models for implementing CMC technologies have only recently started to take form. The aim of this chapter is to discuss, refine, and operationalize existing models of change management with respect to the implementation issues in distributed organizations.

We present a longitudinal case study of the implementation and use of a CMC technology, a generic virtual workspace product. Throughout 18 months, we studied the introduction and use of IBM Lotus® QuickPlace® in a large, distributed financial organization. For reasons of anonymity, we refer to the financial company as "Summa". We have identified four general implementation contexts in which IBM Lotus® QuickPlace® was used, and we have elicited six overall characteristics that influenced the implementation and use. The characteristics describe potentials as well as obstacles for change related to CMC and demonstrate the kind of expectations and conditions for change, that management face, when implementing generic, flexible, and open-ended CMC technologies in distributed organizations.

The empirical findings are related to two models of organizational implementation, the improvisational change management model suggested by Orlikowski and Hofman (1997) and Gallivan's model for organizational adoption and assimilation of complex technological innovations (Gallivan, 2001). We refine and operationalize these change management models by means of identifying and characterizing typical CMC implementation contexts. We generalize our findings and specify managerial challenges and potential strategies for implementing generic, open-ended, and flexible CMC technologies (such as IBM Lotus® QuickPlace®) in distributed organizations.

IBM Lotus® QuickPlace® in Summa

In this section, we describe IBM Lotus® QuickPlace® and its implementation in Summa. For reasons of simplicity, we refer to the individual virtual workspace provided by IBM Lotus® QuickPlace® as a QP.

IBM Lotus® QuickPlace® is a typical representative of virtual workspace products, a group of products that also includes eROOM (http://www.documentum.com/eroom) and BSCW (http://bscw.gmd.de, Bentley, Horstmann, & Trevor, 1997), by being generic products for collaboration and communication in small teams. IBM Lotus® QuickPlace® is a flexible technology that offers users a Web-based shared virtual workspace called a QuickPlace® (QP) with a folder structure, notification functions, support for custom document types, joint editing of documents, shared calendar, and support for simple workflows, including facilities for version and access control. Since QP is open-ended, there is no workflow inscribed within the technology to support, for example, projects, recurrent tasks, and interest groups. The members of a QP need to agree on how to work together using the tool in the particular context, for example, using the tool as a shared archive or as a coordination mechanism for collaborative work (cf. Schmidt & Simone, 1996), and using the tool to design the structure and content of the QP accordingly. Due to its background as an application service provider application (ASP), the system has a distributed security infrastructure. There is no central system administrator role with extensive access rights but instead a very flexible scheme for user management. Once a particular QP is established at the central server and managers for this QP are appointed, any manager can set up a room (a specialized folder type with extra functionality available), invite others to participate, and grant them privileges as managers, authors, or readers.

These characteristics make the technology both cheap to purchase and easy to implement in an organization—from an IT operations point of view. Once the QP server is installed, any users granted with manager rights can initiate a QP and define the structures, folders, document types, as well as apply access rights to other users to each room and folder. Each QP thus consists of various rooms containing documents, which can be reached from a single URL. Users' access to specific documents is defined partly by the managerially-defined user access to rooms and folders, partly by the author of a document who can grant other people access to individual documents as well as rights to edit individual documents.

Summa was created by a merger of a number of financial companies consisting of private, corporate, and investment banks as well as insurance companies located across four European countries. Organizational units at headquarter level were formed spanning the four countries, including core business areas such as corporate banking and support functions like IT, human resources, and communications. Projects were established to merge operations across the national and organizational borders, for example, rolling out a new e-mail system and implementing standards for secure IT infrastructures between company units and customers. The aim of these projects was to create synergy and efficiency by merging complementary business functions at headquarter level, for instance, sharing investment risk data, drawing upon the accumulated expertise of the merged companies. Supporting communication and coordination in these activities was vital, and QP software was deployed approximately one month after the merger for this purpose. IBM Lotus®, the developers of QP software, presents their product as being very easy to implement: "A QP is a place that you can create on the Internet in 30 seconds to communicate with your team, share resources, and keep track of your project" [...and...] "create a Team Workspace on the Web – Instantly" (Lotus®, 2001). In line with this marketing presentation, the implementation process of the technology in Summa was what we choose to call lightweight, without provision of any education or guidelines apart from those on the manufacturer's Web site and the built-in tutorial and help functions.

IBM Lotus® QuickPlace® was chosen for several reasons. The technology was Web-based, thus needing no particular technical efforts to be integrated with the existing IT infrastructures of the pre-merger companies. The product could thus be implemented very quickly from an IT operations point of view. An important factor influencing the decision to go ahead with the technology was that it offered secure (encrypted) communication—unlike conventional e-mail. In the organization, there was a positive experience with other Lotus® products in general. One month after the merger, the technology was installed and made available throughout Summa. The availability of the technology was announced through e-mails and presentations to selected groups of people, typically middle managers at headquarters. A potential QP manager should send an e-mail to Summa's department of IT operations applying for a QP, justifying the request on business terms. In practice, applications were approved provided when members from geographically dispersed organizational units or project teams applied.

Research Activities

Our studies of the implementation and use of QP in Summa took place in 2001-2002 starting one year after the introduction of the technology. The studies concerned the implementation and use of QP in conjunction with distributed work practices and involved interviews, document analysis, a questionnaire survey, and log analysis. All of our analyses of this multi-faceted material were reported on and discussed with management and other informants from Summa on several occasions. On this basis, we present our findings as a characterization of the implementation contexts we encountered, and we propose strategies for implementating CMC from an overall organizational point of view including an outline of the challenges, immediate expectations, and relevant aims to stimulate change processes. Our agreement with Summa did not include testing these strategies and recommendations in practice, thus a concrete intervention informed by our analysis was not part of the study.

The first round of interviews and document analysis were done in parallel over a period of three months in early summer 2001. The interviews lasted between 1 and 2 hours and were based upon an interview guide that was sent to the informant in advance. Interviews were recorded and later transcribed ad verbatim. For the analysis of the interviews, we appropriated a version of the affinity-diagramming technique (Brassard, 1989) to create a common understanding from the empirical material. The logging of all http transactions between client Web browsers and the QP server was initiated at the end of the three-month period of interviewing and lasted for 10 months (see Bøving & Simonsen, 2004, for further details). Our studies showed that the number of active QPs had grown within the first year at Summa. In the first month of our log-period, there were 805 active users in 80 QPs. The growth continued during the 10-month log-period to 1,618 active users in 126 QPs in the last month. All together more than 130 QPs comprising almost 3,000 users and more than 20

Table 1. Development of QP activities in a 10-month period in Summa

Activity measure	Development in activities
No. of active QPs	+58%
No. of active users	+101%
No. of operations	+275%
No. of operations pr. QP	+138%
No. of operations pr. user	+87%

gigabyte of documents accumulated during the first two years. Table 1 summarizes the development in activities as recorded by the log files of the QP server.

The recorded development in activities during the period of our study took place despite the lightweight implementation. Regardless of this rapid proliferation of the CMC technology observed in the organization, no resources were devoted to support and further develop the integration efforts in the local contexts.

Implementation Contexts

Our investigations of the introduction and use of QP lead to the identification of four typical implementation contexts of QP. In autumn 2001, we conducted a survey by distributing a questionnaire by e-mail to 123 QP administrators, who were in charge of a total of 77 QPs, all of which had shown to be active in the first weeks of logging QP related http-transactions. The questionnaire contained 28 closed questions, 3 open questions, and an option for additional comments. The questions all related to the use of QP: who are the users; what is the QP used for; and how is it used. The questionnaires were sent out 18 months after initial deployment of QP in Summa. Fifty-six of the administrators (45%) responded to the survey representing 53 of all QPs (65%).

The survey confirmed the general distribution of the identified implementation contexts—see Table 2—showing the distribution of answers related to the question: "Which group of people is using your QP?"

Table 2 shows that the dominant use of a QP was within the distributed organizational units or projects—accounting for 38% and 32%, respectively, of the total amount of QP use in the survey. Use of QP in a special interest group or a team handling recurrent tasks is much less prevalent—11% and 13% respectively, or 24% of the total amount of QP use. Only 6% of the QP use was reported outside the four implementation

Table 2. Distribution of the four identified implementation contexts in Summa

Implementation context	# of QP	% of QP
Organizational units	20	38
Special interest groups	6	11
Projects	17	32
Teams handling recurrent tasks	7	13
Other	3	6
Total	53	100

contexts identified by the initial interviews. In the following, we characterize each of the four typical implementation contexts as observed in Summa.

Organizational Units

Following the merger, organizational units were reorganized as units from the former organizations with overlapping functions. For example, a new corporate communications department was formed and made responsible for establishing the new name, corporate identity, media relations, and so forth. This department was staffed with 80 employees distributed across four countries. The staff found themselves in this new organizational setting, not knowing their new colleagues, speaking different languages, and spanning multiple organizational and national cultures. The starting point for this unit was typical of the units we studied during the merger, since the basis of the new entity was created by the appointment of a top manager and the production of a charter (in the form of a PowerPoint® presentation), outlining of the overall areas of responsibility along with an organizational chart, and the names of the managers and employees allocated to each section in the unit.

The content of the typical QP within an organizational unit was initially structured according to the organizational chart. A member of staff was appointed as the administrator of the QP. Each section was given their own entry: a folder in QP along with a few (or no) stated guidelines for how to use it. The primary use of these QPs was distributing management information such as meeting schedules, agendas and minutes, strategies, and goals for different sections. The QP was also used as an archive, where users uploaded documents that they felt might be useful for others in their organizational unit. However, extensive use patterns did not develop. A reason for this was reported as problems with finding specific information by browsing a structure that reflects the organizational chart and not the content of the documents. Another reason could be that the information provided was of a general nature and not specifically needed by anyone. Thus, we can observe that QP software employed within distributed organizational units provides an information channel, but it seldom succeeds in mediating active interactions among users.

Special Interest Groups

An important aspect of complex organizations is to share knowledge and achieve synergy. In Summa, practitioners that share a professional interest on a specific topic formed special interest groups, and they were encouraged to take active part in knowledge sharing. Examples of such groups of practitioners are project managers, change consultants, and experts within specific technologies such as Oracle®, Java™, and Notes®. Members of the special interest groups are distributed organizationally as well as geographically. The overall aim of establishing special interest groups was argued in knowledge management terms, for example, by enhancing possibilities for the exchange of experience and for gradually building up a kind of "professional handbook" where knowledge would be represented and eventually made broadly accessible within Summa. A typical QP for this implementation context is structured according to topics relevant for the professionals of the special interest group. Their QPs contain, among other things, a bulletin board with news and events of interest, an archive with profession specific articles, and a frequently-asked-questions list.

In our studies, it became clear that the special interest groups' use of QPs is a secondary function compared to the daily work activities of the members. None of the QPs for special interest groups (typically focusing on general issues of interest) offered any kind of "tools" supporting the members' daily work practices. No functions or information were found that were used frequently as an integral part of work procedures. Being a member of the interest group, using the QP must be understood as a detached activity compared to the daily tasks and deadlines, and spending time using the QP had a low priority.

Projects

The merger initiated an instant need for various cross-organizational projects: a new Internet portal presenting the merged organization, establishing a new internal e-mail system, and so forth. In Summa, all projects have to report results within a six-month "time box". Thus, the majority of projects are completed within six months though some projects are extended to, for example, 12 or 18 months. The goals of using QP in the distributed projects have primarily been to support project documentation, but attempts have also been made to use QP to support coordination, problem solving, and negotiation.

One project had the purpose of evaluating the possibility of creating a shared customer security architecture across countries. The project's QP was organized into specific issues and deliveries such as documents describing issues like "Security" and "Infrastructure", or deliverables like a "Project Charter". Working on the subject matter of the project requires a great deal of coordination and negotiation of the means and the goals of the project itself. To the members, representing several IT sections, such negotiations can be a delicate matter of strategic disclosure and non-disclosure. When trying to use a QP to support negotiations of different solutions to problems, members may not wish to lay all of the cards on the table straight away. Thus, attempts to use QP for problem solving and negotiation in this project did not succeed, and also attempts to ease coordination was found difficult. Therefore, our observations of the QPs in development projects reveal how they typically resemble project archives, where the results of the projects are developed and maintained in a post-hoc manner.

Teams Handling Recurrent Tasks

In Summa, a number of teams within the organizational units manage tasks that must be carried out periodically. Teams handling frequent recurrent tasks are often organized as sections within organizational units. In some cases though, such teams consist of members that belong to different organizational units. For example, when the information providers and translators handled the task of translating the financial reports to be published four times a year for the stock markets. Recurrent tasks typically comprise intense efforts performed over a short period of time, requiring a high degree of coordination and critical predefined procedures. The aim of using QP in this context is mainly to support coordination within the team when performing the task.

Consider the task of producing quarterly financial reports for the stock markets. This comprises production and translation of an English master document into four different languages. The completed financial reports are to be released simultaneously in five languages to the different stock exchanges and the press. The translation is initiated about one week before the release deadline. At this time, the master has not reached its complete and final state, and corrections occur several times right up to the deadline. These changes to the English master must be coordinated very tightly and propagated through to the translated versions. The translators work in parallel on the texts in different geographic locations. When a translator has completed parts of the documents, he or she uploads them to QP. They then become available to all others, and the status and progression of the work becomes visible in QP. Thus, QP provides an overview of the process as well as performing some of the tedious legwork that the collaboration entails. QPs for teams handling recurrent tasks are organized in accordance with their deliveries, and they typically also reflect the workflow of the tasks. In this implementation context, we found QP's main function to be as a coordination mechanism supporting the coordinating work by mediating mutual dependencies (Pors & Simonsen, 2003).

Summary

From the description so far, it is clear that the use patterns are quite diverse. Teams handling recurrent tasks have managed to exploit the technology constructively, primarily due to a number of characteristics that inherently enable its use. While in the other three described implementation contexts, the characteristics can to some extent be seen as constraining factors that call for a more deliberate and concentrated effort in order to fully exploit the technology. In the next section, we identify and describe these enabling/constraining characteristics in order to be able to propose strategies for the organizational implementation of CMC technologies.

Characteristics of the Implementation Contexts

In the following, we characterize the four implementation contexts further with respect to managerial potential for initiating, managing, and implementing change related to the implementation of a QP in a distributed organization. Our synthesis from the

Table 3. Characteristics related to QP use in the four implementation contexts identified

Context / *Characteristic*	Organizational units	Special interest groups	Projects	Teams handling recurrent tasks
Management position & role	Hierarchical (personnel mgr.)	Network manager (among peers)	Project manager (among experts)	Team manager (personnel mgr.)
Administration of QP	Delegated to member of staff	Network manager	Project manager or deputy	Team manager
Membership	Heterogeneous	Continuous and homogeneous	Transient and temporary	Continuous and congenial
Evaluation and redesign of QP	Occasionally and ad hoc	Continuous maintenance	Difficult (due to short life cycle)	Regularly (between tasks)
Work practice integration	Low	Low	Medium	High (critical)
Dependency of QP	Nice to have	Nice to have	Nice to have	Need to have

empirical material has resulted in six overall characteristics of the implementation contexts (Simonsen & Pors, 2003). These overall characteristics are summarized in Table 3 and further described in the following by highlighting similarities and differences across the four implementation contexts.

Management Position and Role

An obvious characteristic related to organizational change in general is the position and role of management. Organizational units typically have a hierarchical management structure, where managers take on the traditional role of personnel managers. This is not the case with special interest groups. A special interest group in Summa is allocated as a network manager supporting and maintaining the group. The network manager is the initiator, administrator, and main contributor to the group's QP. However, the management role is different as compared to the organizational unit because the network managers are among peers when considering the practitioners participating in the group. A somewhat similar situation is found in the projects. While the project manager is in charge of the project, the members of the project team are often specialists, and they might also be managers in their respective organizational units. In the customer security architecture project mentioned previously, the team members were managers of the IT sections from each of the companies that went into the merger. The teams handling recurrent tasks are comparable to the organizational units: the teams might indeed be organizational units, or the manager of the team is typically a personnel manager within a team where the other members have the status of subordinates.

Administration of QP

Administrators of QP are responsible for configuring and customizing the technology to fit intended goals and requested needs, including setting up the QP on the basis of the initial standard structure, handing out and adjusting user access rights, and so forth. In organizational units, this task is typically delegated to a member of staff. In larger units, this task might be distributed among several persons. Even though QP might have an important signal effect (in terms of supporting the unit's identity, etc.), the manager's involvement in shaping QP seldom has his or her primary concern. In the other three contexts, this role most often is taken on by either the manager himself or herself, or it is delegated to a deputy working in close cooperation with the manager. Network managers are also QP administrators. The QPs in the projects were typically initiated by the project managers themselves as part of their establishment of the projects. In the teams handling recurrent tasks, QPs take on the role of an important communication tool and a workflow mediator, and the administration of the QP becomes important to keep the structure in place and the content up-to-date, thus the team manager often takes on this responsibility.

Membership

The users of a QP constitute communities that vary significantly across the four contexts. The size of the group and the varying degrees of clear boundaries constitute different conditions for establishing a common understanding. The members of the organizational unit are characterized by the distributed nature of these units: a corporate unit is typically formed by merging similar units across the different merger companies and appointing one manager in charge of the unit. This community might be viewed as heterogeneous since the employees of the units come from different companies, most of which are still located in the original pre-merger settings. The members of a special interest group constitute a relatively stable and homogeneous network. Even though they are distributed throughout different organizational units, they share a specific and highly specialized profession. Thus, they may be characterized as a community of practice (Wenger, 1998). The projects have a transient and temporary membership, since a project ends after a limited period of time, for example, six months. Teams handling recurrent tasks have the most stable membership. The fact that these members share the same aim, and that they typically perform the task with tight deadlines, contributes to maintaining congenial relationships among team members.

Evaluation and Redesign of QP

The open-ended nature of a QP, along with the continuous changes in the organization, necessitate periodical evaluation and redesign of the QP in order to align the configuration and structure of information in the QP with the agreements and practices related to its use. In the organizational units, this seems to happen only occasionally and might, for example, be triggered by a restructuring of the unit or by a sudden managerial initiative, such as making the QP calendar the default introduction page in order to make the QP members aware of upcoming meetings and arrangements. By contrast, the special interest groups' network manager, who is responsible for administrating the QP, approaches evaluation and redesign as part of an overall maintenance, which is conducted in a continuous manner. Redesign within projects is difficult and problematic simply due to the relatively short life cycle of the projects. The initial setup of a QP is thus usually rarely redesigned: the cost of getting acquainted with a new structure is most often considered too high seen in relation to the short time that the team might yield the benefits from this. The teams handling recurrent tasks have a periodically occurring opportunity for reconsidering the use of QP where former experience can be incorporated in the future routines. The recurrent task thus has an advantage in this respect, since it provides such frequent occasions for evaluation and redesign, and because the character of work is well defined and has been tried several times before within a stable membership of a limited size.

Integration with Work Practice

Successful use of IT in general, including CMC technologies, often depends on how tightly these technologies can be integrated with the work practice of the users. It is generally acknowledged that integrating a CMC technology, such as QP, with work practices is a challenging and demanding task requiring that users are able to see the benefits from its use, and that they choose QP instead of other well-established alternative technologies such as e-mail (Grudin, 1994). In our study, we observed QP's integration with work practices in the organizational units as low reflecting the overall aim of offering QP primarily as an information distribution channel and as a shared archive. This is also the case for special interest groups, where the focus on general issues of interest leads QP to have a secondary role when compared to the daily work for the members. The integration varies in projects. Projects might succeed in integrating QP into their work by, for example, using QP as a working library for object-oriented use cases. In most projects, though, the main use of QP remains as an archive for project documentation with little integration with work practices, except for the project manager. On the other hand, the QPs of the teams handling recurrent tasks show a very tight integration with work practice. The ways of coordinating work are well defined and shared among the members, giving an effective basis for using QP as a coordination mechanism. Changes to established agreements have to be carefully prepared in advance, allowing for the necessary coordination and avoiding any misunderstandings or other disruptions in the completion of the task.

Dependency of QP

The dependency of having access to a QP in a given context reflects the integration with work practice. For the organizational units and the special interest groups, it is generally a nice-to-have facility, and work will continue (with only a few irritations) even if the QP server (theoretically) should crash and be out of use for days. This would also be the case for most projects, where the typical project manager needs QP when managing issues and deliverables and where QP is mostly viewed as a nice-to-have service for the project members. In order to get their work done, other means for coordinating project work such as e-mail and phone might even be more immediately gratifying. Dependency on QP is highly critical when considering teams handling recurrent tasks. When the team finalizes the financial reports of the quarterly translation task, this work is considered so critical that the QP server in Summa and central network facilities enters a "frozen zone mode" where other systems are restricted from certain kinds of updates in order to minimize the risk of a server crash.

Theoretical Models

A large body of research is devoted to studying the diffusion and assimilation of technologies in organizations and in societies in general. Fichman (2000) characterizes two strains of research in this field. The first strain is characterized as research identifying factors relevant for the rate, pattern, and extent of diffusion. Rogers (2003) has formulated one of the central theories, the diffusion of innovation theory, which has guided much of this research. The second strain is research aiming at identifying factors relevant to the diffusion and assimilation of technologies in organizations—in general and for specific technologies. The technology-acceptance model (Davis, 1989) is a classical example of such a theory.

The diffusion of innovation theory is being used intensively to study the diffusion of information technologies and is also being used as a framework for understanding the adoption of new technologies in organizations (see Prescott & Conger, 1995, for an early overview). With the classical diffusion of innovation theory, the relation between the technology and use is a binary one—either the technology is adopted, or it is rejected. We should note that the diffusion of innovation theory to some degree does acknowledge that a technology might be changed during the adoption process, captured by the concept *re-invention* (Rogers, 2003). However as we will see, the situation with an open and flexible CMC technology like IBM Lotus® QuickPlace® is more complex. Many studies have shown the value of the diffusion of innovation theory and the technology-acceptance model in explaining individual acceptance of technologies for personal use where the individual has a free choice of whether to accept the technology. But studies have also demonstrated limitations in terms of misfits between the assumptions underlying the models and the actual technology (Gallivan, 2001, p. 55).

Based on a thorough review of literature on diffusion and adoption models, Gallivan (2001) develops a framework for studying and analyzing the implementation of complex technologies in organizations when there is an organizational mandate to adopt the innovation. Gallivan's approach acknowledges that the organizational context of adoption decisions is not well captured by the traditional models, like the diffusion of innovation theory or the technology-acceptance model. His theoretical framework is based on a two-step decision process, the initial decision being taken by an authority at organization, division, or department level, and the secondary adoption process following one of three paths: (a) total commitment—a mandate that the innovation be adopted throughout the organization; (b) support strategy—the necessary infrastructure is provided while the adoption is voluntarily; or (c) advocacy strategy—based on specific pilot projects, observations of their processes and outcomes, decisions are made whether to implement more broadly.

Gallivan's model focuses on the factors influencing the secondary adoption process, and includes a *feedback loop* between what he terms the organizational consequences and the secondary adoption process with the assimilation stage. The content of this feedback loop, which Gallivan does not elaborate on, is intrinsically relevant when the technology in question is highly open-ended, configurable, and context-specific. In some of the local settings, we studied in Summa, experience from using QP provides feedback to make re-configurations of the technology and thus creates input to iterations of the secondary adoption decision. Refining Gallivan's model with respect to this feedback is vital in relation to such open-ended CMC technologies. Especially, we find that the various implementation contexts provide quite different settings and possibilities for this feedback.

Orlikowski and Hofman (1997) suggest a different approach resting on the assumption that changes associated with the implementation are ongoing processes, and that the changes cannot all be anticipated or planned in advance. They suggest distinguishing three kinds of change: anticipated change, emergent change, and opportunity-based change. Our studies clearly demonstrate the validity of Orlikowski and Hofman's improvisational model of change management (Orlikowski & Hofman, 1997). We can identify change processes of all three types: *Anticipated change,* which is, change that is planned ahead and occurring as intended by the originators of the change, is for example the use of QP in organizational units and projects. *Emergent change*, which is local and spontaneous change not originally anticipated or intended, is exemplified in our study by a QP that was started by a newly formed group of people assigned to gather investment risk data from different business units. They started using the QP as a repository where the people involved posted Excel® spreadsheets of risk data, which was consolidated into one risk profile for Summa. They, thus, used QP to support a recurrent task. Such changes did not involve deliberate actions but grew out of practice. The last kind of change identified by Orlikowski and Hofman is *opportunity-based change*, which is purposefully introduced changes resulting from unexpected opportunities that arise after the introduction of the new technology. An example of this kind of change is the use of a QP to support the translation of quarterly financial reports. The idea of using a QP to support this activity appeared as a possibility to the manager of the team of translators. Since e-mail was too insecure for distributing financial draft reports, the team used the fax machine for this purpose. QP offered an alternative secure medium for this distribution. The manager then introduced a QP to the team and carefully designed the structure of the QP to support the progression of the translation process.

Organizational Change Management Levels

With a technology like IBM Lotus® QuickPlace®, the change processes involved in the integration of a QP into the organization can be understood as taking place at two very different levels. Gallivan's model identifies a two-step adoption decision process (Gallivan, 2001), which in relation to the Summa case relates well to changes at the two levels. At one level—in Gallivan's model called the primary authority adoption decision—we can identify the decision to acquire IBM Lotus® QuickPlace® followed by the introduction of the QP service. The change at this level we call an *organization/infrastructure change*. At another level, we find the local change processes related to the introduction of the individual QPs and the dynamic reconfigurations among the users of a QP, which we coin *work group level changes*. In Gallivan's model, this is referred to as secondary adoption and organizational assimilation processes. In relation to Gallivan's model, we should keep in mind that in Summa the decision to use QP on the level of the work group—be it an organizational unit, a project, or a team—is a voluntary decision.

Thus, in order to better understand—and thus better plan and manage—the implementation of CMC technologies like QP we suggest a model combining the distinction between an organization/infrastructure level and a work group level with Orlikowski and Hofman's approach recognizing changes as ongoing processes of three types: anticipated, emergent, and opportunity-based. As argued previously, the centralized introduction of the general CMC technology and the adoption of individual QPs (in, for example, a project) are very different change processes. Yet, they are equally important. Examples of the changes processes at organizational and group level are provided in Table 4.

Activities at both levels are central to the fruitful implementation of flexible CMC technologies. An implication of this distinction is that it could help an organization understand, foresee, and support a wider spectrum of the change processes involved in implementing CMC technologies in particular by directly addressing the work group level. One way of achieving this could be to systematically collect good practices from individual QPs and distributing this advice to others. For example, in a particular QP, some had discovered a shortcut to reverse the order in which documents appeared in a folder. Other users in QPs with comprehensive and cluttered folders could have benefited greatly from this. Such a sharing of experience outside closed circles is an important prerequisite for enabling emergent and opportunity-based change. Thus, a general guideline drawn from our studies is to encourage and provide resources for evaluation throughout the organization by collecting and disseminating accounts of good practices regarding CMC use.

Table 4. Examples of change processes at organization and work group level

	Organization/infrastructure level	Work group level
Anticipated change	defining goals such as to use QP to reduce travel; establishing procedures for issuing, setting up and closing QPs	defining and agreeing on the group's aim of using a QP, defining folder structure, inviting members, managing content and re-configuring
Emergent change	change of criteria for opening a QP from including a business justification to geographical dispersed groups	the establishment of new communication patterns over time (e.g., using a QP to support gathering risk data)
Opportunity-based change	introduction of new generic services in QP like, e.g., archiving functions, search patterns, or various templates	using the QP for supporting the translation of financial reports as a secure technology replacing the fax machine

The overall situation in Summa concerning the implementation of QP is character-ized by a rapid, although not well supported, spread of the technology, where the configuration and customization of the local QPs are distributed to the users of the technology. QP might in this way be considered as a non-strategic CMC technology that spreads "bottom-up" and develops into different local guises. An improvisational change management approach is needed relying on anticipated as well as emergent and opportunity-based change processes as suggested by Orlikowski and Hofman (1997). This makes the first three mainly organization-oriented characteristics (Table 3) of the implementation context (management position and role, administration of QP, and membership) hard to change without the need for investing resources in, for example, major managerial and organizational restructuring that exceed the perceived returns of such an investment. For example, we consider the role of management within special interest groups and projects to be a fixed condition that prevents management from relying on authority (alone) to promote specific uses of QP. A specific way of using QP must be argued in relation to actual needs, as they are experienced by the users, in order to be successfully adopted. Thus it is not considered realistic to initiate changes within these organization-oriented char-acteristics solely in order to obtain a shift from a nice-to-have to a need-to-have use of QP. The latter three work practice-oriented characteristics—evaluation and redesign of QP, integration with work practice, and dependency of QP—might in this respect be more fruitful to consider initially.

Synthesizing Strategies for Organizational Implementation

Next, we refine and operationalize Gallivan's approach, especially with respect to its feedback loop, as well as Orlikowski and Hofman's improvisational change model and describe strategies for organizational implementation based on the four typical implementation contexts as they appear in Tables 3 and 5. The strategies synthesize our studies and empirical experience with regard to open-ended CMC technologies. Each of the four contexts is characterized with regard to the challenges that management face concerning the characteristics of the implementation context, the immediate expectations and aims that management can have for the effect of implementing CMC technologies in a given context, as well as the strategies to stimulate change by means of enabling anticipated and opportunity-based change processes.

Table 5. Organizational implementation of QP in distributed organizations outlining challenges, immediate expectations, and aims, as well as strategies to stimulate change processes related to four types of implementation contexts

Context *Organizational implementation*	Organizational units	Special interest groups	Projects	Teams handling recurrent tasks
Challenges	Most characteristics do not support effective use of QP	Low integration with work practice (no specific collaboration among members)	Transient, temporary membership combined with short life cycle	No serious challenges: All characteristics support effective use of QP
Immediate expectations and aims	QP as information distribution channel with low effect on collaboration	QP as information distribution channel and "information of interest" archive	QP as information distribution channel and post hoc project documentation archive	QP as coordination mechanism effectively reducing complexity in collaboration
Strategies to stimulate change processes [A]: Anticipated [O]: Opportunity-based	[A]: QP as shared archive developed by regular evaluations and redesigns [O]: QP use reflecting teams handling recurrent tasks as such teams evolve	[A]: QP as means for promoting "best practices" [O]: QP as indispensable tool provider integrated with daily work practice	[A]: QP as a strategic application across projects, supporting (mandatory) concepts, models, tools, techniques, and deliveries	[O]: QP as local strategic application, requiring full commitment to using QP and aligning work practices to obtain tight integration

Organizational Units

Most characteristics (see Table 3) do not support extensive use of QP. The focus is on clarifying and establishing processes and collaboration across the units' distributed sections, rather than supporting existing work practices by integrating QP. A potential strategy for change could include aiming for a comprehensive shared archive. This requires a well planned process of anticipated change to develop a comprehensive and shared categorization system for the archive, established by regular evaluations and redesigns. If parts of the organizational unit over time evolve into specialized sections and teams, an opportunity-based change process could be initiated including sub-structures with "private" folders. Such specialized sections might finally resemble teams handling recurrent tasks, and (like the group of translators) teams within the unit might thus use QP to support coordination of their work.

Special Interest Groups

The members within a special interest group potentially do share a professional interest, but this does not entail any specific collaboration or mutual dependencies. This hinders integration of QP and work practices, and the need to use QP is therefore modest. Expectations for using QP to reach beyond a "nice-to-have" facility depend on the possibilities for a more tight integration of QP with the daily work practices of the group members. Two potential strategies might be considered, a "tool" strategy and a "best practices" strategy. Developing the technology into an indispensable tool requires that opportunities arise where QP might provide functionality that is more closely integrated with daily work practices, for example, by offering resource management services for the project managers, by creating mutual commenting and editing procedures for the change consultants, by providing facilities for software configuration management for the Java™ developers, and so forth. Promoting and establishing so called "best practices" requires an anticipated and ambitious change strategy with wide-ranging implications, including requirements for an organizational transformation of the groups into single, uniform entities, or coherent communities of practice, as suggested by Bansler and Havn (2001).

Projects

The immediate challenge related to projects is to deal with the risk of investing effort to establish and maintain a QP in a situation that can be characterized as a temporary endeavor involving busy project members, and hereby gain advantage from the investment. Transient and temporary memberships combined with short life cycles are characteristics that seriously restrict ambitious use of CMC technologies beyond a "nice-to-have" system. Establishing a QP as a "need-to-have" coordination mechanism within a specific project requires that the collaboration between mutual dependent project members has been established, that a general need to reduce the complexity of collaboration has been experienced and recognized, and that the QP is designed and configured to support the collaboration. This is almost impossible within a short time frame. A realistic expectation for a project is using QP on a relatively low ambition level as an information distribution channel and as an archive for project documentation. Strategies for a more ambitious use of QP, such as using QP as a coordination mechanism, should include elements that project members recurrently face in every consecutive project. This could include support for concepts, project models, selected tools and techniques, and deliverables that are required in all projects. In this way, QP could be turned into a strategic application that supports using and coordinating shared (mandatory) elements across projects. In a longer perspective, consecutive projects might in this way resemble teams handling recurrent tasks. Such an initiative could be supplemented by allocating change agents that evaluate use of QP across several projects, identify opportunities and emergent practices for QP use, and support the disseminating and handing over to new projects.

Teams Handling Recurrent Tasks

This is the only implementation context observed in Summa where QP has evolved into a critical technology having the effect of seriously reducing the complexity involved in communication and collaboration within a geographically distributed team. All aspects of the special characteristics of this implementation context are inherently in favor of using QP. Recurrent tasks with an embedded feedback loop naturally open for opportunities to reflect on and further develop procedures and practices for using QP as well as re-configurations of the QP. The strategies for an ambitious and successful use of QP for recurrent tasks include a full commitment to the technology and potentially a dramatic change in work practices in order to obtain the opportunities. Supporting the mutual dependencies embedded in a coordination mechanism also differentiates this implementation context from the other three by establishing a situation where a CMC technology develops into a local strategic application.

Conclusion

In this chapter, we have presented results from an empirical study of the use and implementation of a particular CMC technology, a commercial virtual workspace product used to support communication in a distributed organization. We saw that the implementation contexts were quite diverse, and we further offered six characteristics as essential factors in understanding the implementation of open-ended and flexible CMC technologies: management position and role, administration, membership, evaluation and redesign, work practice integration, and dependency.

Combining Orlikowski and Hofman's improvisational model for change management (Orlikowski & Hofman, 1997) with Gallivan's elaborate model for organizational adoption of complex technological innovations (Gallivan, 2001), we identified typical changes of three types—anticipated, emergent, and opportunity-based change—at two levels: an organization/infrastructure level where the introduction of the technology is prepared, and a work group level where the particular application close to the existing work practice takes place. Linking these change management models to the findings from the empirical study, we synthesize implementation strategies on the premise that these levels are mutually interdependent. Organizational units might evolve and include sub-units with local teams handling recurrent tasks, while special interest groups might be highly organized. Effective use of CMC technologies, however, is dependent on the possibilities of providing indispensable tools integrated with local daily work practices. We have identified that the special characteristics of technologies for networked communication entail successive changes including configuration and re-configuration of the technology used in local organizational contexts. In this light, the options for organizational implementation are further operationalized by identifying challenges, immediate expectations, and aims, as well as strategies to stimulate change beyond the immediate effects of implementing CMC technology.

Acknowledgments

We would like to thank the informants in Summa, who provided opportunities for studying networked communication in practice, and our colleagues in the DIWA research program, which was funded by the Danish Research Councils (grant no. 99-00-092). The chapter in particular draws upon earlier work by the authors in cooperation with Kristian B. Bøving.

References

Bansler, J., & Havn, E. (2001). Sharing best practices: An empirical study of IT-support for knowledge sharing. In *Proceedings of the 9th European Confer-

ence on Information Systems, Bled, Slovenia, June 27-29 (pp. 653-664). Bled, Slovenia: University of Maribor.

Bentley, R. T., Horstmann, T., & Trevor, J. (1997). The World Wide Web as enabling technology for CSCW: The case of BSCW. *CSCW: The Journal of Computer-Supported Cooperative Work, 6*(2-3), 111-134.

Brassard, M. (1989). *The Memory Jogger Plus+™. Featuring the seven management and planning tools*. Methuen, Massachusetts: GOAL/QPC.

Bullen, C. V., & Bennett, J. L. (1990). Learning from user experience with groupware. In F. Halasz (Ed.), *Proceedings of the Conference on Computer-Supported Cooperative Work*, Los Angeles, CA, October 7-10 (pp. 291-302). New York: ACM.

Bøving, K. B., & Simonsen, J. (2004). Http log analysis: An approach to studying the use of Web-based information systems. *Scandinavian Journal of Information Systems, 16*, 145–174.

Davis, F. (1989). Perceived usefulness, perceived ease of use and user acceptance of information technology. *MIS Quarterly, 13*(3), 319-340.

Fichman, R. G. (2000). The diffusion and assimilation of information technology innovations. In R. W. Zmud (Ed.), *Framing the domains of IT management: Projecting the future through the past* (pp. 105-128). Cincinnati, OH: Pinnaflex Educational Resources, Inc.

Gallivan, M. J. (2001). Adoption, diffusion, and infusion of IT: Organizational adoption and assimilation of complex technological innovations: Development and application of a new framework. *ACM SIGMIS Database, 32*(3), 51-85.

Grudin, J. (1994). Groupware and social dynamics: Eight challenges for developers. *Communications of the ACM, 37*(1), 92-105.

Kwon, T. K., & Zmud, R. W. (1987). Unifying the fragmented models of information systems implementation. In R. J. Boland, & R. A. Hirschheim (Eds.), *Critical issues in information systems research* (pp. 227-251). New York: John Wiley and Sons.

Lotus®. (2001). Retrieved November 10, 2001, from www.lotus.com/home.snf/welcome/quickplace

Massetti, B., & Zmud, R. W. (1996). Measuring the extent of EDI usage in complex organizations: Strategies and illustrative examples. *MIS Quarterly, 20*(3), 331-345.

Orlikowski, W., & Hofman, D. (1997). An improvisational model for change management: The case of groupware technologies. *Sloan Management Review, 38*(2), 11-22.

Orlikowski, W. J. (1993). Learning from notes: Organizational issues in groupware implementation. *Information Society, 9*(3), 237-250.

Orlikowski, W. J. (2000). Using technology and constituting structures: A practice lens for studying technology in organizations. *Organizational Science, 11*(4), 404-428.

Pors, J. K., & Simonsen, J. (2003). Coordinating work with groupware: The challenge of integrating protocol and artefact. In M. Korpela, R. Montealegre, & A. Poulymenakou (Eds.), *Organizational information systems in the context of globalization* (pp. 53-68). Dordrecht: Kluwer.

Prescott, M. B., & Conger, S. A. (1995). Information technology innovations: A classification by IT locus of impact and research approach. *Data Base Advances, 26*(2&3), 20-41.

Rogers, E. M. (2003). *Diffusion of Innovations* (5th ed.). New York: Free Press.

Schmidt, K., & Simone, C. (1996). Coordination mechanisms: Towards a conceptual foundation of CSCW systems design. *Computer Supported Cooperative Work. The Journal of Collaborative Computing, 5*(2-3), 155-200.

Simonsen, J., & Pors, J. K. (2003). Conditions for change related to groupware in a distributed organization – A case study. In C. Ciborra, R. Mercurio, M. D. Marco, M. Martinez, & A. Carignani (Eds.), *Proceedings of the 11th European Conference on Information Systems, ECIS'2003: New Paradigms in Organizations, Markets and Society*, Naples, Italy, June 19-21. Naples, Italy: Università di Napoli Federico II.

Wenger, E. (1998). *Communities of practice: Learning, meaning, and identity.* Cambridge, MA: Cambridge University Press.

Chapter IV

Participatory Design and Creativity in Development of Information and Communication Technologies

Nette Schultz
Technical University of Denmark, Denmark

Lene Sørensen
Technical University of Denmark, Denmark

Dan Saugstrup
Technical University of Denmark, Denmark

Abstract

This chapter presents and discusses a new design framework for involving users at an early stage in a mobile ICT development project. A user-centered design process, in which participatory design principles are combined with creativity techniques, is used in order to create scenarios as a communication tool between users and system designers. The theoretical basis for the framework is described, leading to a new participatory design and creativity framework. Empirical insight into how the framework has been developed and used in practice is presented based on the experiences and results from a large ICT development project within the field of mobile communication. Finally, the value of applying creativity as part of a participatory design process is discussed.

Introduction

Many information and communication technology (ICT) projects have experienced a gap between the system design itself and the needs and visions expressed when users have been introduced to the system developments. Within the field of human-computer interaction (HCI), several design methods and techniques have been developed to involve users in the design process and to bridge the gap between what users want and what is technically possible. Employing participatory design methods, like PICTIVE (Muller, 1991), means that users are actively involved in the design process, aiming at gathering user requirements and reflecting them in system design. The design process very much depends on how designers collaborate with users. There are several challenges in this process: the vocabulary used between designers and users, and to what extent user requirements are expressed in usable and understandable terms for the designers. Often, it is difficult for users to express their ICT design needs, especially when referring to a future state. On the other hand, designers have a technological insight that may take the ICT system designs and services much further than anticipated by the users. Finding the right balance between the two is a challenge.

In developing familiar applications that directly interact with users (e.g., Web pages) the traditional tools for deriving user needs are methods such as contextual inquiries, participatory design meetings, focus-group meetings, surveys, and interviews (Zappen & Harrison, 2005). All these methods possess advantages and limitations that have to be taken into consideration when using them. However, when addressing mobile, wireless technologies and networks, the tradition has so far been to develop these applications without paying much attention to user needs—in other words, a technology-driven development approach.

This chapter addresses mobile and wireless ICT development and presents a framework for how user requirements can be derived from users regarding design of technology, applications, and services within this area. A basic idea is to apply the principles from participatory design and focus on scenarios in particular as the technique for establishing designer/user communication. The use of scenarios is commonly used within ICT development and design, often presented as narratives about how people use technology in different situations and attempting to explain what, when, and how events and actions take place.

When using scenarios for innovation and identifying challenging technological ideas, it is fruitful to build these on creative thinking. Creativity is needed to support users in thinking ahead of and beyond their present needs, and to identify needs and situations in which current technology does not adequately support users. There is no firmly established scenario technique for ICT project design and developments (Alexander & Maiden, 2004, presents different techniques), and the aspect of creativity is traditionally not directly part of this process. Little research has been carried out in linking creativity and participatory design. Most theories of creativity are linked to either the individual or a group of people working together (Kazanjian, Dradin, & Glynn, 2000). In this chapter, creativity is used as an active component in setting up user-centred scenarios and is thus an effective factor in identifying user requirements—focusing on both the individual and the team creativity of a group of users.

The overall purpose is to present a participatory design and creativity framework developed in order to support and produce user-centered design in the development of innovative mobile, wireless ICT systems within the IST EU project "My personal Adaptive Global Net" (MAGNET, 2004). The framework has been built upon scenario construction and a set-up of successive workshops developed through practical project work.

The MAGNET project has a strong emphasis on user centricity, personalization, and personal networking. The end goal of the project has been to enable commercially viable personal networks that are affordable, user-friendly, and beneficial for all kinds of users in all aspects of their everyday lives. It addresses research issues within personal distributed environments, where users interact with a multitude of entities in their near vicinity, although potentially anywhere. These systems are defined as personal networks and constitute a category of distributed systems with very specific characteristics (Niemegeers & Groot, 2002). The concept of personal networks is related to personal communication environments, consisting of a large number of devices, which can all interconnect independently of time and place. They enable a collaborative environment within a distributed network setting, which supports users in both their professional and private activities. Figure 1 illustrates a generic set-up for a personal network and communication environment that can be interconnected through different ad hoc or infrastructure-based networks.

The specific design process addressed is the process of developing personal network services and applications, progressing through system layers from the top layer consisting of devices, user interfaces, and functionality and down through the layers to hardware components. By involving users in the development process, the written system requirements specifications for networks and platforms,

Figure 1. A personal network illustrating the user and how (s)he communicates with other environments

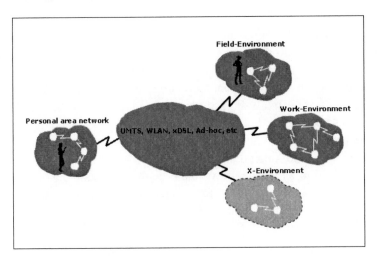

which induce constraints and limitations on the final services and applications, can be anticipated and already addressed when defining the first specifications. In this process, it is important to remember that "users" is a broad concept covering not only end users but also other stakeholders such as service providers, service operators, and different types of communities. In the present context, users will be understood as end users.

The chapter is divided into the following sections. First, the relevant theory within the fields of mobile systems development, participatory design, and creativity is discussed as the theoretical basis for a new participatory design and creativity framework. The new framework is then described with specific focus on different workshops structured according to creativity and participatory design principles. The practical implementation of the framework is illustrated by the MAGNET project. Focus is on how the theoretical framework has been applied to a specific case study dealing with improving the handling of health care related situations. The chapter concludes with reflections on both the theoretical framework and the practical experiences the application has provided for understanding the use of this framework.

Mobile System Development

In the past decade, mobile system developments have been researched extensively from an engineering system development and organizational point of view. However, during the last couple of years, a new perspective has emerged—the user perspective, which as the name implies focuses on user perspective and involvement. This means actively involving users, drawing social aspects into the development process, and creating a high level of user acceptance and usefulness in practice. Based on early research concerning nomadicity, mobility concepts, and later mobile system development literature, the present section briefly describes some of the important developments in this area and gives a short overview of important research carried out within the field.

Today, the combination of mobile computing and communication is rapidly changing the way we think about information processing and communication in general, and it is taken for granted that access to computing and communication is necessary from all locations, for example, office, home, and so forth, but also while in transit and when arriving at unfamiliar destinations.

The basis for some of these ideas and concepts has been discussed by computer scientist Kleinrock (1996a, 1996b), who describes and outlines the essence of nomadicity (nomadic computing and communications). This he defines as the system support needed to provide a rich set of computing and communication capabilities and services to nomads in a transparent, integrated, and convenient form as they move from place to place. From an engineer's perspective, this approach and concept are more or less based on making computers and computer communication systems mobile. According to Kleinrock, nomadic computing and communication described from a system perspective should support capabilities that enable independence of: location, motion, computing platform, communication device, and communication bandwidth, meaning that specific mobile computing environments should automatically adjust to the processing power, communication, and bandwidth available at any given time.

User Needs and Requirements

The overall viewpoint on mobile system development is mainly related to user needs and requirements and, more specifically, to design studies and HCI perspectives. In general, the number of wireless communication technologies and communication devices, services, and applications has increased dramatically over the last decade, albeit most of these developed and designed based on what was technologically possible with little attention being paid to specific user needs. However, during the last couple of years, increasing attention has been allocated to actually defining real user needs and designing and developing services and applications accordingly within the limits of the available technology. The big challenge within mobile system development and design is to develop mobile services and applications that actually support users in their everyday lives and also support professional working environments.

In a review of mobile HCI methods, Kjeldskov and Graham (2003) found a bias towards engineering systems using applied approaches and evaluating them, if at all, only in laboratory settings. Furthermore, they identified some gaps in the commonly used research approaches; for instance, action research, case studies, and basic research were identified as being applied rarely. The bulk of papers researched fall within the category of applied research (56 of 102 papers) and lab experiments (32 of 102 papers), whereas the remaining categories—case studies, field studies, action research, basic research, and normative writings—account for only 14 papers altogether. Based on their findings, Kjeldskov and Graham suggest a change of research focus within the area of mobile HCI in order to achieve a better understanding of the limits on design and application.

From a different perspective, Krogstie, Lyytinen, Opdahl, Pernici, Sian and Smolander (2004) explore the challenges in developing mobile information systems at the conceptual and logical levels and with a special focus on mobile knowledge workers and a user-oriented perspective. A major characteristic of mobile knowledge workers is the required ability to communicate and interact either synchronously or asynchronously with different information systems and persons independently of time and location. According to Krogstie et al. (2004), one of the main challenges regarding future mobile information systems is related to user orientation and personalization. Specifically, the separation of content and medium is very important in relation to delivering a maximum level of user personalization, as the systems should automatically adapt to the preferences of the user.

Participatory Design

Applying user-centered design to mobile system development does not necessarily mean that users actually participate in the design process. There are many different methods and techniques within interaction design that aim at a successful transition from the identification of user needs and requirements to the development of the final product. Using participatory design means that users are actively involved in the design process phase where new design ideas are generated. Users may be involved at different levels: the focus here is on the beginning of the design process dealing with scenario construction, low-fidelity prototyping, and simple mock-ups with the overall goal of capturing and exploring user needs and requirements.

Human Values

Participatory design in accordance with the Scandinavian approach has been centred on democracy issues and was, as described in Ehn (1988), developed in close collaboration with trade unions. Activity theory used as a high-level framework for understanding of the design process, as described in Kuuti (1996), was linked together with participatory design in Bødker, Greenbaum, and Kyng (1991). The definition of functional organs and mediation from activity theory means that all human experience is shaped by the tools and sign systems we use. This leads directly to users being actively involved in the design process. Participatory design is used in order to ensure that the finally developed applications and services will be adaptive to the users and not the other way around. In accordance with an activity theory framework (Kuuti, 1996), it is important to consider carefully how to set up a participatory design process because the results will be greatly influenced by how this is done.

Asaro (2000) presents a discussion of the different approaches to the participatory design process. Here, the conclusion seems to be that the technological rationalization perspective, including joint application design (Carmel, Whitaker, & George, 1993) and contextual design (Beyer & Holtzblatt, 1998), and the socialist and humanist perspectives—putting the sociotechnical (Mumford, 1987) and Scandinavian (Kensing & Blomberg, 1998) approaches under the same hat—have converged. The different approaches to the participatory design process have altogether converged to form a current heterogeneous field claiming the twin goals of increasing efficiency and increasing democracy. In the present context, the use of participatory design is not only aiming at more efficient and usable products but also at human values. However, focus has shifted from the original ideas of Scandinavian participatory design, in which democracy and workers' rights were at issue, to the private emotional life of the user. Today, new possibilities within ubiquitous computing and attentive environments and threats of surveillance and emotional manipulation and persuasion (Fogg, 2003) call for engineering designers who are able to perceive, understand, and communicate personal feelings and emotions. This new paradigm also calls for new experimental ways of prototyping using external cognitive aids developed as a language within the design team.

It is important to stimulate communication and learning in multi-disciplinary teams. A shared design language using external cognitive aids such as pictures and different kinds of elements for prototyping can be used with inspiration from Muller (1991), where the PICTIVE approach guides the users with the help of predefined elements, and from Gaver, Dunne, and Pacenti (1999), where the content of cultural probes is obtained by getting the users to create their own personal stories. During a participatory design workshop, the users are asked to envision future possible products within a case. This may be rather difficult for many users, and with inspiration from future workshops (Jungk & Müllert, 1987), the approach of starting with the present can be used as a good way of initiating the development of a shared communication language within a team.

Team Work

We design the products, and the products shape our living; therefore, engineering designers must be able to contribute to the connection between human values and technology. Design tools as external cognitive aids are good to have, but the primary source of success is the team members: engineers, designers, users, and other stakeholders. A good engineering designer is curious, open-minded, and creative while having technical, design process and teamwork skills. It is challenging to facilitate team development in order to achieve a creative and innovative blend of human values and technology in the design process. One approach in developing ICT products for the future is to use development methods that facilitate creativity, human values, user participation, and heterogeneous design teams. Furthermore, it may be necessary to accept design processes that might seem somewhat unstructured while in the exploration phases. Within design teams, the agreement of a code of cooperation is also important (FoundationCoalition, 2002). This may be predefined or formulated by the team itself. It is essential that team members get to know and trust one another, and feel secure and at ease. They must also be able to recognize and handle the trade-off that can exist between designers and participating users.

A team member must be able to understand the trade-offs inside the team, and this is commonly achieved by the use of transparency. The ability to see things from the point of view of other people is important. The concept of cognitive congruence, that is, the ability to understand and express ideas and solutions at the same level of knowledge, is also important when communicating with users, stakeholders, or other team members. These team skills are closely related to two of Howard Gardner's multiple intelligences (Gardner, 1983), the so-called interpersonal and intrapersonal intelligences. Interpersonal intelligence is the ability to understand the feelings of others, observe what is going on in a group, behave in an open and social manner, and communicate with people at an appropriate level. This intelligence is closely related to cognitive congruence. Intrapersonal intelligence is the ability to look within oneself, recognize whether emotions belong to oneself or another person, and situate these emotions where they belong. The ability to exhibit transparency is closely related to this intelligence. A person with an accurate view of him or herself possesses this skill. It is therefore necessary to spend time on the facilitation of such an environment. It does not just occur because people are put together in a team, but requires that team members learn to connect with one another in an open and positive framework.

Creativity

All innovation begins with creative ideas. Successful implementations of new products or services depend on a person or a team's ability to come up with a good idea in order to develop that idea beyond its initial state (Amabile, Conti, Coon, Lazenby, & Herron, 1996). The following descriptions focus on the theoretical perspectives and techniques used, completely or partly, for the proposed framework.

Creativity is a broad concept not easily defined and often based on combinations between theoretical foundations and beliefs of the user of the concept (see Pope, 2005). Here, we apply the definition presented by Amabile et al. (1996), in which "creativity is seen as the production of novel and useful ideas in any domain". Innovation is defined as the successful implementation of creative ideas within an organization, project, or given situation. This means that the starting point for any innovation is creativity exercised by individuals and teams.

Within the literature, Torrance (Millar, 1997) stands out with his research on creativity as a process; he views each individual as creative, and this creativity can be enhanced or blocked in many ways. Torrance believes that all persons are born creative, and it is possible to use activities, methods, and motivation to maintain and even increase a person's creativity.

When it comes to being creative in problem solving (and design can be seen as a problem solving process), research dates back to Wallas (1926), where he described a model for the process of the individual's creative thinking. This process has four phases:

- **Preparation:** The problem is defined and a starting attempt is made to solve the problem.
- **Incubation:** The problem is left while thinking about something else and doing something else.
- **Insight:** The person experiences (often suddenly) an insight into solving the problem.
- **Verification:** The solution is tested and can be accepted by others.

Behind this process lies the idea that creativity comes from the unconscious, leading to sudden insight, and that analytic thinking and creativity are complementary.

In an organizational context, models have been developed for the creative process that focuses systematically on the combination of techniques in order to generate ideas and techniques for analyses and selection of alternative solutions. The models have clear similarities to the Wallas model presented earlier. One such model can be seen in Leonart and Swap (1999).

Creativity Techniques

From characterizing and researching creativity, it is a step to actually enhancing and supporting creativity. There are a large number of different methods and techniques to increase and support creativity in different situations (see, for example, Higgins 1994). One of the central principles in working with creativity is the principle of divergent and convergent thinking. Divergent thinking is characterized by the generation of as many ideas as possible regarding a specific problem or theme. After some time (and a lot of ideas produced), it can be constructive to look at the ideas produced and select a few promising ones to work on. In the divergent phase, techniques such as brainstorming and picture stimulation can be used. In the convergent phase, more structure, systematic thinking, and patterns must be recognized as well as rules and prioritizations (Vidal, 2003). In the framework that follows, the focus is on techniques supporting divergent thinking, and, as such, it is relevant to consider some details on brainstorming and picture stimulation techniques.

Brainstorming is perhaps one of the most successful and often used creativity techniques. Brainstorming was introduced by Osborn (1953) as an element of creative problem solving to stimulate the generation of ideas and facilitate their expression. The technique is excellent for strengthening fluency, imagination, and communication skills (Goff, 1998) and can be used any time there is a problem or gap and within groups or with individuals. Brainstorming generates and stimulates enthusiasm as well as spontaneity and creativity (Goff, 1998) and is often used in combination with other techniques.

The picture stimulation technique (Vidal, 2003) encourages participants to think in completely different terms. The participants look at a particular problem from different and sometimes contrasting perspectives. Pictures are used to stimulate ideas and thoughts that break away from the normal way of thinking. This technique will enhance the production of original ideas and tends to break up established paradigms (Vidal, 2003).

Creating a Creative Environment

Amabile (1989; Amabile et al., 1996) has focused much of her research on the work environment and how it affects creativity. Many factors can be identified within organizations (as well as in the individual) that may inhibit and even block creativity. Therefore, it is also important to focus on the work environment when creativity is needed. There are no specific rules for setting up a creative environment, but often it is necessary to establish physical work environments that encourage participants to relax, move around, and work in other ways than they customarily do. All aspects that stimulate the brain to become creative can be included—such as pleasant surroundings, music, good food, opportunities to walk around and sit in different positions, and being able to have a general overview of the ideas produced. These principles have been brought into the design of the workshops that are described in the creative framework.

A Participatory Design and Creativity Framework

In the following, the participatory design and creativity theories described previously will be used and explored in relation to the MAGNET project, in which the new participatory design and creativity framework was developed and applied in order to derive valid user requirements for personal networks. The MAGNET project focuses on three case studies which together cover different societal themes relating to areas such as "health care", "business and working life" and "the home and private sphere". The following is based on the case study associated with health care, more specifically, on identifying situations in which personal networks will potentially be able to improve the monitoring and management of diabetes.

The collection of data in MAGNET was mainly based on qualitative methods, especially from workshops, in order to gain some insight into the information and communication patterns within the different case studies. In general, the aim of using qualitative research methods is to gain firm empirical knowledge of a social or natural phenomenon and to construct a coherent, internally consistent argument from sequences of empirical data in the form of texts, perceptions, and social acts (Denzin & Lincoln, 2000).

Within the participatory design and creativity framework, scenarios are the preferred tool for communication between users and designers. An example of another use of scenarios is the closely related IST project MobiLife (www.ist-mobilife.org). There is, however, no specific way in which to develop scenarios so that they represent the user's wishes optimally and, at the same time, address the technology issues needed for the designers. Alexander and Maiden (2004) present different scenario developments for different purposes in the systems development life cycle. Here, focus is on developing a scenario construction method which can: involve users, actively, in parts of a design process; ensure that the scenarios focus on relevant information such as user requirements in different situations, user needs, relevant user interfaces, and device interaction, as well as the social implications of the use and development of technology; link user requirements and needs with technical specifications and be based on possible and expected trends in society that may influence user needs and technological possibilities and developments.

The overall principle for scenario construction is the participatory design process, which focuses on interaction between users in particular situations and technicians and engineers designing future technologies and applications. Scenarios are used as the central communication tool between the users and the technical designers—and for deriving user needs and requirements. Scenarios create a possible picture of how the users anticipate themselves in the future using one or more technologies, applications, or services. The scenarios can include both aspects of wishful thinking and also situations that the users have not necessarily evaluated positively or negatively. In order to ensure that the scenarios will provide valuable input for technologies designed for the future, scenario construction focuses on providing a general overview of trends and situations that could be part of the future while at the same time freeing users from the present-day state of technology. Since the users have to think about the future, it is essential that they are able to do so. Therefore, the design methodology includes workshops based on creativity methods that encourage users to fantasize and extend their world to possible situations in the future. There are two types of workshops that together generate the information needed—the user workshop and the expert workshop. The user workshop includes users and their wishes for the future. The expert workshop, with technical developers and engineering designers as participants, works with these ideas to make sure that user needs and visions are brought to a state in which, technology-wise, they are challenging and interesting and may be discussed in terms of possibilities and limitations for the technical design.

In the following, scenarios will be defined (based on Van der Heijden 1996) as: ... *a descriptive set of plausible and possible different futures.* These futures are based on users representing different situations using a particular technology or service. It is assumed that the scenarios focus on longer-term ICT developments (5 years or more). In order to create scenarios that are usable for the design process, the scenarios must be relevant, likely, transparent, and coherent (Godet & Roubelat, 1999).

Scenario Construction in the MAGNET Project

The application of the participatory design and creativity framework made some practical demands on how to construct the scenarios. A scenario template was applied consisting of various steps in which descriptions and trends from the present time as well as expectations for the future were mixed together into scenarios. The approach used in the MAGNET project was based primarily on Schwartz (1991) and Van der Heijden (1996) and adapted for use as a communication tool in an ICT development project. Central to this scenario template is the direct representation of users and technicians/engineers as part of the scenario construction process through the application of participatory design principles and using creativity to focus on innovative ideas. The outcome of the scenarios is a mixture of narratives that can form the basis for creating use cases (Unified Modeling Language, UML), mock-ups of low-fidelity prototypes of devices, and pictures and graphs showing technical requirements based on the user needs and requirements.

Since the personal network architecture was to be developed over the coming years, it could be expected that trends in society would have an impact on the usage and acceptance of low fidelity devices, transmission possibilities, and the architecture itself. In order to obtain insight into expected trends, a questionnaire was therefore designed and structured according to the STEEP methodology (Johnson & Scholes, 1999). STEEP is short for Society, Technology, Economy, Environment, and Policy. For each factor, a number of questions were posed to shed light on the recipients' expectations of future developments within that particular area. The questionnaire was sent to all MAGNET participants (technical as well as non-technical). The questionnaire resulted in a number of statements and expectations that not only provided support for the project idea in the anticipated direction, but also revealed some expectations that could limit the idea or change its perspective. One such example was the concern about technology use and the potential risk of increasing the number of "throw away" devices. This could lead to thinking in terms of more recyclable products and an increased focus on battery lifetime and alternative fuels. The results of the questionnaire were used as input to the workshops in the form of questions.

Workshops and Results

In the participatory design and creativity framework, the creative user workshops are an essential part of user centricity. This is where the participatory design and creativity methods and techniques are fully intertwined. A conceptual text-based scenario landscape relating the case study must be created prior to a creative user workshop. This will be the first story users are told and acts as a prototype to be developed further during the workshop before finally becoming a complete scenario landscape. The scenario landscape should be understood as a conceptual, physical paper landscape showing different situations and pictures of how users think about the future. During a workshop, the users will be given additional external cognitive prototyping aids in the form of so-called image elements consisting of pictures, words, or short sentences. They are produced for each workshop on the basis of the case study's conceptual scenario landscape, the environmental trends (identified in the questionnaire), case study context, human activities, and important high-level user requirements. Pictures and perhaps a word will typically represent the related contexts and human activities.

At the creative user workshop for the "health care" case study, it was decided to divide the scenario landscape into four phases, each representing different life cycles and disease treatment for a diabetic person. The four phases were: babies, teenagers, adults, and elderly people. The image elements and questions used represented predefined contexts and user situations, as well as user requirements. Predefined contexts and user situations covered: shopping, education, travel, community, collaborative work, surveillance, emergency, health care, society in general, transportation, and home. Each of these contexts was represented by a number of pictures intended to stimulate the participants in remembering and discussing their needs and requirements in these situations. They covered areas such as: usability perspectives, personalization, user experience, user interface, economy, ethical issues, security, and legal issues. These requirements were presented as questions to the participants by the facilitator at different times during the workshop. The first activity in the workshop was a shared user evaluation of aids and devices available today. The purpose was to start at a level that was familiar to users so that they could feel at ease and gain confidence in contributing to the workshop. It was also a way of establishing and acknowledging a common, shared design language that was understandable for non-engineers. The predefined conceptual landscape scenario and its life cycle phases were then introduced during a fantasy journey. The fantasy journey was a short guided meditation and was used in order to stimulate the participants' creativity while thinking about the future. Construction of the life landscape scenarios took place within teams. The participants were divided into

Figure 2. A landscape scenario is under construction

two teams, each containing users with diabetes, health care personnel, men, and women. Each team was placed around a table where image elements were placed together with plenty of prototyping materials. They were asked to physically place pictures, notes, and other prototyping material on large pieces of white paper and to describe their thinking about different situations. A landscape scenario created by one of the teams is shown in Figure 2. After the workshop, all ideas presented were analyzed and used as the basis for describing four narrative user scenarios of important situations and ideas from each life cycle phase.

After the creative user workshop from the "health care" case study, the expert workshop was held. Its purpose was to discuss different technological solutions to support the visions expressed in the user scenarios. This meant that the experts had a more specific task and that the teamwork atmosphere was stimulated more than the general creativity in the first workshop. The second workshop started with a lecture about diabetics and open discussions concerning important technical aspects to consider, focusing on core activities that were interesting for the project. The experts were then divided into two teams equally representing the project's working groups and based on specific technological expertise and company profiles. The teams were guided by the facilitators and note takers and each given two different user scenarios, which they were given time to read. The teams started the prototyping of a conceptual system architecture based on the specific user scenarios they had been introduced to. The teams were sequentially given questions based on subsets of previously defined, high-level system requirements. This continued until all requirements had been dealt with. The teams were encouraged to add possible sub-scenarios to the user scenarios. This was facilitated by brainstorming on activities and tasks from user scenarios accompanied by suggestions for possible new activities and tasks in the given context. Finally, the teams had to select and explore the most important/interesting activities and tasks. The results from the expert workshop were conceptual personal network architectures based on user needs and requirements expressed in user scenarios. These were then used to formulate "rich" scenarios that would sum up the findings of both workshops and be a mixture of narratives, use cases, graphic network schemes, requirements specifications, and tables containing quantitative parameters.

Within the project, creative user workshops and expert workshops have been conducted for three case studies. All workshops ended with an open informal plenum evaluation of the workshop day, and in general the participants were satisfied with the results and felt that the day had been meaningful. Starting with the creative user workshop, the comments from the users were mainly about the process and techniques that had been applied. Some comments revealed that the process was confusing in the beginning, but by the end, a structure actually appeared in the landscape scenarios. Other comments were about the fantasy journey as being really interesting and something never tried before. The fantasy journey created a special atmosphere of awareness seldom seen before in ICT project workshops or meetings.

The internal evaluation among the engineering designers was also positive; all felt that the workshops had been successful and useful. However, it was clear that it was important to find the right persons for the different workshop roles (facilitators and note takers), and that these persons were well prepared. Regarding the expert workshops, participants found the workshops interesting, and no one answered the direct question as to whether they felt that some of the activities were silly or meaningless in the affirmative.

The principles and techniques from creativity theory were applied most comprehensively in the creative user workshops. The application of the creativity techniques allowed for the participants to be surprised and to establish a common basis for discussing the future ICT ideas on the same premises. The use of the image elements introduced common and even perhaps overly divergent thinking in the scenario landscape. Many ideas were expressed using only the image elements, and no other ideas for the use of new technologies came up. However, the image elements did support the participants in thinking about new technologies and ideas they were not used to considering—or were not even aware of—within this particular context.

The brainstorming techniques were easily applied, and all participants were able to use them. The participants had never tried a fantasy journey before. The application of this technique was perhaps the most challenging aspect for them. Whether the journey actually supported their creative thinking is difficult to assess. However, the participants were asked immediately after the fantasy journey to start their work on the scenario landscape, and this process was relatively easy for most of them. The participants subsequently expressed their positive (and surprised) attitude to the fantasy journey, and it would appear that this journey did support the creativity process.

It must be mentioned that the expert workshop participants were in a sense eager to evaluate the ideas expressed at the creative workshops only from a technically demanding point of view. However, the users did not express many innovative and technically challenging ideas, which was a disappointment to the experts. On the other hand, these experts perhaps never really understood that their task was to create technological challenges based on the users' ideas, and that they were allowed to elaborate on the users' ideas and create new ideas. In this process, the lack of focus on creativity in the expert workshop may have been an important factor for its outcome. Another issue that could be raised in this connection is the lack of open-mindedness exhibited by the participants on arriving at the workshop. The expert workshop participants were clearly reluctant, and some irritation was even expressed about the exercise before it started. After the workshop, most participants were more positive, but during the process the atmosphere was more forced and less relaxed than in the creative user workshops. It may be that the results of the workshops (and the mixing of participatory design and creativity techniques) could have been even more beneficial, if it had been possible to overcome the reluctance of expert workshop participants. It must be emphasized that in the course of the expert workshop, a teamwork atmosphere was built up during the day and that in itself can be seen as a substantial achievement. Furthermore, the experts did express a growing understanding for the user visions expressed, which in itself supported a better link between the user-centricity and the technological perceptions and visions of the project.

During the workshops, participants were able to establish a shared communication language and feeling of ownership and responsibility for the created prototypes. All users participating in the creative user workshops contributed to the process. The participants in the expert workshop communicated well together even though they had different technological competences and were very different multi-, inter-, and trans-disciplinarily. At the creative user workshops, the core human activities in each case study were illuminated through the landscape scenarios. Based on this, user scenarios were composed and passed on to the expert workshops for further elaboration and inquiry into technical issues raised. The results from the expert workshop were conceptual personal network architectures, fulfilling the user needs and requirements in the user scenarios, and new sub-scenarios, putting additional focus on specific technological development issues. These results have then been used as a basis for deriving use cases and a final requirements specification.

The final applications and services have not been developed yet, so it has not been possible to evaluate whether the project results will be ultimately usable and make a difference. Internally in the project, however, the results based on the design framework have been used as a basis for deriving system requirements in other parts of the project. Future work will focus on how to take the participatory design and creativity approach into usability evaluations of the applications to be developed. When dealing with mobile ICT usability testing, the traditional highly controlled laboratory user testing has too many drawbacks not only in relation to real human behavior but also to changes in context. New valuable insights may therefore be obtained from exploring a complementary but very different approach.

Conclusions and Discussions

In this chapter, a new participatory design and creativity framework has been presented and described through a project case study within the area of mobile ICT development. The framework is based on methods and techniques from participatory design and creativity and consists of scenario construction carried out through workshops. The set-up of successive workshops has been useful in regard of generating ideas and building a "bridge" between the user focus and the technical focus represented in the project. In particular, the expert workshops have played a role in building up the team atmosphere that is necessary for major ICT projects.

The participatory design and creativity framework has to be evaluated in terms of its contribution to the real world—and the MAGNET project. The theoretical base constitutes a mixture of techniques and principles from different fields, and it is only in its practical application that it can be really tested. Three primary areas reveal something about performance and how well the framework worked in a real application. These are: workshop participants' feedback, the experience from the mix of techniques that was used in the MAGNET project, and the extent to which the results have been useful for the project in respect of the implementation of ideas. The user and expert evaluations stated clearly that the participants felt that they had established a shared design language in the workshops. The internal project evaluation and use have shown that a transition medium between the successive workshops and the system requirements specification has been established. It is not yet possible to measure the level to which the methodology has facilitated the generation of innovative design ideas. However, both users and engineering designers found the participatory design and creativity methods and techniques useful and meaningful, which indicates that they did work together stimulating each other's approach. Participatory design, teamwork, and creativity have many things in common, and during the workshops, it was often very difficult to say whether participatory design or creativity was the dominating approach as a combination of both blended together in the applied techniques.

The research conducted within the MAGNET project showed that creative techniques such as brainstorming and picture stimulation were useful, easy to apply, and well received by the workshop participants. The techniques worked in two almost contradictory ways: as a source of stimulation and, at the same time, a tool for structuring thoughts and ideas. The brainstorming that was used to support fluency and volume of ideas worked both in the discussion of today's use of technology and in the construction of future landscape scenarios. However, the brainstorming session could easily have turned out to provide overly general ideas that would not necessarily be useful for the project. The image elements were used both to stimulate the participants into thinking in particular directions and to generate new ideas based on the pictures and elaborating on them.

The methods used could not have been applied without proper input from the team facilitators and note takers to structure the overall process. In the user workshops, the note takers were allowed to take a more active role and support the creation of ideas in the teams—without being dominating in any way. This clearly also stimulated the participants in thinking about future technologies and situations where technology could support them. In all workshops, it has been clear that the incubation phase was an important factor. The breaks during the workshops functioned as relaxing phases in which the participants on one hand relaxed from the "job" they were asked to do, and on the other hand "working" (perhaps unconsciously) with ideas, sometimes producing new ideas when returning from the breaks.

There is no doubt that the proper evaluation of the new design framework ought to take place repeating the framework in different projects and with different participants. This evaluation is based on user and expert workshops held as part of the same project. However, a final evaluation of the framework cannot be performed before the project has concluded, and the results have been implemented. Then it will be possible to see the value of the ideas and the user interaction that were generated in the project design phase. Applications have been produced with a direct link to the users, since they also contributed to testing these. By looking at this whole process, we could learn something more about the value of using participatory design and the creativity techniques. However, the need for envisioning a new personal network concept together with users has clearly indicated a necessity for incorporating creativity techniques more explicitly in more traditional participatory design methods.

Using participatory design principles is challenging for all ICT projects in the sense that the engineering designers do not necessarily believe that this kind of user involvement is a good idea. However, the application of participatory design principles and creativity techniques in MAGNET has provided an understanding of new aspects that has been acknowledged by some of the engineering designers. The new participatory design and creativity framework presented here addresses many valuable aspects of technology project development. One often-overlooked aspect is the need for teamwork skills to establish a team spirit atmosphere. The experience within the MAGNET context is that the framework ideas support the development of teamwork skills, and perhaps that it in itself will increase the possibility of successful future development projects.

Acknowledgments

Acknowledgments should be given to all of the user and MAGNET expert participants in the workshops, especially to the diabetic persons and staff from Aalborg University. The research was carried out within the IST MAGNET project, FP6-IST-IP-507102, www.ist-magnet.org.

References

Alexander, I. F., & Maiden, N. (2004). *Scenarios, stories, use cases. Through the systems development life-cycle.* Chichester: John Wiley & Sons.

Amabile, T. M. (1989). *How work environments affect creativity.* Paper presented at the IEEE International Conference on Systems, Man and Cybernetics, November 14-17.

Amabile, T. M., Conti, R., Coon, H., Lazenby, J., & Herron, M. (1996). Assessing the work environment for creativity. *Academy of Management Journal, 39*(5), 1154-1184.

Asaro, P. M. (2000). Transforming society by transforming technology: the science and politics of participatory design. *Accounting Management and Information Technologies,* (10), 257-290.

Beyer, H., & Holtzblatt, K. (1998). *Contextual design: Defining costumer-centered systems.* San Francisco: Morgan Kauffman.

Bødker, S., Greenbaum, J., & Kyng, M. (1991). Setting the stage for design as action. In J. Greenbaum, & M. Kyng (Eds.), *Design at work: Cooperative design of computer systems* (pp. 139-154). Hillsdale, NJ: Lawrence Erlbaum Associates.

Carmel, E., Whitaker, R., & George, J. (1993). PD and joint application design: A transatlantic comparison. *Communications of the ACM, 36*(4), 40-48.

Denzin, N. K., & Lincoln, Y. S. (2000). *Handbook of qualitative research* (2nd ed.). Thousand Oaks, CA: Sage Publications.

Ehn, P. (1988). *Work-oriented design of computer artifacts.* Stockholm: Arbeitslivscentrum.

Fogg, B. J. (2003). *Persuasive technology: Using computers to change what we think and do.* Amsterdam; Boston: Morgan Kaufmann Publishers.

FoundationCoalition. (2002). Preparing a new generation of engineers. Retrieved June 15, 2005, from http://www.foundationcoalition.org

Gardner, H. (1983). *Frames of mind: The theory of multiple intelligences.* New York: Basic Books.

Gaver, B., Dunne, T., & Pacenti, E. (1999). Cultural probes. *Interactions,* (Jan + Feb).

Godet, M., & Roubelat, F. (1999). Creating the future: The use and misuse of scenarios. *Long Range Planning, 29*(2), 164-171.

Goff, K. (1998). *Everyday creativity.* Stillwater: Little Ox Books.

Higgins, J. M. (1994). *101 creative problem solving techniques: The handbook of new ideas for business.* Winter Park, FL: New Management Pub. Co.

Johnson, G., & Scholes, K. (1999). *Exploring corporate strategy* (5th ed.). London; New York: Prentice Hall Europe.

Jungk, R., & Müllert, N. (1987). *Future workshops: How to create desirable futures.* London: Institute for Social Inventions.

Kazanjian, R. K., Dradin, R., & Glynn, M. A. (2000). Creativity and technological learning: The roles of organization architecture and crisis in large-scale projects. *Journal of Engineering and Technology Management, 17,* 273-298.

Kensing, F., & Blomberg, J. (1998). Participatory design: Issues and concerns. *Computer Supported Cooperative Work, 7*(3-4), 167-185.

Kjeldskov, J., & Graham, C. (2003). A review of mobile HCI research methods. Paper presented at the *5th International Mobile HCI,* Udine, Italy, September 8-11 (pp. 317-335).

Kleinrock, L. (1996a). Nomadic computing, information network and data communication. Paper presented at the *International Conference on Information Network and Data Communication,* Trondheim, Norway, June (pp. 223-233).

Kleinrock, L. (1996b). Nomadicity: Anytime, anywhere in a disconnected world. *Mobile Networks and Applications, 1*(4), 351-357.

Krogstie, J., Lyytinen, K., Opdahl, A. L., Pernici, B., Sian, K., & Smolander, K. (2004). Research areas and challenges for mobile information systems. *International Journal of Mobile Communications, 2*(3), 220-234.

Kuuti, K. (1996). Activity theory as a potential framework for human-computer interaction research. In B. E. Nardi (Ed.), *Context and consciousness: Activity theory and human-computer interaction* (pp. 17-44). Cambridge, MA: The MIT Press.

Leonart, A. D., & Swap, C. W. (1999). *When sparks fly.* Boston, MA: Harvard Business School Press.

MAGNET. (2004). *MAGNET Technical Annex.* Retrieved June 15, 2004, from http://www.ist-magnet.org

Millar, W. (1997). *E. Paul Torrance - "The creativity man".* New Jersey: Ablex Publishing.

Muller, M. J. (1991). *PICTIVE – An exploration in participatory design.* Paper presented at the Computer-Human Interaction Conference, Australia, April 27-May 2.

Mumford, E. (1987). The collective resource approach to systems design. In G. Bjerknes, P. Ehn, & M. Kyng (Eds.), *Sociotechnical systems design: Evolving theory and practice* (pp. 59-76). Brookfield, VT: Avebury.

Niemegeers, I., & Groot, S. M. H. d. (2002). From personal area networks to personal networks: A user oriented approach. *Personal Wireless Communications, 22*(2), 175-186.

Osborn, A. (1953). *Applied imagination.* New York: Schreibners.

Pope, R. (2005). *Creativity, theory, history, practice.* London: Routledge.

Schwartz, P. (1991). *The art of the long view.* New York: Currency Doubleday.

Van der Heijden, K. (1996). *Scenarios: The art of strategic conversation.* Chichester: John Wiley & Sons.

Vidal, R. V. V. (2003). *Creativity and problem solving* (No. 2002-3). Kgs. Lyngby: Technical University of Denmark.

Wallas, G. (1926). *The art of thought.* London: J. Cape.

Zappen, J. P., & Harrison, T. M. (2005). Intention and motive in information-system design: Toward a theory and method for assessing users' needs. In P. Van der Besselaar, & S. Koizumi (Eds.), *Digital cities 2003* (pp. 354-368). Berlin; Heidelberg: Springer-Verlag.

Chapter V

Information and Function Chunks as Building Blocks in the Control Room of Life

Georg Strøm
University of Copenhagen, Denmark

Abstract

Inspired by work on systems for control rooms, this chapter describes how working with information on the Internet and other types of network-based information systems can be made easier by applying five principles:

1. *by providing information to the user about any changes to the information that may affect him or her;*

2. *by dividing information and functions into chunks—the smallest possible meaningful units;*

3. *by automatically synchronizing navigation and parameters in different chunks;*

4. *by using views that each gives access to chunks that are relevant in a specific situation or for a specific task; and*

5. *by sharing information from one terminal to another as needed.*

Introduction

The owner of a Web site may upload information that later is downloaded by other users. This is an example of a networked communication where one or more information providers push information out into a space from which users of that information may later pull it.

In contrast to phone calls and chat, it is not possible to ask a question and get an immediate answer through this type of networked communication. However, it offers other advantages:

- Information providers can provide information at the moment when it is most convenient for them.

- Users of the information can get access to it when they need it and when it is convenient for them to deal with it. In some cases, that may be many years after it was made available by the information providers.

- It is not necessary for the information providers to specify in advance or even to know all users of the information.

This type of communication is much older than the Internet. We find similar combinations of push and pull in the publication of newspapers, magazines, books, and in the establishment of libraries. Our organization of information on the Internet reflects these older types of communication: we organize information as Web pages, even though the concept of a page containing a number of sometimes-unrelated pieces of information makes most sense when information is distributed on paper. We imitate the principles and characteristics of a displaced type of technology, not unlike the first passenger carriages for trains that were shaped as three horse-drawn carriages on a common set of wheels. Archaeologists use the phrase "Skeumorphism" to describe such imitations of a displaced technology (Basalla, 1988).

One common consequence of imitating displaced technology is that the new technology becomes less flexible than the older technology it replaces. Often, a user can easily cut out or make a photocopy of any part of paper-based information that he or she needs, and there are a number of tools readily available for making annotations or indicating relationships on each piece of information. In most cases, these actions are much more difficult on electronic information.

On a desktop in the physical world we are forced to distinguish between tools—such as a calculator or a ruler—and pieces of paper with information on them, and we have similarly implemented that distinction in computer interfaces (spreadsheets being one of the few exceptions). As a result, the computer interface is actually less versatile than the physical desktop. We have implemented the limitations of an older type of technology, even though it is much faster to move the eyes from a calculator to a piece of paper on a physical desktop than to open a new window on a computer.

Instead of copying the limitations and characteristics of older types of technology, it is better to focus on the needs and habits of users, and on how we can make the work easier without imposing any additional limitations. This is necessary because future network-based communication may copy not only the appearances and limitations of pre-computer technologies, but also some of the limitations of present computer technology.

Today's personal computers are based on monolithic applications. They can be set up by the ordinary user, but he or she is forced to think about file formats when using them, even though users are not normally interested in how information is stored if it can be used for the intended activity. It is also impossible for personal computers to share processing power or other resources, and ordinary transfer of information from one application to another may similarly be cumbersome or even impossible.

In contrast, it is feasible today to design software that allows users to exchange information between a multitude of processes both on the same computer and between computers. Grid-computing is reaching a stage where it is possible to reliably borrow processing power and transfer processes and tasks from one device to another. It is also possible—for instance, through the use of XML—to define information formats that are much more usable, which makes it much easier for the user to organize information according to his or her own categories.

Over the last 30 years, the prices of cell phones (today in reality small portable computers) have dropped about 95%, and the prices of personal computers have dropped about 85% (for computers with much stronger processors and with more features), and these changes have affected the way we think about and use cell phones and personal computers. We work faster and more effectively, we process much more information, we work across applications and information sources, and we increasingly use the technology to liberate us from the office with its shelves of papers and binders. We try to complete more complex tasks in a shorter period of time, and it is likely that we make more mistakes, in particular when the current tools stress our short-term memory and our ability to recall something.

As society becomes more complex and more diverse, the needs of different users are also becoming more diverse. It is becoming increasingly difficult to make a single organization of information that fits a significant proportion of the user group. This makes it necessary to find ways to make it easier for a single user or group of users to combine and integrate information and functions from different elements in personal networks.

Over the next decade, it is possible that new types of plastic-based computers will emerge at prices below ten dollars (Collins, 2004; Howard, 2004). Once again, our view of computers and how they are used may change. With such small, low-cost computers, it may become common for a user to work on a number of computers in his or her work area, to use some of them as notebooks and others to display information that may be useful as a reference while working, not unlike the way paper is used on a physical desktop today.

In the following sections, I will describe some principles for organizing information and functions in ways that make it possible to utilize more of the benefits of future network-based communication. In doing so, I will take into account the limitations of the human memory and suggest how we may regain some of the flexibility we lost when moving from paper-based to computer-based information processing.

Background: A Control Room of Life

I first got the inspiration for the following principles for networked communication in 2001 when working as usability specialist in Ericsson—a leading worldwide manufacturer of telecommunication equipment. One of the areas I worked in was control systems for telecommunication networks. Such systems are designed to make it possible to supervise and control networks with a multitude of different pieces of equipment and to react quickly and correctly when something happens. This situation is actually quite similar to what an ordinary user may experience when using a number of applications spread on an intranet or other communication network. Other users of the networks are continuously providing new information and modifying or deleting existing information, and the user must identify and react to any changes to the information that affect him or her.

At the same time, it is easier to understand the problems when discussing a control system than when discussing an intranet or the Internet. We have grown accustomed to the Internet and have learned to live with its limitations, so it is difficult to imagine that it might work in a different manner. In the following sections, I will therefore first discuss control systems and then use that discussion to highlight the limitations of the Internet and most or all intranet applications.

Software for controlling telecommunication networks rarely looks like what we see in movies, with maps and graphical overviews, where it is possible to zoom in with lightning speed and where everything is integrated and easy to survey. The reality is that the pieces of equipment supervised through a control system come from a number of different manufacturers, and they all come with their own control applications with proprietary interfaces. This is a situation that the operators must live with; in general, it is too costly to integrate all information from different control applications, and an integration may distort critical information that cannot be presented properly in an integrated display.

The only truly integrated function in a control system is the presentation of alarms. However, in addition to a few alarms that indicate serious problems, the exchanges and equipment in the network tend to transmit a large number of alarms because of minor irregularities that normally go away within a few minutes. This creates a mental load similar to that experienced by a manager with one hundred e-mails in his inbox: even though the manager is forced to disregard most of the e-mails because of time pressure, it is essential that he act on the few that demand immediate action. In essence, the e-mails are alarms that indicate problems that may affect the operation of his or her information network.

When an operator in a control room perceives an alarm that indicates a serious problem, he must immediately access an application that makes it possible to diagnose and control the piece of equipment that has sounded the alarm. He will often have to go into another application to access the documentation of the equipment to identify the causes and possible corrections of the error. He may have to look up the standard operating procedure for the particular type of incident, and he may finally have to go into yet another application to document what he has done. (Most administrative problem-solving is done in a similar fashion: the user must find more detailed information about the problem, check applicable rules if necessary, and document his or her results.)

Through my work, I have seen that cell phones and other portable devices tend to become similar to equipment in control rooms. Users of cell phones and operators in a control room both need facilities that may draw their attention or provide a quick overview, and an interface that makes it possible to react quickly and in an appropriate manner.

Modern cell phones can give access to a number of different communication channels and services from different providers with different interfaces, for instance, music, movies, games, or Web-like services that are either offered by the telecommunication service provider or by other information providers. A cell phone will typically contain a clock and appointments on a calendar with built-in alarm, a camera and stored pictures, communication through e-mail, SMS or MMS (multimedia messaging service), and perhaps even chat-like services that make it possible for the user to keep track of what his or her friends are doing.

Instead of having one integrated interface, the cell phone begins to resemble what you see in a control room: something that gives access to a number of different elements with different interfaces in a network. We may regard the modern cell phone as a control room of daily life, where the user stores information about earlier events, gets an overview of his or her daily life and social network, receives from other persons messages or alarms that he or she must react upon, interacts with the environment in different manners, and tries to influence it.

The most important difference between the cell phone and the interface in a control room is that whereas the operator in a control room has access to the network through at least one full-size computer screen, the user of a cell phone has access through a PDA-size screen at the most, or less than 5% of the display area that is available to the operator in the control room. In spite of these limitations, some control room applications are today implemented on PDAs. It is easier for an operator to diagnose errors when he can move around and make direct observations while having access to information from the control system (Nielsen & Søndergaard, 2000), and a technician who drives around making repairs may supervise the state of a small network from his PDA or portable computer.

Administrative workplaces are following the same trends as cell phones and applications for control rooms. They are becoming increasingly complex and incorporating functions for getting an overview of schedules and work to be done and access to an intranet or a number of servers with different applications. At the same time, some functions that were once available only on a tabletop computer are today also available on a PDA or small tablet PC.

What may happen in the years to come with the advent of new low-cost computers and probably large, inexpensive, and even flexible displays is that fixed workplaces and portable applications may merge. When working in an office, we may use a workstation with a large display, while the table is cluttered with one or more small, expensive, and comparatively fast computers and a number of slower and cheaper computers. When moving around, we may use the small computers together with a flexible display that we carry along or some inexpensive, fixed computers connected to large wall displays.

Networks accessed through cell phones and networks accessed through administrative workplaces are created through what Law (1987) calls "heterogeneous engineering". Those who build the networks are not only concerned with artifacts but take also social, economic, and political factors into account. This means that the networks in particular are shaped by the designers' previous experiences (see Naur, 1985), and by the users' perception of how valuable and useful they are. Law (1987) includes both artifacts such as servers and software and social factors in the network, so a network that is disregarded by users and not used in reality ceases to exist, much like a ghost city that has been deserted by its inhabitants.

Law (1987) describes how networks are constructed by putting together heterogeneous elements that can be shaped into a stable network, one that is well adapted to its environment. According to Law, the builders—which include users who shape the network to fit their own needs—try to dissociate hostile elements that may threaten the stability of the network, and encourage or force elements that have become part of the network to act in a way that contributes to its stability.

Law's (1987) description fits networks used in control systems, networks accessible through cell phones, and the network of resources that may be available for an office worker through the Internet and an intranet. Such networks are complex, shaped by a number of different forces, and are difficult to change. Therefore, I will not discuss how it is possible to create a better network. Instead, I will discuss some principles that make it easier to access the information and resources that are contained in them.

Five Principles that Facilitate the Use of Network-Based Information

The following describes five design principles that make it possible to work effectively and effortlessly with networked information and resources:

- informing the user about changes in the network;
- information or function chunks as basic units;
- automatic synchronization between chunks;
- views giving access to situation or task specific groups of chunks; and
- the ability to pull or push views from one terminal to another.

I will describe each specific principle, the psychological background of each of these principles, previous work in the same area, and in some cases, possible adverse consequences of a principle.

Informing the User about Changes in the Network

One problem faced by the user of network-based communication is that he or she must be aware whether any changes to elements or information in the network exist that may affect his activities or require a response. This may be impossible even if the user continuously scrolls around looking for changes. Already, William James (1890) observed that we have a tendency to notice what we expect to see. This means that we also have a tendency of not noting any changes we do not expect to see.

Another problem is that the user sometimes has to recall that he or she should react to specific information in the network at a specific time. However, that is not easy. Schacter (1996) describes how it is difficult to recall, for instance, an appointment or a task that has to be done during the day.

Shneiderman (1998) describes the following order of activities when users shall visualize large amounts of data: "Overview first, zoom and filter, then details on demand."

This is fine if the user knows what he or she is looking for. However, it is not sufficient if the user cannot recall that he or she should look after a critical piece of information, as, for instance, whether any appointments are noted in the calendar. It is also insufficient if the user is working in a network of information that may continuously change. In such cases, the user must be made aware of any changes that are relevant for his or her work or situation in general.

I have seen how operators in control rooms had to zoom in on different parts of a network to ensure that there had not been any changes that needed their attention, but this is only feasible if the total network is fairly small. In most cases, the user will miss any changes until he or she finds them by accident or is made aware of them by someone else. Most people working in an organization experience this when they complain that they have not been informed about something, and are then told that the information has been on the Web for a long time, and that they could have gone to a specific Web page to look it up.

An interface should draw a user's attention to any elements that need to be addressed, but if it attempts to draw the user's attention for no obvious reason, the user will become annoyed, ignore the warnings, or try to disable the function that issues warnings. This is similar to what happens when information about changes is sent out by e-mail. It is the sender, not the user, who decides what information should be included in a message, and it is extremely unlikely that the e-mail arrives at a time when the user wants to be informed about any changes. Also, even if the user saves all e-mails about changes to the network, the information is likely not ordered according to the elements in the network, so it is almost impossible to get an overview of it.

Indicators are needed that can make the user aware of the states of elements in the network and draw his or her attention as strongly as necessary:

States that the user should only be aware of without paying any attention to them. Such an indicator basically assures the user that access to the network and the network in general functions the way it is supposed to.

Changes of the state of an element that it is important the user is aware of, but where it is not necessary that the user react immediately. One example is an overview that shows which part of the information used by the user has been updated within the last month (this could be a useful feature on many intranets).

Changes of the state of an element that the user should react to within a very short time, as, for instance, when a meeting in the calendar is about to begin, or when something urgently needs approval. Then it is necessary to attract his or her attention. This may be done by a flashing signal or a symbol that moves on the screen because the eye, in particular, is sensitive to movements (Humphreys & Bruce, 1989).

Changes of state that require an immediate reaction, and that the user has ignored. This may be the case if the user does not enter a decision on something that urgently needs his or her response. Such changes of state must attract the user's attention so strongly that he or she can perceive that they are urgent. This may be done by using tones with a high pitch or fast intermittent repetitions (Hellier, Edworthy, & Dennis, 1993).

The principles of such indicators are obvious for anyone who has used a cell phone. The battery and field strength icons are examples of indicators that assure the user that the network in general functions as it is supposed to, and the ringing tone which gradually increases in volume is an example of both an indicator that the user has to react to within a very short time and an indicator that the user has ignored and therefore must react to immediately.

However, when used in a network where a large number of elements may simultaneously signal that a change of state has occurred, some sort of intelligent control is needed. The indicators must be correlated and coordinated such that the user is not overwhelmed when they all announce the same event at the same time. (It is easy to imagine that the calendar in the computer, the calendar in the cell phone, and the departmental bulletin board simultaneously announce an upcoming meeting.)

There is also a need for prioritization because the user can react to only one indicator at a time. Ideally, the prioritization should be so intelligent that an announcement informing the user that a meeting has been cancelled takes precedence over the indicator that announces that the meeting begins soon.

As mentioned, it is not feasible to continuously browse through a large network looking for changes, nor is it possible to look up every piece of information every time we need it. The consequences of using an information network without any change indicators are that decisions may be based on outdated information and that critical changes to elements in the network might be overlooked.

However, it is crucial that change indicators draw the attention of the user only when it is necessary; otherwise the indicators interrupt the user in his or her work, and may even become so overwhelming that the user is forced to disregard them in order to get any work done at all.

Information or Function Chunks as Basic Units

According to Bartlett (1932), our thinking is based on the use of schemas—actively developed patterns of past reactions and past experiences—and we can only capture or recognize a schema if it has a certain minimal content. Bartlett mentions as an example that a picture often appears to be meaningless without a caption describing the context in which it was taken. The concept of schemas in interaction design is mentioned by Miyata and Norman (1986) who describe principles for interfaces that support multiple activities. It is necessary in such cases to provide a context so a user who has been interrupted can recognize the point where he or she should resume activity. Compared to the use of network-based information, that is a fairly simple case. The user of network-based information not only needs to recognize the point he or she has reached in an ongoing process, he or she also needs sufficient context information to understand how each new piece of information may fit into his or her past reactions and experiences. In addition, Bartlett (1932) describes how aspects that do not fit into a schema are easily forgotten or corrupted. This means that it is necessary not only to provide background information, but also to divide the information into units that feel natural for the user with his or her background and experiences.

This is a problem today. When a picture is transferred from a digital camera to a database, the stored technical information about when and how the picture was taken may be lost, and when the picture is transferred from the database to a Web page, for example, any captions or comments added to the picture in the database will be lost. The unit of information that feels natural for the user is broken up.

In a similar example, when re-organizing text where the meaningful units are not clearly marked, the editor in each case must determine what the meaningful units are; otherwise, it is possible that the text will be divided into meaningless pieces. (A lack of well-defined meaningful units also means that it is almost impossible to make a database that lists all the units in a text for use as a reference or as support when editing.)

Horn (1989) describes how these problems can be solved by organizing the information as information blocks, where each block is something that the user has learned to see as one unit, independently of the medium used to present it. Such an information block may consist of a few sentences with a headline or a table or a drawing with a caption.

However, the term "block" is already used to label a number of different concepts in software development. Horn (1989) uses the term "chunking principle" to describe the organization of information into blocks, and I will therefore use the term "information chunks" to describe the organization into meaningful units of information with explanations or captions. This is in accordance with Simon (1974), who uses the term "chunk" about an amount of information that is familiar to a person and therefore easier to perceive and remember.

Henrik Hvid Jensen (2004) discusses the use of Web services as basic units in an interface. He describes a Web service as (translated from Danish):

"Encapsulated loosely coupled software components that in a semantically well-defined manner describe their functionality and behavior and that can be accessed through other programs."

If such a Web service has a headline, caption, or explanatory text that makes it possible for the user to understand or recognize its context, it is a function chunk. Function and information chunks may consist of information and different functions for input, data processing and output, and a headline, caption, or explanatory text that makes it possible for the user to understand or recognize its context. They are the smallest meaningful assemblages of information—assemblages where any single part may be meaningless if the other elements are not known. Some examples are:

- pictures with a date, different technical information, and captions;
- a headline followed by a paragraph or a section in a text (typically, the amount of text that a reader will reread from the beginning if he or she is interrupted in the middle of it);
- a short, uninterrupted video-clip with a time-stamp and location;
- a function for doing one specific calculation, for instance, calculating total interest when the amount, the interest rate, and the period are entered;
- a window for seeing part of a digital picture with a caption, and with buttons that make it possible for the user to zoom in and to scroll horizontally and vertically; and
- a browser window giving access to an information chunk somewhere on the Internet.

The last two examples illustrate one important aspect of how information and sometimes function chunks are presented to users. They may be layered so the user sees an information or function chunk through a function chunk that is designed to display other chunks. An information chunk containing a picture with a caption, for example, may be seen through a function chunk designed to display pictures, and an information chunk or a Web service somewhere on the Internet may be seen through a function chunk—a chunk browser—designed to show Web-based chunks.

A consequence of the use of information and function chunks as basic units is that applications and Web pages become much more flexible units than they are today. Instead of Web pages, we may have collections of information chunks where it is easy for the user to add or remove a chunk; an application could be a combination of a viewer, perhaps a copy-and-paste chunk and a search-and-replace chunk and other function chunks that the user or someone else has put together. Then, it may be possible for the user to take a spell-checking function chunk from the word processor and use it to check the texts included in a drawing. (The use of chunks may also solve some of the problems caused by bloated applications where the user is overwhelmed by the large number of functions. When the application consists of a number of chunks, it is possible to add or remove chunks, and thereby functions, to create an application that fits a particular user.)

Another consequence of the use of information and function chunks as basic units is that the structuring of information becomes much more spontaneous and situation-oriented. When working on a paper, the user commonly selects and organizes notes with the information he or she needs. When using information chunks, it is easy for the user to organize electronic chunks of information in a similar manner, and even to distribute them on different computers and interfaces in his or her work area.

A third consequence of the use of information and function chunks is that it becomes easier for information brokers to organize information in useful ways. Today, the organization of Web-based information tends to become an abstract and technical activity. It is likely that it would be much easier to organize information if it were possible to move chunks around when needed and immediately see the result. Compared to the design of Web pages, it becomes easier for users to organize information for other users. This means that the organization of information can be done by writers or communication specialists with only a minimal technical background, and that it will be so easy that it can be done to meet unique requirements.

Automatic Synchronization Between Chunks

Grudin (1983) reports that skilled typists have error rates of about 1%. Even though the user may detect and correct some errors, the figure is so high that any operations where the user must read the content of one part of display and type it into another are likely causes of errors. In addition, some of the most obviously time-wasting and frustrating work probably occurs when you are forced to spend time reading what is shown on one part of the screen and typing it onto another.

Aran Lunzer presents a creative and intriguing solution to this problem. He introduces the term "subjunctive interfaces" to describe interfaces where the user may adjust several scenarios in parallel so that "... any adjustment in a parameter value should be applicable to more than one query at a time. This would allow, for example, simultaneous exploration of the effect of different departure dates on the results for several different destinations" (Lunzer & Hornbæk, 2003).

Fujima, Lunzer, Hornbæk, and Tanaka (2004) describe how subjunctive interfaces can be applied to what they describe as C3W—Clip Connect and Clone for the Web. They describe a tool that makes it possible to copy single elements from Web pages, paste them into a new window, and connect them so the output parameter from one element is automatically transferred and used as input parameter in the next. As an example, they show how it is possible to copy a currency conversion calculator and a stock price query and link them together to see stock prices in different currencies.

One interesting aspect described by Fujima et al. (2004) is the possibility of cloning or duplicating a copied element. This means that it is possible to have two elements with the same programming code and where some of the parameters are the same. For instance, it is possible to have two currency calculators set to different currencies but connected to the same stock price query, so the actual stock price is shown simultaneously in two different currencies. This points to fairly advanced methods for handling function chunks, methods where function chunks are copied and moved around as freely as pictures or pieces of text.

However, elements that are cut out of Web pages cannot be considered proper function chunks. The examples shown by Fujima et al. (2004) do not have any labels or explanatory text, and the elements shown cannot be regarded as natural functional units. As one example, it is not possible to see that the field showing the currency has anything to do with the field where the result of the conversion is shown. This means that the C3W is well suited for someone who wants to put together a function for a specific purpose quickly, but it may be difficult for the same person to later remember exactly what the elements are and how they are connected. (This is a problem because current experience with spreadsheets suggests that calculations are often used many times by the same user or distributed to other users.)

There is also a need for an improved method of establishing synchronization between function chunks. In C3W, synchronization is set up through a procedure similar to entering formulas in a spreadsheet. However, ideally the synchronization should be almost as simple to establish as copying the contents of one field into another. One possible way of doing that may be through a sort of drag-and-synchronize, where:

- The user drags a connection showing the possible direction of the dataflow from one chunk to another.
- The possible output and input parameters for each function chunk are shown.
- The user drags the connections between the output and input parameters that shall be connected.

In addition, it may be possible to include a function that automatically synchronizes or suggests possible synchronizations, for instance, based on XML tags indicating output and input elements with information of the same type.

Subjunctive interfaces deal with the synchronization of parameters. When the value of a parameter is changed in one element, the change is automatically and immediately reflected in the value of the same parameter in another element.

Another case is the synchronization of navigation, where any navigation done by the user in one chunk is immediately reflected in another. This is similar to what has been described for contextual help functions, where the help function automatically opens information about the part of an application that is open in the specific moment (Silveira, Barbosa, & de Souza, 2001). When used in a system for a control room, a similar function may synchronize a viewer of the documentation with the navigation in the system that is controlled, so the viewer automatically shows the documentation that is related to what the operator is working on. Another example may be an office caseworker who must use two different sets of regulations to make a decision. It may then be convenient if he or she needs to navigate only to the particulars of the case in one set of regulations and the other automatically follows the same navigation information.

Synchronization may also provide input for an inspector chunk—a function chunk that displays parameters about an item that is shown or highlighted in another chunk. An inspector chunk may, for instance, show information about color balance and highlights based on inputs from a function chunk that displays a digital picture.

Two outcomes of an automatic synchronization are substantially lower error rates and a substantially lower number of manual operations that the user must perform to complete a task.

If automatic synchronization is combined with a method that makes it easy to move function chunks around and synchronize them, users who have the proper function chunks and know how to put them together may easily set up complex calculations even if they do not know the precise formulas that are used. An electronics technician, for example, may put together sets of function chunks to determine the parameters for the components in an electronic circuit and their power consumption, and he may synchronize the results with a catalogue from a component supplier to get the total costs of the components used in the filter. (In electronic design, it is a common challenge to design a circuit with specific characteristics while minimizing both the power consumption and the cost.)

Another possible consequence is confusion when the user does not know how the different function chunks are synchronized and how changes in one chunk affect another. There may even be unintended or unforeseen changes because of relations between function chunks that the user is unaware of. This is similar to the problem we experience today when using spreadsheets. It is much easier to write formulas directly into a spreadsheet than to verify that the calculations and relations between all figures are correct, which increases the risk of hidden errors in the calculations. When using function chunks, it is therefore necessary to include some means of indicating the relations between the different information and function chunks.

Views Giving Access to Situation or Task Specific Groups of Chunks

The information and functions needed by a user depend on his or her actual situation and any tasks he or she wants to complete. In the control room I described earlier, the operator needs access to functions to control a piece of equipment, and he needs access to manuals for that piece of equipment, perhaps to standard operating procedures, as well as to a log to register what he has done.

One way of solving this problem may be to synchronize navigation in the manuals, standard operating procedures, and the log with navigation in the function chunks that are used to control elements in the network. However, such synchronization is not sufficient when navigating between function chunks that are used to control different types of equipment, and probably several systems for accessing the manuals. It is then also necessary to include a function to enable the synchronization to be handed over when the user navigates to an area that is covered by another function chunk.

This problem is similar to the situation when an Internet user wishes to work with information from several different Web sites. It may be possible to synchronize the navigation in one Web site with the navigation in another, for example, to synchronize a database of book reviews with an Internet bookshop, but it is difficult to set up a function that automatically switches to another database of book reviews when the user selects a book that is outside the scope of the first database.

A solution that is technically much simpler than synchronized navigation with handover was designed by Thomas Albrink, a software engineer in Ericsson (Albrink & Strom, 2002).

In a traditional tool for managing a telecommunication network, the user must work his way down through the levels of a navigation tool until he can open a new window that gives access to the application used to control, for instance, one of the 200 telephone switches in a network. If the user then needs any documentation he must work his way down through an application that gives access to the documentation for the specific switch. If the user closes windows on his way, he or she may spend a lot of time closing and opening windows as he chases a problem through the network, but if he does not close windows, he may end up with more than 20 open windows.

Albrink's interface looks like Windows Explorer® and is built so that each branch contains both an interface to control a particular piece of equipment, information about it, and the different tools the operator needs to work on its software, so the operator easily can change back and forth between the different functions and information he or she needs when working on a particular piece of equipment.

Such a collection of function and information chunks may be called a "view", similar to the term "point of view", which covers how a person at a specific moment sees the interface.

An example of a task where a view may be used is the writing of a scientific article. The writer needs access to his or her manuscript, maybe to more than one version of it, as well as direct access to different pieces of information stored at different Web sites, and perhaps also to a statistical application or to remote measuring equipment. Of course, the natural method is to put together everything that is needed for the specific task in one view, no matter the types of information or function chunks or where in the network they are stored.

To some extent, this is possible in current window-based interfaces. However, the usefulness is often reduced because the distances between the different elements are too large. According to the gestalt principle (Bruce & Green, 1990), we perceive two items as unrelated if they are placed some distance apart, and it is likely that the same principle is even stronger when the distance is in time instead of space. Even if it only takes a few seconds to close one element and open another, this is much more than it takes to shift focus in the physical space from one element to another. This means that even if the elements or their icons are placed next to each other, the user will perceive them to be distant if it takes time to change from one to the other. (This problem is even larger when some of the material is placed on the Internet. The browser will normally open on a default setting, and the user must then focus his or her attention on navigating to the appropriate book-marked page.)

Another problem may arise when synchronizing navigation conflicts with the selection of information that is done to support a specific task or for use in a specific situation. Imagine that the user who has created a view by selecting and synchronizing a large amount of information makes a detour in his or her navigation and follows an advertisement or goes to a news site. All the other settings that have been set up in the synchronized view may then be lost.

This may be solved by making it possible to save a view with its actual settings, similar to when a document is saved, so that no matter how the user navigates around, the settings will revert to the former ones when the view is closed unless the user specifies that the settings have to be saved. (This will even make it possible to create new views based on existing ones by using a "Save as..." function.)

The Ability to Pull or Push Views from one Terminal to Another

When the user accesses a network, he or she views it through the terminal he or she uses at the particular moment. However, the view the user needs for a particular task may be situated somewhere else in the network, or the user may need to move his or her work to another interface, for instance, from a handheld computer to a large screen in order to read his or her e-mail.

It is therefore necessary that the user can both pull and push views: pull a view that is needed from somewhere else in the network, or push a view that is meant for another interface onto the current one (or onto a storage device or a portable device that the user may bring with him or her).

It should be possible to handle views in the same manner as we handle files today: to access another computer in the network and a view stored on it, to move a view from the currently used computer to another, and possibly even to send a view as an attachment to an e-mail.

However, this may have one unforeseen consequence. As the user pushes views out to different devices, such as big screens used to read mail or intelligent whiteboards used at meetings, the user may inadvertently leave copies behind. This is a privacy issue because some of the information in the view may be private; it is a security issue because the view may be used to gain illicit access to the user's computer; and it is a storage issue because devices used by a large number of users may run out of memory space. It is, therefore, necessary to include some functions in each view that ensure that it deletes itself when appropriate. For example, if a view has been pushed to a public screen, it may delete itself when the screen loses contact with the device that the view has been pushed from.

Conclusion and Future Trends

For many years, control room operators have faced the challenges that users of network-based information face today: they must perceive and react to changes to information that are placed at different locations in the network, and they must navigate between different information sources and work areas in order to complete their tasks.

Tasks done on a computer today are done by working on whole files or pages of information and through applications, where each application may offer a subset of functions that do not quite fit the task that the user wants to accomplish. In contrast, the five principles described in this chapter may offer the same flexibility as when a user is working with pieces of paper and open books on a physical desktop. Compared to existing ways of organizing electronic information, these principles reduce the workload and the cognitive load on the short-term memory of the user by actively making him or her aware when something happens that may impact an ongoing task or the user's situation in general, and by reducing the effort the user must devote to copying information from one part of the display to another or navigating between different functions and pieces of information when performing a task.

Spreadsheets are already well known, so users may think about the new principles for networked communication as a sort of super spreadsheet. It is, therefore, interesting to discuss the relationship between the five principles and the way a spreadsheet is organized and used. The ability to set up views that present precisely the information that is needed in a particular situation or for a specific task is the core functionality of a spreadsheet. The automatic synchronization between different information units is also already a basic principle of a spreadsheet. When a value is changed, all other values that depend on it are also changed automatically. It may also be possible to support synchronous navigation between two spreadsheets with the same organization and to add a function to a spreadsheet that informs the user about changes to values in it, in particular if one of the values is outside a set of pre-defined parameters (for instance, if the company is losing money). It may also be possible to pull or push views or pages of a spreadsheet from one terminal to another. To some extent, this is already possible in some existing systems. In contrast, the current structure of spreadsheets is in direct contrast to the use of information or function chunks as basic units. If a numerical value in a spreadsheet is calculated by a formula, the parameters in the formula change if the cell is moved. The contents of the cell are not an independent unit of information that can be moved around. In addition, each cell in a spreadsheet may contain only text or some sort of numerical value. This means that anything that may be perceived as a schema by the user is chopped up by the cell structure, so information about the background and context of each piece of information easily are separated.

It is technically feasible to implement the five principles in a Web-based network. However, as described earlier, today's networks of electronic information are heterogeneous, so if and how the five principles are implemented depend also on market forces and their compatibility with the existing organization of electronic information.

This means that the first principle (making users aware of changes in the network) is probably the most likely to be implemented. It is fairly easy to make an application that can scan a number of Web pages and inform the user if any of them have been changed, and it may be both possible and desirable to design content-management systems that can alert users automatically when specific changes or other events happen to the information and functions organized in them.

It is also likely that we will see tools that implement situation-specific views of information and function chunks, such that the user can create and store a view that gives access to the information and functions he or she needs in a specific situation or to solve a specific task. This may be done in addition to existing operating systems. The main challenge will then be to make it possible for the user to move fast enough between the different elements presented in the view. The value of the view is substantially reduced if it takes several seconds before an element is accessible after the user has clicked on it.

This means that an introduction of the ability to pull and push views also is fairly likely. This is a valuable addition to the concept of views. With view formats with absolute addresses (so the definitions of the chunks that are accessible through a view do not depend on the specific computer on which it is situated or accessed), it is possible in principle to move views similarly to the way files are moved today.

The most difficult developments are the introduction of information chunks as basic units and facilities that support the automatic synchronization between them.

When using the current systems, which are based on files and applications, we can be almost certain that a file can be accessed through the application it is created by or for. It may not be possible to access it in any other manner, but at least we have one way of accessing it. In contrast, the use of information and function chunks requires public standards for the interfaces required to create views with a number of information and function chunks and to synchronize the chunks in a view.

In addition, both browsers and the Web-design industry are accustomed to pages that each contain a conglomerate of information, and the software industry is used to thinking in terms of high-cost, multi-function applications. The use of information and function chunks requires a different way of thinking and a different way of doing business, similar to the way the music industry is moving from selling CDs to selling single songs for download.

However, it is possible that disintegration tools such as C3W, which makes it possible for users to cut information apart, may force information providers to change their way of doing business. Another possibility is that function chunks may become used in specific areas, for instance, for building applications for control rooms, for simulations, or for teaching environments. It is then possible that established software developers will also have to contend with providers of function and information chunks, in particular if the chunk providers can provide additional high value functions, or functions that make it possible for users to do most of what they want to do, but at a lower cost than if they were to buy a full-scale application.

Designers often copy elements from earlier types of technology. In addition, we also have a legacy in technological development. Once a decision is taken and implemented in information systems, most changes require that a number of implementations are changed and that backward compatibility is ensured.

If the concept of information chunks is realized, it will probably be through interfaces and networks that mix the current organization of information and tools into applications, pages, and files, and information and function chunks. One consequence is that even though the principles described in this chapter look simple and sensible, if any of them are realized, the future may look even messier than our networks today.

References

Albrink, T., & Strom, G. (2002). *The network explorer: A compact view of a telecom network.* Paper presented at the ECUE 2002 (Ericsson Conference on Usability Engineering 2002), Ericsson, Copenhagen, Denmark, March 6-8.

Bartlett, F. C. (1932). *Remembering, A study in experimental and social psychology.* Cambridge: Cambridge University Press.

Basalla, G. (1988). *The evolution of technology.* Cambridge: Cambridge University Press.

Bruce, V., & P. R. Green (1990). *Visual perception.* Hove, UK; Hillsdale, NJ: Lawrence Erlbaum Associates.

Collins, G. P. (2004). Next stretch for plastic electronics. *Scientific American, 291*(2), 58-65.

Fujima, J., Lunzer, A., Hornbæk, K., & Tanaka, Y. (2004). Clip, connect, clone: Combining application elements to build custom interfaces for information access. In *Proceedings of UIST '04,* Santa Fe, New Mexico, USA, October 24-27 (pp. 175-184). New York: ACM Press.

Grudin, J. T. (1983). Error patterns in novice and skilled transcription typing. In W. E. Cooper (Ed.), *Cognitive aspects of skilled typewriting* (pp. 121-139). New York: Springer-Verlag.

Hellier, E. J., Edworthy, J., & Dennis, I. (1993). Improving auditory warning design: Quantifying and predicting the effects of different warning parameters on perceived urgency. *Human Factors, 35*(4), 693-706.

Horn, R. E. (1989). *Mapping hypertext: The analysis, organization, and display of knowledge for the next generation of on-line text and graphics.* Lexington, MA: The Lexington Institute.

Howard, W. E. (2004). Better displays with organic films. *Scientific American, 290*(2), 64-69.

Humphreys, G. W., & Bruce, W. (1989). *Visual cognition.* Hove, UK; Hillsdale, NJ: Lawrence Erlbaum Associates.

James, W. (1890). *The principles of psychology.* New York: H. Holt and company.

Jensen, H. H. (2004). *Service orienteret arkitektur – Integration som konkurrenceparameter.* Allerød: Litera.

Law, J. (1987). Technology and heterogeneous engineering; The case of portuguese expansion. In W. E. Bijker, T. P. Hughes, & T. Pinch (Eds.), *The social construction of technological systems: New directions in the sociology and history of technology* (pp. 111-134). Cambridge, MA: The MIT Press.

Lunzer, A., & Hornbæk, K. (2003). Side-by-side display and control of multiple scenarios: Subjunctive interfaces for exploring multi-attribute data. In *Proceedings of OZCHI 2003,* Brisbane, Australia, November 26-28 (pp. 202-210). Brisbane: CHISIG.

Miyata, Y., & Norman, D. A. (1986). Psychological issues in support of multiple activities. In D. A. Norman, & S. W. Draper (Eds.), *User centered system design* (pp. 265-284). Hove, UK; Hillsdale, NJ: Lawrence Erlbaum Associates.

Naur, P. (1985). Programming as theory building. *Microprocessing and Micropro-gramming, 15*, 253-261. (Also published in: Naur, P. (1995). *Knowing and the mystique of logic and rules: Including true statements in knowing and action, computer modelling of human knowing activity, coherent description as the core of scholarship and science.* Dordrecht; Boston: Kluwer Academic Publishers.)

Nielsen, C., & Søndergaard, A. (2000). *Designing for mobility – An integration approach supporting multiple technologies.* Paper presented at the Nordichi 2000: Design vs. Design, Stockholm, October 23-25.

Schacter, D. L. (1996). *Searching for memory: The brain, the mind, and the past.* New York: BasicBooks.

Shneiderman, B. (1998). *Designing the user interface: Strategies for effective human-computer-interaction* (3rd ed.). Reading, MA: Addison Wesley Longman.

Silveira, M. S., Barbosa, S. D. J., & Souza, C. S. d. (2001). Augmenting the affordance of online help content. In A. Blandford, J. Vanderdockt, & P. Gray (Eds.), *People and computers XV - Interaction without frontiers* (pp. 279-296). UK: Springer.

Simon, H. A. (1974). How big is a chunk? *Science, 183*, 482-488.

Chapter VI

A Short History of Designing for Communication on the Web

Simon B. Heilesen
Roskilde University, Denmark

Abstract

Web design is important for how we communicate on the Internet, and it also has an influence on computer interface design in general. Taking a very literal view of the theme of "designing for communication", this chapter examines the development of Web design as a prerequisite for understanding what it has become today, and it concludes by offering some reflections on the future of Web design. In the first part of the chapter, the history of Web design is outlined in terms of the complex interplay of various social, cultural, economic, technological, and communicative factors. This section concludes with the presentation of a framework for Web design that allows for—if not actually reconciles—the many existing approaches to the subject. In the second part of the chapter, it is suggested that Web design, as it has developed so far, may be facing major changes as the requirements of users and the technologies employed to meet them are changing.

Introduction

In most technologically-advanced societies, the Internet has become an extremely important means of distributing, exchanging, and finding information, and the World Wide Web (WWW) has become the all-dominant service on the Internet. The Web browser is the de facto interface to the Net, and through the Web pages displayed in them, the user is able to operate in the digital universe. Increasingly, we are experiencing the world through the Web browser interface. "Web design" comprises not only *documents*, but also *applications* of many kinds. As more and more computer programs are becoming available on the Net or are in some way being integrated with it, the conventions for designing Web pages are also having a pronounced impact on user interface design in general.

"Web design" is a vague term referring to a complex subject that has evolved over time. It covers the layout, content, and behaviours of individual Web pages as well as the information architecture of entire Web sites. Normally, it is not concerned with the design of the software that is used for displaying Web pages (browsers and plugins)—other than the technical limitations imposed by different software products and versions. The term "Web design" does not distinguish between documents (static or dynamically-created Web pages) and applications running in the browser window (e-mail, games, simulations, groupware, etc.), nor does it usually distinguish between the various technologies employed to create visual design and content (HTML, XML, VRML, and multimedia applications such as Flash™, Shockwave™, etc.).

Web design obviously matters greatly when we are designing for networked communication—as is evidenced by the already vast body of popular, technical, and scholarly literature on the subject. It is a developing discipline characterized by a great diversity of approaches that in some cases seem to be at odds with one another.

It is our contention that Web design as we know it today is the result of a development involving complex interrelations between many different factors and actors. A consequence of this development is that designing for the Web involves considerations that are sometimes weighted somewhat differently than is the case when designing other kinds of information technology solutions. Another consequence is that in order to understand what Web design has become and in which direction it might be moving it is necessary be familiar with the history of Web design. The aim of this chapter is to explore the history of Web design in some detail in order to arrive at a framework for Web design that allows for—if not actually reconciles—the many existing approaches to the subject.

In the historical account, Web design will be understood as an aspect of the history of the World Wide Web, and it will be interpreted in line with the recent tradition of technology history writing that approaches the subject from the point of view of social and cultural history (Klüver, 1986). Specifically, the historical development will be presented as the complex interplay between several factors, the most prominent of them being technology, organizations and regulations, market forces, theoretical background, producers, purpose, consumers, and our overall understanding of the medium. A few comments on each of these factors are required before we proceed with the historical account.

Technology should be understood in a highly inclusive sense as comprising hardware (network and computers), software (browsers, plug-ins) as well as programming languages and mark-up languages (e.g., HTML, XML, Flash™, JavaScript®). A steady stream of new technological features have been introduced both to meet existing needs and to create new ones, and ultimately technology sets the limits for what it is possible to achieve.

The *organizations* responsible for developing and maintaining the World Wide Web and the official *regulations* concerning ownership, distribution, and use all have been decisive for the dissemination of the Web and for imposing some order on a fairly indomitable medium.

The *market forces* have been very much in evidence since the privatization of the Internet. In a practical sense, they exert influence on availability and access. In a broader sense, they have been instrumental in the rise of a Web industry, commercial exploitation, and more.

The *theoretical background* consists of not just engineering and computer science, which have been essential for implementing the hypertext technology, that is the fabric of the Web, but also to a host of other disciplines that have contributed to our practices for designing Web products that make use of multi-semiotic forms of expression.

By *producers* of Web material should be understood both those who commission and own Web sites (referred to as "senders" in the context of communication) and those who do the actual designing and coding (amateurs as well as professionals). A noteworthy characteristic of the producers of Web design has been that all practitioners in this emerging field initially have had to rely on competencies acquired in other disciplines that in some way have proven relevant to Web design.

The *purpose* of creating Web materials refers to the intentions for publishing material or offering a service as well as business plans for organizational or commercial use. Purpose is a factor particularly important to design. We will deal with it both in terms of genre, and in a more general way in terms of the concepts "looking through" and "looking at" introduced by Richard Lanham (1993) and developed by J. David Bolter (Bolter & Gromala, 2003). These concepts aptly illustrate two different understandings of communication, and they go a long way in explaining a prominent and much publicized division in Web design. When you are *looking through*, ideally the interface should be completely transparent so that you can concentrate fully on the task or content at hand. In the analogue world, layout and typography for a textbook should support "looking through", and if it does not, then that is commonly thought to detract from the credibility of the book. When you are *looking at* the interface, you are conscious of and probably appreciative of the visual design. An analogue example would be the brochure advertising a product. In this case, the user is to be persuaded by being imbued with an emotional and even sensuous experience. This contrast between functional and aesthetic design is not at all new, nor of course is it absolute. An important point to be made later is that, given a minimum of Web literacy, consumers (users) are just as capable of dealing with both kinds of "looking" in the Web medium as they are in conventional media.

The *consumers* of Web material—usually referred to as "users"—is a vast, ever growing, and entirely heterogeneous "target group". By searching for information or conducting transactions on the Web, users by their presence and preferences to a large extent shape the direction that Web design is taking.

Our understanding of the World Wide Web as a medium and more broadly as a phenomenon is what frames the values we attribute to it and the uses we make of it, right down to the actual design of products. As Mark Stefik (1996) noted quite early on in the "Internet revolution", the way we think about the Internet will help determine the way we develop it.

All of the factors enumerated previously in the text are highly dynamic. They have developed dramatically in the short-time span that we have had the Web. The various factors are also closely interrelated. Any one of them has some bearings on all of the others in intricate patterns of cause and effect, as we will try to demonstrate in the next section.

The Development of Web Design

In February 1991, the World Wide Web was introduced as a character-based system. At the time, it was in fact already running with a graphical user interface on the inventor's own NeXT computer (Berners-Lee, 1999; W3C, 2003), but the graphical Web user interface, so essential for the eventual success of WWW, became common only after the launch of the Mosaic® Web-browser two years later (February 1993). To the early users, WWW primarily offered a new, simple, and efficient way of organizing information: In the words of the Web's creator: "The WWW project merges the techniques of information retrieval and hypertext to make an easy but powerful global information system" (Berners-Lee, 1991). Web page authors were concerned with structuring and writing hypertext. The tool most often used was a text editor, and the early versions of HTML offered only very few and simple means of formatting the document. Since the vast majority of early users were members of the academic community, most writing for the Web was professional in nature. That is, it was the kind of communication that usually is meant to be transparent. Hence, the primitive design features even if somewhat limiting were not critically so.

The theoretical background for the new means of expression was threefold. First of all, there was hypertext research, an emerging field that had organized its first conference a few years earlier (1987). Hypertext research combined various disciplines ranging from computer science, driving the technological development, and to theology and the humanities, providing showcase applications such as a hypertext New Testament and a hypertext anthology of Tang poetry (Delany & Landow, 1991). A characteristic of the early years was the literary approach to hypertext. This contributed greatly to our understanding of the nature of hypertext and its relation to writing. But in the long run, the literary approach may have contributed more to the emerging fields of interactive entertainment and computer game research than to practical design of Web sites for professional or commercial use (e.g., Aarseth, 1997; Bolter, 2001; Landow, 1997).

Another important early approach to handling information on the Web was that of the documentalist and librarian. Years before the World Wide Web was created for purposes of archiving at the CERN research facility, hypertext had been used successfully for creating manuals, documentation, online help systems, and archives. This tradition has contributed to our knowledge about writing hypertext documents and structuring Web sites (e.g., Horton, 1994; Rosenfeld & Morville, 1998).

Last but not least, HCI research (human-computer interaction) was applied to Web design right from the start (e.g., Nielsen, 1995; Shneiderman, 1997). Focus was on the practically-oriented research in system acceptability, and in the context of the Web, *usability* became a key concept (Nielsen, 1993; Norman, 1988). Also in this research area, interest in hypertext pre-dated the Web, and the HCI principles invoked were in fact developed for stand-alone software products and not for the Net medium. A case in point is *heuristic evaluation*. In the beginning, pre-Web heuristics had to be interpreted more or less successfully in Web terms (e.g., Instone, 1997), and it took years before new heuristics suitable for the Web were developed. Still, in early Web design, even poorly adapted guidelines were better than none at all. In a new medium offering seemingly endless opportunities and hardly any norms, the practical and easily applicable guidelines drawn from the HCI field became trendsetting. Even today, the strict HCI approach is frequently clearly reflected in public sector guidelines for Web design.

A major HCI school contribution to Web design is the notion of and the methods for involving end users in the creation of Web sites. In its most basic form, it is practiced as product testing by end users at various stages in the process of implementation. But it can also be extended to the early phases of analysis and planning, and it can be combined profitably with various methods for target group analysis.

In the various approaches to early Web design mentioned earlier, the literary/librarian and computer science/HCI may be found as the origin of two prevalent conceptions of the WWW as being either a publishing tool or a software system. A Web site may be understood as being primarily a communication product or a tool; it can be a vehicle for experiencing or just an object to work with; it can be meant to look at or to look through.

The Universal Web

The free graphical Web browser has contributed greatly to WWW's phenomenal success since 1993. It offered Windows®- and Mac®-users a familiar interface, and it suddenly made it simple to access the Internet. So much so that the World Wide Web soon began incorporating most other Internet services. In just one year, it grew into the most popular service on the Net, and eventually it has become synonymous with "Internet". Equally important, however, was the gradual privatization of the Internet that was completed in 1995. This led to a commercialization of Internet access, Internet software, and Internet content. Thus, in 1994, the first local communities made their way to the Web, and the first Internet shops and banks opened. Almost overnight, branding, marketing, and retailing became important issues in Web design. Web use kept increasing at an overwhelming rate, and soon the Web became universal both in terms of users and content. Over a very short period of time, rushing to fulfill actual needs as well as a good many potential needs that no one had ever imagined before, just about everything that could be produced in any other medium was re-mediated on the Web—more or less successfully, to be true. One of the persistent problems in Web design has been the misconception that any kind of material can simply be "translated" for use on the Web without any regard for the characteristics of the new medium.

The triumphant flotation of Netscape® in August 1995 marked the beginning of the dotcom-bubble, and it is symbolic of the hectic development of Web technology driven first by Mosaic®, then by Netscape® and finally by Microsoft® when Internet Explorer® emerged victorious from "the browser wars". Initially, the software companies were leading the development of new tags and attributes necessary for creating ever more sophisticated Web pages. New browser versions with important new features (not always compatible with the competitors' browsers) appeared every few months, and only gradually was the World Wide Web Consortium (W3C, founded October 1994) able to enforce standards and take charge of an orderly development of the medium.

There were two main characteristics in this technological development: (a) improved control with the user interface providing for advanced layout reminiscent of desktop publishing or word processing; and (b) higher degrees of interactivity empowering the users to perform all kinds of transactions on the Web, making it an extremely versatile tool. Important inventions were Java® and JavaScript® (1995), the first of several programming languages facilitating the creation of dynamic Web pages; the implementation of style sheets giving the designer advanced control over typography and layout—cascading style sheets in 1996 (Lie & Bos, 1999); the availability of tags for embedding multimedia objects such as Shockwave™- and Flash™-animations (standardized in HTML 4.0, 1997). This rapid development of means of expression meant that the "Web page" ceased to be a simple, fairly uniform kind of document. Now it could have any imaginable form, ranging from a short text with a minimum of formatting to the presentation of an advanced multimedia application with sound, images, and animations.

The division of Web design into content, form (layout by means of style sheets), and behaviour (scripts and programs) that was established in the mid-1990s may be the single most important technical development in the history of Web design. It added logic and flexibility to Web design; it paved the way for the content management systems that since have become indispensable in professional Web use; and it provided the foundation for a better understanding in the broader Web community of the proper relationship between information and the presentation of it.

In the early years, Web authors cumbersomely wrote HTML-code using a plain text editor. But as the Web gained popularity, text based and graphical HTML-editors automating the process started appearing, encouraging the designer to place more emphasis on the visual design. Soon, all moderately computer literate users were able to publish on the Web, and we witnessed an outburst of creative, but untrained talent, somewhat reminiscent of the early years of self-publishing with desktop publishing and word processing. Back then in the 1980s, every typographical rule ever established was joyfully violated while the craft of typography all but perished. A decade later, even the technical limitations offered by the print medium were gone. Guides to HTML-coding typically focused on the technical aspects, dealing with the finer points of design mainly in terms of norms for usability. More reflected introductions to Web design started appearing only in the late 1990s when the technical challenge had become minimal and Web design had evolved into a global professional industry.

With widespread use of WWW, an ever-increasing range of uses and the greatly improved tools for designing, more and more new professional groups embraced Web design: graphics artists, designers, people involved in marketing and retailing, artists working in old and new media, multimedia developers and others who would typically work with images as much as with text, and to whom expression and aesthetics matter as much if not more than functionality. Best known among the pioneers of this direction of Web design was David Siegel (1996), whose Web sites were revelations and whose first book became an international bestseller. Siegel and his self-proclaimed third generation Web design emphasized design rather than technology, experience rather than functionality, creativity rather than conformity. It was a rebellion against the established and "correct" HCI-functionalism (which can, of course, also be designed in an aesthetically pleasing way). Like so many other rebellions, it went over the top in an unrestrained use of images and "tunnels" of screens meant to put the user in the right mood for viewing the actual Web page content. However, Siegel (who later moderated his position—Siegel, 1998) and many like-minded designers did establish firmly that the Net medium is suitable for visual as well as textual communication, and that things need not always be done in a particular manner.

Since the mid-1990s, graphical Web design has been characterized by rapid changes of fashion. Interactive images, frames, a coloured stripe as left margin, curved decorative lines, flash introductions (reminiscent of Siegel's tunnels), and much more have come and (sometimes) gone. To some extent, these experiments with expression represent a playful and unrestrained use of the technical facilities—"Why not use them, now that it is possible?" But the changing and quite often enormously widespread whims of fashion also illustrate how Web designers typically learn from one another by copying innovative technical solutions and designs. When the Web was still almost exclusively a medium for enthusiasts, good ideas were usually free. But even if many still subscribe to the spirit of the "electronic frontier", the commercialization of the Web has led to a stricter enforcement of intellectual and property rights. Web design has developed into an industry, and innovative design consequently has become a key asset.

Seen in an overall perspective, it may be held that certain styles have evolved on the Web since the mid-1990s, and Web style certainly has become a subject for design experts and art historians (Cloninger, 2002; Engholm, 2002). Most obvious are the styles associated with particular professional approaches to the Web, notably the HCI/usability approach. Other styles can perhaps best be associated with a particular line of business or purpose. Banks and insurance companies, for example, tend to use certain visual elements to signal solidity and credibility, and search engines typically favour a minimalist design that does not detract attention from the search results. Yet, other proclaimed styles are more likely to be the result of exciting creative work done by high profile designers who have managed to generate high visibility and perhaps a following.

A Page for Every Purpose

Looking back at Web design in the 1990s, it is striking that there was not more focus on the existence of genres and target groups. The idea of using "genre" as a means of investigating uses of new media was suggested already at the beginning of the decade (referring to organizations; Orlikowski & Yates, 1994; Yates & Orlikowski, 1992). Probably the earliest example of a reflected practical use of genres in relation to Web design was offered by Jennifer Fleming (1998). She investigated Web design in the light of intended purpose, establishing some broad "content domains". Genre has since been recognized as a useful tool for planning and analyzing Web sites (Crowston & Williams, 2000). We have even seen the introduction of the concept of *cybergenre*, which combines form and content with functionality, thus allowing for the dynamic nature of Web pages (Shepherd & Watters, 1998).

The explosive development of the Web in the 1990s combined with unfamiliarity with the new medium may have made it difficult to fully understand that the Web was developing into a universal medium as rich in genres as all the conventional media combined. Yet even in the new millennium, the notion has persisted that Web sites can and should be designed in accordance with a limited set of norms. A case in point is an influential publication by Jacob Nielsen & Marie Tahir (2001) suggesting that Web sites, for example, IBM, Disney, Victoria's Secret, and New Scientist, should be deconstructed according to a set of detailed usability rules with no apparent concern for intended target group, purpose, or content.

This example illustrates the fundamental problem in approaching Web design from a purely functionalist point of view. Usability (and in a wider sense system accept-ability) is of course central and indispensable to Web design whether or not you agree that the ultimate goal is to "practice simplicity" (Nielsen, 2000a). But once you transform usability into a formula, for example, the 113 universal guidelines in the Nielsen & Tahir book, there is a risk that Web design becomes trivialized and institutionalized. There is a rather thin line between advocating tested and useful guidelines and claiming—explicitly or implicitly—that there is a "correct" way of doing things (and hence many incorrect ways). Still, it cannot be denied that guidelines are extremely helpful in avoiding design disasters, and they also lend themselves to quantification so that Web sites may be measured and compared for user friendliness by authorities and customers.

Responses by the HCI community to the criticism of conventional usability guide-lines have been at least twofold. One important trend has been to refine usability guidelines by taking into consideration the role of the sender (government, business, etc.), some simple characteristics of the users (e.g., age, disabilities) or distribution (Internet, intranet), greatly increasing the number of available guidelines (1.277 by a recent count; Nielsen, 2005). It may be a useful ad hoc approach, but it does not bring much coherence to Web design, and a wild proliferation of guidelines, eventually providing us with a set for every situation, may end up being counter-productive. Another important trend has been the recognition of the significance of emotional user response. Thus one line of HCI research has focused on the user experience, and the importance of making it pleasurable (Green & Jordan, 2001; Jordan, 2000), while others in a more general way have been exploring affective design (Norman, 2004).

One aspect of the interest in affective Web design has been an increasing emphasis on visual design focusing on the aesthetic qualities. Aesthetic qualities have been discussed in a HCI context since the mid-1980s, and it is common knowledge that visual first impressions "tune" the user—just as they do in every other medium. It has also been demonstrated that visual design is important for establishing credibility for a Web site, although it is not the single most important factor (Fogg, 2003). So, it is mainly a question of how to combine considerations of functionality and those of aesthetics. According to some writers, aesthetics and usability (as in looking at/ looking through) seem to represent opposites (Hoffmann & Krauss, 2004). Others, more constructively, point out that discussions of design issues and usability in fact often explicitly or implicitly involve aesthetics (Karvonen, 2000). Yet others wish to bridge the possible divisions by differentiating between "classical aesthetics" (i.e., clear and orderly design that agrees perfectly well with usability considerations) and "expressive aesthetics", which being creative and unconventional in nature may violate established norms—in effect trying to combine "looking through" and "looking at" (Lavie & Tractinsky, 2004).

A not yet fully resolved issue in the propagation of aesthetics in Web design is the fact that the understanding of aesthetic qualities differs widely not just across the cultures of the world, but also between different social groups in a country. Even if the audience for a given Web site may be a good deal less global than is commonly claimed (Halavais, 2000), still not only "social acceptability" has to be taken into account (Nielsen, 1993) when globalizing or localizing a Web product, but also a number of quite pronounced cultural factors (Marcus & Gould, 2000; Simon, 2001; Tractinsky, 1997).

Whereas usability immediately caught on as a dominant concept in Web design, the equally important concept of "utility" for long remained somewhat neglected. In the early years, when the Web primarily was a body of texts, utility was not much of a problem, because the suitability of the Web for organizing documents was obvious. But since the mid-1990s, the Web has been used for every conceivable purpose, and sometimes it seems that being on the Net is an end in itself, few if any questions asked about why or how. One of the first to demonstrate how to implement utility convincingly in Web design was Jennifer Fleming (1998). Her model for developing Web sites demonstrates a faceted understanding of their function, and it assigns to classical usability the role as the basis upon which is added both functionality appropriate to the particular content domain and a particular content. Fleming also argues in favour of the (good) user experience that results from thoroughly understanding the needs of the user and designing so as to meet them.

The overriding problem with having user experience as a criterion is that "user" is a wildly heterogeneous concept. Users approach the Web with different aims and needs, different backgrounds and values, and, not to forget, different technologies. An elaborate Flash™ animation and lots fancy visual stuff demanding a state-of-the-art browser is likely to annoy a user searching some particular piece of information and wanting to get at it fast, while it may be experienced in a positive way by a technophile Net-surfer looking for excitement.

An important aspect of utility is the content of the Web site. In discussions of Web design, content is frequently viewed in relatively simple terms of site architecture or particular styles of writing. Perhaps the fact that a Web site should have something to offer is too trivial to mention. Still, the Web being in principle a vast hypertext database, the relation between archived information and its presentation should not be ignored. Nor has it been by those Web designers who have worked with back end databases and storing and retrieving the information to be displayed on Web pages (e.g., Greenspun, 1999). Given the complex nature of the tasks, the design of content management is often the domain of computer scientists and professional Web designers working on professional solutions. The implementation of content management, on the other hand, has been spread out to the actual producers of information, who operate advanced content management systems that divide the creation and maintenance of Web sites into storage (in databases), visual design (in templates), and the production of content (in an editor). The professionalization of Web design is also evidenced in recent literature on Web design that emphasizes the creation of communication solutions within organizations and between organizations and the surrounding world. Web design, once a maverick trade, has finally matured into a type of system development actively involving representatives of the commissioning organization as well as the intended end users (e.g., Garrett, 2003).

In traditional usability and also in the more recent user experience perspective, emphasis is very much on the user. It seems to be assumed that the sender's purpose has been served if the user is able to navigate a given Web site and has a pleasant "user experience" in the process. A more balanced understanding of how to serve the needs and intensions of both the owner and the user of a Web site has been introduced, drawing on general communication theories (e.g., Heilesen & Wille, 2001). Other writers have tried to describe Web-based communication in terms of (sometimes modified) conventional communication models. The results tend to be unconvincing, for as Burch (2001) has noted, conventional communication models do not apply well to communication on the Internet, and new ones may yet have to be developed so as to accommodate the characteristics of the medium.

Also representing a broader communications perspective, the recent and promising field of captology offers a quite concrete approach to serving the needs and intensions of site owners as well as users (Fogg, 2003). Focusing on credibility and persuasiveness, captology is related to many earlier writings tying Web design with the three classical principles of rhetoric—ethos in this case. Captology examines how information on the Web is perceived and what mechanisms foster trust. Persuasive design is perhaps of particular relevance to e-commerce, but most of the findings are applicable to other types of senders—government, organizations, special interest groups, and individuals.

Striking a Balance

As the preceding pages have amply demonstrated, there is no silver bullet in Web design. The many and sometimes conflicting views on the subject offered with confidence by a great many practitioners as well as theorists simply reflect that Web design is an emerging discipline—and a continuously developing one. Being a new field, it has attracted people from many different professions, each one bringing and naturally employing the theories and methods of the particular field in which he or she was trained. Different points of view have been prevalent at different times, matching broadly, as it has been suggested, the technological and social develop-ment of the Web. Just as no particular approach to Web design offers an absolute truth, not one of these many approaches is superfluous. Together they constitute Web design, each one of them being a legitimate facet of a truly interdisciplinary field. When designing for the Web, decisions on whether to emphasize one or more facets and tone down (but not ignore) others should depend on an analysis of genre, objectives, and intended audience for the product at hand.

To sum up the preceding historical presentation, Figure 1 presents an attempt to visualize in the form of a set of Chinese boxes the complex framework of the de-veloping field of Web design. It should be emphasized that the figure is meant to

Figure 1. Web design framework

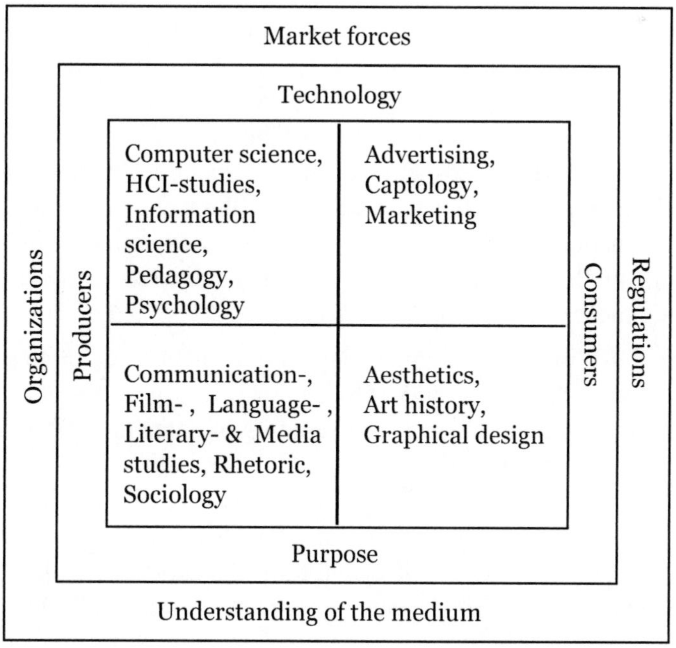

provide an overview of the complexities of Web design—qualifying, as does this chapter, hopefully, the sometimes naïve discussion of what constitutes the "correct" approach to Web design. It is *not* a communication model, and it is *not* meant to be yet another set of useful recommendations for Web design.

At the centre of the figure are grouped in four boxes the more prominent of the disciplines (nearly all of them conventional) that in some way, alone or combined, are relevant to the various aspects of Web design—as described in the historical overview. The grouping is meant to illustrate similarities in the professional background that are likely to be reflected in the approach to Web design. Stated roughly, and at the risk of over-simplifying matters, the disciplines in the boxes on left hand side and on right hand side of the figure respectively can be characterized as follows in terms of the qualities in Web design that they emphasize:

Left hand side	**Right hand side**
Effect,	Affect,
Functionality,	Experience,
Narrative,	Immersion,
Navigation,	Layout,
Perception,	Reception,
Structure,	Persuasiveness,
Textual design,	User response,
User behaviour.	Visual design.

Surrounding these four boxes listing disciplines are two concentric boxes enumerating the various factors, introduced at the beginning of this chapter, that help shape Web design both in a practical manner and in a general way. The inner box deals with the practical aspects of designing for an act of communication, that is: taking into account the intentions of the sender, the purpose (including content) of the act of communication, the needs and response of the target group (not necessarily identical with the actual users), and the choice of the technology most suitable for the particular situation. The outer box lists some of the economic, political and organizational, and intellectual factors that in a very general way provide the foundation for the development of the World Wide Web.

Web products, just like "multimedia", may well be incunabula of an as yet poorly understood medium (Murray, 1997). If so, a figure like Figure 1 is bound to become much simpler as we develop a true understanding of the nature of the medium and start basing Web design on such an insight. However, at the time of writing there is little agreement as to what constitutes the nature of the Web medium. A common method for characterizing WWW is to enumerate its most important qualities such as intertextuality, nonlinearity, multimedia forms of expression, global reach, and more (e.g., Mitra & Cohen, 1999). But more recently, scholars have been trying to identify general defining characteristics of the Web and the Internet, a particularly attractive example being Finnemann's (2001, 2005) simple suggestion that the most basic defining characteristic of the Internet is that it combines high-speed communication with an unlimited potential for archiving.

Still, perhaps we should not believe too firmly in a linear, logical, and fully predictable future development of the Web medium. In the final section of this chapter, we will consider some factors likely to bring major changes to our understanding of Web design as it has developed in the first 15 or so years since the introduction of the World Wide Web.

The Future of Web Design

Some years ago, in a much-debated newsletter posting, Web guru Jacob Nielsen predicted the "End of Web Design" (Nielsen, 2000b). Web design is still around, technology has developed a bit differently from what was predicted, and Nielsen's argument that Web design must be standardized because users prefer familiar interfaces obviously is biased and insufficient. Granted that, however, there may still be some truth to the claim. So, in conclusion, let us consider some of the current trends that are likely to help reduce Web design to a very mundane matter.

As noted earlier, Web design became an industry in the late 1990s. High-quality commercial Web design is now the domain of professionals, or more often teams of professionals where each member contributes some of the competencies we discussed in the previous section. Their primary objective is to provide for easy communication between site owners and end users, and producing mainstream solutions is a safe and effective way of realizing that goal. Inevitably therefore, as the Web has become all-embracing, some conventions—and genres—have emerged making it possible for the trained user to recognize quickly the look and feel of common types of Web sites such as the corporate Web site, the news site, the fashion site, the e-commerce site, and so forth. However, even if a broad consensus has been reached as to what is required for a particular kind of Web site, there is still great latitude when it comes to the details of form of expression. Also, it is worth noting that in the Web design community, there are a great many influential individual professional designers and artists as well as numerous avant garde companies who challenge the mainstream concepts of what a Web page should look like, who continually expand the limits of Web design, and who experiment with the latest technical tools.

Untamed creativity has also been the hallmark of the large segment of hobbyist, semi-professional, and small office Web designers who continue to produce huge quantities of personal home pages, community Web sites and small business solutions. A significant agent of change in this popular segment of Web design, however, is the recent availability of tools that make publishing on the Web an extremely simple matter. In fact, the advent of Web logs and similar social software are blurring the distinction traditionally made between Web publishing and computer-mediated communication (Herring, Scheidt, Wright, & Bonus, 2005), thus also challenging the notion that Web design is something unique.

A Web log or a wiki is the obvious choice if the ambition is simply to publish some text and images on the Net. "You do not have to build a car in order to know how to drive one" was the 1980s argument against everyone having to learn to write computer programs. It now also applies to the Web. The user of wikis, blogs, and similar kinds of social software can concentrate on producing content. Page design and functionality come off-the-shelf in the form of ready-made templates ("skins") that can be freely chosen according to individual taste. It would seem that from a cursory inspection such templates are not to any large extent customized by ordinary users, for why should they bother with code if the page looks neat and works well. Design becoming a commodity or an added feature does not bring an end to Web design as such. But the decline of the tradition of amateur users and small-time professionals designing Web sites from scratch inevitably must contribute to increasing product uniformity.

In terms of visual design, the new social software generally seems to favour simplicity—sometimes bordering on the bland. Content is what counts. At the time of writing, it is not possible to tell whether the renewed preference for the simplicity of functionalism is just a fad like many trends in Web design have been before. But it might be a hint that the medium is reaching a stage where purpose more clearly than before dictates the choice of form of expression. If so, we are getting to the point where Web literate users effortlessly understand the different forms of expressions that have developed on the Web and are quite able to distinguish between "looking at" and "looking through" just as they are when using conventional media. Thus, for example, communicating ideas or collaborating is best done in a simple and clear way, just as it is by now customary that a fancy design is required for a life style or fashion Web site, that a corporate Web site needs the particular kind of restrained elegance with a human touch that helps establish credibility, that a professional publication or an official form must offer clarity, easy reading, and navigation, and so on.

The growing emphasis on content is also supported by the success of Web syndication, that is, the popular RSS feeds (rich site summary, RDF site summary, or really simple syndication) that "push" updated material to a Web page or a Web log. RSS delivers content that is completely separated from the particular design used for presentation of it on the original site.

It is a basic condition in Web design that the presentation of a Web page ultimately is determined by the hardware and software used to display it. An important practical task in Web design, therefore, is to make Web pages' browsers compatible and adaptable to different screen resolutions. The complexity of this task has increased immensely, however, as the Internet increasingly is accessed by means of handheld devices such as PDAs and cell phones. The small screen formats require page layout adaptation. In the present context, the actual strategies for adapting Web pages are not particularly significant, but the outcome is: Content (effectively text and links) can be displayed without problems, advanced layout and embellishments cannot. We are just witnessing the early stages of pervasive, wireless networked computing, where Internet access will be integrated in all kinds of electronic devices. Of course, this seriously challenges the conventions of Web design that have been developed in the first decade or two of the WWW era on the assumption that the Iinternet user interface invariably is a 14-inch or larger monitor with 4:3 proportions and a screen resolution measured in many hundreds of thousands of pixels.

References

Aarseth, E. (1997). *Cybertext: Perspectives on ergodic literature.* Baltimore, MD: Johns Hopkins University Press.

Berners-Lee, T. (1991). *WorldWideWeb – Executive summary.* Retrieved August 23, 2005, from http://groups.google.com/group/alt.hypertext/msg/395f282a67a1916c

Berners-Lee, T. (1999). *Weaving the Web. The past, present and future of the World Wide Web by its inventor.* London: Orion Books.

Bolter, J. D. (2001). *Writing space. Computers, hypertext and the remediation of print* (2nd ed.). Mahwah, NJ; London: Lawrence Erlbaum Associates.

Bolter, J. D., & Gromala, D. (2003). *Windows and mirrors: Interaction design, digital art, and the myth of transparency.* Cambridge, MA: MIT Press.

Burch, R. O. (2001). Effective Web design and core communication issues: The missing components in Web based distance education. *Journal of Educational Multimedia and Hypermedia, 10*(4), 357-367.

Cloninger, C. (2002). *Fresh styles for Web designers: Eye candy from the underground.* Indianapolis: New Riders Publishing.

Crowston, K., & Williams, M. (2000). Reproduced and emergent genres of communication on the World-Wide Web. *The Information Society, 16*(3), 201-216.

Delany, P., & Landow, G. P. (1991). *Hypermedia and literary studies.* Cambridge, MA: MIT Press.

Engholm, I. (2002). Digital style history: The development of graphic design on the Internet. *Digital Creativity, 14*(4), 193-211.

Finnemann, N. O. (2001). *The Internet—A new communicational infrastructure* (Papers from The Centre for Internet Research, Vol. 2). Aarhus: The Centre for Internet Research, Department of Information and Media Studies, Aarhus University.

Finnemann, N. O. (2005). *Internettet i mediehistorisk perspektiv* (1st ed.). Frederiksberg: Samfundslitteratur.

Fleming, J. (1998). *Web navigation. Designing the user experience.* Sebastopol, CA; Cambridge: O'Reilly.

Fogg, B. J. (2003). *Persuasive technology: Using computers to change what we think and do.* Amsterdam; Boston: Morgan Kaufmann Publishers.

Garrett, J. J. (2003). *The elements of user experience. User-centered design for the Web.* Indianapolis: New Riders Publishing.

Green, W. S., & Jordan, P. W. (2001). *Pleasure with products: Beyond usability.* London; New York: Taylor & Francis.

Greenspun, P. (1999). *Philip and Alex's guide to Web publishing.* San Fransisco: Morgan Kaufmann.

Halavais, A. (2000). National borders on the World Wide Web. *New Media & Society, 2*(1), 7-28.

Heilesen, S. B., & Wille, N. E. (2001). *Design for WWW.* København: Dansk Design Center.

Herring, S. C., Scheidt, L. A., Wright, E., & Bonus, S. (2005). Weblogs as a bridging genre. *Information Technology & People, 18*(2), 142-171.

Hoffmann, R., & Krauss, K. (2004). *A critical evaluation of literature on visual aesthetics for the Web.* Paper presented at the 2004 Annual Research Conference of the South African Institute of Computer Scientists and Information Technologists on IT Research in Developing Countries, Stellenbosch, Western Cape, South Africa, October 4-6.

Horton, W. (1994). *Designing and writing online documentation.* New York: John Wiley & Sons.

Instone, K. (1997). *Usability engineering for the Web.* Retrieved July 23, 2005, from http://www.w3j.com/5/s3.instone.html

Jordan, P. W. (2000). *Designing pleasurable products: An introduction to the new human factors.* London; Philadelphia: Taylor & Francis.

Karvonen, K. (2000). The beauty of simplicity. Paper presented at the *Proceedings on the 2000 Conference on Universal Usability,* Arlington, Virginia, November 16-17 (pp. 85-90). New York: ACM Press.

Klüver, P. V. (1986). Kavalleriet kommer altid til tiden – træk af teknologihistoriens og – opfattelsernes historie. *Den jyske Historiker, 35-36,* 8-23.

Landow, G. P. (1997). *Hypertext 2.0: The convergence of contemporary critical theory and technology*. Baltimore, MD: Johns Hopkins University Press.

Lanham, R. A. (1993). *The electronic word: Democracy, technology and the arts*. Chicago: University of Chicago Press.

Lavie, T., & Tractinsky, N. (2004). Assessing dimensions of perceived visual aesthetics of Web sites. *International Journal of Human-Computer Studies, 60*, 269-298.

Lie, H. W., & Bos, B. (1999 (1997)). *Cascading style sheets, designing for the Web* (2nd ed.). New York; London: Addison-Wesley.

Marcus, A., & Gould, E. W. (2000). Crosscurrents: Cultural dimensions and global Web user-interface design. *Interactions, 7*(4), 32-46.

Mitra, A., & Cohen, E. (1999). Analyzing the Web. Directions and challenges. In S. Jones (Ed.), *Doing Internet research. Critical issues and methods for examining the Net* (pp. 179-202). Thousand Oaks; London; New Delhi: Sage.

Murray, J. H. (1997). *Hamlet on the holodeck: The future of narrative in cyberspace*. New York: Free Press.

Nielsen, J. (1993). *Usability engineering*. Boston: Academic Press.

Nielsen, J. (1995). *Multimedia and hypertext. The Internet and beyond*. Boston ; London: Academic Press.

Nielsen, J. (2000a). *Designing Web usability*. Indianapolis: New Riders Publishing.

Nielsen, J. (2000b). End of Web design. *Jakob Nielsen's Alertbox*, July 23. Retrieved July 21, 2005, from http://www.useit.com/alertbox/20000723.html

Nielsen, J. (2005). Durability of usability guidelines. *Jacob Nielsen's Alertbox,* January 17. Retrieved July 21, 2005, from http://www.useit.com/alertbox/20050117.html

Nielsen, J., & Tahir, M. (2001). *Homepage usability. 50 Websites deconstructed*. Indianapolis: New Riders Publishing.

Norman, D. A. (1988). *The psychology of everyday things*. New York: Basic Books.

Norman, D. A. (2004). *Emotional design: Why we love (or hate) everyday things*. New York: Basic Books.

Orlikowski, W. J., & Yates, J. (1994). Genre repertoire: The structuring of communicative practices in organizations. *Administrative Science Quarterly, 39*(4), 541-574.

Rosenfeld, L., & Morville, P. (1998). *Information architecture for the World Wide Web*. Sebastopol, CA: O'Reilly.

Shepherd, M., & Watters., C. (1998). The evolution of cybergenres. *Thirty-First Annual Hawaii International Conference on System Sciences, 2, no. 2*, 97.

Shneiderman, B. (1997). *Designing the user interface: Strategies for effective human-computer interaction* (3rd ed.). Reading, MA: Addison-Wesley.

Siegel, D. (1998, November 3). Siegel goes for sensible. *Sydney Morning Herald*. Retrieved July 23, 2005, from http://www.shorewalker.com/design/design100.html

Siegel, D. (1996). *Creating killer Web sites. The art of third-generation site design*. Indianapolis: Hayden.

Simon, S. J. (2001). The impact of culture and gender on Web sites: An empirical study. *The DATA BASE for Advances in Information Systems, 32*(1), 18-37.

Stefik, M. (1996). *Internet dreams: Archetypes, myths, and metophors*. Cambridge, MA: MIT Press.

Tractinsky, N. (1997). Aesthetics and apparent usability: Empirically assessing cultural and methodological issues. Paper presented at the *CHI 97 Conference on Human Factors in Computing Systems*, Atlanta, GA, March 22-27 (pp. 115-122).

W3C. (2003; 1995). *Some early ideas for HTML*. Retrieved July 23, 2005, from http://www.w3.org/MarkUp/historical

Yates, J., & Orlikowski, W. J. (1992). Genres of organizational communication: A structurational approach to studying communication and media. *The Academy of Management Review, 17*(2), 299-326.

Chapter VII

Fostering Innovation in Networked Communications:
Test and Experimentation Platforms for Broadband Systems

Pieter Ballon
Vrije Universiteit Brussel, Belgium

Jo Pierson
Vrije Universiteit Brussel, Belgium

Simon Delaere
Vrije Universiteit Brussel, Belgium

Abstract

This chapter examines how to foster innovation in networked communications by setting up broadband environments for joint testing and experimenting. It identifies six types of test and experimentation platforms (TEPs), based on criteria such as technological maturity, openness, and focus. The typology is matched with the characteristics of real-life TEPs in three European benchmark countries, that is, Finland, The Netherlands, and the UK. The authors argue that the creation of open platforms furthers the interplay between business actors in the value chain, helping to tackle the systemic failures associated with broadband innovation. They demonstrate that the strategic relevance of TEPs lies in the extent to which networked communications between all stakeholders, including users, is made possible in the establishment of a trusted setting that resembles real-life situations (as closely as possible) and in the support of non-linear, mutual shaping innovation processes with semi-mature technology.

Introduction

Modern mediated communication is networked through various systems composed of complementary artefacts such as infrastructures, devices, services, and applications. While most research on networked communications recognises the mutual influence between these artefacts and the communications enabled by them, it has a marked tendency to take changes (in other words: innovation) in these artefacts for granted. As a result, this research has generally paid little attention to the optimal preconditions and circumstances for fostering "systemic" innovations of these artefacts, even though such innovations can be expected to have deep repercussions on the nature of communications mediated by them.

Innovation in broadband systems and services is the primary example of such systemic innovation currently taking place. In a digitised and converged world, an increasing part of mediated communication is happening via fixed or wireless broadband systems, that is, systems that enable "rich" multimedia communication. Innovation in broadband systems and services is regarded as one of the cornerstones of strategies and policies to innovate and ameliorate networked communications in general (see also the following sections). This chapter examines whether current approaches to achieve this do justice to the goals and specific characteristics of networked communications. The objective is to find out how to implement innovation in broadband technologies and applications, in order to optimise networked communications among people and communities. In this way, broadband innovation is defined as innovating multimedia and high bandwidth technologies and applications in close interplay with social, economic, and policy developments.

It is increasingly apparent that broadband innovation requires experimentation with a large variety of technologies, and between a wide range of potential service providers and users, from early on in the development phase. That is, the innovation process of broadband technologies and services is to be regarded as a process of networked communication in itself. This often surpasses the capacity of a single firm or even a single sector of firms. Therefore, policy makers on all sorts of levels are rushing to establish or support joint test and experimentation facilities as pivotal tools to drive broadband innovation. This chapter examines experiences with these facilities on regional, national, and supra-national levels across Europe.

In addition to technological and innovation support, these facilities are set up for understanding and guiding the social and economic changes as well as networked communications related to digital technologies and ICT developments. This refers to experimental settings, often imitating real-life user contexts, where ICT developers and users interact and exchange views for optimal technological introduction.

However, we should not only look at innovation in the configuration of (broadband) networks but also involve the concept of networked communications in the differentiation and assessment of platforms for broadband innovations. More particularly, three different layers can be identified in this regard. The first and most important layer refers to the networked communications between (potential) users and the technology developers. The degree to which these users are involved (early on) in the design and development process will support successful mobilisation of the broadband network and applications later on. Second, we examine how different stakeholders communicate and cooperate in a networked open environment. Finally, networked communications will thrive especially in a technological environment that is "semi-mature". Immature technology, linked to fundamental research findings from engineers and technology developers, has not yet taken a form that is fully "understandable" for future users. Mature technology, close to market-launch, makes more sense to (possible) users. Yet, this kind of technology offers few possibilities for technological changes, except for some minor adaptations. Hence, this phase is of less relevance for technology developers. Therefore, fully immature or fully mature technologies are not adequate to act as a so-called "*objet frontière*" (frontier object) (Flichy, 1995) for networked communications between different stakeholders. Semi-mature technologies do have the opportunity to act as "boundary objects" in this regard, enabling all actors involved to discuss the meaning and further development of the artefact.

A lot of confusion exists as to what types of facilities for broadband innovation can be distinguished and which of those, if any, are best suited to fulfil the goals in relation to networked communications. Therefore, the objective of this chapter is to provide a conceptualisation and examination of these facilities as they currently exist throughout Europe. The chapter introduces the generic term of "test and experimentation platforms" (TEPs) to indicate all facilities and environments for joint innovation including testing, prototyping, and confronting technology with usage situations. It focuses on open and innovation-oriented platforms that involve various technology and service providers as well as users in different stages of technology design, development, and testing.

As TEPs constitute a new and relatively uncharted territory, an extensive exploratory research effort was undertaken, both in terms of theoretical literature and in terms of empirical data. The main research objectives addressed in this chapter are as follows:

- to provide a conceptualisation and typology of test and experimentation platforms;

- to provide an analysis of the potential added value of these platforms for innovation through networked communications; and

- to provide a comparative examination of the actual characteristics of current TEPs in a number of European benchmark countries.

Typology of TEPs

A quick scan of 15 European joint facilities and initiatives to accelerate innovation in broadband infrastructures and services (Ballon et al., 2005) reveals a wide range of terminology used including usability labs, experience and application research centres (EARCs), experience prototyping, living labs, prototyping environments, field trials, societal pilots, testbeds, co-development environments, demonstration centers, user trials, pilot networks, and commercial pilots. While no consistent or uniform terminology seems to be employed, it seems that in general, a distinction is present between environments aimed at testing versus environments aimed at design and development. The extent to which the technology in question is mature (and more or less dependent on this) or pre-competitive operates on a more or less gliding scale. There also seem to be considerable differences between initiatives that involve users and ones that do not, as well as between TEPs in a business-to-business versus a business-to-consumer environment.

A rare systematic overview of joint innovation facilities (Niitamo, 2005) describes the following types: (1) innovation platforms—organised collaborative network for venturing and exploitation/"project incubator", (2) living labs—broad regional development programmes where testing, developing, and validating new products and services indicate future systemic innovation needs, (3) open testbeds—enhanced/interoperable technology infrastructure which will be offered to users, (4) closed testbeds—specific technology for testing purposes, (5) software platforms—interface to software development.

However, while this overview brings together a number of recognisable types of joint innovation environments, more flexible or even fluid joint innovation forms such as joint field trials and pilots are not included. No overarching concept or common denominator is provided. Also, the different types of joint innovation do not appear to be situated on the same level. While some have a rather broad conceptual scope (innovation-platform or living lab), others focus more on the technology level (software platform) or are differentiated by their openness (open versus closed testbeds). This chapter attempts to deal with these issues by presenting a conceptual framework capable of uniting the different instances, adopting a general focus on open, joint, facilities, and considering both (semi-)permanent and more fluid collaborative innovation platforms. We introduce the generic term of "test and experimentation platforms" (TEPs) to indicate all facilities and environments for joint innovation including testing, prototyping, and confronting technology with usage situations. This term focuses on open and innovation-oriented platforms that involve various technology and service providers as well as users in different stages of technology design, development, and testing, enabled by networked communications.

More specifically, we distinguish six types of TEPs: (1) prototyping platforms (including usability labs, software development environments), (2) testbeds, (3) field trials, (4) living labs, (5) market pilots, and (6) societal pilots. These are typified in Table 1. It should be noted that a so-called demonstrator function is often combined with several, if not all, of these types. This chapter will not consider demonstration as an innovative activity in itself.

In order to combine these types within a general conceptual framework, three central characteristics of TEPs are taken into account. First, the technological readiness (as is also considered by Niitamo) is represented on the horizontal axis. Are we dealing with rather mature technologies or applications that are (almost) market ready, or are they more immature? Second, on the vertical axis, the scale goes from a focus on testing technology to a focus on the design aspects. Do we look

Table 1. Typology of test and experimentation platforms

TEP type	Definition
Prototyping platform	A design and development facility used prior to mass production and resulting in the first proof-of-concept of a new technology, product, or service
Testbed	A standardised laboratory environment used for testing new technologies, products, and services and protected from the hazards of testing in a live or production environment
Field trial	A test of technical and other aspects of a new technology, product, or service in a limited, but real-life environment
Living lab	An experimentation environment in which technology is given shape in real-life contexts and in which (end) users are considered "co-producers"
Market pilot	A pilot project in which new products or services that are considered to be rather mature, are released to a certain number of end users in order to obtain marketing data or to make final adjustments before the commercial launch
Societal pilot	A pilot project in which the introduction of new products and services into a real-life environment is intended to result in societal innovation

Figure 1. Conceptual framework of test and experimentation platforms

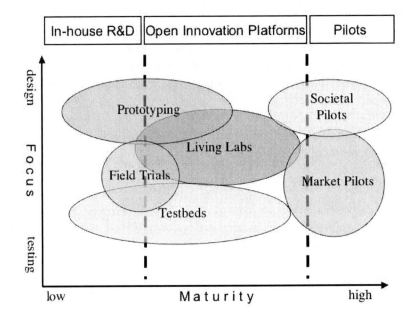

at the extent that the technology works properly in technical terms or do we look at what the technology should look like and what it should be capable of doing? Finally, a differentiation is made between the degree of openness, ranging from in-house activities to open platforms. These aspects are illustrated in Figure 1. The subsequent sections will attempt to substantiate this conceptual framework in two ways. The next section, *Relevance of TEPs for Innovation*, considers the relevance and added value of the concept of TEPs in the light of current thinking on technology use, innovation policy, and innovation economics. In the *Benchmark Cases* section, the TEP requirements that can be derived from this are matched with the actual characteristics of present-day TEPs throughout Europe.

Relevance of TEPs for Innovation

Test and experimentation platforms are aimed at supporting innovation through networked communications between different stakeholders and thus mostly transcending individual companies' initiatives. Based on a succinct survey of various strands of innovation-related literature, this section identifies three major rationales for establishing TEPs: involving users in the innovation process, increasing policy awareness of the importance of innovation activities for competitiveness, and overcoming systemic failures in innovation.

User-Centric Innovation

A first rationale behind the establishment of TEPs is the involvement of users in the innovation process. Understanding the (potential) user can help in minimising risks of technology introduction. Furthering design and development of future technologies and services that are well adapted to potential users will lower the threshold for acceptance and increase the potential for e-inclusion. In addition, it can help to understand why certain innovations can be "disruptive" for existing technology paths.

The (technology) user as a scientific research object is rooted in a range of disciplines (informatics, sociology, economics, and ethnography). In general, a division is made between three schools of thought: the usability approach ("human-computer interface"), domestication approach ("social context as everyday life experiences"), and diffusionist approach ("user as consumer"). The first school, that is, usability or human-computer interaction (HCI), has its roots in the field of informatics, more specifically in the design of software and interfaces. The focus on the "human" in this field has shifted in recent years from a focus on the individual (e.g., drawing on concepts from cognitive psychology) to a focus on the contexts of use (e.g., experience prototyping).

The domestication school of thought is rooted in science and technology studies and the social sciences. This school originates from a critique on technological determinism, pointing to the social dimension of technological change and to the user specifically, as a subject of investigation instead of a mere static factor.

The third school of thought (diffusionist approach) is embedded within economics and aims particularly at understanding factors that explain the adoption and the diffusion of ICTs within society (Burgelman, Tuomi, Punie, & van Bavel, 2004). These different user approaches, stemming initially from informatics, sociology, and economics respectively, gradually advance toward each other. This enables a "richer" understanding of user behaviour.

Yet, users of ICT often behave unpredictably and engage in creative and sometimes unanticipated ways. This is especially the case when engineers or product developers themselves postulate a specific image of the possible user of their particular technology or service. In order to get a better grip on innovatory use and how this can contribute to the technological landscape, these users are increasingly investigated in direct contact with the technological prototype or service (that is being developed). The "virtual user" (Flichy, 1995) is replaced by the "real" user in the innovation process. The technology is confronted with the user during the technological development process. The experiences of these users are used as feedback in the different stages of technological design and development. This requires test and experimentation platforms where the (potential) user is actively involved.

A central element with regard to user involvement in TEPs is the degree to which a "real-life" environment is created and can inform strategic decisions of technology developers and decision makers with regard to user insights. Therefore, understanding the use of technological innovations implies a thorough understanding of the social "real-life" context of groups of people in everyday life, as has been amply demonstrated in social constructivist literature, such as domestication research (Berker, Hartmann, Punie, & Ward, in press). Starting from the idea of mutual shaping, it is essential to look at how technology and social behaviour configure each other. This refers to a double question:

- How is the social enabled or constrained by technological innovation?
- How is technological innovation enabled or constrained by the social?

To understand social changes and to integrate them in the design process, it is crucial to investigate the social life of (potential) users and how this is linked with the adoption and appropriation of communication devices and services. In a ubiquitous networked environment in particular, understanding the social community basis of innovations becomes crucial because these ICTs are appropriated in social practices through social learning processes. In order to investigate this appropriately, a research setting is required that encompasses these social uses in everyday life.

In particular, the "living lab" as an open innovation platform aims at reconstructing the natural user environment as closely as possible. This TEP is based on the notion of users as co-producers of ICT. The living lab is characterised by confronting (potential) users with (prototypes or demonstrators of) technology early in the innovation process. This approach has three main advantages. First, it helps in developing more context-specific insights on development and acceptance processes and especially the interaction between both. Second, these experiments inform us about possible conditions for stimulating the societal and economic embedding of technology. Third, embedding technology in real-life situations generates images of potential societal impacts of innovation (Frissen & van Lieshout, 2004).

Notwithstanding the relatively new nature of this concept, some guidelines on how to construct a living lab for optimal research exist already. It needs to be created as an "experimental field" with specific goals and with a uni-vocal structure, but simultaneously dealing with the uncontrollable dynamics of everyday life. As a consequence, a living lab is characterised by its openness. It also creates opportunities for technologies to be shaped by specific social contexts and needs, where users are perceived as co-producers. Its origin can be traced back to the first social experiments in Scandinavian countries in the '70s and '80s. It fits within the broader constructivist framework of science and technology studies as well as the tradition of constructive technology assessment, now being re-applied in the context of user-oriented technology design. The living lab approach also has strong links with the human-computer interface (HCI) research tradition, referring to notions like participatory design and experience prototyping. Recent illustrations of living labs are the "experience and application research centres" (EARCs). This refers to the research, development, and design by, with, and for users of future technologies like ambient intelligence. It also covers research into methods and tools to enable this (ISTAG, 2004). The novel aspect is that it involves users in all stages of R&D and all stages of the product development life cycle, not just at the end phases as, for example, in more classical field trials or user testing of products.

Taking stock of these developments and guidelines, the relevance to user-centric innovation of TEPs in general, and living labs, in particular, arguably lies in the extent to which (end) user participation is made possible by TEPs, the establishment of an experimental setting that resembles real-life situations as closely as possible, and the enabling and support of non-linear, mutual shaping innovation processes.

Innovation Policy

There is an increasing awareness that we are in the midst of a techno-economic paradigm shift leading to major transformations in economy and society (Perez, 2004). The driving forces behind this shift are information and communication technologies and services. Policy makers are more and more won over by the idea that the degree to which societies take advantage of these changes will depend on the extent that innovations such as fixed and wireless broadband technologies and services are embedded in the economic and societal system. There is also widespread recognition of the fact that, instead of fostering a straightforward belief in the blessings of technological innovations per se, an adequate innovation policy needs to be set out ensuring a close match between technology, society, and economy. In Europe, various Directorate Generals (DGs) of the European Commission have implemented policies aimed at promoting broadband innovation and competitiveness. The European Framework Programmes, the eEurope (and future iEurope) action plans, the Competitiveness and Innovation Framework Programme (CIP), and the Community Framework for State Aid for Research and Development are among the main instruments employed towards this objective.

In order to realise the match between technology, society, and economy, adequate environments need to be created in various projects, in particular, environments that facilitate the interplay and networked communications between different innovation stakeholders: engineers, users, business people, social scientists, and policy. This development reflects the real-world shift in importance from intra-muros R&D to all sorts of extra-muros innovative activities, including the establishment of joint test and experimentation platforms. As argued by Megerian and Potkonjak (2002), almost all modern science and engineering has been built using compound experiment-theory iteration steps. Typically, the experiments have been the expensive and slow components of the iterations. Thus, the existence of flexible yet economic experimentation platforms often results in great conceptual and theoretical breakthroughs. Megerian and Potkonjak cite the example of how advanced optical and infrared telescopes enabled spectacular progress in the understanding of large-scale cosmology theory. Particle accelerators and colliders enabled great progress in the understanding of the ultra-small world of elementary particles. Furthermore, progress in computer science, information theory, and nonparametric statistics has been greatly facilitated by the ability to compile and execute programs quickly on general-purpose computers.

The proliferation of joint test and experimentation facilities (see also the *Benchmark Cases* section) demonstrates that TEPs for broadband innovation are expected to have a similarly positive effect. In light of the innovation policy concerns highlighted earlier, it seems that TEPs may be relevant in three major ways: by enabling industrial research, pre-competitive development, and other innovation activities; by introducing innovations in a specific competitive milieu; and by spreading and mitigating the cost and risk associated with innovation activities. In terms of active policy support, it has become clear that one of the primary issues in this respect is the "distance" to the market of the TEP-related activities. This means that TEPs should be used in support of innovation activities, rather than in support of fundamental research or commercial development. It also implies the primary use of TEPs for technologies, products, and services that could be labelled as "semi-mature" in terms of their market readiness and can thereby be perceived as "boundary objects" between different innovation stakeholders.

Systems of Innovations

Another closely related rationale to establish and support TEPs is to overcome a number of systemic failures in the innovation process. Recent literature on so-called systems of innovations has heightened the awareness, among business stakeholders as well as policy makers, that most innovation processes are characterised by a systemic nature. As argued by scholars such as Edquist (2001), innovation is a complex phenomenon, embracing both new processes (technological and organisational) and new products (goods and services). Similarly, the processes through which innovations emerge are extremely complex. These processes concern not only the emergence, diffusion, and combination of knowledge elements, but also the translation of these into new products and production processes. This translation from basic research to applied research, and to the development and implementation of new processes and new products, by no means follows a linear path. Instead, it is characterised by complicated feedback mechanisms, networked communications, and interactive relations involving science, technology, learning, production, institutions, organisations, policy, and demand.

Also, Edquist notes that while most innovations occur in firms, innovation is a collective effort whereby innovating firms normally communicate and interact with other organisations in the context of existing institutional rules and via networks. Innovations emerge, therefore, in systems where organisational actors and institutional rules are important elements. Systems approaches to innovation are essentially an attempt to think through and analyse the nature and implications of the collective character of innovation.

Of particular importance are inter-firm relations involving sustained interaction between users and producers of technology. Here, the argument is that inter-firm linkages are far more than arm's-length market relationships. In fact, they often constitute ongoing cooperative relationships that shape learning and technology creation through networked communications. Firms also interact with non-firm organisations such as universities, research institutes, private foundations, financing organisations, schools, government agencies, and so forth.

In this complex innovation context, various problems may occur. Hers and Nahuis (2004) provide a critical overview of these problems. First of all, they distinguish a number of market failures, which lead to suboptimal outcomes for society as a whole. External effects, information failures, market power, and incomplete markets may cause too little (knowledge) or too much production (pollution). In addition, there may be system failures, that is, too much or too little interaction, path dependency, and lock-in, missing, or inadequate institutions. It is these system failures that are generally a motivation to intervene in the innovation process.

There is little literature offering an in-depth exploration of potential systemic failures in broadband innovation. However, a considerable number of authors have pointed at market failures, so-called "chicken and egg" problems and lagging services and applications development, all plaguing the broadband infrastructure and services sectors (Ferguson, 2002; Varian, 2002). In an emerging broadband world characterised by high uncertainty, large up-front investments in new technology and complex interdependencies between infrastructure provision and service development, it may be expected that joint test and experimentation platforms will reduce systemic failures in broadband application domains such as information, health, mobility, education, and entertainment. If used for this purpose, it may also be expected that TEPs focus on stimulating interactions and networked communications, creating institutional support for innovation and accelerating the emergence of new technological systems. This implies that TEPs should be open to various business stakeholders while actively building trust, allowing business model experimentation and promoting the formation of clusters.

Benchmark Cases

The empirical part of this chapter involves the examination of a series of examples of TEPs in three EU member states that are broadly accepted as being among the world's leading countries in terms of broadband penetration and innovation as well as policy attention devoted to broadband[1]. To reflect contrasting policy traditions and approaches to broadband innovation processes, the selected benchmark countries are the Netherlands, Finland, and the UK. For each of them, six TEP cases were identified, mirroring the six-type typology described in the *Typology of TEPs* section. The main criterion in selecting individual cases was the (observed or expected) impact of the TEP—in terms of visibility, policy and/or business stakeholder commitment, and economic and societal spill over. Also, a number of cases demonstrating important bottlenecks or negative experiences were included. Table 2 provides an overview of the selected cases.

Table 2. Overview of selected benchmark cases

Type of TEP	Selected Cases	Short Description
Prototyping platform	Philips HomeLab (NL)	Feasibility and usability test lab for ambient intelligence, home care, and advanced multimedia and gaming applications, open to selected partners.
	Silicon Hill (FIN)	Partnership between telco and university to create an open testbed and field trial facility, evolving into a joint prototyping platform for next generation wireless and mobile technologies, new services as well as innovative devices.
	Virtual Engineering Centre and ENABLED (UK)	Prestigious university platform, specialising in validated simulation of complex engineering systems, with EU Integrated Project partly run on the platform.
Testbed	Gigaport NG Network (NL)	Large-scale, successful testbed, in which a 10 Gbit/s backbone and state-of-the-art technologies are used to conduct diverse tests in the domains of authentication, security, directories, and mobility.
	TestbedFinland (FIN)	Public-private partnership to create various open multi-channel development and testing platform environments in the domains of mobile, proximity, and broadcast technologies.
	TV Anytime testbed (UK)	Joint testbed of the TV Anytime standards consortium involving various competitors in the digital TV sector.
Field trial	Surfnet / Kennisnet project (NL)	Experimental settings at schools to pilot e-learning and other educational services.
	Rotuaari (FIN)	University and municipality cooperation for wireless applications field trials including market research.
	Buckfastleigh Broadband (UK)	Combination of a fixed wireless broadband technology field trial and market pilot in a small rural community.

Table 2. (continued)

Type of TEP	Selected Cases	Short Description
Living Lab	Kenniswijk (NL)	Large-scale, high profile living lab, aimed at Fibre-to-the-Home infrastructure, innovative broadband services, and an extensive user community.
	Arabianranta Helsinki Virtual Village (FIN).	Large newly-developed urban area, exhibiting societal pilot and living lab functions in the domain of wireless broadband.
	@PPLe (UK)	Multi-disciplinary user-centred project, involving different research centres as well as private partners, and aimed at a virtual learning environment for people with learning disabilities.
Market pilot	Damsternet (NL)	Combination of research platform and Fibre-to-the-Home infrastructure rollout, under review for compliance with EU state aid rules.
	Octopus (FIN)	Open city testbed project growing into public-private business platform for mobile applications and services.
	Scottish Borders Rural Broadband (UK)	Wireless broadband infrastructure platform offered by local community.
Societal pilot	Digitaal Trapveld (NL)	Pilot project providing ICT access and education to people living in disadvantaged neighbourhoods.
	SparkNet (FIN)	Cooperative testbed evolving into a city wide Wi-Fi multi-operator network.
	EverybodyOnline Glasgow (UK)	Range of small scale ICT infrastructure projects aimed at homeless people in Glasgow.

The aim of the case studies (reflected here in a highly condensed manner) is to highlight the main characteristics that enable a comparison between different TEPs. This is done in order to substantiate the definitions of the TEPs, to identify the ways in which they are most used, and to hint at any specific objectives for which the different types of TEPs may be most suited. Before going into any detail, the case studies have been classified according to two basic criteria. The horizontal axis refers to the focus in terms of being aimed primarily at testing or at design and development. The vertical axis relates to the technological setting in terms of being aimed at testing and developing infrastructures versus services. The results are shown in Figure 2.

As Figure 2 demonstrates, the large majority of TEPs reviewed are concerned with both testing and design and development. This involved all living labs and all pro-totyping platforms as well as most field trials and market pilots. Some societal pilots understandably did not show any testing of technologies, products, or services (as they are designed to introduce mature and duly tested artefacts into new environments). By contrast, a number of testbeds, market pilots, or field trials were predominantly about the testing of technologies or services. In addition, as can be seen from Figure 2, the majority of TEPs are concerned with the testing and development of services

Figure 2. Classification of TEP case studies

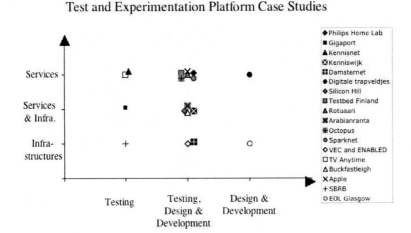

and applications. These TEPs generally provide a standard (but usually very in-novative) infrastructure and consider this as a "given" in their experimentations. A sizeable minority of TEPs (a number of living labs), are concerned with testing and developing of both services and infrastructures.

The subsequent sections further compare characteristics of the different types of platforms according to six axes that were devised so as to measure and compare TEP characteristics:

- **Openness:** The degree to which TEPs are open (including openness regarding results as well as partnership) and thus enabling networked communications between different stakeholders.

- **Public Involvement:** The degree to which policy makers are actively sup-porting and controlling the TEP.

- **Commercial Maturity:** The degrees to which technologies, products, and services tested and developed are close to market introduction. This will also give an indication of their adequacy for configuring networked communica-tions.

- **Vertical Scope:** The degree to which TEPs involve stakeholders from dif-ferent levels in the value chain (i.e., technology providers, service providers, businesses using the technology, and end users). Especially the involvement of users creates opportunities for setting up networked communications between developers and real users. This is also linked with the next characteristic (virtual user versus real-life user).

- **Scale:** The degree to which TEPs have a large and spread-out scale (including laboratory versus real-life, and centralised versus distributed settings).

- **Duration:** The degree to which TEPs are set up as permanent facilities.

Values range from low (1), medium low (1.5), medium (2), medium high (2.5), to high (3).[2] We will complement these characteristics data with case study findings on the value generated by the different types of TEPs. Naturally, due to the small number of case studies and parameters involved, the results cannot be considered as generally valid outcomes. Also, some cases, in particular the Finnish ones, constitute a blend or evolution of TEP types. However, the findings do present indications on the nature of the different types of TEPs as they are currently used in the three EU benchmark countries, and as such may provide a starting point for further research into this matter.

Prototyping Platforms

In this study, we define prototyping platforms as *design and development facilities used prior to mass production and resulting in the first proof-of-concept of a new technology, product, or service.* In general, this activity happens in closed, in-house environments. However, as has been demonstrated by the benchmark case studies, there are successful examples of open, joint prototyping platforms to be found throughout Europe.

Figure 3 illustrates the main characteristics of the prototyping platforms under review. Philips HomeLab in The Netherlands is a high profile lab, driven by a single, large technology-producing firm, but it is increasingly used in collaboration with selected partners. As is also demonstrated in this diagram (Figure 3), this makes it a semi-open environment for joint, open innovation activities. While it is clear that this platform is limited in scale and scope, it is considered to be one of the world's leading research facilities into users' needs and responses related to ambient intelligence (see, e.g., ISTAG, 2004). It is estimated that 80% of the research activities connected to HomeLab are carried out exclusively by Philips, and the remaining 20% in cooperation with various other partners (e.g., research projects within the EU Framework Programmes; Philips is contributing to over 100 EU projects). Recently, Philips started to explore and apply the concept of "open innovation". It implies that Philips shares knowledge and competencies with selected research institutions and industrial parties to improve its R&D. A pilot project is about to start with several

Figure 3. Main characteristics of prototyping platform cases

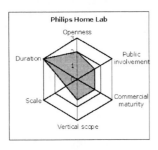
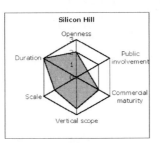
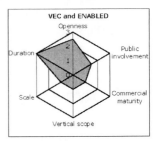

local SMEs. It is expected that in these SME projects, the HomeLab will be both a (open) research facility and a demonstration platform.

Silicon Hill in Finland originated as a partnership between a telecommunications operator and a university to create an open testbed and field trial facility, and gradually integrated joint prototyping platform features. It exhibits features similar to the HomeLab case, but has a larger scale and vertical scope. It is characterised by a specific focus on technology and service innovation related to WLAN combined with mobile cellular networks and has been successful in developing a citizen's electronic identity card.

The Virtual Engineering Centre and ENABLED Integrated Project in the UK is a prestigious university engineering and prototyping platform, specialising in validated simulation of complex engineering systems. It is successful in the sense that it is used for many projects in a wide range of application domains and with various international partners, including an EU Integrated Project partly run on the platform, involving several leading EU companies. It is again very similar to the previous cases, but is more open, as would be expected of an academically driven facility.

In general, it can be said that the prototyping platforms considered exhibit quite similar characteristics. They constitute a more or less permanent setting for joint prototyping between large firms, SMEs and/or academia, on a limited scale and generally with limited vertical scope. Public involvement is also limited, pointing to the business or academic-driven nature of the platforms reviewed.

Even though these platforms are evidently used primarily for designing technologies, products, and services in early stages of development, they also serve as environments for jointly testing and developing more market-ready concepts. This is evidenced by the elaborated rules and guidelines that are often available for the use of these platforms, the active building of trust between participants, and the attention to experimentation with new business models between different partners. Therefore, it comes as no surprise that our case studies show that prototyping platforms can be very successfully combined with field trials, or even with living labs and market pilots.

In addition, the joint testing and developing of semi-mature technologies makes this an adequate platform for networked communications between stakeholders on different levels in the value chain, using technologies in a rather early development stage as boundary object between different actors. The cases demonstrate that users are involved in different degrees in these networked communications, while forms of co-design represent the most intensive user interaction.

Testbeds

Testbeds have been defined as *standardised laboratory environments used for testing new technologies, products, and services and protected from the hazards of testing in a live or production environment*. It can be argued that together with living labs, open testbeds constitute the most visible and recognised TEP-related concept encountered in our case studies.

Figure 4 demonstrates the main characteristics of the testbed cases in our sample. Gigaport NG Network is a large-scale, successful, and comprehensive testbed used for testing very advanced infrastructures while at the same time providing a highly performant backbone for the knowledge base in The Netherlands. Gigaport NG Network demonstrates intensive cooperation between scientific organisations, government, and the private sector. Apart from considerable public funding, it was able to attract even higher funding from private companies (well in excess of expectations) while retaining an open character to a wide range of users. Some typical aspects are the limited commercial maturity, as well as the large scale and scope of this project.

Testbed Finland is an ambitious public-private partnership to create open multi-channel development and testing platform environments for mobile services. It

Figure 4. Main characteristics of testbed cases

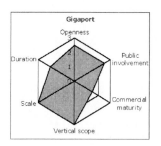
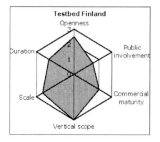
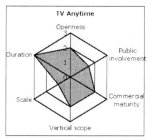

is distributed over three cities, each location specialising in certain testbed and prototype platform aspects. As illustrated by Figure 4, it is not driven mainly by the public sector, but is an extensive cooperation between private, public, and semi-public entities including Nokia, various network operators, many SMEs, and leading academic knowledge centers. The TBF Core Agreement Model, as detailed in the case study, is an interesting model for open collaboration with many stakeholders, and is based on EU 6th Framework Programme rules. It demonstrates characteristics quite similar to Gigaport.

The TV Anytime testbed is a successful open testbed involving high profile competitors in the digital TV sector in the UK. It is an interesting example of the potential value of open testbeds for technology producers and service providers including many competitors, that is, in order to drive standardisation and interoperability in this field. It displays quite similar characteristics to prototyping platforms, which is probably explained by its business-driven nature, limited scale, and permanent set-up.

In general, the testbeds reviewed here are used as semi-open environments for commercially not yet mature technologies, products, and services. They show diverging characteristics in terms of public involvement, scale, and scope, demonstrating the wide variety of ways in which open testbeds are deployed and used throughout Europe today. The testbeds are not only used for technical testing, there are also instances of testing of services and even some marketing concepts. Consequently, they need not be strictly horizontal and limited to technology producers, but can involve vertical chains with technology producers, service providers and even end users, as is demonstrated by the Testbed Finland case. Furthermore, open testbeds that involve all major stakeholders within a sector appear able to provide guidance and (re)orient a whole sector to innovative new technologies.

The testbeds create an environment that initially enables networked communications among technology producers on the horizontal level. This makes collaboration on this level quite intense but at the same time somewhat closed off from other stakeholders. Nevertheless, the analysis of cases of innovative broadband testbeds shows more vertical integration and in some cases even the user is involved in the cooperation and communications. One of the challenges in establishing this cooperation is to offer prototypes of technologies that are mature enough to be understood and tested by common users.

Field Trials

Field trials have been defined here as *tests of technical and other aspects of a new technology, product, or service in a limited, but real-life environment*. We have found several instances of successful attempts to create environments and facilities

Figure 5. Main characteristics of field trial cases

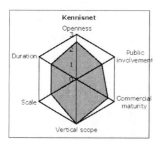 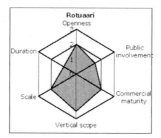 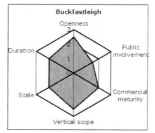

for open field trials involving several stakeholders and even users. Figure 5 shows the characteristics of the field trial cases.

The Kennisnet case involved experimental settings at schools to test e-learning and other educational services. It was primarily aimed at testing the extent to which advanced network applications can be useful for primary and secondary schools and to provide a platform for innovative services of so-called education service providers. In the case of a successful field trial, results may be scaled up to all interested schools. This TEP is characterised by a limited duration, rather high commercial maturity of products and services employed, and a vertical scope.

The Rotuaari case involves university and municipality cooperation for wireless field trials, including market research. Rotuaari shows similar characteristics in terms of permanence, maturity, and scope. Interestingly, this field trial environment is combined not just with joint prototyping, but also joint market pilot features—the field trials involve consumers as end users and yield not just technical test results but also user and market-related data. These findings are used for further service development in subsequent trials. The project's open R&D environment for field trials, successfully involving several companies based in the proximity of the field trial area, is part of a local cluster innovation policy that characterises many of the Finnish cases featured here.

Buckfastleigh Broadband is a combination of a wireless broadband technologies field trial and market pilot in a small rural community. It is interesting because of its attempts to combine rollout strategies in a rural community with open innovation activities such as the development of broadband health and education services. While it demonstrates the potential of such initiatives as a demand articulation tool, it also reveals their vulnerability to commercial strategies, as it is facing difficulties following the commercial provision of fixed broadband access in the area. It has somewhat similar characteristics to the previous cases in the sense of limited duration, semi-maturity, and rather high vertical scope.

Even though, in theory, field trials may seem hard to organise collectively or in an open setting, our benchmark cases demonstrate it is possible. As we have shown, these open field trials can also combine the involvement of end users. They are used as flexible, temporary facilities for specific, relatively small-scale tests. But as collective, open environments involving several subsequent field trials, they can take on a more stable stature and become the nucleus for structural innovative cooperation.

In order to embed the testbed environment in a limited real-life setting, field trials are the preferred platforms of innovation. Here the networked communications are often limited to the personnel directly involved in the trial. The relative lack of openness presents a risk on the involvement of sufficient stakeholders when striving for open innovation. A lot of networked communications take place among professional people, which links it to the origins of computer-mediated communication (CMC) found in the sphere of collaborative working. However, the selected benchmark cases also show the involvement of other actors and thereby extending the vertical scope.

Living Labs

Living labs have been defined as *experimentation environments in which technology is given shape in real-life contexts and in which (end) users are considered "co-producers"*. They are at the core of current new concepts for open innovation platforms. As was argued previously, a living lab is characterised by confronting (potential) users with (prototypes or demonstrators of) technology early on in the innovation process.

Figure 6 illustrates the main features of the living lab cases that were analysed. Kenniswijk is a large-scale, high profile living lab in the region of Eindhoven in The Netherlands, aimed at developing innovative broadband applications and

Figure 6. Main characteristics of living lab cases

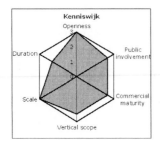 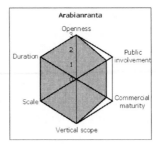 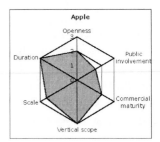

speeding up fibre-to-the-home penetration. It has been discontinued in its present form following a series of critical evaluation reports. It is a very interesting case, not just because of several evaluations that were conducted and published, enabling several changes in the organisation and modalities of the initiative, but also because of a number of problems, such as conflicting and possibly unrealistic objectives (i.e., the combination of TEPs with technology-specific infrastructure roll-out objectives). Its characteristics include high openness and a large scale, as well as relatively high public involvement, maturity, and a vertical scope, while being limited in duration.

Arabianranta/Helsinki Virtual Village is a societal pilot involving a large, newly-developed area and living lab for innovative service development. Even though no formal evaluations have been published, it appears to constitute a successful illustration of a cluster initiative aimed at small enterprises and innovative end users rather than at large ICT firms. Apart from being a more permanent facility (even being recognised as a "New Century City"), it has similar characteristics to Kenniswijk, that is, large scale, vertical scope, high degree of openness, and rather high public involvement and commercial maturity of technologies, products, and services.

The @PPLe case is a multi-disciplinary user-centred project, involving different research centres, a large charity organisation, and private partners. It is aimed at fundamental and applied research as well as the pre-commercial development of a learning environment for disabled people. In comparison with the previous examples of living labs, it is semi-open, involves more "immature" technologies and is driven more by academic, business, and semi-public stakeholders.

The living labs in this sample are characterised by a large scale, a vertical scope, and a medium-to-long-term time horizon. They offer the possibility of bringing the end user as active co-producers of value into a large-scale, real-life testing and design environment. As such, they are capable of providing more user-centric and context-specific insights on development and acceptance processes than traditional methods. They can be combined with market pilots and societal pilots, as is evidenced by our cases. In some instances, their semi-permanent status, and the possibilities they offer to create a large innovative user base, are employed to directly pursue objectives of accelerating adoption and penetration in society as a whole, but experiences up to now have been mixed. In any case, they appear to be able to make innovation processes highly visible and more embedded in society.

These living labs represent the most adequate platforms for networked communications between all stakeholders in the value chain. While the technology is not yet stabilised and thus immature enough to be still negotiable for technological change, it is also mature enough to be useful in confrontation within a real-life user context. Therefore, the living lab forms an ideal opportunity for social innovation based on mutual shaping between technological setting and social context.

Market Pilots

We have defined market pilots as *pilot projects in which new products or services that are considered to be rather mature, are released to a certain number of end users in order to obtain marketing data or to make final adjustments before the commercial launch.* While it is clear that most market pilots will be outside the scope of this report, as they are primarily used as commercialisation tools with a closed and exclusive character, we have found several instances of joint market pilots that display some open innovation characteristics. However, a cautious approach to supporting these "grey area" initiatives is necessary.

Figure 7 illustrates three market pilot cases. In the Damsternet case, which is a regional project started by the Dutch municipality of Appingedam, a close link was established between a broadband innovation platform and fibre-to-the-home infrastructure rollout. Following a lawsuit introduced by a commercial cable operator, it is currently under scrutiny by the European Commission because of state aid issues. Other similar initiatives in The Netherlands have subsequently adopted a less municipality-led approach to joint broadband innovation market pilots. The main characteristics of this case include high public involvement, permanent status of the facilities, and high commercial maturity.

Octopus was started as a temporary open city testbed project and grew into a public-private partnership offering a comprehensive "end-to-end" platform. More than 60 companies and organisations are reported to have joined the network. The core of Octopus is a technologically highly advanced testing platform. It enables testing of mobile services in real-life situations. Around this platform, services are developed and tested, even up to the business cases behind them. Octopus displays similar characteristics to Damsternet in the sense of long duration, vertical scope, and relatively high public involvement, but it differs in that it also includes less mature technologies.

The SBRB case involves a wireless broadband infrastructure platform exploited by a local community. This is a very similar case to Damsternet in the sense that it

Figure 7. Main characteristics of market pilot cases

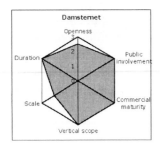
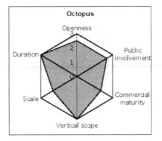
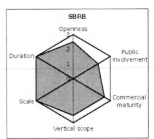

mixes an innovation platform with an infrastructure rollout strategy. Most characteristics are therefore very similar, except for less public involvement as this has been a community initiative. Similar to the Buckfastleigh Broadband case, SBRB has proved vulnerable to commercial rollout strategies.

In general, it can be said that the market pilots reviewed here are constituted by semi-open platforms for piloting usually mature commercial products and services in a permanent setting. Experiences with open market pilots have been more positive for services than for infrastructure. With regards to services there is still more uncertainty prior to commercialisation and, thus, more scope for joint innovative activities; with infrastructure, these roll out pilots are vulnerable to commercial strategies and sometimes questionable in the light of unjustified state aid issues. Therefore, the change potential of networked communications between stakeholders is mainly situated on the level of services development and less on infrastructure level.

Societal Pilots

Finally, societal pilots have been defined as *pilot projects in which the introduction of new products and services into a real-life environment is intended to result in societal innovation.* Figure 8 illustrates the main characteristics of the societal pilot cases.

The Digitale trapveldjes case was a large-scale pilot with mixed results, involving many initiatives to bring ICT to disadvantaged neighbourhoods. It demonstrated a large flexibility for individual initiatives to organise public-private cooperation, but also experienced continuous issues over the continuation of the pilot. In the end, only a small number of initiatives were able to continue. Unsurprisingly, this societal pilot is limited in duration, scale, and vertical scope, exhibiting few technological challenges that require the involvement of technology producers.

In contrast, Sparknet can be characterised as a co-operative testbed that has evolved into a wireless community, promoting societal innovation. As it has grown into a

Figure 8. Main characteristics of societal pilot cases

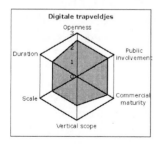 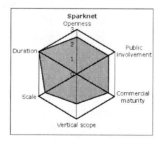 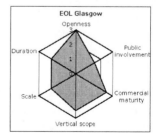

large WiFi network operated by three universities, one polytechnic, two cities, and one science park, it differs from the previous case mainly as to duration and scale. Because of its open, decentralised nature and its use of open source software, it has continued to constitute an innovative platform for testing and development.

EOL Glasgow is a range of small-scale ICT infrastructure projects aimed at home-less people in Glasgow. Involving many major ICT producers and service providers, it further demonstrates that societal pilots need not be driven by public authorities per se. Similarly to Digitale trapveldjes, it is limited in duration and scale, and uses relatively mature technologies and services.

In general, it can be concluded that societal pilots are typically limited in scope and scale, and involve rather highly mature technology. Public involvement need not be high per se, and also large variations regarding their time horizons have also been recorded. It is true that societal pilots are not central to what constitutes open innovation platforms, but, as an educated user base and user-driven innova-tions become more important for innovation processes, they can increasingly be regarded as innovation platforms in their own right, particularly when combined with other TEPs. In addition, they can be tools for the inclusion of societal goals into innovation processes. In this way, networked communications in societal pilots are predominantly situated among different societal stakeholders and less in interaction with technology developers. The technologies and services give little possibility for fundamental changes and the focus is more on how different players cooperate together to enable innovation on a societal, community, or individual user level.

Conclusion

As demonstrated in this chapter, various public and private stakeholders are creating, supporting, and using environments for joint testing and experimenting of broadband innovations. This chapter has proposed a conceptual framework of test and experi-mentation platforms that differentiates six types of TEPs, based on technological maturity, openness and focus, and consisting of testbeds, field trials, prototyping platforms, living labs, market pilots, and societal pilots. At least half of the different characteristics for differentiating TEPs are closely linked to the notion of networked communications. This refers to: openness in results and partnerships, the objective of open innovation activities, stakeholder involvement (technology producers, service providers, professional users, and/or private users), real-life organisational settings, and the involvement of "medium immature" technology.

An analysis of various strands of innovation-related literature identified three major rationales to establish TEPs: involving users in the innovation process; increasing policy awareness of the importance of innovation activities for competitiveness;

and overcoming systemic failures in innovation. From these rationales, a number of a priori requirements for TEPs can be deduced. First, there is the need for adopting a user-centric innovation rationale. TEPs would benefit from involving users of the technologies, products, and services, emulating real-life circumstances, and employing non-linear development trajectories and feedback loops to ensure active user involvement. Second, adopting an innovation policy rationale, TEPs should be used to support innovation activities rather than to enable fundamental research or commercial development. This implies the primary use of TEPs for technologies, products, and services that could be labelled as "semi-mature" in terms of "distance to the market". Finally, adopting a system of innovation rationale, TEPs should be open to various business stakeholders, actively building trust, allowing business model experimentation, and promoting the formation of clusters through networked communications.

Case Studies

While these requirements generally appear to reinforce, rather than contradict each other, it can be expected that they will not be equally present in every (type of) test and experimentation platform. The *Benchmark Cases* section has attempted to match them with the actual characteristics of typical TEPs as they are being set up and used in three European benchmark countries today. In general, it can be said that while specific context and country influences are obvious, the TEPs that were examined exhibit a remarkable commonality in that for all types of TEPs, we have found ample instances of valuable, open initiatives aimed at joint innovation and mostly involving (business or individual) users. In these instances, the relevance of networked communications between all actors involved is apparent.

Despite the differentiation made between the six types of TEPs, there are obvious overlaps with regard to objectives and approach. As illustrated by the cases, there are also various useful and successful combinations or evolutions of different types of TEPs. Therefore, the TEP classification presented here should be seen as ideal-typical rather than as absolute. Living labs, open testbeds, and, to a lesser extent, joint prototyping platforms appear to be the most central and recognisable concepts of what constitutes open TEPs, while the combination of these platforms with open field trials, joint market pilots, or societal pilots appears to have the potential to yield considerable additional value. The *Benchmark Cases* section has further detailed the specific characteristics and potential added value of the six types of TEPs that were identified.

Overall, there appears to be a relationship between the type of TEP employed and the commercial maturity of the artefact, as is indicated by the conceptual framework. However, there is no longer absolute linearity in innovation processes and TEPs can even be regarded as instruments to dissolve this linearity. The fact that joint prototyping platforms or field trials in the examples cited were often combined with involving users or trialing new business models, just as living labs or market pilots included technology testing as part of their activities, demonstrate that R&D and innovation can include user aspects or even business models in quite early stages of development, just as technology testing can run up to the pre-commercialisation phase.

When focusing on the user-centric aspect in this regard, we find that the involvement of (end) users is certainly not limited to those TEPs that are close to the market. Even in more technically-oriented TEPs, like testbeds (e.g., Testbed Finland) and field trials (e.g., Kennisnet), users can be included as part of a vertical stakeholders chain. So the user-centric orientation can be generalised as an overarching potential characteristic of TEPs that is not dependent on a specific type of TEP. The degree of networked communications that involves users will depend on the particular project objectives and business model. This also means that users in a TEP can be confronted with less mature technology, which makes the impact on further (user-centric) technological developments by active user feedback more substantial.

We find that the creation of open platforms also furthers the interplay and networked communications between the business actors in the value chain, as evidenced by the (horizontal) scale and (vertical) scope preferred by many of the TEPs cited. TEPs appear to enable business model experimentation in a trusted, reduced-risk environment. Therefore, they may be positioned at the centre of the debate about the systemic nature of innovation, that is, innovation as a collective effort of different stakeholders, prompting actors that normally have only limited contact, to cooperate in the innovation process. This interaction and networked communications of stakeholders in an early stage of the technology development process may be instrumental in helping to remove the major systemic failures associated with broadband innovation. The open character of TEPs, combined with adequate rules to regulate their exploitation and use, can be seen as the main prerequisites for this.

Value of TEPs for Networked Communications

The advantages of extended networked communications between stakeholders are situated on the technological (system) level and on the social level. On a technological level, it helps in developing more social context-specific insights on ICT use in relation to technology and user interface design. In the field of design and HCI-research, this relates to the shift of "user-centred" design to "people-centred" design. The fundamental source of innovation then, is people using computer-mediated communication in their social context instead of the more task-oriented view based on cognitive psychology (Wakeford, 2004). This entails the shift in usability research on CMC from a "product-oriented" model to a "sociotechnical model" of research. In the latter, ethnography is employed as a research tool for exploring the social aspects of innovative technologies (Crabtree & Rodden, 2002). The research on different cases of test and experimentation platforms has demonstrated that each of them to some degree enables networked communications between developers and users. Even the most technologically-oriented platforms (like testbeds and field trials) often organise the involvement of potential users. However, the most optimal form for creating mutual shaping based on networked communications is found in the living lab platforms. The outcome from a living lab is not primarily aimed at user requirement specifications. This kind of sociotechnical approach is predominantly meant for developing and elaborating sensitising concepts that draw attention to central characteristics of sociality implicated in ICT usage. The latter may then be further explored through continued design. In this way—underscoring the notion of mutual shaping—ICT becomes a vehicle for social research, the results of which in turn drive design.

On the social level of computer-mediated communication, these experiments inform us about possible conditions for stimulating the societal and economic embedding of technology. Embedding technology in real-life situations also generates images of potential societal impacts of innovation. Ideally, the living lab is created as an "experimental field" within a socio-technological scope with specific goals and structures while simultaneously dealing with the uncontrollable dynamics of everyday life. The distinguishing feature is that users are involved in all stages of the product development life cycle through networked communications, not just at the end phases as, for example, in classical field trials or user testing of products.

To conclude, the strategic relevance to people-centred innovation of TEPs like living labs, arguably lies in the extent to which networked communications with users and other stakeholders is made possible, in the establishment of an experimental setting that resembles real-life situations as closely as possible and in the enabling and support of non-linear, mutual shaping innovation processes with semi-mature technology.

Acknowledgments and Disclaimer

This chapter is based partly of the results of a research project carried out on behalf of the Interdisciplinary Institute for BroadBand Technology in Flanders, Belgium, at the request of the Flemish Minister for Economy, Enterprise, Science, Innovation and Foreign Trade. The statements and opinions expressed in this chapter are the authors' alone and should not in any way be considered as a reflection of the opinions of the IBBT or the Minister.

The authors gratefully acknowledge the valuable and substantial contributions of their co-authors to the full research report (Ballon et al., 2005): Martijn Poel (TNO),

Mijke Slot (TNO), Jan Bierhof (ECDC), and Myriam Diocaretz (ECDC); as well as the research assistance of Wendy Van Den Broeck (SMIT), Alice Frangoulis (SMIT), Jan Jaap Badon Ghijben (TNO), and Silvain De Munck (TNO).

References

Primary Case Study References

The Netherlands

www.philips.com

www.gigaport.nl

corporate.kennisnet.nl

www.kenniswijk.nl

www.damsternet.nl

www.trapveld.nl (currently no longer accessible)

Finland

www.hightechfinland.com/2001/information-communications/elisa_corporation. php3

www.testbedfinland.com

www.rotuaari.net/

www.helsinkivirtualvillage.fi

www.mobileforum.org/octopus

www.tiedetoimittaja.com/english/pages/sparknet.html

UK

www.vec.qub.ac.uk

www.tv-anytime.org

www.broadband-buckfastleigh.org/

www.thebigtree.org/p_apple/

*www.scottish-enterprise.com/sedotcom_home/services-to-business/broadband/
broadband-news/borders-rural-broadband/*

www.citizensonline.org.uk

General References

Ballon, P., Delaere, S., Pierson, J., Poel, M., Slot, M., Bierhof, J., & Diocaretz, M. (2005). Test and experimentation platforms for broadband innovation: Conceptualizing and benchmarking international best practice. IBBT/VUB-SMIT Report.

Berker, T., Hartmann, M., Punie, Y., & Ward, K. (In press). *Taming the technology? Domestication – A key concept in media and technology studies revisited.* Berkshire: Open University Press.

Burgelman, J.-C., Tuomi, I., Punie, Y., & van Bavel, R. (Eds.) (2004). Mapping the European knowledge base of socio-economic impact studies on IST (EKB-SEIS) (EUR 21375 EN). Sevilla: EU-IPTS-ESTO, 42.

Crabtree, A., & Rodden, T. (2002). Ethnography and design? Paper presented at the *International Workshop on "Interpretive" Approaches to Information Systems and Computing Research*, London, July (pp. 70-74). London: Association of Information Systems (Brunel University).

Edquist, C. (2001). Innovation policy – A systemic approach. In B.Å. Lundvall, & D. Archibugi (Eds.), *Major socio-economic trends and European innovation policy* (pp. 219-238). Oxford: Oxford University Press.

Ferguson, C. (2002). *The broadband problem: Anatomy of a market failure and a policy dilemma.* Washington: Brookings Institution Press.

Flichy, P. (1995). *L'innovation technique – Récents développements en sciences sociales: Vers une nouvelle théorie de l'innovation.* Paris: La Découverte.

Frissen, V., & van Lieshout, M. (2004). *To user-centred innovation processes: The role of living labs.* Delft: TNO-ICT.

Hers, J., & Nahuis, N. (2004). The Tower of Babel? The innovation system approach versus mainstream economics. *Method and Hist of Econ Thought*, 0403001. Economics Working Paper Archive, WUSTL.

ISTAG. (2004). *ISTAG report on experience and application research: Involving users in the development of ambient intelligence.* Luxembourg: European Commission.

Megerian, S. & Potkonjak, M. (2002). Wireless sensor networks. In J. G. Proakis (Ed.), *Wiley Encyclopedia of Telecommunications*. Hoboken, NJ: Wiley-Interscience.

Niitamo, V.-P. (2005). *Living labs*. Retrieved April 27, 2005, from http://www. arksuominen.com/livinglab

Perez, C. (2004). *The new techno-economic paradigm and the importance of ICT policy for the competitiveness of the whole economy*. Paper presented at Working on Growth with Europe: Looking into the Future of ICT, Amsterdam, September 29-30.

Varian, H. (2002). The demand for bandwidth: Evidence from the INDEX experiment (Revised version). *Mimeo*. University of California, Berkeley.

Wakeford, N. (2004). *Innovation through people-centred design: Lessons from the USA*. Guildford: University of Surrey.

Endnotes

[1]   The full report analyses additional TEP cases outside of Europe, that is, in Korea and Canada.

[2]   Based on a detailed assessment and scoring of 13 parameters in total, in the full report. These consist of: degree of openness regarding results; degree of openness regarding partnership; objective (aimed primarily at in-house R&D, open innovation, or at commercial introduction); focus (primarily on testing, versus primarily for design and development); horizontal (involving mainly technology producers or mainly service providers) or vertical (involving both technology producers and service providers) scope; extent of user involvement; extent of public support; degree of public control; laboratory versus real-life setting; central versus distributed setting; aimed at infrastructures versus services; maturity of technology; dynamic aspects.

Chapter VIII

Envisioning Potential:
Stories of Networked Learning Designs from a UK University

Frances Deepwell
Coventry University, UK

Kathy Courtney
Coventry University, UK

Abstract

*In this chapter, we explore how the design of networked learning can contribute to building a shared understanding of the applications of new technologies. We draw on our own experiences of the managed introduction of a virtual learning environment (VLE) in a higher education institution and apply techniques of narrative inquiry to aid our understanding. We have explored narrative accounts from different stakeholders in terms of an overarching theme of "building shared understandings", which we have organised around three areas of our experience, namely **designing for a community, developing a discourse,** and **developing artefacts**. We argue that design decisions in these three areas have been highly significant in terms of the levels of acceptance and future direction of an online learning implementation.*

Introduction

The chapter explores the ways in which new understandings of the potential of technologies in higher education may be developed and shared within communities within an organisation. As well as emphasising the importance of community-building in a networked learning implementation, a particular focus of the chapter is the way in which the design of artefacts and processes can enable these shared understandings of new technologies to spread within a complex organisational context. The chapter is based on the authors' experiences in implementing a university-wide strategy of rolling out a Web-based learning environment. Both authors are educational developers with a special interest in learning technologies.

We consider how new understandings emerge though changing discourse, practice, and beliefs within an organisational community and beyond. We draw on Wenger's theory of a community of practice, in particular the facilities of engagement, imagination, and alignment (Wenger, 1998) as a useful way of conceptualising pedagogical and cultural processes and the role of artefacts as mechanisms for understanding. The discussion will centre around the following questions:

What are the benefits of involving communities of practice in designing for networked learning?

How can we enable conversations to develop around virtual design issues?

What artefacts might be useful in developing shared understandings of the potential of networked learning?

On Methodology and Method

The data that informs this chapter was collected as part of the EU project EQUEL (EQUEL, 2004). The EQUEL project brought together European researchers and practitioners to collaborate in research into aspects of e-learning. The present authors collaborated in a special interest group within the EQUEL project that sought to "bring together European research on the implementation of e-learning from an institutional perspective" (EQUEL, 2004).

The research from our own institution was action research into the management of change as the VLE was implemented across the organisation. This approach to research enabled us to involve colleagues in engaging with the processes of change as a collaborative venture, which in turn helped them "to raise their own awareness of the significance of what they are doing as a form of social change, and have confidence in its legitimacy and importance" (McNiff & Whitehead, 2002). In our research, we were furthermore guided by the phases of appreciative inquiry, which is a mode of action research that celebrates what is working within an organisation and helps members of the organisation envision and then bring about an improved future through shared commitment and collaborative development. Ludema, Cooperrider and Barrett (2001) make a claim for the method that accords with our understanding of the research we are doing: "Appreciative inquiry recognises that inquiry and change are not truly separate moments but are simultaneous. Inquiry **is** intervention" (Ludema et al., 2001).

Appreciative inquiry organises its data collection and analysis around 4Ds, namely:

- Discovery
- Dream
- Design
- Destiny (Ludema et al., 2001).

In this chapter, we report mainly on the "design" phase of our inquiry, where a "pragmatic vision" of the future state of an organisation is constructed.

To illustrate our considerations, we will be interweaving accounts from a range of stakeholders in a specific implementation of technology. We gathered stories of change from individuals with different perspectives on the learning situation (learners, technicians, managers, librarians, tutors). The stories were generated either at research workshops or through in-depth interviews. They have been used to identify concurrent themes in the experience of implementing new technologies. These accounts have helped to reveal some of the intricacies of introducing and embedding a large-scale implementation of a networked technology, namely an integrated virtual learning environment, into a UK university. For succinctness, we will refer to this case as the "networked learning implementation".

Narrative accounts are used widely in areas of qualitative research that are trying to discover the emotional dimensions of social and political phenomena (Elliot, 2005). In the case presented here, we are drawing on individual stories to reveal insights into how administrative and management decisions made at the macro-level play out at the meso- or micro-level. Our analysis highlights areas where attention should be paid in an implementation of networked technology for learning. We have grouped the accounts around three areas of our experience, namely **designing for a community**, **developing a discourse,** and **developing artefacts**. We argue that design decisions in these three areas have been highly significant in terms of future direction of the networked learning implementation.

Setting the Scene

In order to set the scene, it is first necessary to scope the nature of the organisation prior to the campus-wide online learning implementation described in this chapter and the strategic imperatives for embarking on a large-scale initiative of this kind.

Coventry University is typified as a modern university, one of the former polytechnics that gained a university title in 1992. The culture is predominantly that of a teaching organisation with strong affiliations to regional transport and engineering industries. Most of its research activity is in the applied and industrial sphere, and knowledge transfer activities are highly regarded. The university has a tradition of being at the forefront of new developments in the higher education sector, in terms of its infrastructure and technology, as well as its pedagogy. While it had grown under the massification of higher education in the UK during the 1990s (Dearing, 1997), the university had not sufficiently altered its courses and infrastructure to adapt to new and diversified student needs and more flexible patterns of delivery.

In 1997, the University formulated a learning and teaching strategy that set out a forward-looking response to the new realities in the UK as the sector moves from a mass system towards a universal system of higher education with a target of 50% of young people in higher education. This shift necessarily has an impact on teaching and learning practice, namely in terms of massification, diversification, marketisation, modularisation, and interdisciplinarity (CHERI, 2004). The learning and teaching strategy was the catalyst for a local management of change initiative called the Taskforce for Learning, Teaching and Assessment (hereafter called the Taskforce) (Beaty & Cousin, 2002).

The Taskforce was an internally-funded initiative and brought together experienced colleagues from across more than 20 subject disciplines and support areas in the university to develop and disseminate innovation projects. Over time, the membership of the Taskforce changed and new members were absorbed into the group. One of the key roles of the Taskforce was to mediate between the centre (where strategies were devised and policies formulated) and the faculty base within departments (where the implications of change were felt most acutely). This network of people provided the central educational development unit with a route directly into many of the departments, and likewise a route from the departments to the centre. Essential to the effectiveness of the Taskforce was strong support from senior management, who actively listened to the concerns of this group and sought to remove "blocks" to development where they were identified, as evidenced in Beaty and Cousin (2002). The members of this Taskforce played a significant role in informing the design processes of networked learning, as outlined in the following text.

Design as a Conversation with a Community of Practice

In developing our own understanding of networked learning design, we have been guided by a number of different theories regarding technology implementation, learning development, organisational change, and cultural practices (Alvesson, 2002; IVETTE, 2002; Laurillard, 2002; Steeples & Jones, 2002; Sturdy & Grey, 2003). These theories, together with our own observations and empirical data, bring four broad dimensions into perspective: **technology**, **pedagogy**, **organisation,** and **culture**. Each of these dimensions contributes to an overall framework, which (Cousin, Deepwell, Land, & Ponti, 2004) have attempted to define for the implementation of networked learning. Within these four dimensions, there are forces at play that influence developments at different layers within the change process. The authors argue that an ecological metaphor provides a useful explanatory framework for the

Figure 1. Elements in an ecology of learning technology implementation (Deepwell et al., 2004)

Organisational
rules and procedures
policies and strategies
reward structures
jobs and resources
quality assurance and enhancement

Technological
IT support and access
virtual learning environments and other tools
software and licensing conditions

Pedagogical
disciplinary cultures
teaching, learning and assessment regimes
educational development
profile of students

Cultural
language (discourse)
visions and personalities
resistances
communities of practice
perceived roles and change agency

---

implementation process, with interdependencies and external as well as internal balances to be maintained. Elements within the framework are shown in Figure 1, and the implications of this for design, in particular the pedagogical and cultural practices, will be developed through the rest of this chapter.

According to this theory of implementation, it is essential to recognise and to build on existing patterns, communities, and structures such that the technology is seen as an enhancement of current practice rather than a replacement of it. Laurillard (2002) similarly uses a biological metaphor to describe the emergence of new technologies in teaching within an institutional context: "The implementation of new technology methods cannot take place without the system around it adjusting to the intrusions of this new organism" (p. 214). Laurillard argues for an adaptive learning environment, one that is based upon a "learning conversation", learning from its own experience and able to adapt to its environment (p. 215).

In order to allow scope for change, there also needs to be a certain amount of "slack" in the system (Courtney, 2004). "Slack" within an organisation, in the form of time and financial resources (required to support networking), is necessary to allow the precious resource of local knowledge of individuals and small groups to come into play. This local knowledge is precious because it is unique as well as topical—it needs to be exploited while it is relevant.

In terms of our experience at Coventry University, "slack" was introduced through the establishment of the Taskforce. In our understanding of how this particular group has supported the design process, we have found the conceptual tools provided by Wenger (1998) and the notion of a community of practice to be particularly useful.

Specifically, Wenger's concepts of facilities of engagement, imagination, and alignment draw our attention to the importance of community participation in an iterative design process. "There is an inherent uncertainty between design and its realisation in practice, since practice is not the result of design but rather a response to it" (Wenger, 1998, p. 233).

The increased communication channels that the Taskforce provided directly informed policy decisions relating to learning and teaching, including the networked learning aspects.

"Lots of conversations ... and listening to each other about some of the issues, that's been quite an important way of working." (Story 1: Head of Educational Development Unit)

The initial networked learning implementation was designed to fit with the understandings and practices of this particular community of practice, an inter-disciplinary group of teachers and learning support professionals with a drive to innovate and

enhance the student learning experience. The overall intention of the implementation was to make the learning design as unobtrusive as possible and to automate or
predefine as many administrative and learner support processes as possible before
launching the design across the university.

Developing a Discourse: Enabling the Conversation

We now come to discuss some of the details of our experience of the emerging
discourse of Web-enhanced learning in our organisation, including the use of metaphor in envisioning change, communication networks, and the role of an annual
conference.

Use of Metaphors in Envisioning Change

Over the past seven years and with the growth in the number and range of tools for
online learning, there has come to be a far greater awareness of the facilities and
terms associated with online learning in higher education. Most universities in the
UK now have fairly widespread access to online learning delivery platforms in the
form of VLEs and other Web-based mechanisms for engaging learners in education
processes. In the early phases of the implementation (1998-1999), however, there
was little understanding of what an online learning environment might look like, and
hence it was necessary to construct a metaphor that related to current experience of
learning and teaching in our context. The importance of metaphors for learning new
concepts is widely acknowledged, and in our case, it proved productive as a means
to bridge the technical/pedagogical divide. The metaphor of a virtual classroom
was used at many consultations, discussions, and awareness-raising presentations
to groups around the institution.

Through the metaphor of a virtual classroom, educational developers and Taskforce members were able to convey the online space as an image of a place (Ponti
& Ryberg, 2004), where learners came together with a door that was open only to
members of the course. Others could only come into the space when invited, and
their presence would be known. The learners would be able to hold discussions either
among themselves or with the tutor. Smaller groups could be set up within the larger
group for private discussions. There would be learning materials within the virtual
classroom, as well as presentational facilities for both learners and tutors. Learners
could be assessed in a number of ways, and tutors could record and distribute grades
in the virtual classroom. The potential for offering any time, any place learning was

made possible, but the tutor would still be able to declare their own availability through clearly defining "office hours". By using the simple metaphor of the virtual classroom, teachers in the institution, who had previously had little engagement with technology, were able to start to consider terms and concepts of networked learning. They were thus able to envision the possibility of employing these new tools and ways of integrating them into their learning and teaching practice.

Communication Networks Within and Without the Community

In order to bridge the gaps between intensive communications available at the periodic large group meetings, an internal university e-mail list was established to service the members of the Taskforce initiative. In the current age of mass e-mail communications and online services, this may not appear to be a significant move, but at the time, in 1998, it was unusual within a university setting for a cross-disciplinary, multi-layered network of this kind. Membership of the list has been cumulative and has grown as the membership of the Taskforce has changed. Significantly, membership included senior management. While the list is closed to those who are or have ever been members of the Taskforce initiative and only members can initiate messages, the circulation is far wider since members judiciously forward selected comments, observations, or announcements to other individuals and groups within their own networks. Similarly, members of the list communicate external information to others within the network. The list continues to be empowering and over the past seven years has worked to share knowledge and information about events, build profiles, instigate collaborations and writing projects as well as provide a social forum and a political lobby within the organisation. It furthermore serves to keep a community up to date with national and strategic developments, mainly around learning and teaching innovations.

Annual Conference and Exhibition as a Focus

A second communication mechanism, designed to help envision the potential of the implemented technologies, has been an annual, local university staff conference on learning and teaching innovations called ELATE, **E**nhancing **L**earning **A**nd **T**eaching **E**nvironments. The first ELATE conference was held in 1999, building on a teaching exhibition the previous year. This has become a key professional development activity and a particular design characteristic of the conference itself is significant here, namely the collaborative planning process. At every stage, working groups comprising members of the Taskforce and the Centre for Higher Education Development are communicating with colleagues from across the university and using the conference itself as a vehicle for driving innovations. Examples include introducing the university's first functional online booking system; a learning and teaching exhibition by a group of technicians (reported in Courtney, 2004, and Grant et al., 2002); a panel debate on the pros and cons of the proposed virtual learning implementation strategy; a joint presentation by subject librarians with their respective subject tutors; a conference Web site built as an exemplar of accessible Web design; and interactive demonstrations of technologies of tomorrow.

In part due to the push for innovations and the large size and varied availability of the planning group, there have been a number of attempts over the years to sustain a networked communication channel for the conference planning group, and a further channel for the 150 or so delegates at the conference each year. E-mail remains the most popular medium for discussion, alongside a discussion in the university's virtual learning environment. The online environment has proved to be a useful repository and archive, for example, of the items in the conference pack.

Developing Artefacts: Viewing Templates as Reified Objects

In Wenger's (1998) terms, a community of practice needs at certain times to bring together its shared understandings in the form of reified objects, artefacts, or processes. "Reification occupies much of our collective energy... aspects of human experience and practice are congealed into fixed forms and given the status of object" (Wenger, 1998, p. 59). These objects, or artefacts, are vital to a community in order to affirm its shared understandings and to consolidate the participation by all in the community. This indeed concurs with our experience. We will now outline three examples where this has happened in the form of a template design, which symbolises the ideas shared by this community of practice. Each one, we argue, has benefited a wider community through exemplifying good practice: the "module" template, developed for all taught modules at the university, a "content display" template, embodying concepts for online language teaching, and a template for teaching information skills by subject librarians. These artefacts are all viewed as templates, in the sense that they offer a pattern which can be re-used, as well as adapted.

The first and possibly the most influential of the templates to be introduced here is the "module template", which defines the initial design of every online space created for each of the modules taught at Coventry University. This design has been a vehicle for the community of practice to spread its understanding of networked learning as a communication medium with and between students and tutors.

The template design is such that faculty can use it for teaching purposes without making any modifications to its design. Once a module based on the template is

*Figure 2. The three core screens of the "module template": **HOMEPAGE** (primarily communication tools); **RESOURCES** (links to support the learner); **STUDENT AREA** (learner-centred tools)*

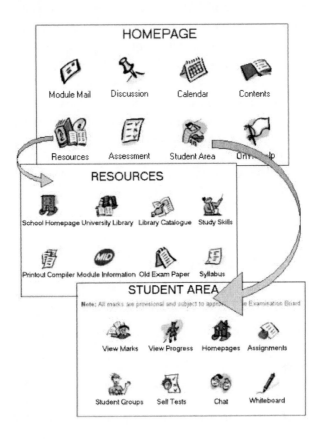

actively used, it naturally fills up with data that is unique to each module. For example, as teachers and students make use of the discussion forum, it is populated with conversations unique to this teaching and learning context. In this sense, the "template" both enables discussions and functions as a container for the unique content that is being generated.

A second example of a template design exhibits slightly different properties. It defines a format for displaying information on screen, but one which demands new content at the design stage. We will call this a "content display" template. This design represents the use of networked learning as a discovery medium.

Figure 3. A "content display" template

Riassunto	Grammatica
Testo di Partenza	La cena a villa Salina era servita con il fasto sbrecciato che allora era lo stile del Regno delle Due Sicilie. Il numero dei commensali (quattordici erano fra padroni di casa, figli, governanti e precettori) bastava da solo a conferire imponenza alla tavola. Ricoperta da una rattoppata tovaglia finissima, (1) essa splendeva sotto la luce di una potente "carsella" precariamente appesa sotto la "ninfa," sotto il lampadario di Murano. Dalle finestre entrava ancora luce ma le figure bianche sul fondo scuro delle sovrapporte, simulanti dei bassorilievi, si perdevano già nell'ombra. (2) Massiccia l'argenteria e splendidi i bicchieri recanti sul medaglione liscio fra i bugnati di Boemia le cifre F.D. (Ferdinandus dedit) in ricordo di una munificenza regale, ma i piatti, ciascuno segnato da una sigla illustre, non erano che dei superstiti delle stragi compiute dagli sguatteri e provenivano da servizi disparati. Quelli di formato piú grande. Capodimonte vaghissimi con la larga bordura verde-mandorla segnata da ancorette dorate, erano
Contesto	
Registro	
Stile	
Grammatica	
Vocabolario	
Tema – La famigila	
Tema – la religione	
Tema – l'aristocrazia	
Tema – larte	
Tema – l'epoca e la morte	*Essa* - E la forma antica del pronome personale femminile. Oggigiono, si usa questa parola soltanto nella letteratura. Contribuisce allo stilo formale del libro.

The re-usable part of this template lies in the way it splits the screen into three separate parts or frames and the way it defines relationships between content in one part to content in another. This "content display" template offers a menu list on the left, and depending on what a user selects from the list, the content in the main section of the screen changes accordingly. Furthermore, the text in the main section includes shaded phrases, and selecting any one of these will cause additional relevant information to appear in the small frame at the bottom of the screen.

This template does not change, once it has been populated with content, other than in the predetermined ways which are a combined function of its underlying design and specific content.

Finally, we refer to a more complex and a more complete example of a design of an online space as a template because it played a key role in serving as an example to colleagues, suggesting to them how they might use the VLE themselves. In this example, the "module template" has been adapted and then populated with content specific to the teaching of information skills. This design embodied an approach which handled assessment online, thereby relieving the subject librarian of a very substantial marking task. Once this had been accomplished, the librarian's close colleagues could immediately see how they might use the VLE for their own teaching. It is in this sense that the design functioned as a template.

We see all of these templates as reified objects, as defined in Wenger's theory of communities of practice. Each design has played a part in providing insight and vision to an emerging community of practice which was searching for ways of making use of newly available technologies.

Template Design in Sharing Good Practice

In software design, templates are an efficient way of scaling up from local or bespoke designs to system-wide implementations. The notion of a template, however, can be regarded with ambiguity in a number of ways. They provide a **stability** and **reliability** to the look and feel of the screen across the spectrum of users, which is not only **reassuring** to novice or hesitant users of the system, but also makes it easier for the development team to write and illustrate manuals, for example. Templates can be seen as **liberating**: since the design work has been done, it remains simply for the user to provide the textual or graphical detail. They can appear **restrictive**: irrespective of the content, there can be no deviation from the prepared template. There is a danger that they quickly become **outdated**: as needs change, the template remains fixed and no longer satisfies the pedagogical, usability, or aesthetic requirements. The template may also become **obsolete**: if technology advances beyond the current horizon, then the template is unlikely to remain functional.

Prior to the online learning implementation, there had been much individualised and resource-intensive investment in content-rich learning packages, such as CD-ROM or lab-installed packages. As the speed of technological change increases, however, it becomes imperative that the tools and techniques can be sustained either through adaptation or re-versioning. What remains from a technological innovation are the merits of the underlying design, enriched and endorsed through feedback from teachers and students.

The "Module Template": Emphasising the Potential for Communication

The design of the online module template brought to the fore the communication tools of the virtual learning environment as a clear indication to faculty members that these were the priority tools to consider when adopting the online environment. The collaborative development of this template design, we argue, did in itself foster a generative learning perspective to software developments within an educational setting. Through discussions over which Web-based tools from the available toolkit would be most useful and widely used in learning settings across the widest possible range of disciplines and levels in the university, the emphasis shifted away from product toward process, away from interaction with the computer toward interaction within a community of learners. The online module template was designed in consultation with the Taskforce and was intended to satisfy the basic demands of any module taught at the university. It was therefore based on the **communication tools** of mail, discussions, and calendar; the **learner tools** of tracking progress and retrieving marks; and on **customised links** with external (reliable) resources within the organisation such as the library, student support materials, the central module information (syllabus) database and a system for displaying past exam papers for revision purposes. The template provided a consistent layout, customised to Coventry University's organisational context and with a certain level of personalisation. Once the template gained acceptance among the user base of Taskforce members, it was rolled out across the organisation, ready for use with students. Overnight over 2,000 instances of the template were generated automatically and 17,500 students were given access to the online modules for which they were enrolled (some 95,000 "registrations").

Another significant benefit of having the template available is that teachers could come to a system that was up and running with their specific module available instantly online. There was no initial uncertainty over the page layout and headings or over what tools to include and what to exclude, or over the colour scheme and icon types. Those who were using the technology did not therefore need to assume the role of instructional designer and could concentrate on how to teach, or foster learning within this new environment. Those who wanted to were still able to re-model the environment if they so wished, but many teachers were able to add further content and learning activities to the template as it was delivered.

The module template has lasted over six years with only minor modifications being introduced across the board. However, the template has been designed to be open to modification by the teachers themselves. In our experience of reviewing and assisting developments of the module spaces, it is mostly the case that new tools or links are added to the existing base template rather than complete re-designs. This suggests that the template finds general acceptance. In addition, it has succeeded in part in promoting the communication and learner-centred aspects of the online collaborative space.

The "Content Display" Template: Evolving Practice in Language Teaching Online

A basic conception of "sharing good practice" manifests itself in the form of showcasing, giving examples and offering case studies (Courtney, Davidson, Deepwell, & Grantham, 2003). There is clearly a place for this kind of "sharing of good practice". Here, however, we trace the role of the "content display" template (see Figure 3) as a means of sharing good practice. Orsini-Jones (1999) describes her adoption and adaptation of the template to a student-centred, technology-based approach for teaching Italian—one which required the construction of online grammar exercises by students for the benefit of their peers. Orsini-Jones had seen the "content display" template used for teaching aspects of German grammar, an approach originally developed in the context an early CAL project at Coventry, called TIGER (which has since been developed and marketed by the TELL Consortium, 1996). Making use of the template's power for displaying content in an interactive format, Orsini-Jones adapted it to a "role-reversal" pedagogy, which tasked students with the creation of grammar content. Students prepared an Italian text and annotated it in various ways to highlight its grammatical structure. Orsini-Jones was able to draw on the services of a programmer to embed the content provided by the students in the "content display" template. This pedagogical approach ensures a high level of student participation and involvement. The framed Web page with its predefined relationships between the frames represents a basic template. In combination with the "role-reversal" pedagogy, a new, more complex template for teaching and learning emerged, but remains one which requires little or no adaptation for use in a different language context (Orsini-Jones, 1999). This approach proved very popular with students, as the technology enabled them to become in part the authors of their own learning.

In a fast-moving world, it is ideas and new insights that prove the most valuable and enduring. It is this more abstract notion of "good practice" which has become evident and important in the journey of cultural, pedagogical, technological, and organisational changes which are of interest in this chapter. This example of the adoption of a practice developed elsewhere demonstrates that where abstract patterns can be embedded in templates, they can be much more easily adopted as well as adapted by others, thereby functioning as significant enablers to the sharing of good practice.

The Power of a First Example: Shared Practice in Information Skills Teaching Online

Our third example of a template was developed in the context of information skills teaching by a subject librarian, whose teaching load had become unsustainable due to increased student numbers. In search of a solution, she sought to investigate the use of the newly available VLE for the purpose of teaching and assessing information skills.

Tutorials on using online databases were developed and offered online to students in addition to the face-to-face information skills sessions. Importantly, information skills assessment was placed online and presented in a format which could be computer-marked. The important consequence of this was that it relieved the subject librarian of the immense burden of marking several hundred scripts.

These online resources were developed in close collaboration between one subject librarian and an educational developer (Courtney & Patalong, 2002). The project had grown from an initial meeting between the two women, in which the subject librarian's difficult teaching context was revealed and the decision was made to explore the potential of the VLE to remedy the situation. It turns out that this was a productive encounter, given the subsequent success of the project. The educational developer recalls in one of her stories:

"[this e-learning] project came in at a point when it [the VLE] was ready to go. Because so many other things had happened [in the institutional set-up], it worked really well. So if we hadn't had [the VLE], you know, what [solution] would I have offered her? I don't know." (Story 2: Educational Developer)

From the outset, there had been the idea that if an approach could be developed which would work for one subject librarian, it would define a practice that would be of interest to other subject librarians. In this sense, the project embodied the design of a template—the development of an approach to teaching information skills which could be adopted and adapted in other subject areas because it had been designed in harmony with the needs of this community of practice. Interest in the project grew, both within the institution and beyond, and by 2003, six other subject librarians at Coventry University had adopted the approach to teaching information skills in their subject areas (Patalong, 2002).

Gains for Stakeholders Across the University

The example of the information skills usage of the VLE serves to show how one particular template has had considerable impact across the university. One group of stakeholders benefiting from the approach were other subject librarians at Coventry University. Patalong (2003) mentions **timeliness** of the availability of the online tutorials for revision purposes as one of the major benefits to students. In general, large numbers of **students have felt more supported** with information skills teaching, as the online space is offered in different subject areas, in addition to the face-to-face sessions, thereby representing an enhancement.

Patalong (2003) further emphasises how the use of the VLE for information skills teaching has **promoted collaboration** among faculty and library staff at Coventry. This is echoed by comments made in one of the stories from the time:

"..I remember the ELATE conference session we had, and in the past when you have put things in about the library, you know, you get two or three people turning up and what was amazing about that session was not only that it was full, you could hardly get another person into the room, but there were a number of librarians in the room who had never actually met before, subject librarians and people from the academic community. And the potential partnership working between these groups, because of this project, really was enriching." (Story 1: Head of Educational Development Unit)

Analysing the impact of the adoption of the VLE for information skills teaching and its effect of increased collaboration between subject librarians and academic staff, Patalong (2003) concludes:

"It (the online information skills resource) has also contributed to the process of getting information skills recognised in the University and having them written into the curriculum. All the literature points to the fact that it is only when this happens that the skills sessions are truly effective."

These comments demonstrate that the benefits of this library-based development had a considerable impact institution-wide, positively affecting staff and students alike. This part of the online learning implementation has contributed significantly to Coventry University's ability to serve the lifelong learning agenda, preparing students with vital skills for finding and evaluating information in our information-rich society.

Through collaboration with an educational developer, a vision eventually crystallised for a specific use of networked learning for the teaching and assessing of information skills. The resulting design of the online space and embedded resources represented the reification of this envisioning process and a template which other subject librarians could readily and unambiguously interpret and understand. So while previously, networked learning may have been something nebulous and vague to librarians who previously never even had access to the VLE, it had now become a case of "Ah—so that is what we could do with it—that is what we could use it for". Writing a story about this development, the head of the library had stated that prior to the project, he "wanted the Library to be connected to [the VLE], but did not know how" (Story 3: Librarian). Now colleagues in this area understood the nature of the VLE to a level which allowed them to see how they might adapt the existing template to their own teaching contexts.

Building a Shared Understanding and the Role of Meaning-Makers

The faculty base at Coventry University is far from homogeneous; it comprises many different disciplinary cultures, professional group allegiances, pedagogical and technical skill levels, roles and functions, motivations and efficacy beliefs, research interests, teaching loads, personal commitments, and cultural affiliations, to name but a few categories of distinction. Acceptance of directives from the top, moreover, cannot be presumed, particularly in relation to their own domain of control, namely their teaching and learning practice.

In order to better address the needs of these groups, therefore, and to ensure that there is a sense of ownership of the processes, the implementation strategies wove themselves into a network of experienced and innovative teachers in the Taskforce initiative. It is in these flows of activity that we can perceive the ecologies at play. The mechanisms and processes that were used included the three examples of rei-fied artefacts in the form of the templates described here. Artefacts such as these have helped the broad, local community to envision what networked learning might signify to the learning and teaching cultures prevalent in the university. The work has been assisted by a number of individuals who have taken on the role of mean-ing-makers in the history of Coventry University's online implementation through a community of practice. This community includes members of the Taskforce, faculty members who were not part of the Taskforce, librarians, members of staff of the Centre for Higher Education Development, and senior managers with responsibili-ties for learning and teaching developments.

Convergence of Macro-, Meso- and Micro-Levels

In this chapter, we have sought to present a collage of perspectives documenting some of the changes within Coventry University that have taken place in rela-tion to the implementation of online learning and its underlying design elements. Multiple influences have been sited, from macro- to meso- to micro-levels. At the macro-level, it is prudent to mention the impact on institutions in the UK of the Dearing Inquiry (1997), an influential report which recommended an increased use of information technology in teaching and learning. At the meso-level, Coventry University's Teaching and Learning Strategy (Coventry University, 1998) focused strongly on the "maximisation of opportunities afforded by C&IT and innovation" and the "building (of) capacity for change". It named the Task Force and the avail-ability of an electronic learning environment as key enablers for achieving these strategic objectives.

The efforts invested by members of staff in central units, such as the Centre for Higher Education Development, and agents for change in the departments, such as members of the Taskforce, can be classed at the meso-level. The authors have shown how considerable effort was focused on simplifying the "terrain" of the online learning implementation through the design of the module template, thereby helping to create a virtual landscape which sustained a metaphorical analogy with the classroom, presented familiar features and shielded users from the more intri-cate interface design aspects of the software as it would have been delivered "out of the box".

Some interesting stories have emerged at the micro-level, the journeys of discovery by individual members of staff, who explored the affordances of online learning in the context of their teaching needs and their readiness to embrace technology for teaching purposes. The people behind the developments sited as examples—practitioners in language and information skills teaching, represent meaning-makers who have communicated through the construction of templates which are meaningful and accessible to their existing communities of practice.

The interrelatedness of influences between these different levels emerges strongly from these fragments of stories gathered, referencing as they do the frame-setting forces of macro- and meso-level policies and strategies and the significant and decisive contributions of individuals on the ground. From the vantage point of understanding their contexts, they have interpreted the strategies and directive, weaving together multiple demands and pressures, taking advantage of opportunities they can see but which cannot be anticipated by others.

Concluding Remarks

Returning now to the three questions posed at the start, we close the chapter with a discussion of: the benefits of involving communities of practice; the ways of enabling conversations to develop; and the usefulness of artefacts in developing shared understandings of the potential for networked learning. In generating the stories for the purposes of the research, the appreciative inquiry method itself has provided opportunities to articulate the positive and creative aspects to the implementation of the VLE and has also strengthened the construct of the Taskforce as a community of practice.

The **need for meaning-making** in a complex world is central to Wenger's (1998) notion of communities of practice. Scope for generating solutions to problems is generally the mark of a professional context, where people operate within guidelines and work with heuristics to a large extent, rather than follow hard and fast rules. In this context, we have shown the powerful effect of a community of practice for shaping a networked learning design that appears to have been fit for purpose.

Both in the Taskforce and in the context of language teaching and in information skills teaching, there have been innovators at the centre of developments, operating within a network where they can influence immediate colleagues and, through this network, create ripples which are felt across the entire organisation.

The **consolidating force of reification** in the form of artefacts and specifically that of collaboratively designed templates has emerged as a significant factor in driving innovations forward, influencing practice, discourse, and community ties all at the same time. The nurturing of these networks is of paramount importance in **building a shared understanding** of the networked learning implementation and its design. Only through conversations and collaboration can individuals within a network come to envision some of the potential of what might be achieved using the new learning technologies.

Concurring with Wenger's (1998) argument that "you cannot design learning, but only design for learning", we recognise that any design is based on presuppositions, and that on implementation it takes on a life of its own. It is no longer under the designer's control. The initial expectations are not necessarily met, while other purposes are discovered along the way. However, the designs have given meaningful insight into the potential of the networked learning technology and prompted many to become educators in the new connected academic reality. It is hoped that this chapter has outlined just some of what this might be in a UK modern university.

References

Alvesson, M. (2002). *Understanding organisational culture.* London: Sage Publications.

Beaty, L., & Cousin, G. (2002). An action research approach to strategic development. In R. Macdonald, & H. Eggins (Eds.), *The scholarship of academic development.* Buckingham: SRHE/Open University Press.

CHERI. (2004). *Ten years on: Changing higher education in a changing world.* Booklet. Retrieved March 5, 2006, from www.open.ac.uk/cheri/pdfs/cheritenyears.pdf

Courtney, K. (2004). *Constellations of collaboration: The hidden foundations of a successful e-learning project.* Paper presented at the 4th International Conference on Networked Learning, Lancaster, April 5-7.

Courtney, K., Davidson, A., Deepwell, F., & Grantham, D. (2003). *Sharing our Webs with the world.* Paper presented at the WebCT European Conference, London, January 13-15.

Courtney, K., & Patalong, S. (2002). Integrated information skills: A case study using the virtual learning environment WebCT. *Education Libraries Journal, 45*(1), 7-11.

Cousin, G., Deepwell, F., Land, R., & Ponti, M. (2004). *Theorising implementation: Variation and commonality in European approaches to e-learning.* Paper presented at the Networked Learning 2004, Lancaster, April 5-7.

Coventry University (1998). Coventry University learning and teaching strategy 1997-2002.

Dearing, R. (1997). *Higher education in the learning society.* London: HMSO.

Deepwell, F. (2004). Implementing e-learning at the institutional level in EQUEL.

Position papers EQUEL project. Retrieved November 1, 2005, from http://equel.net

Elliot, J. (2005). *Using narrative in social research. Qualitative and quantitative approaches.* London: Sage.

EQUEL. (2004). Implementing e-learning at the institutional level. EQUEL project.

Grant, E., Courtney, K., & Bhanot, R. (2002). Out of the shadows: Responding to the changing role of technical staff at Coventry School of Art & Design. Coventry University. *Educational Developments, 3*(3).

IVETTE. (2002). Implementation of virtual environments in training and education. Final report. European Commission TSER programme.

Laurillard, D. (2002). *Rethinking university teaching: A conversational framework for the effective use of learning technologies* (2nd ed.). London; New York: Routledge/Falmer.

Ludema, J., Cooperrider, D., & Barrett, F. (2001). Appreciative inquiry; The power of the unconditional positive question. In P. Reason, & H. Bradbury (Eds.), *Handbook of action-research: Participative inquiry and practice* (pp. 189-200). London: Sage.

McNiff, J., & Whitehead, J. (2002). *Action research: Principles and practice* (2nd ed.). London; New York: RoutledgeFalmer.

Orsini-Jones, M. (1999). Implementing institutional change for languages: Online collaborative learning environments at Coventry University. *ReCALL, 11*(2), 61-73.

Patalong, S. (2002). Using WebCT in the library. Retrieved September 5, 2002, from http://www.lse.ac.uk/library/other_sites/aliss/patalong.ppt

Patalong, S. (2003). Using the virtual learning environment WebCT to enhance information skills teaching at Coventry University. *Library Review, 52*(3), 103-110.

Ponti, M., & Ryberg, T. (2004). *Rethinking virtual space as a place for sociability: Theory and design implications.* Paper presented at the Networked Learning 2004, Lancaster, April 5-7.

Steeples, C., & Jones, C. (2002). *Networked learning: Perspectives and issues.* London; New York: Springer.

Sturdy, A., & Grey, C. (2003). Beneath and beyond organizational change management: Exploring alternatives. *Organization, 10*(4), 651-662.

TELL Consortium (1996). Retrieved August 21, 2006, from http://www.hull.ac.uk/cti/tell/

Wenger, E. (1998). *Communities of practice: Learning, meaning and identity.* Cambridge: Cambridge University Press.

Chapter IX

Reflective Designing for Actors and Avatars in Virtual Worlds

Sisse Siggaard Jensen
Roskilde University, Denmark

Abstract

This chapter proposes a designing strategy referred to as "virtual 3D exploratories". It is a strategy by which to facilitate knowledge sharing and social innovation, activities important to many postmodern organizations and work groups—be they educational or commercial. The strategy will allow us to build virtual worlds, and universes, aimed at exploration—virtual worlds, where actors interact and communicate with each other by the means of avatars. To substantiate the designing strategy, this chapter calls attention to virtual phenomena such as: avatar-based interaction, communication, and scenarios designed for reflective practices. Taking a first step, the chapter presents narratives and video-based self-observations from 12 experiential sessions undertaken by the "Virtual 3D Agora-world" SIG as part of the EQUEL EU research project (2002-2004). Based on findings and reflections from these sessions, the designing strategy of virtual "exploratories" is outlined with reference to the "sense-making" theory (Dervin & Foreman-Wernet, 2003) and summarized in a "designing triangle".

Introduction

This chapter proposes the development of virtual 3D "exploratories" to bring about virtual and creative activity-systems to complement the prevailing file sharing systems of computer-supported collaboration. Virtual activity-systems emphasize the importance of actually "doing" something together in concurrent action and interaction. Moreover, the notion of exploratories, or "virtual laboratories", stands for a *reflective designing strategy* by which to support knowledge intensive and creative activity such as organizational knowledge sharing and social innovation. Some of the worlds and games of virtual universes, and particularly advanced multi-user online role-playing games, inspire this strategy of virtual exploratories. Being present in virtual worlds implies, among other things, that human interaction and communication is avatar-based. Avatars thus condition the development of exploratories, and they play an important part in the reflections of this chapter.

In virtual worlds, actors present themselves in the shape of an avatar. Choosing an avatar is the very basis for action. It is also a precondition for interaction. The avatars may take the shape of fictitious creations, such as human beings merged with creatures, dragons, mythological heroes and gods, mermaids, rats, demons, or atoms. They may also depict familiar roles such as craftsmen, businessmen, merchants, or stockbrokers but in an imaginative framing whether fantastic or dystopian. This chapter deals with questions of how it feels to act as an avatar and to interact with other avatars, and also, how by communicating as avatars conditions social interaction and knowledge sharing. As I see it, this is a matter of general interest, as advanced multi-user online role-playing games have become pervasive platforms for networked communication, especially among younger generations.

In this chapter, I do not presume to present a general theory about communicating as avatars in virtual worlds. I will, however, take a step towards understanding such virtual phenomena by presenting some of the findings from empirical research carried out in the project "The Virtual 3D Agora-world"[1]. In this project, several questions were explored: Is it possible to enact complex processes of knowledge sharing and social innovation in a 3D virtual world based on interaction with avatars, building a meeting place consisting of only virtual 3D building objects? How does communicating with avatars influence social interaction and knowledge sharing? Is it possible for actors acting as avatars to collaborate as a team while actually building a virtual meeting place, a virtual agora?[2] With such questions in mind, 12 explorative sessions have been undertaken to explore if the energy, fun, and eventful experiences of virtual worlds may also be utilized in support of reflective and creative activity.

Virtual worlds come from open-ended, innovative and fantastic, time and money consuming, online role-playing games. With these games, virtual experiences have been designed for, and also, they are *designing* networked communication as they condition the expectations of many young actors. However, the purpose of exploring virtual worlds and avatar-based social interaction in this chapter is not to understand the online games as such. Rather, the intention is to inquire if and how the design, energy, and virtual experiences may be remediated into other domains. In a comparison between findings from the virtual 3D Agora-world project, and some of the general features of advanced multi-user online role-playing games, I will therefore refer to these games, but the games as such will not be dealt with.

Background

Millions of actors and players "inhabit" the virtual worlds of today. They are, most likely, acting, interacting and communicating in so-called multi-user online role-playing games. The inhabitants are mostly young. They are the future generation of university students, who will expect to learn about virtual worlds, and avatar-based communication and interaction, when studying subject areas such as communication studies, interactive media, and design.

As early as 1985, Chip Morningstar coined the usage of the term "avatar" to denote *"...the image of a person in virtual reality: a movable three-dimensional image that can be used to represent somebody in cyberspace, for example, an Internet user"* (Castranova, 2001, p. 6). Seen from the perspective of virtual worlds, avatars may thus be described as the inhabitants of these worlds. Basically, a virtual world is a computer program with defining features such as interactivity, physicality—in a virtual sense of the word, and persistence. The program combines a graphical 3D environment with chat-based social interaction and systems developed in the world of multi-user domains (MUDs). The history of virtual worlds is briefly summarized by Castranova (2001):

"In 'Tomb Raider'®, you run a little person around on your screen and do things; in a VW (Virtual World), other people are running around in the same virtual space as you are, and they can talk to you. VWs can trace their history back to online-games on the ARPA-Net in the 1980s. The game that started the recent explosion of VWs was Meridian 59™, or M59 (Colker, 2001), begun in 1995 by Andrew and Chris Kirmse, two Microsoft® interns. They made a town and an open field and let users manipulate the environment by issuing keyboard and mouse commands to a graphical representation of themselves. This virtual persona, now known as an avatar, could be told to walk here and there, pick up a sword, look behind a bush, and hit whatever was there." (Castranova, 2001, p. 6-7)

Ultima Online™ (1997) was one of the first advanced virtual worlds, or multi-user online role-playing games, and a few years later *Everquest*® (1999) caused a break-through and gave rise to the distinction between "Earthlings" and the "inhabitants of Narrath" (Castranova, 2001). Later, games such as *Neochron*™ and *Dark Ages of Camelot*® appeared and recently the game of *World of Warcraft*™ has been in-troduced. In an interview, Malte, a young and very skilled player of such advanced games, says: *" ... you almost feel as free as is the case in real life, free to choose and decide either alone or in mutual action without any constraints..."* (Interview with Malte, 2004). This feeling of being free to choose how to present yourself, where to meet with others, and with whom to interact while organizing and collaborating opens up the possibility of playing with the perception of self and identity in the social interactions of virtual worlds.

In 1995, Sherry Turkle (1995) pointed out that playing with identity might become one of the most important aspects of online games. From a theoretical perspective, Espen Aarseth in 1997 described games as "ergodic texts" in trying to understand games as new kind of computer-based texts (Aarseth, 1997). In 2002, Lars Qvor-trup published comprehensive findings from a Danish research project on virtual reality, also covering some early studies of avatars' social interaction (Qvortrup, 2001, 2002). In the anthology, *The Social Life of Avatars*, Ralph Schroeder (2002) has published the findings from several international projects on avatars' interac-tion. Recently, a Lacanian psychoanalytic perspective has been applied to better understand subjectivity and avatars (Rehak, 2003). Such research-based publica-tions indicate that the acts of interacting and communicating with avatars in virtual worlds have become pervasive platforms for networked communication as well as important areas of research if we are to understand the recent "state-of-the-art" and the future potentials.

Theoretical Approaches

The presentation that follows is meant to shed light on knowledge sharing, forms of interaction, experience and self-consciousness when communicating with avatars in virtual worlds, and focus points that are essential to the explorative sessions of the Agora-world project. Also, the ontology of the sense-making theory and methodology is briefly introduced as it grounds the designing strategy of exploratories. In other words, no general and overall frame of reference as regards theory has guided the sessions of the Agora-world project; on the contrary, pieces of a puzzle or a mosaic form the basis for reflection. Areas such as knowledge-sociology, social interaction theory, and communication and media theory influence the theoretical approach. The focus points are briefly introduced next.

Knowledge Sharing

In the Agora-world project, knowledge is understood as a living phenomenon en-acted with the human body and social interaction between people as their "media" (Goffman, 1986; Jensen, 2005b; Jensen, Olsen, & Mønsted, 2004b; Mead & Mor-ris, 1934/1970; Stacey, 2001). In other words, knowledge is seen as a phenomenon based on social interaction and not from representational perspectives prevalent in information and systemic theory. Based on the interactional understanding of knowledge, the sharing of knowledge is seen as a process that has to be kept alive and constantly nourished. It is by nourishing the constant "flow" (Csikszentmihalyi, 1996, 1999) of human communication and interaction that the medium in which knowledge and creativity develop and unfold can be continuously created. This flow also includes knowledge artefacts as a form of non-human actants (Latour, 1988, 1998, 2005), meaning that they are important actants. However, they *are* not the knowledge, they merely act as the intermediaries of knowledge (Latour, 2005).

In an interaction-based understanding of knowledge, dialogue is essential for the process of knowledge sharing, and this also applies to social interaction mediated in virtual worlds as well as with avatars. It is not communication intended explicitly to convey tacit knowledge with a view to copying, storing, and sharing (thereby making it available as organizational knowledge, for example, via an intranet) as has characterized the theoretical discussion of knowledge sharing and knowledge management for many years (Boisot, 1995, 1998; Nonaka & Takeuchi, 1995; Non-aka, Toyoma, & Byosière, 2001; Tsoukas & Vladimirou, 2001). Rather, it is com-munication intended to nourish the reflective dialogue relevant to a certain group and its practice and therefore also the group's ignorance as these two aspects of knowledge are closely linked.

One of the central themes in knowledge sharing and knowledge management liter-ature is the fact that it is difficult to be aware of one's own knowledge, and with that also one's ignorance (Davenport & Prusak, 1998; Gourlay, 2001). Agents of a given practice are themselves rarely aware of what they actually know. Very often, this does not become clear until others ask questions or problems arise that have to be dealt with in cooperation with others. This is particularly true if the cooperation takes place across practices or maybe even across knowledge cultures (e.g., practice/ theory; natural science/the arts; artistic/commercial). Knowledge communication is thus a method by which to create the self-consciousness that enables the individual to be aware of his/her own knowledge and hence ignorance. That is, the dialogue and reflective practices (Dewey, 1933), or reflection-in-action (Schön, 1983) by which to reflect on matters otherwise un-reflected. Such processes of (self-)reflection-in-(inter)action thus form the basis for the understanding of knowledge sharing in this chapter (Jensen, 2005b; Jensen et al., 2004b).

Forms of Interaction

It takes experience and new knowledge to create a virtual environment as a basis for knowledge sharing in dialogues on the Net in order to maintain dialogues that are inspiring and motivational for the actors. This is the "lesson learnt" from previous experience with computer-mediated communication in project-organized university study-programmes at the master level (Jensen, 2001; Jensen & Heilesen, 2005a). In networked communication, a new context for social interaction and therefore cooperation, coordination and dialogue is created. Activities such as these play important parts in long-term projects and knowledge-based cooperation on the Net, for example, in study programs and other types of knowledge-intensive activities.

The computer medium and networked communication have the potential to integrate and remediate (Bolter & Grusin, 1999) all other types of mediated interaction. However, there are several significant limitations to remediation, and furthermore, it leads to other and new considerations. The decoupling of interaction and communication from the body is the most significant difference between face-to-face interaction and three other types of interaction: mediated, quasi-mediated, and computer-mediated interaction (Jensen & Heilesen, 2005a; Thompson, 1995). One can perceive the body as a medium for emotions which are closely linked to the many rhythmic layers of the body (Damasio, 2003; Stacey, 2001). Examples of this connection between the body's mediation and emotions are when we smile and blush. In virtual worlds, the body is decoupled as the medium for interaction. Regardless of how many multimedia, Web cams, videoconferences or virtual worlds, and avatars that are included, the body is present only in the "background" of social interaction. The body itself is not the medium of interaction; however, it is of course a prerequisite for dealing with the symbolic mediation. In order to activate the mediation, the body must control the input and output devices.

What makes networked communication special is the potential integration of both the mediated and quasi-mediated interaction, and the capacity to remediate them in a new medium. This remediation creates a broader spectrum of symbolic mediation than is the case for other mediated types of interaction, albeit a narrower one than is the case for physical presence. The decisive factor, however, is the creation of a new context with new relations between time and place. In computer-mediated interaction, physical presence has become face-to-interface, and this presence is a significant element of what can be perceived as *practice time*—a context of time and place that is local and meaningful (Mead, 1932/1959). This practice time is, however, in constant interplay with a *system time*, which is abstract. System time can be, for example, a chat environment, online communities, or avatar-based virtual worlds. In computer-mediated interaction, participants therefore constantly shift or oscillate between practice time and system time, each referring to a different context in time and place (Jensen & Heilesen, 2005a). It is in this oscillation between different references of time and place that the mediated interaction's separation of context can now be coupled to an extended accessibility so that a new context specific for networked communication arises in remediated interaction.

Avatars of the Self-Conscious

An actor's identity is transformed or remodelled when there are changes in the time and place of the context, for example, when entering into a dialogue and collaborating on the Net. The simplest way of summing up this transformation is to introduce a distinction between the narrator and the author (Latour, 1998). The *narrator's* actions are real and take place in the living now—s/he sweats, cries, thinks, writes, and contemplates how to create a new meaning in and with a new text. When the text is written, the narrator assumes a new identity as the *author*, and the text takes on its own life in social interaction. The relationship between the narrator and the author can be said to reflect the "I" and "me" of the self-conscious; that is, the "I" that others see compared with the way that the "I" perceives other people's perception of the self same "I". This is what the social psychologist and philosopher Mead calls the "me" (Mead & Morris, 1934/70). On the Net, this relationship takes place as a dynamic shifting or oscillation between practice time and system time, and this shift creates a *marked shift* between the two sides of the self-conscious (Jensen & Heilesen, 2005a). This marking of the way that the self-conscious constantly shifts between the "I" and the "me" in social interaction on the Net can be visualized through a designed character: an avatar.

In networked communication, social interaction can be acted out simultaneously in two different meetings: the physical presence and meetings between avatars in a virtual world. In other words, this type of interaction enables one to meet oneself in a situation on the screen in the form of an avatar, while at the same time meeting other people in a place "out there" and in a simultaneous "here". This meeting between the two sides of the self-conscious can therefore be seen in new ways, which make it possible to approach the different sides of the self-conscious reflectively and to do this together with others (see also Taylor, 2002).

Several focus points that form the basis for the theoretical understanding of knowledge sharing and avatar-based social interaction have now been presented. Focus points that in particular concern the new context of time and place, which creates presence and distance in a simultaneous process, as well as the reflective potential created in and with the marked shift between the two sides of the self-conscious. This reflective potential is well worth exploring so as to understand the conditions for social interaction in virtual worlds and thus in the meeting between avatars.

Sense-Making Ontology

As mentioned previously, the designing strategy of exploratories is inspired by sense-making theory and methodology as developed by the communication researcher Brenda Dervin. In a Dervin inspired ontology (2003), human beings are seen as continuously moving from situation to situation in a world sometimes chaotic and at other times orderly, but always filled with "gaps"—be they physical or mental. Movements occur in a flow of which we are not conscious. In many situations, we do, however, become conscious of our own movements in time and place and particularly if the movement is stopped. "Gaps" most often cause such stops, and the "bridging" of gaps is the human activity undertaken in trying to overcome such "situation movement stops". They are general patterns of human action and social interaction developed by Dervin with reference to her extensive empirical research. Some of these patterns are: "*decision*—being at a point where you need to chose between two or more roads that lie ahead; *problematic*—being dragged down a road not of your own choosing; *spin out*—not having a road; *wash-out*—being on a road suddenly having it disappear; *barrier*—knowing where you want to go but someone or something is blocking the way; *being led*—following another on the road because he or she knows more and can show you the way; *waiting*—spending time waiting for something in particular; *passing time*—spending time without waiting for something in particular; *out to lunch*—tuning out; *observing*—watching without being concerned with movement". In a "sense-making" approach, examples such as those are seen as opposed to: "*moving*—seeing self as proceeding unblocked in any way and without need to observe" (Dervin et al., 2003, p. 262). "Situation move-

Figure 1. The sense-making triangle and metaphor (Dervin et al., 2003, p. 277)

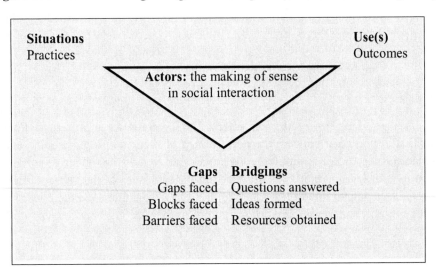

ment stops" such as these are patterns by which to configure some of the general features of a virtual exploratory.

Seen from a sense-making perspective, human bridging strategies when facing "gaps" are potentially innovative, even if only in minor scales. Such bridging strategies are at the centre of interest to the designing strategy of virtual exploratories. Finding new ways, or simply minor variations of usual ones, can be said to allow us to move on in time and place and to do so in a flow of unconscious energy. The "sense-making triangle" is the metaphor and model summing up this ontology, and it is briefly illustrated in Figure 1.

In a later part of this chapter, the sense-making triangle and metaphor will be modified to the "designing triangle" on the basis of which the reflective designing strategy of exploratories is then outlined.

Methodological Approaches

A universe of different 3D virtual worlds (Activeworlds Education™, awedu) formed the basis for 12 explorative sessions undertaken in the virtual 3D Agora-world project. It is a universe of open-ended virtual meeting places, not games. In awedu, the actors, presented as avatars, can build different worlds or universes of their own using 3D building objects and thus create and visualize different scenarios for interaction and communication. The awedu universe is simple yet the design idea of the system with an open virtual space to build in, a stock of 3D building objects, and a broad range of avatars to choose from, inspires the exploration of knowledge sharing and social innovation. In building a virtual meeting place with 3D objects as avatars, the awedu universe enables the experience of reflective practices involved in coordinating, organizing, shaping, creating, deciding, problem-solving, discussing, and so forth. These practices are important to organizational knowledge sharing and social innovation. Results from other 3D research projects have also documented the history, background, and activity of some of the worlds of the Activeworlds'™ universe (Hansen, 2002).

The virtual Agora-world was thus set up in awedu, and as a starting point, a horizon, blue sky, and ground with simple signs indicating directions (such as the four cardinal points of the compass) were created. In setting up the Agora-world, the intention was not to focus on the actual system design in itself, but to use the Agora-world as a *thinking tool* and thus enable and facilitate a collaborative process of (self-)reflection-in-(inter)action (Schön, 1983; Stacey, 2001), while *engaging* in knowledge sharing, that is, getting *involved*. The design idea was to explore the virtual world *to get a feeling* for the environment and new forms of interaction in recorded and reported first-hand experiences and self-observations. Joint explorative sessions facilitated the sharing of experience among actors, the underlying assumption being that first hand experience is essential if we are to get a feeling for the situation in these new, complex and somewhat unfamiliar virtual worlds. This feeling for the situation proved to be essential to reflective practices and knowledge sharing. Thus, it was assumed that first-hand experience with the virtual 3D world would be a precondition for building shared knowledge of access, navigation, action, building, interaction, and communication. The approach to research was therefore based on self-observation and self-reporting activities. In other words, the methodological approach was experiential and explorative, the idea being to use ourselves in the research—an approach inspired by the methods of personal and narrative inquiry (Claudinin & Connelly, 2000; Heron, 1996; Mann, 2003), and also by visual anthropology (Banks, 2001; Grimshaw, 2001; Howard, 2002; Pink, 2001) as video recordings played an important part.

Some of these first-hand experiences refer to: *presence* in a virtual world presenting yourself in the shape of an avatar; *sensation* in avatar-based interaction; and *conventions* in avatar meetings. They are reported in narratives that reflect the narrator's own choice and selection as to what to communicate. "Being a novice" is a narrative based on a personal inquiry approach, identifying critical incidents in the experience. "My initial experience" is about exploring the Agora-world experience from a relatively un-theorized position in terms of how it is possible to present a self within an avatar-enabled setting. "My learning process" is based on a narrative approach dealing with preconceptions, understandings, engagement, and learning, as well as the influence of social, contextual, and personal factors. "Different locations" is an account of attending the Agora-world from two different physical locations in a personal inquiry approach that explores co-location, presence, and attention. In the narrative "From novice to skilled avatar", the progress of starting out in the 3D universe with the uncertainty of a novice and the progress of skills while becoming a more skilled avatar is dealt with based on a personal inquiry approach.

In addition to the reporting of these first-hand narratives, comprehensive documentation serving the purpose of self-observation was also made available for reflection. In this documentation, sessions and walkthroughs were reported immediately after the explorative sessions supported by loggings of the chat activities. Also, several explorative sessions were video-recorded (see Table 1, sessions 2, 3, 5, 6, 7, 8, 11, 12 & 14) and video-logs made, the purpose being to provide evidence for collaborative reflection in a qualitative methodological approach. In the analysis of the video recordings, the method of reversed storyboarding has been applied. That is, the video recordings are deconstructed so as to identify beginnings and endings of situations and situation types, interaction patterns, breakdown situations, rhythm, and so forth, all with reference to the video interaction analysis method (VIA) (Henderson & Jordan, 1994; Jensen, 2001, 2004a, 2005b; Jensen et al., 2004b). The video-recordings are not aimed at covering all the activities of the Agora-world in a panoptic set-up. Rather, they are produced to visually support the participants' collective and individual memory so as to facilitate a process of (self-)reflection-in-(inter)action. An overview of the sessions undertaken is summarized in Table 1.

Table 1. The explorative sessions of the virtual 3D Agora-world project (2002-2004). Abbreviations: Roskilde University (RUC), Learning Lab Denmark (LLD), Special Interest Group (SIG), Personal Inquiry (PI), face-to-face (F2F)

	Context and documentation	Objective/ participation	Observations
1	F2F workshop	Introductory session	Discussing the idea of bridging gaps between different knowledge cultures supported by virtual worlds; different from usual text-based cscl/cscw-systems. Games, roleplaying, 3D and avatars, etc.
2	F2F workshop/ Net-based session Videologs, chatlogs, and observation logs	Introduction to the 3D Agora-world and the awedu universe. 3D Agora SIG	It took a lot of preparation, time, and support to introduce the 3D Agora-world in the awedu universe. Too short time-span to really try out the system together. Had a feeling for the system after the workshop, had fun, felt that navigation and movements of the avatars were under control.
3	Net-based session in Agora Videologs, chatlogs, and observation logs	Navigation and interaction with avatars. 3D Agora SIG	Avatars joined in at different times. Problems with gathering the avatars at the same place and at the same time. Difficult to get avatars' attention, and chat communication was also difficult. The chat was new for some avatars. No exploration, no fun and play.
4	Net-based session in Showcase Observation logs	Knowledge sharing; avatar meeting with AW expert. LLD Showcase	Learned about and decided on a chat dot system. Were told about 3D object market places on the Internet and visited the Showcase 3D object warehouse.
5	Net-based session in Agora Videologs, chatlogs, and observation logs	Information centre and voyages of discovery. 3D Agora SIG	Problems with gathering avatars left little time to take the recommended tours or to see how bumps and clicks could be built into signs. Difficult to coordinate avatars' interaction and to focus communication in the ongoing chat.
6	Net-based session in Agora Videologs, chatlogs, and observation logs	Avatar meeting about chat norms and chat language. 3D Agora SIG	Difficult to coordinate avatar interactions and negotiate a common understanding of chat norms and language. Technical problems with "gravity". Building activities introduced.
7	Net-based session in Agora Videologs, chatlogs, and observation logs	Joint building activity with avatars. 3D Agora SIG	Building activities take place collaboratively and in a playful atmosphere. Technical problems for one participant are dealt with by one of the other avatars. Different roles develop, which means that building activities can take place.

Table 1. (continued)

	Context and documentation	Objective/ participation	Observations
8	Net-based session in Agora Videologs, chatlogs, and observation logs	Joint building activity with avatars. 3D Agora SIG	Building activities continue collaboratively with avatars now experienced in navigation and building. Still technical problems for some avatars. One avatar takes other participants on a tour to Showcase. Very difficult to build together—using each others' objects. Rules are needed. Also, the building space is limited when it comes to number of objects.
9	Net-based session in the EQUEL project's collaboration system. Netlogs	Evaluation. 3D Agora SIG	Much harder to operate the worlds than first anticipated—feelings of being a novice, the multi-tasking aspect is difficult to deal with—very difficult—feelings like being neglected stem from this. You cannot just build—it takes time to learn how to navigate and communicate.
10	Net-based sessions in Agora Videologs, chatlogs, and observation logs	Joint building activity with avatars. LLD/RUC	Very hard to build collaboratively—technical limitations and no set of rules even for experienced avatars.
11	F2F workshop/ Net-based session Videologs, chatlogs, and observation logs	Design of the voyage of discovery and the visualizing meeting. 3D Agora SIG	Many differences appear. (1) Different preconceptions and meta-understandings of Agora activities; (2) Different approaches to research; (3) Different perceptions of design: the analogy-to-real-world design versus the abstract design different-from-real-world. One avatar brings up issues in the avatar meeting not discussed F2F. Issues not pleasant but necessary to discuss. Things that might be avoided in F2F situations due to politeness and eagerness to avoid conflicts. The avatar meeting allowed this to appear.
12	F2F workshop Observation logs	Exchange of experience understandings	Open discussion of different approaches and understandings as to the design and purpose

First-Hand Experience and Narratives

The reflections about narratives and first-hand experiences that follow are based on five narratives: "Being a novice", "My initial experience", "My learning process", "Different locations", and "From novice to skilled avatar", all of which have different authors (Olsen & Jensen, 2004). The narratives are based on each of the narrators' own evaluations and choices as to what to communicate from their first-hand experiences with the exploration of the Agora-world.

Copyright © 2007, Idea Group Inc. Copying or distributing in print or electronic forms without written permission of Idea Group Inc. is prohibited.

Presence

The choice of avatar and avatar name is commented on in the narratives. Some of the actors feel very comfortable with the appearance of their avatar and also feel some kind of attachment to the figure, either because of a resemblance or difference from themselves: "*... so I learned to change my appearance and become the elegant woman I can only dream of being outside of Agora*" (Different locations). Others cannot find an avatar matching the personality they want to project, and they feel uncomfortable about being imaged by an avatar: "*My initial sense was of a mild constraint having to select and adapt rather than display my own identity or construct an identity*" (My initial experience). However, it seems that the choice of name for an avatar makes up for the lack of personality in its figurative representation: "*In the end, I came to like my strange name which I gave to myself on an impulse, but I never found an avatar that I really wanted to be*" (Being a novice). The focus on choice of avatar and/or name seems to point to an awareness of self-presentation and thus self-consciousness. This awareness indicates that there is a strong sense of presence felt when being in the Agora-world. This presence and awareness is also reported in research literature of relevance to the explorations (Becker & Mark, 2002; Hudson-Smith, 2002). The feeling of being present is, however, also a feeling of being volatile due to potential anonymity. If the virtual presence, and with that the feeling of being able to "*sink into the ground*" (From novice to skilled avatar), is combined with the ability to change avatar/self-presentation then it seems to create an atmosphere of freedom to speak: "*I could express myself more easily*" (My learning process). This virtual presence played a major role for some novice avatars in the Agora-world. At that point, the focus was very much on the mediation itself, the environment, the appearance of avatars, and the movements, and it seemed as if the richness of the Agora-world, and the awedu universe in itself, was enough to attract attention. However, as time went by, this virtual presence was replaced by the activity itself as it became more focused. As purposeful interactions became more and more important, communication changed and the text/chat area became the focus. In this process of adaptation, the medium receded into the background, and as the environment became implicit, the feeling of presence grew stronger (Becker & Mark, 2002).

Sensation

In interactions with more than two avatars, it also became obvious just how difficult it was to know what the other avatars felt, wanted to do, and so forth: "*I also felt deflected from this at times by ... colleagues who took on a teaching/facilitation role towards me to help me make best use of the environment*" (Being a novice). The richness of information in real-world vision, sensation, perception, and body language tells us, or rather shows us, in an instant what others feel, what they are doing, and what they expect. We can *sense and feel* the situation and the responses. This is not possible in the Agora-world and misunderstandings among avatars easily occur: "[I was] *torn between the pursuit of my own agenda to build, and being 'good' and available to be co-operative with and supportive of others who might be experiencing difficulties*" (Being a novice). Help and guidance might thus be perceived as being intrusive. On the other hand, failure to help and offer guidance easily gave rise to a feeling of being isolated or neglected in this world of avatars. What is obvious in social practice and in real-world settings due to physical sensation and perception had to be expressed explicitly. This is demanding, as one's feelings are not always explicit to oneself in the virtual world.

Conventions

The process of adaptation is an important theme identified in most of the narratives; it is also a theme in the research literature in which Nilsson sees it as significant behaviour (Nilsson, Heldal, Axelsson, & Schroeder, 2002). The first avatar meetings in the Agora-world, and in the awedu universe as such, created an awareness of not only one's presence, but also of social conventions and communication strategies as these were made explicit simply *by not being there*; or rather, the system did not support the many conventions that are implicit in everyday interactions in the real world. This creates an innovative and explorative awareness of having to overcome problems and constraints: *"...using a person's name and so specifically addressing one's sentences, it is possible to "see" who is speaking to who"* (From novice to skilled avatar). In this case, adaptation is not just a question of overcoming problems and constraints as to communication, appearance, collaboration, and so forth, it is also a process of learning the conventions of virtual worlds, and these are rather similar to those in the real world (Jakobsson, 2002). The need for a zone of proximity is a virtual reality for avatars (Becker & Mark, 2002), and social roles and status are adopted over time in addition to the corresponding behaviour (Jakobsson, 2002). When avatars behave inappropriately, conventions break down, and this situation is very difficult to deal with: *"My perception of the distress levels within our virtual community was increasing. Constructive communication was breaking down"* (Different locations). Feelings and responses in the Agora-world became almost as real and strong as in real-life settings (Jakobsson, 2002).

Multi-Faceted Interaction

In the sessions, collaboration was mediated in different media, settings, and locations: face-to-face workshops, Net-based avatar meetings, text-based Net sessions, and co-location in a computer lab while acting "out there" in a virtual distance. This multiplicity of mediations is commented on in one of the narratives: *"... that variation of media where I express myself can be of value and support a develop-ment of confidence in a different way, or perhaps different direction, than it would have been if there were only one medium"* (My learning process). Different media might thus open up the possibility to see more facets of oneself in social interaction. I will describe this as "a multiplicity of mediations". Moreover, this multiplicity might help reflect more facets of one's self-presentation, reflection, and response in social interaction, and thus new understandings and new lines of action. When viewed in this way, I will conclude these reflections on the first-hand narratives by suggesting the concept of "multi-faceted interaction" to denote interrelations between a multiplicity of mediations and different facets of self-consciousness in social interaction.

Video-Based Observations

In this section, I will first summarize some of the findings from the project's in-troductory workshop (Table 1, session 2), the following Net-based Agora sessions (Table 1, sessions 3, 5, 6, 7 & 8) and the four days of online sessions of evaluation undertaken at the EQUEL project's site (equel.net). Then different situations or rather situation types are identified in the outline of three scenarios. These scenarios and prototypes rely on a series of self-observations based on the comprehensive video-recordings and with that the videologs.

A Playful Atmosphere of Fun

The introductory session took place as a workshop where participants from Sweden, Scotland, England, and Denmark were gathered. Several things stand out when watching the video material from the workshop. The activities within the Agora-world took place in a single shared room, where each participant had his/her own computer. The atmosphere was very intense. It is clear that the participants had a good time "playing" with their avatars while navigating in the various 3D worlds of the virtual universe. As the Agora-world was still new, it was an uninhabited and empty space that had to be built-up. Many of the avatars were therefore encouraged to explore other developed and imaginative 3D worlds. The playful atmosphere on these voyages was partly because the participants were able to communicate and interact across two temporal and spatial zones. There was a constant commentary across two temporal zones and worlds in the Agora-world's system time, as well as in the concrete practice time in the shared workshop room. That is, a "setting", a situation, or context with many parallels to the setting that constitutes the context for players of online games, who sit together in a local context while acting in union in another virtual world somewhere "out there" simultaneously interacting with other actors in the shape of avatars.

A Cold and Lonely World

The playful atmosphere of community changed in the second phase of the explorative sessions, which took place after the workshop. The research project continued to have a number of distributed and Net-based shared sessions, where all participants entered the Agora-world together from different physical locations with the objective of experiencing and building. A feeling of being lost spread among several of the participants, who were also experiencing technical problems. Some members began feeling left out and neglected, while others were rendered powerless as they were having problems navigating or communicating. It was difficult to multi-task when the level of complexity increased in the transition from embarking on a voyage of discovery, experiencing interesting and imaginative ideas in advanced virtual 3D worlds, to actually coordinating a building activity alone, yet as part of a group. It turned out to be difficult to coordinate the avatars' attention in this system, even though it is a system that emphasizes the intensity of the experience. Simultaneously, the avatar must be navigated at several levels; the participant must keep an eye on what the other avatars are doing, while at the same time communicating in the new language used in the chat. If you can keep up, it is a lot of fun; if you cannot, then it quickly becomes very cold and lonely in a virtual world.

Three Scenarios

In the third phase of the explorative sessions, experiences and observations have been summarized in three scenarios which distinguish between different types of activity and modes of interaction in the Agora-world: 1) the voyage of discovery, 2) the playful meeting, and 3) the purposeful meeting. The *Voyage of Discovery* is the first activity that springs to mind when you log on to the virtual universe. It is a voyage through the many different worlds in the awedu universe, full of experiences, surprises, and inspiration due to the many imaginative and innovative ideas that have been visualized. You can embark on a voyage of discovery on your own or travel with other participants in small groups of 2-3 or meet other travellers. There is also the *Playful Meeting*, which expresses a desire to meet other avatars. In the playful meeting, it is the meeting itself, through avatars and in chat that motivates activity. You chat together to explore and experiment with the new mode of communication itself; this also applies to the interaction between avatars. You can dance, wave, and imitate others to experience how the movement develops and affects the meeting between avatars. Building activities can be done just for fun, so experiments can easily be deleted or associated to one another. The objective is to have fun and to meet in a new way. Finally, there is the *Purposeful Meeting* where the meeting includes planned activities and avatars meet to do something together—that is, when the meeting has a defined objective. If this includes building activities, a learning element of knowledge communication and knowledge sharing is linked to an otherwise playful activity. Examples could be meetings where the objective is to build something in particular together, or meetings that deal with navigating and building as such, or a meeting that uses the system to visualize ideas or develop role-plays based on different framings and avatars.

Findings from the Sessions

The narratives and video-based observations show that it is difficult to get avatars to meet, to coordinate their attention, and to create a shared focus point in a larger group of avatars (4-8). When avatars meet two at a time, they can work together. Groups of up to four can just manage; however, when larger groups of avatars get together, they often experience difficulties coordinating, focusing, and communicating if they are doing anything more demanding than playing and exploring or going through the "rituals" of meeting. This is particularly true, when they cannot split up into onlookers and active participants. These conclusions supplement experience from other research projects on 3D and avatar-based interaction (Schroeder, 2002). It is difficult to create an actual dialogue that can uphold a longer chain of thought between two or more avatars in chat while navigating in the virtual world. Moreover, the avatar's movements are a poor reflection of the signs and symbols that the body uses to coordinate social interaction as the participant has so little control over the movements. This soon becomes evident when requirements and complexity increase. This is typically the case for purposeful activities that require knowledge sharing and collaboration, for example, building a new world together in the shape of a meeting place. The building activity in the sessions started from scratch and participants had no design as their starting point. In that way, the tasks were very complex and difficult.

As a result of this, the philosophy had to be changed mid-passage and two design examples, "the Cube" and "the Visualizing Meeting" (see the *Appendix*), were developed and subsequently explored. The design examples can be seen as an "intermediate form" (Latour, 1998): they visualize a framing of social interaction while, at the same time, eliminating the very same framing. In this sense, they express a conclusion that on the one hand emphasizes the necessity of a minimalist design that helps shape the social interaction between avatars—a design perceived as a basic framework (Goffman, 1986), which connects the design with familiar forms of interaction. On the other hand, the two examples are also shaped as *reflective designs*, which are abstract and "contra-intuitive"—designs that emphasize the difference from the real-world settings with a view to seeing what is otherwise taken for granted in a new light, and by which the virtual meeting between avatars can contribute to rendering the un-reflected reflected as it is possible to frame social interaction in contra-intuitive ways. The significant shift between the two marked sides of the self-conscious can thus unfold in a new context of simultaneous physical presence and virtual distance as the participants constantly shift between practice time and system time. In other words, it is a design that inspires new knowledge about the balance between, first, the basic frameworks of the minimalist design, which shapes the social interaction of different situation types and, second, the reflective design that adds dynamism to the same basic frameworks by provoking the framing, roles, and conventions of social interaction and practices.

Exploring the Agora-world shows how difficult it is for avatars to move from playful to more purposeful activities. In playful activities, such as voyages of discovery, avatars very often have fun while playing around in imaginative and inspiring 3D worlds. They imitate each others' movements using non-verbal communication while jumping, waving, and dancing or communicating in a chat-mode; it is brief, humorous, and funny and characterized by playing with words, signs, and languages. In contrast, the purposeful activity of building a meeting place requires joint and focused attention, mutual coordination, and a shared understanding of the activity undertaken. This is where the limitations of the avatar-based social interaction become apparent.

The choice of an avatar is a self-conscious process of presenting yourself (Goffman, 1959). It seems that either the preferred avatar character or the avatar name, or both, are important identifiers charged with meaning and significance to the actors. There are close bonds between the avatars—be it the character or the name—and the actors. These bonds are so close that avatars adhere to conventions as regards to communication and interaction (proximity zone, pursuit, tapping, staring). Breakdown of conventions occur, however, in virtual worlds as well as in the real world, but the framing is different. In the virtual world, you act at a distance with your avatar as an intermediary. This framing might encourage an explorative attitude and a willingness to speak out. We should further research the framing of knowledge sharing in which breakdown situations and "gaps" are purposefully planned to make explicit what is taken for granted, to enable reflection on what is otherwise un-reflected, and to make explicit what is implicit.

In view of this, one of the important findings from the Agora-world sessions is the idea of a *reflective design* by which to challenge the borders of social conventions and question what is otherwise taken for granted. In simulations and reconstructions, the virtual design remediates well-known and physical spaces, navigation, arrangement, expressions, and so forth. Conversely, in a reflective design, we should utilize the differences between physical and virtual worlds to promote and *provoke* the awareness of explorative activity, that is, to do things otherwise not possible. Multi-faceted interaction marks the shift between the two sides of the self-conscious in social interaction and in a multiplicity of mediations. In a process of oscillating between different mediations, more facets of oneself in relation to social interaction are made visible and explicit. If we are to challenge and provoke existing practices and related roles by a strategy of reflective designing, then it might prove to be promising to explore such oscillations between different time zones of practice time and system time, and with that multi-faceted interactions.

Exploratories: Designing for Reflection

The laboratory is a generally recognized framing of experiments, research, and innovation in many natural sciences. In parallel to this, the *exploratory* can be said to offer an analogy to the laboratory only within the humanities and social sciences. In the laboratory as well as the exploratory, actors are preoccupied with innovation, the difference being that laboratory experiments are chiefly concerned with medical, biological, or technological innovations, whereas the activities of an exploratory are concerned with *social* innovation and creativity. An exploratory may thus be described as: a virtual and avatar-based reflective design framing (Goffman, 1986) or staging (Latour, 1998) a flow of creativity (Csikszsentmihayli, 1996, 1999) in social interaction provoking a process of knowledge sharing and/or social innovation, either in a collaborative or a competitive way, or in a combination of both. To further develop this description, findings from the Agora-world project are now compared with general features of the multi-user online role-playing games. Subsequently, the idea of a reflective design is seen in relation to the outcome of this comparison. On the basis of this, a reflective designing strategy of exploratories is then suggested with reference to the sense-making methodology (Dervin et al., 2003).

A Comparison with Multi-User Online Role-Playing Games

In light of the findings from the Agora-world project, it appears that purposeful as opposed to playful activity may cause problems and breakdown situations as regards to communication and social interaction. Also, the reflective design prototypes tested in the project prove to be confusing rather than challenging. They are too abstract, bringing about only minimal orientation as to patterns of social interaction. For the purpose of re-evaluation, findings are now briefly compared with virtual worlds in the shape of multi-user online role-playing games.

"Quests" like "killing the monster" or fighting for your life, are basic activities of role-playing games. Also, the development of one's avatar and the organizing of cooperative activity among avatars to kill the monster, fight the dragon, or beat a hostile clan or tribe seems to be almost as important as the game itself. In games, avatars play predefined roles with certain abilities. In choosing an avatar, a spectrum of abilities and roles are at the actor's disposal as well as different "levels" facilitating the development of one's avatar. It takes time and effort to develop an avatar, for example, with the ability to "forge swords" to the highest of levels. Raising the avatar's level requires laborious "work", training abilities while solving sub-quests. Actors with high-level and well-developed avatars may also sell their avatar for maximum virtual or real profit, or in service of a good cause. Laborious work and developing avatars to certain high-level skills and abilities in accordance with urgent demands is of central importance to the actors, together with organizing collaboration between avatars. Being able to "read the game", and thus meet the demands and needs of different situations—very often characterized by fighting for survival—are some of the most challenging features of the role-playing games to many actors.

Compared to this, the set up of the virtual Agora-world was "open" in almost every way. The actors were expected to build a virtual world together and from scratch. No quest defined the situation and the challenges that avatars had to deal with. The avatars had no predefined role to play and practice, and no levels facilitated their development and training. The problems with coordination and sharing of attention, both of which are basic to purposeful activity, indicate that rule-based and predefined behaviours are, to some extent, necessary features. Building a virtual world in a collaborative effort with open-ended negotiations of meaning is an activity too complex when acting as avatars. Avatars do not yet have the ability to read and sense a situation, to respond to the situation, and to adjust their communication and action to this reading. In other words, the important part played by tacit knowing in social interaction becomes obvious, as it is absent when acting and interacting with avatars. For a shared focus to emerge in purposeful activity, explicit rules of the game or "rituals" are necessary. In designing the Agora-world's sessions, the intention was to explore the potential of virtual worlds in an open space as opposed to the predefined worlds, quests, roles, levels, and so forth, of games. However, it appears that we will still have to learn from the games in rethinking the design.

In view of this, the reflective design of an exploratory should challenge the actors in concrete "quests" and preferably in challenges for fight and survival. To meet these challenges, collaboration and organization of resources in mutual action are also of crucial importance to the activity of exploratories. Also, avatars should have defined and different roles, and be able to collaborate and adjust to social interaction, as well as develop certain skills and abilities to a high level. The open "cast list" of the virtual Agora-world's design seems to cause problems. Considering this, reflective design should create the basic framing for social interaction, roles, and practices in a recognizable and familiar framing, while at the same time make use of the reflective potential in a provocative design, challenging the actor's usual roles and practices. A designing strategy of exploratories should deal with and balance this contradiction.

The Designing Triangle

Exploratories are virtual worlds aimed at disturbing existing practices, for example, in organizational knowledge sharing, by provoking well-established procedures, mentalities, ways of thinking, and not least, roles related to those practices—activities that have a part to play in, for example, management education, project management, teamwork, teambuilding, communication practices, and education. To frame a designing strategy for such activities, the sense-making triangle, (introduced earlier) is now modified to a designing triangle (Figure 2) that constitutes the designing principle of virtual exploratories.

The triangle consists of the following general features: scenarios with quests and avatar roles, gaps with built-in choices, bridging strategies by which to overcome the gaps, and innovative outcomes resulting from the overcoming of gaps. A virtual scenario with certain quests and related avatars with roles, possible actions, skills, and levels of development is the framing of social interaction and "gaps" or "situation movement stops" are the disturbances that provoke action and interaction. In this way, quests, avatar roles, and "gapiness" together define the virtual scenarios. Also, choosing is an activity essential to the "bridging" of gaps of different scenarios, particularly if the designed gaps make more specific the general patterns of "situation movement stops", that is, for example, decision, problems, spin out, wash-out, barrier, being led, waiting, passing time, tuning out, and observing. Setting up a range of choices of relevance to both the different gaps or "situation movement stops", and the bridging strategies aimed at provoking reflective practices, is therefore one of the most important steps to be taken in the designing of an exploratory. Virtual teleports may make visible the built-in choices of virtual scenarios and quests. As compared to hypertext links, teleports may be seen as visualizing the choices to be made in and between scenarios. Overcoming built-in quests while bridging the gaps should furthermore produce an innovative outcome that creates something new, even if of only minor variations.

Facing gaps and choosing different ways by which to "bridge" these gaps is the core activity of an exploratory and the part played by the avatars is to challenge the actor's self-perception by marking the shift between the "I" and "me" of social interaction. This marking of the shift unfolds in a simultaneous "out there" at a virtual distance, and "in here" in an attentive presence with avatars acting as the intermediaries. Presenting oneself by an intermediary in the shape of an avatar makes possible the observation of this distinction between the "I" acting "in here" in front of the screen, and the "me" in interaction with other avatars "out there" on the screen. Even if interacting at a distance, a sense of attachment and presence is created in this process, as close bonds seem to form between actors and the avatars acting as their intermediaries. This double-layered process of observing oneself at a distance while at the same time feeling attached to one's intermediary forms the very basis for the reflective potential to be designed for in virtual exploratories. The general features of the designing triangle of exploratories are summarized in Figure 2.

The designing triangle can be seen as a thinking tool. It is a tool by which to consider the question of how to balance the underlying contradiction between a minimalist design framing the social interaction with avatars in familiar ways, and a contra-intuitive reflective design that provocatively encourages (self-)reflection-in-(inter)action. In the minimalist design, the general features of the triangle are recommended to form the framing of social interaction, and in complementing those features, a reflective design should allow for actors to co-construct the exploratory, taking action when provoked and reflecting on existing strategies when challenged. In deciding to what extent the actors are allowed to co-construct the virtual exploratory, reference may be made to ascending scales from concrete to abstract: the more abstract the less familiarity with the framing of social interaction, and vice versa; similarly, the more concrete, the less open to co-construction, and vice versa.

Finally, in relating the designing triangle to different areas of application, it is important to emphasize that the "situation movement stops" of the sense-making approach are to be seen as general patterns essential to human *practices*—patterns that appear differently when applied to more specific practices such as organiza-

Figure 2. The designing triangle of exploratories

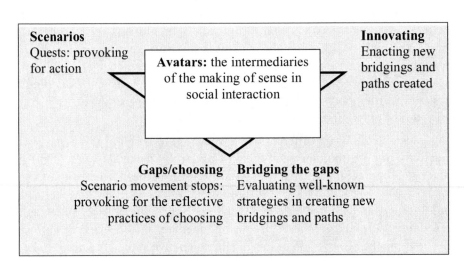

tional knowledge sharing. In transforming general patterns to concrete gaps, the designing strategy should therefore rely on careful studies of the practices designed for. Qualitative field-studies are thus to be seen as the anticipated starting point in relating the designing of exploratories to certain organizational practices, be they educational or commercial.

Future Research

To further develop the reflective designing strategy, the next step will be taken in practice. In a future design workshop, students of subject areas such as communication studies, interactive media, and design will be asked to apply the general features of the triangle to organizational practices. In this way, the idea and concept will be subject to thorough testing and possibly subsequent redesign. Besides the testing of the triangle in practice, further research is carried out in the ongoing research project: "Actors and avatars communicating in virtual worlds—an empirical study of actors' sense-making strategies based on communication theory" (2006-2007)—a project supported by the Danish Research Council for Culture and Communication. In this project, the focus is changed as compared to the virtual Agora-world. Being present "inside" the worlds, acting as avatars, was an important experience, but in the ongoing project about actors and avatars, the focus is turned towards the actors while acting. Iterative videoviews, that is, qualitative (inter)views carried out with video-recordings in recurrent sessions, are conducted in field studies to answer questions such as: Which are the sense-making strategies developed by actors as regards communication and social interaction in virtual worlds? Do avatars have a part to play in the shaping of actor's self-perception, and if so, how? Which are the communication strategies enacted by actors in handling the movement to and from virtual worlds and real world? As regards to theory, the project will contribute to the phenomenology of experience in reflecting on how to understand the experience of avatar-based communication and interaction. Also, sense-making theory will be applied to critically question the "tradition" of user-oriented design and communication, and with that, suggest an *actor*-oriented approach.

Conclusion

Actors identify themselves with their avatars. Playing around while exploring virtual worlds, taking on different identities and roles while solving problems together with other avatars is fun because the attachment to the avatars brings about a feeling of presence; you can almost sense the worlds and the other avatars, even so thoroughly as to adhere to real-world conventions of, for example, proximity, staring, and so forth. It seems that actors get deeply involved with their avatars and the activity undertaken, and thus it makes sense to explore the remediation of role-playing games into other domains. However, the findings from the Agora-world sessions also indicate that problems seem to arise from this process of remediation. In the first place, a reflective designing strategy should emphasize the difference between virtual and real-world framings to challenge and provoke existing ideas, practices, expectations, mentalities, and strategies; second, in communicating and interacting with avatars, actors also need a well-known framing in support of their activity. In this chapter, a reflective designing strategy of "exploratories" by which to reflect on and balance this contradiction is therefore introduced and summarized in the "designing triangle of exploratories". The triangle is developed with reference to findings from the Agora-world sessions in comparison with some of the general features of multi-user online role-playing games, and it is based on the sense-making triangle of sense-making theory. The designing triangle can thus be said to act as a thinking tool for the designing of virtual worlds, if such worlds are to be developed in support of knowledge intensive activity such as, for example, organizational knowledge sharing and social innovation.

References

Aarseth, E. (1997). *Cybertext: Perspectives on ergodic literature*. Baltimore, MD: Johns Hopkins University Press.

Banks, M. (2001). *Visual methods in social research*. Thousand Oaks, CA; London: Sage Publications.

Becker, B., & Mark, G. (2002). Social conventions in computer-mediated communication: A comparison of three online shared virtual environments. In R. Schroeder (Ed.), *The social life of avatars* (pp. 19-40). London; New York: Springer.

Boisot, M. (1995). *Information space. A framework for learning in organizations, institutions and culture*. London: Routledge.

Boisot, M. (1998). *Knowledge assets. Securing competitive advantage in the information economy*. Oxford: Oxford University Press.

Bolter, J., & Grusin, R. (1999*). Remediation – Understanding new media*. Boston: MIT Press.

Castranova, E. (2001). *Virtual worlds: A first-hand account of market and society on the cyberian frontier.* CESifo Working Paper No. 618.

Claudinin, J., & Connelly, M. (2000). *Narrative inquiry*. San Francisco: John Wiley & Sons.

Csikszentmihalyi, M. (1996). *Creativity: Flow and the psychology of discovery and invention*. New York: HarperCollins.

Csikszentmihalyi, M. (1999). Implications of a systems perspective for the study of creativity. In R. J. Sternberg (Ed.), *Handbook of creativity* (pp. 313-339). Cambridge: Cambridge University Press.

Damasio, A. (2003). *Looking for Spinoza. Joy, sorrow and the feeling brain*. London: Vintage.

Davenport, T. H., & Prusak, L. (1998). *Working knowledge. How organizations manage what they know*. Boston: Harvard Business School.

Dervin, B., & Foreman-Wernet, L. (2003). *Sense-making methodology reader*. New Jersey: Hampton Press.

Dewey, J. (1933). *How we think. A restatement of the relation of reflective thinking to the educative process*. Boston: D.C. Heath and Company.

Goffman, E.(1959). *The presentation of self in everyday life*. London: Penguin Books.

Goffman, E. (1986). *Frame analysis: An essay on the organization of experience* (Northeastern University Press ed.). Boston: Northeastern University Press.

Gourlay, S. (2001). Knowledge management and HRD. *Human Resource Development International, 4*(1), 27-46.

Grimshaw, A. (2001). *The ethnographer's eye. Ways of seeing in modern anthropology*. Cambridge; New York; Melbourne: Cambridge University Press.

Hansen, K. (2002). The design of public virtual spaces in 3D virtual worlds on the Internet. In L. Qvortrup (Ed.), *Virtual space: Spaciality in virtual inhibited 3D worlds* (pp. 145-171). London: Springer.

Henderson, A., & Jordan, B. (1994). *Interaction analysis: Foundation and practice*. San Francisco: Xerox Palo Alto Research Center & Institute for Research on Learning.

Heron, J. (1996). *Co-operative inquiry: Research into the human condition*. London; New Delhi: Sage Publications.

Howard, P. N. (2002). Network ethnography and the hypermedia organization: New media, new organizations, new methods. *New Media & Society, 4*(4), 550-574.

Hudson-Smith, A. (2002). 30 days in active worlds – Community, design and terrorism in a virtual world. In R. Schroeder (Ed.), *The social life of avatars* (pp. 77-90). London: Springer.

Interview with Malte, 2004 (to be published).

Jakobsson, M. (2002). Rest in peace, Bill the Bot: Death and life in virtual worlds. In R. Schroeder (Ed.), *The social life of avatars* (pp. 63-76). London: Springer.

Jensen, S. S. (2001). *De digitale delegater – Tekst og tanke i netuddannelse. En afhandling om hyperlinks i refleksiv praksis, der er face-to-interface.* København: Multivers.

Jensen, S. S. (2004a). *Knowledge sharing in the 3D Agora-world.* Paper presented at the Networked Learning Conference, Lancaster University, Lancaster, April 4-7.

Jensen S. S. (2005b). Video views of knowing in action. Analytical views in situ in an IT firm's development department. In A. F. Buono, & F. Poulfelt (Eds.), *Challenges and issues in knowledge management* (pp. 249-270). Greenwich, CT: Information Age Publishing.

Jensen, S. S., & Heilesen, S. B. (2005a). Time, place and identity in project work on the Net. In T. S. Roberts (Ed.), *Computer-supported collaborative learning in higher education* (pp. 51-69). Hershey; London; Melbourne; Singapore: Idea Group.

Jensen, S. S., Olsen, S. F., & Mønsted, M. (2004b). *Viden, ledelse og kommunikation.* København: Samfundslitteratur.

Latour, B. (1988). The politics of explanation. In S. Woolgar (Ed.), *Knowledge and reflexivity: New frontiers in the sociology of knowledge* (pp. 155-176). London: Sage Publications.

Latour, B. (1998). Artefaktens återkomst. Ett möte mellan organisationsteori och tingens sociologi. *Studier i företagsekonomi 5.* Stockholm: Nerenius & Santerus Förlag.

Latour, B. (2005). *Reassembling the social. An introduction to actor-network theory.* Oxford: Oxford University Press.

Mann, S. (2003). A personal inquiry into an experience of adult learning on-line. *Instructional Science, 31,* 111-125.

Mead, G. H. (1932/1959). *The philosophy of the present.* Chicago; London: La Salle, Ill: Open Court.

Mead, G. H., & Morris, C. W. (1934/1970). *Mind, self & society.* Chicago: University of Chicago Press.

Nilsson, A., Heldal, I., Axelsson, A., & Schroeder, R. (2002). The long-term uses of shared virtual environments: An exploratory study. In R. Schroeder (Ed.), *The social life of avatars* (pp. 12-125). London: Springer.

Nonaka, I., & Takeuchi, H. (1995). *The knowledge creating company. How Japanese companies create the dynamics of innovation.* Oxford: Oxford University Press.

Nonaka, I., Toyoma, R., & Byosière, P. (2001). A theory of organizational knowledge creation: Understanding the dynamic process of creating knowledge. In M. Dierkes, A. Antal, J. Child, & I. Nonaka (Eds.), *Handbook of organizational learning and knowledge* (pp. 491-517). Oxford: Oxford University Press.

Olsen, S. F., & Jensen, S. S. (2004). *Narratives from the 3D Agora-world*. Paper presented at the Networked Learning Conference, Lancaster University, Lancaster, April 4-7.

Pink, S. (2001). *Doing visual ethnography: Images, media and representation in research*. London; Thousand Oaks; New Delhi: Sage Publications.

Qvortrup, L. (Ed.) (2001). *Virtual interaction: Interaction in virtual inhabited 3D worlds*. London: Springer.

Qvortrup, L. (2002). *Virtual space: Spatiality in virtual inhabited 3D worlds*. London: Springer.

Rehak, B. (2003). Playing at being: Psychoanalysis and the avatar. In M. Wolf, & B. Perron (Eds.), *The video game theory reader* (pp. 103-127). New York: Routledge.

Schroeder, R. (Ed.). (2002). *The social life of avatars*. London: Springer.

Schön, D. (1983). *The reflectice practitioner*. Aldershot: Avebury.

Stacey, R. D. (2001). *Complex responsive processes in organizations. Learning and knowledge creation. Complexity and emergence in organizations*. London; New York: Routledge.

Taylor, T. L. (2002). Living digitally: Embodiment in virtual worlds. In R. Schroeder (Ed.), *The social life of avatars* (pp. 40-63). London: Springer.

Thompson, J. B. (1995). *The media and modernity: A social theory of the media*. Cambridge: Polity Press.

Tsoukas, H., & Vladimirou, E. (2001). What is organizational knowledge? *Journal of Management Studies, 38*(7), 973-993.

Turkle, S. (1995*). Life on the screen: Identity in the age of the Internet*. New York: Simon & Schuster.

Endnotes

[1]   The project: "Virtual 3D Agora-world" was one of seven special interest groups in the EU EQUEL project on e-learning (equel.net). Fourteen universities from seven EU countries took part in the project from 2002-2004. The virtual 3D Agora-world research project was undertaken by special interest group 5: Sanne Fejfer Olsen and Nina Tange, Learning Lab Denmark; Sisse Siggaard Jensen, Center for Knowledge and Design in New Media, Communication Studies, Roskilde

University; Chris Jones, Center for Studies in Advanced Learning Technology, Educational Research, Lancaster University; Frances Deepwell, Center for Higher Education Development, Coventry University; Sara Mann, Teaching and Learning Service, Glasgow University; Klara Bolander, Dept. of Learning, Informatics, Management and Ethics, Karolinska Instituttet and Vic Lally, School of Education, Sheffield University

[2]   The agora was the ancient Greek public meeting place for free citizens.

Appendix: Reflective Design Prototypes

The *Cube*: A Reflective Design Prototype

The *Cube* is a point of entry and a ground zero design based on the voyage of discovery scenario. The point of entry will open up adventurous worlds only through exploration of the VW features such as bumping into the walls, clicking, or teleporting to other locations. The *Cube* is twisted to emphasize the difference between physical space and the virtual worlds. The twisting of the angle leaves the avatars with no possibility to rest in the room—there is nowhere to settle down; this is to promote an urge to explore how to move on and where to go.

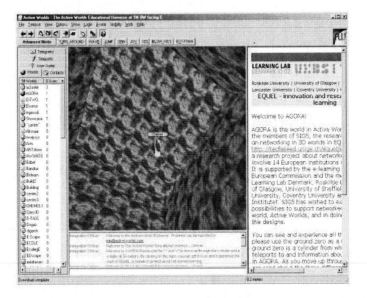

The 3D Vincent world is one of the adventurous worlds the avatars can bump into while exploring the *Cube*. This world is a 3D model of Vincent van Gogh's paintings. Avatars can move around inside locations and sceneries painted by Vincent van Gogh. Other bumps in the *Cube* will teleport avatars to virtual worlds such as the Luna-world in space, to locations in the Agora-world, or click active different urls.

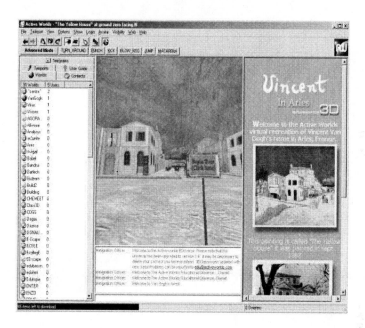

The *Visualizing Meeting*: A Reflective Design Prototype

The *Visualizing Meeting* is a design based on the purposeful meeting scenario. It is designed with a violet scene or an arena at the centre, which is easy to identify. When standing at the violet scene, the avatar is asking the others to pay attention and direct their action towards the centre. The scene is thus the framing of coordination, attention, and action.

216   Siggaard Jensen

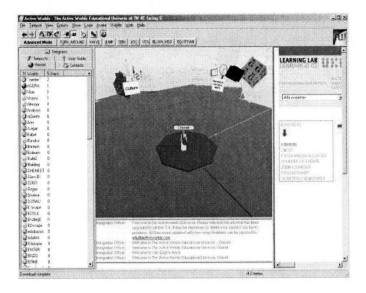

In the periphery of the violet scene there are objects from eight different categories: language, technology, culture, emotions, social issues, mathematics, and texture objects. The design idea being that when avatars hold purposeful meetings in this scenery their intentions, ideas, attitudes, and so forth, are to be visualized when choosing among the objects to match an idea with a visual signifier.

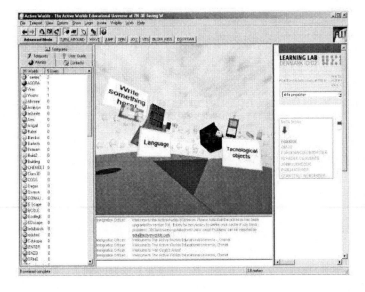

Chapter X

The Psychology of Online Sociability:
Theory and Examples

Torkil Clemmensen
Copenhagen Business School, Denmark

Abstract

In this chapter, I will review current approaches to online sociability and present and exemplify the psychological social reality theory of online sociability. By analyzing sociability in a university-level virtual world course, I will present and analyze examples on how to understand the students' design of conditions for sociability as communication of cultural symbols, such as avatars and virtual landscapes, and the social reality of perceived groups of people. The results of the analysis will be used to illustrate different kinds of online sociability: superficial, convivial, and negative sociability. The chapter suggests solutions and recommendations to designers and researchers with a focus on online communities and networked communication.

Introduction

This chapter deals with the design of sociability for human encounters in online environments. By analyzing sociability in a university-level virtual world course,

I will present a psychological perspective on users' design and practice of online sociability. I will present and analyze examples of how students' design of bodily aspects of the virtual world, for example, their choice between a limited and insufficient number of different avatars, contributes to shape the roles and rules of their social interaction. In the context of basic, everyday classroom activities, students' social interaction and communication in the virtual world take unexpected and interesting forms. For example, in the virtual world course analyzed in this chapter, one form of student interaction resembled the famous Wild West gunfight between the gangs at the OK Corral in Tombstone. Such unexpected projections in time and place of groups of people will be psychologically real and unpleasant to the participants, who are surprised by the scenarios in which they suddenly become involved. Furthermore, such unusual forms of online social class interaction are difficult to understand if we look at the communication only from a mass media perspective or interface design perspective. We need to find a concept that bridges the two areas. One useful bridging concept between computer-mediated communication and human computer interaction is the concept of online "sociability", which has been investigated from sociological, technological, and mass communication perspectives (Preece, 2000). In this chapter, I wish to add to the knowledge of online sociability by presenting a psychological perspective on sociability to support the analysis, design, and evaluation of online communities and networked communication.

Background

Since the beginning of the information and communication technology era, the concept of sociability has been important to practitioners and researchers. For example, Willoughby (1972) described the individual software programmer's personal ability to socially interact with other people as a sociability issue, and Mantei (1981) discussed the sociability requirements of small teams of computer consultants who should be able to communicate with users as well as technical specialists. This early psychological view of sociability within information and communication technology environments needs to be updated in the light of recent technological and theoretical advances.

With the emergence of the Internet, the concept of sociability has gained a renewed interest within information and communication technology design as an approach to express and study (mostly negative) social aspects of technology (Kiesler, 1998). Studies show that users do not become more sociable by the new networked communication facilities offered by the Internet, and that the time Internet users spend online actually reduces interpersonal interaction and communication in much the same way as watching television does (Nie, 2001; Nie & Hillygus, 2002). It is argued that it is a fundamental mistake to think that the role of networked communication is to maintain or develop spatially remote social ties; we will not acquire new friends simply because we have access to the Internet, and most of the social ties that we maintain by telephone are based on blood relations (Gourna & Smoreda, 2003).

However, there are also positive social effects from participating in dedicated social activities on the Internet, that is, activities aimed at social interaction where the alternative is little or no social interaction. Today, a great deal of the (inter-)networked communication takes place within various online communities: communities of practice, communities of interest, communities of learning, health support communities, and so forth. New technology for networked communication seems to work as a principle that organizes the social ties where urban mechanisms no longer work (in big cities, large buildings, institutions and companies, etc.). It provides new facilities for creating a convivial proximity requiring coordination of time among family members and friends (meeting friends in town, women's night work, etc.) (Gourna & Smoreda, 2003). However, planning and designing successful networked communication in emergent online communities requires more than just designing human-computer interaction (usability); it requires planning of sociability (de Souza & Preece, 2004).

The planning of sociability in online communities has been well researched in recent years. We now know how sociability is related to networked communication in terms of the success of online communities. The success of an online community can be measured in terms of the numbers of participating people, the number and interactivity of the discussions, and the kind of policies employed (Preece, 2001). Relevant sociability measures of success include classification and counting of uncivil communication behaviour, such as abusive language, and issues of trustworthiness, such as adherence to procedures to make the trustworthiness of e-commerce action vendors explicit. Other sociability measures of success include counting the number of "lurkers", that is, people who read or see the communication content without contributing with own messages, counting the amount of on-topic conversations, the reciprocity in giving and taking questions and answers in discussion threads, and so forth (Preece, 2001). A further development of the environment measures designed specifically to enhance social interaction may be based on validated instruments, such as the social space scale, the social presence scale, and the sociability scales (Kreijns, Kirschner, Jochems, & Van Buuren, 2004). It is argued that we will soon have valid and reliable measures of sociability.

However, measures of sociability need to be interpreted within theoretical frameworks. Currently, a semiotic and sociological framework may be used to support evaluators, designers, moderators, and users in identifying and understanding sociability problems (de Souza & Preece, 2004). The idea is that online communities have three constituents. First, an online community constituent with four ontological elements: community, people, purposes, and policies. Second, an interpretative constituent, testing the adequacy of the community's communication behaviour by applying a base of culturally determined signs systems (signs in the semiotic sense, such as common conversational signs familiar to any speaker of a given language). Third, the usability and sociability constituent examining both individual attributes, such as trust and reciprocity, and collective sociability attributes, such as community culture (de Souza & Preece, 2004). This framework can be used to analyze particular instantiations of the general online community concept. For example, it has been used to analyze an education support community and suggest changes in the design of the community's software (de Souza & Preece, 2004). Further research related to the framework may locate it within other theories, for example, within a psychological theory (de Souza & Preece, 2004).

Empirical studies, in particular ethnographic research into online sociability on the Internet and in virtual worlds, have helped unveil sociability phenomena in networked communication. In all their complexity and unpredictability, these online phenomena are to some degree similar to phenomena known from sociability in off-line settings. For example, the off-line sociability emerging in American-Israeli family dinner conversations (Blum-Kulka, 1997) resembles the complex composition of roles and behaviours that may emerge in the communication behaviour in online communities, even in an online community with an undifferentiated technology for support of sociability (Maloney-Krichmar & Preece, 2005). Emergence of such complex behaviour makes externally-driven governance of the community unnecessary, because newcomers will learn to behave simply by deducing suitable roles (e.g. task roles, socio-emotional roles, individualistic roles) from reading the existing threads in the community and following the norms suggested by the roles (Maloney-Krichmar & Preece, 2005).

Another example of the complexity and unpredictability involved in online sociability is the effect of Internet usage (Kiesler, 1998), which, contrary to early predictions, shows that people actually benefit socially from participating in online communities. They find information, emotional and esteem support as well as humour in their exchanges with other community members (Braithwaite et al. in Maloney-Krichmar & Preece, 2005).

A third example of the complexity of online sociability and its comparability with off-line sociability involves studies of online communication acts in the home, which shows that people plan the time and place of personal conversations, even telephoning the other person to arrange the best time for a personal exchange. In addition to the specialization of space, there seems to be a homophily of contacts, that is, people mostly communicate online with people of the same sex they already know and are actually quite inaccessible to other possible communication partners (Gourna & Smoreda, 2003).

A fourth example of the complexity of online sociability is the identification of dedicated places for sociability in massive multiplayer games, which shows that online "cantinas", just like off-line cantinas, help facilitate the long periods of inactivity that may be necessary to enable sociability to occur. This indicates that it is important for the development of sociability to promote regularity, maintain the most active socializers among the community members, and partition the social space by making separate rooms in the cantina.

A fifth example of online sociability's complexity is the (positive and negative) evident changes in thinking and values of first-time participants in an (online) community, which by design allows culturally non-accepted behaviour, despite the participants' intention to use the communication medium in accordance with their original cultural values (Al-Saggaf & Weckert, 2004).

A sixth example is a lower sociability threshold (do not talk about personal issues) and an upper sociability threshold (do not discuss general differences among people) supporting newsgroup participants' sociability in the original, playful, sociological sense of the word (see Rutter & Smith, 1999; Simmel & Hughes, 1949).

These examples of ethnographic research into online social interaction suggest that it may be better to focus on the development of strong group norms through moderation and reinforcement of positive group behaviour and partition of the conversational space by a good design, rather than inhibiting inappropriate behaviour by rules and policies to support emerging online communities. Such a focus underscores the need for a psychological study of group perception and the role of communication in sociability.

Technology studies of social support technology illustrate various design possibilities to support sociability. Attempts have been made to develop a technology with "social affordances"—that is, a technology with properties that facilitate a social context by providing salient information to all about users and enabling communication with other users for example (Kreijns, Kirschner, & Jochems, 2002). A concrete attempt to develop such a technology is the design of personal devices with built-in "social functionality", that is, the aspects of a device explicitly designed for eliciting sociability (Constas & Papadopoulos, 2001). Sociability does not even have to be an explicit goal for a user of a product, but the design brings it to a user's mind when he or she uses the device. An example is the design of a bracelet that allows the user to withdraw money from an ATM and functions as a piece of jewelry as well. In addition, the latter function may increase the enjoyment of being together with others (Constas & Papadopoulos, 2001).

Another example of a technology that appropriates social affordances is the support of online shopping by developing shared browsers designed to allow people to enjoy (developing) common ground while shopping together online (Farnham, Zaner, & Cheng, 2001) and by adhering to usability and sociability principles in the design of an online customer service chat (Andrews & Haworth, 2002). Similarly, the sociability of computer-supported collaborative learning may be supported by social contextual facilitators such as a group awareness widget providing a learner group with awareness of the other group members and, furthermore, providing the learner group with a particular focus on off-task interactions of central importance to the social and psychological experience of sociability (Kreijns et al., 2002). Communities of science teachers may be supported by a Web-based tool designed in relation to the "visiting-the-classroom" metaphor aiming to foster sustained participation and a sense of ownership (Barab, MaKinster, Moore, & Cunningham, 2001). Students in classrooms may be supported by software allowing them to be co-constructors of their own learning environment, which makes them perceive the tasks as more fun and sociable (Ryberg & Ponti, 2004). In summary, technology studies have identified design possibilities for technology that support social interaction and pointed to the importance of technology that allows the human user an active role in the design of online sociability.

We, therefore, have a sociological concept of sociability in online communities, a semiotic framework for analyzing and understanding sociability in communities and measures for evaluating online communities. We also have ethnographic accounts of online sociability phenomena as well as technological solutions to a number of sociability problems in a diverse set of environments. The rest of this chapter will present an updated psychological concept of sociability that takes up the thread from an early understanding of sociability within the information and communication field by looking at the social skills and knowledge of individuals and small groups.

A Social Reality Theory of Online Sociability

In this section, I will present a social reality theory of online sociability based on the role of psychological essentialism and group perception in online sociability. Group perception, or the social ontology of groups, deals with how to determine whether an aggregate of individuals is an entity or not. From a psychological viewpoint, the process involves a human capacity for visually analyzing very rapidly whether we confront a group-like entity, that is, whether a number of individuals really is a group in our eyes. In order to visually experience groups of people rapidly, we use gestalt principles such as proximity, similarity, and common fate in much the same way as we use gestalt principles to perceive groups of objects (Campbell, 1958).

Our psychological sense of the reality of a social group is strengthened by ongoing mutual verification of collective intentionality. We always confirm each other in a group where we share the same target. How do we do that? Symbols are cultural; they are entities based on implicit or explicit social agreements. However, they are also used to create such social agreements. In other words, cultural symbols and social agreements are locked together in a seamless process that verifies our collective intentionality. In this process, human language communication plays a major role as an activity that binds culture and social reality together (Kashima, 2004).

Culture produces shared symbols that enable people to construct their social reality. In turn, social reality underpins the cultural symbols that helped construct the social reality in the first place. It is the communicative act that launches the process. This cycle creates the psychological sense of social reality. For example, an Indian student may discuss a drawing of Ganesh, the Hindu elephant god, with me, a visiting researcher. The nature of this drawing (new to me, familiar to the student, etc.) provides the opportunity for creating a social reality with me as a guest and the student as a representative for the host. The possible social relation is underscored and supported by our communication, which reveals that the student considers me and my knowledge to be on the tourist level and thus different from and inferior to the other Indian students' and professors' knowledge of Ganesh. Subsequently, our communication about the Ganesh symbol and our tiny, dyadic social reality will maintain and perhaps develop the newly created social reality. Figure 1 shows a visual illustration of the process. The figure has been adapted and developed from the figure in Kashima (2004, p. 263) to focus on the production of various forms of online sociability. Figure 1 illustrates the triadic relationship between *cultural symbols* (such as the Ganesh symbol in the earlier example), *social reality* (in networked communication enabled by the technologies of human-computer interaction (HCI) & computer-supported cooperative work (CSCW)) and *communication* processes (which in networked communication is synonymous with computer-mediated communication (CMC)). Placing online sociability between social reality and communication indicates how online sociability emerges both from computer-mediated communication between humans and from individual and cooperative computer-supported interaction with environments. Figure 1 also illustrates how the processes may result in various forms of online sociability.

I call my adaptation of the psychological group perception theory to online sociability issues, as illustrated in Figure 1, the "social reality theory of online sociability". With this theory, I suggest that we think of sociability as the psychological sense of social reality. Therefore, measuring sociability means measuring the psychological

Figure 1. The production of various forms of online sociability

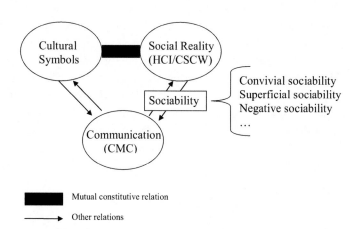

sense of social reality, which is not a component of a theoretical framework but rather an emerging, dynamic phenomenon. Being sociable means displaying a good personal sense of social reality, and designing support of sociability means designing support for the psychological sense of reality. If we take into account that cultural symbols are mutual constitutive with HCI/CSCW realities, sociability becomes a bridge between CMC and HCI/CSCW in various ways.

Social reality theory of sociability focuses on the human experience of social reality. This makes the theory different from other attempts to formulate a social psychological theory of online sociability. For example, the theory of social affordance and sociability of computer-supported cooperative learning environments (Kreijns et al., 2002) defines sociability as *the extent* to which the computer-supported cooperative learning environment gives rise to a social space. If we compare this theory with the social reality model of sociability, the computer-supported cooperative learning environment including the social affordances may be understood as a repository of cultural symbols and the social space as a kind of social reality emerging from communication in media that allows and supports social presence. However, this affordance-based concept of sociability is not psychological in nature, but only an environment attribute: "Sociability is a strength or potential associated with an environment", (Kreijns et al., 2002, p. 10). While the social affordance theory argues that sociability is a quality of an environment, the social reality theory maintains that sociability is a human experience.

This chapter advocates that sociability in a psychological sense depends on specific cultural symbols and social reality(ies) as well as the concrete communication processes that develop and maintain the relations. As researchers, we are part of this communication. Depending on which relations in the social reality model (arrows in Figure 1) we choose to investigate, we will obtain a certain view of online sociability. Conversely, our perspective will become focused on particular relations in the model if we investigate particular phenomena of social reality.

When a group becomes part of a social reality, people develop a sense that the group's existence is out of their control or beyond manipulation. This describes psychological essentialism (Kashima, 2004). In other words, the existence of a particular group with (a) a perceived similarity in the members' goal-directed activity, (b) perceived member characteristics such as appearance and character, and (c) a perceived physical location may gradually become an implicit assumption in peoples' everyday reasoning. Subsequently, it becomes very hard for the group and group members to alter the group's characteristics (Kashima, 2004). For online sociability, psychological essentialism means that groups seemingly exist outside human control or manipulation by HCI/CSCW design or CMC activities and that any online group may become just as real and hard to alter as any off-line group.

Illustrating the Social Reality Theory of Online Sociability

In this section, I will illustrate and apply the social reality theory of online sociability to unexpected and seemingly unusual social interactions in a university-level virtual world course (which I offered) on computer-supported cooperative work and online communities. I will present my perspective on the forms of interaction and communication that emerge in networked communication and relate these to the thesis of sociability as a bridge between HCI/CSCW and CMC. In addition, I will advance my position that this bridge can only be built if we include cultural symbols in the model of social reality. Furthermore, the analysis will show that users are active in designing their own sociability experiences. However, they are not successful in all cases, and therefore it is important to consider what designers and researchers may do to help users improve their sociability experiences.

In the following, I draw on material from a virtual world (Active World®) session that I held with my graduate students at a course on CSCW and online communities. At this session, they were supposed to present their experiments with online and off-line small-group cooperation about a task (Towers of Hanoi). Their presentations were to be made in the Active World® online environment during a two-hour long session, where everyone was physically located either at home or at various computers at the university campus. As part of the setup, I conducted a post-session evaluation the following week when all the students met me face-to-face in the classroom. In the evaluation, I interviewed and moderated the students and discussed their experiences during the online session, while I showed them the screen dumps presented and discussed next.

First, I discussed the "Meeting at the OK Corral", in which three male students presented a group of uniform gun-slingers confronting an unidentified enemy (see Figure 2). I introduced the non-verbal, implicit, silent, gender-specific, media-oriented, and cultural thinking that these young men revealed when I asked them in the classroom after the session why they chose their appearance as they did. Second, I analyzed the ways in which the students moved from presentation to presentation in the virtual world, and I reflected on why this very simple problem of moving together in a virtual world is considerably harder to solve than it appears to be at first. Third, I reported on an event, which was afterwards characterized as sexual harassment by an unknown student's avatar towards a female student who was the victim of the other avatar's closeness. Then I presented my observations on the students' implicit rules and roles of interactions in a case where one group had chosen to do their presentation high above the ground in the virtual world. Finally, I reported on how the students presented their results as facts in their poster sessions using unusually large poster formats. Together, these forms of interaction and communication may be explained by different aspects of sociability, but not without considering the context provided by the students' activation of highly diverse and sometimes misplaced cultural symbols.

Superficial Sociability: Meeting at the OK Corral

An important point in the social reality theory of sociability presented in Figure 1 is how cultural symbols and an HCI/CSCW-enabled social reality are mutual referents and together form a basis for experiencing a form of sociability in the CMC communication. This point will be illustrated by an analysis of an odd sociability experience related to the beginning of the course session when the students had gathered to watch the first group present their work (see Figure 2). The example illustrates and introduces what I call superficial sociability.

In the situation shown in Figure 2, three male students take a position as a group of uniform gun-slingers confronting an unidentified enemy, much like the standard configuration on the street of a small Western town in a Western movie. The three male avatars are at the same physical location and are similar in appearance, and the other participants in the virtual world session rapidly perceive them as a uniform group. Furthermore, their group activates the cultural symbol of Wild West gun-

Figure 2. Meeting at the OK Corral: An illustration of superficial sociability

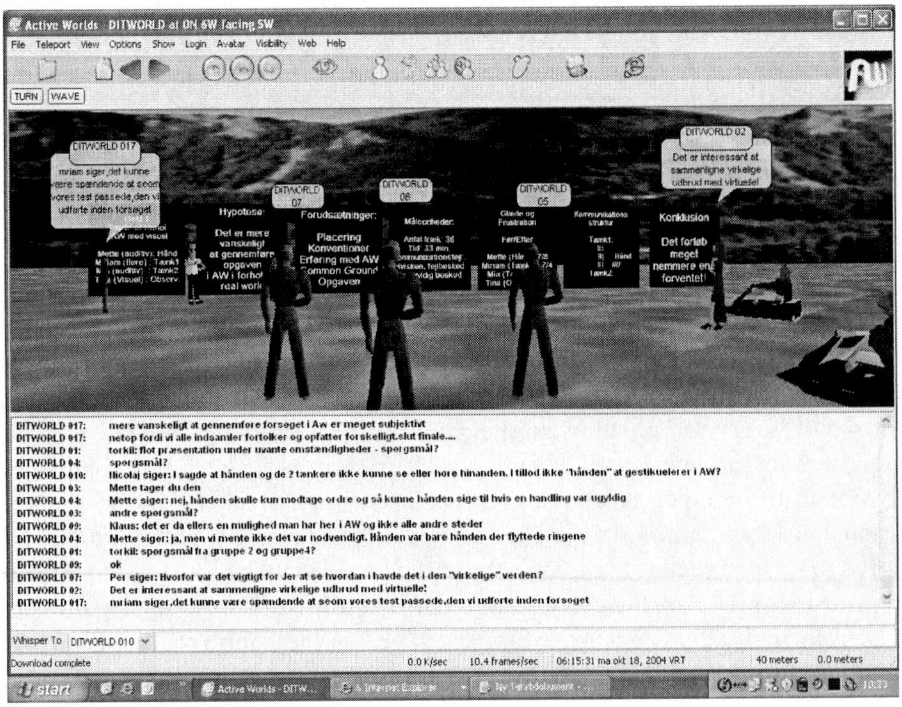

slingers due to their "spread out" position, "strong man" appearance, and similar names with subsequent numbering and visual cues suggesting a surrounding Wild West nature. If the group and the other students had been sitting on rows of chairs in a room with walls, that is, in a classroom-like setting instead of being surrounded by Wild West nature with mountains, and so forth, we would have known that they shared the same purpose, namely listening to a student presentation. None of this ambivalent reality, "Wild West social reality" vs. "listening student reality", is communicated in the online chat text, which only deals with the ongoing presentation and related questions and answers. However, in the discussion about their "Wild West appearance" following the virtual world session, the three students explained that they had selected three identical avatars in order to appear as a group, and the reason for their "spread out" location was to make the presentation appear more clearly. They had not attempted to design their common appearance at the presentation as a "threatening group" of gunslingers, as some of the participants said they were. On the other hand, they had not considered how they should look if they were to appear as "listeners" to other participants in the student presentation.

It is clear that the three students' psychological sense of social reality, their sociability, was only superficial. Their sociability was based on an apparent similarity in appearance and location, but lacked a clear common fate. Furthermore, it suffered from the wrong cultural symbols, that is, it suffered from the "Wild West nature" in the HCI/CSCW environment of the "Active World"®, and from a lack of a "listener" avatar or other cultural symbols that might be useful in the construction of a suitable social reality. Obviously, the students were not supported or encouraged to communicate about this during the session, for example, by being asked if they were a group, and if yes, what kind of group they were. Hence, the Wild West cultural symbols in the HCI/CSCW-enabled social reality formed a basis for experiencing a superficial sociability via the CMC communication. By their own explicit design and through very simple means of choosing similarity in appearance and physical location, the students managed to stand out as a group.

In contrast to the students' accomplishment, we know from previous work that so-called "third places", that is, online places dedicated to online sociability in particular and online environments in general, tend to erase individual distinctions between participants (Ducheneaut, Moore, & Nickell, 2004). Intuitively, this generalized experience always seems to be true. In virtual worlds, everybody tends to have a limited number of avatars to choose from, and they can do more or less similar things. However, the three gunslinger students in the Wild West example successfully designed and communicated a superficial sociability that made them stand out as a group compared to the other students. By supporting the production of this particular superficial sociability, they actually counteracted a potential levelling of all individual distinctions between the participants.

However, through the design of their appearance as a group, the students gained something they had not planned for: they appeared to be a threatening group. The idea of importing forms of social interaction from outside the online social reality is well known—and warned against—in research on sociability in computer-supported cooperative learning (Kreijns et al., 2002). The OK Corral example shows the importance of the social psychological dimension of social interaction outside the task context and how the (non-)communication about cultural symbols affects online sociability.

Convivial Sociability: Moving Collectively

According to the social reality theory of sociability, the CMC communication facilitates the participants' psychological sense of social reality, thus partly constructing their social reality and cultural symbols. This point will be illustrated by an analysis of an odd sociability experience in the course session when the students had finished their first group presentation and needed to move to another place in the virtual world to watch the next student group present their work (see Figure 3). As the

Figure 3. The communication and social situation after students and teacher had moved collectively to a new presentation site (The situation illustrates convivial sociability.)

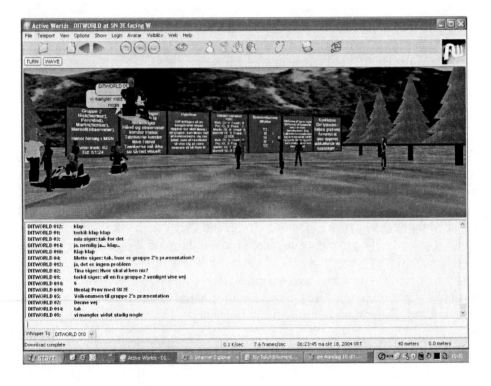

example shows, the students experienced convivial sociability, which I attempt to exemplify by indicating that the students' extensive communication allowed them to experience a common fate without superficially having to appear similar or be proximal in their location.

In the following excerpt from the chat communication (and in Danish in Figure 3), two students ask where they have to go now to watch the next presentation, and people begin to move away from the location in a scattered way. Out of the blue, the teacher asks for directions and a student from the presenting group provides geographical coordinates (see the following translation of this part of the communication in Figure 3):

> DITWORLD 04: Mette says: where is group 2's presentation?
>
> DITWORLD 012: Tina says: where are we going now?
>
> DITWORLD 01: Torkil (teacher) says: will somebody from group 2 please show the way?
>
> DITWORLD 010: Nicolaj says: try SH 2E
>
> DITWORLD 05: welcome to group 2's presentation
>
> DITWORLD 07: this way
>
> DITWORLD 014: thank you
>
> DITWORLD 05: apparently we are still missing some

Without warning and in a glimpse, we are in the social reality illustrated by Figure 3. The information from Nicolai appeared to be an address in the virtual world, which allowed participants to move immediately from the location of the first group presentation to the location of the next group presentation. In the new location, two of the presenting group members (DITWORLD 05 and DITWORLD 07) bid the participants welcome. While they were on their way, they have changed their avatars from the previous "gunslinger" avatars to "motorcycle" avatars. In the middle of the picture, we also see an avatar standing on its head. In other words, several quite different avatars are present. However, not all the students have arrived at the site yet—those who cannot figure out how to use the software to teleport themselves to the presentation site are "out", that is, they are left behind.

In the example, the students' limited and misplaced (out-of-class-room) vocabulary in the computer-mediated communication, the avatar-changing class-mates, and the social reality of the student presentation combine in an unusual sociability experience. It is unusual because the participants are in a world with a blue sky and have to find their way by using geographical coordinates instead of classroom numbers, and also because some of the students suddenly become motorcyclists. In an off-line class of students, who would ever ask a student on a motorcycle to make a presentation at, say, 56 degrees north, 10 degrees east? However, the students seem happy, positive, and polite towards each other. They say "this way" and "thank you" and they care for each other: "we are apparently still missing somebody". In their communication, they seem to make it clear that they are a student group. In this particular case, the students seem to regard the collective moving around as emotionally positive and rewarding.

In research on the rituals of sociability in CMC in health communities, it has been found that the enactment potential of "netiquette" is closely associated with the production of at least five features of positive, convivial sociability: "discussion thread" organization and content (standard discussion thread lengths will be borne out of the participants' everyday experience in the discussions), terms and techniques of address (recognizing who is being addressed, etc.), broadcast requests (such requests are met by advice and responses to advice), playful re-contextualization (to find new twists and turns in the development of a thread), and sociability thresholds (not too personal, e.g., report on one's own divorce problems, etc., and political and religious issues should not be discussed) (Rutter & Smith, 1999).

If we compare these research findings from the production of convivial sociability in health communities with the example presented in Figure 3, it is possible to see the rituals of sociability in the virtual world course and how they relate to communication: First, the (word) length of the statements by the students seems to be similar. Second, they make it clear who speaks by entering their real name as the first word in the statement—which is a very fast ritualization of communicative behaviour, since the students have only been online together for less than half an hour and it is the first time in their lives. Third, advice is given in terms of addresses and directions and acknowledged by the responding students. Fourth, the neutral addressing of the missing students (no names of fellow students and no positive or negative generalization of the missing students) in Figure 3 may be seen as an example of sociability thresholds in action.

A theoretical understanding of convivial sociability will help us define online sociability qualitatively in contrast to definitions of *degrees* or *extent* of sociability (Kreijns et al., 2004). Convivence, "living together" in the working environment, in organizations is a human experience that should not result in any degree of suffering and human intolerance (Avallone, Sinangil, & Caetano, 2005). In contrast to the current theoretical interpretation of the enactment of netiquette in online communities, which merely suggests that an appropriate netiquette leads to "discourses of friendliness" (see Rutter & Smith, 1999), the social reality theory of online sociability offers an interpretation rooted in an understanding of the importance of communicating about cultural symbols and social reality to produce online sociability.

Negative (Violent) Sociability: What's Going On?

The part of the psychological model of sociability in Figure 1 illustrated in the next example deals with how the nature of the available cultural symbols obstructs a human-like CMC communication. This creates a stiff social reality, which some experience as an odd or even violent sociability.

The (odd) sociability experience presented in the next example involves the students' second group presentation (see Figure 4). In the left hand side of the picture, one of the students has changed into an airship avatar, which hovers over the ground. In the central part of the picture, the student who uses a male motorcycle avatar DITWORLD 012 runs his avatar into the female avatar DITWORLD 017, who does not react to being run over. Otherwise, the presentation proceeds as shown in the written communication. However, the next time the class met face-to-face, the student whose avatar had been run over explained upon being asked that she had felt it unpleasant and obtrusive to be hit by the motorcycle avatar, but she did not know what to do about it. When the female student delivered her term report one month later, she had written about the incident and her experience of being run down several times although she luckily survived. When presented with the

Figure 4. What's going on? The experience of violent online sociability

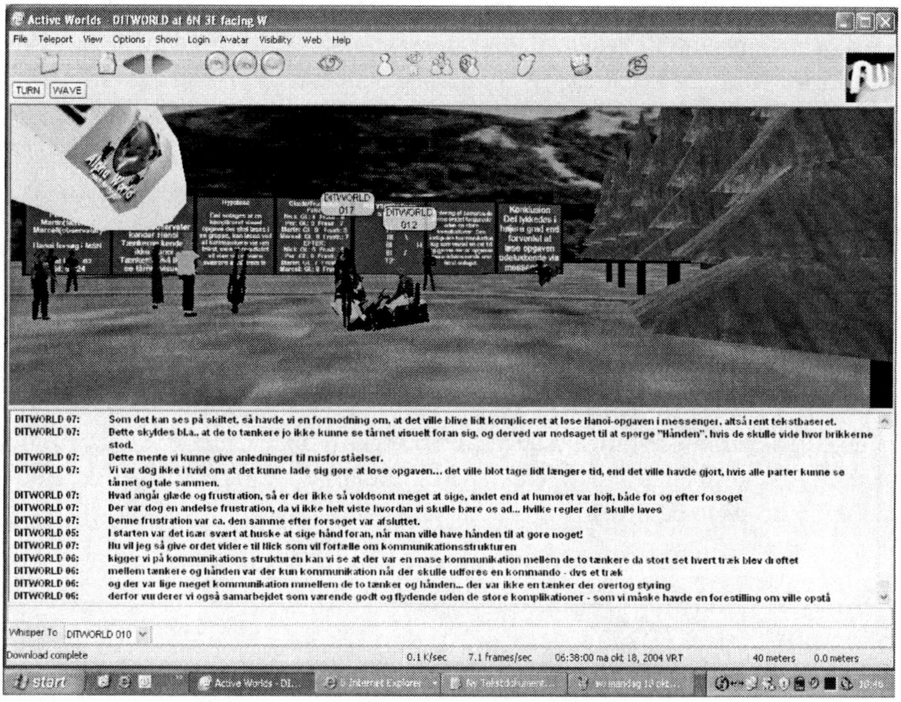

chance to speak about this again two months later at the individual oral exam, she voluntarily returned to the event and spoke about it as molestation. In this way, the social reality to which she referred had extended beyond a brief event, and it was still not entirely clear what had actually happened.

The airship avatar as well as the motorcycle avatar refer to a peculiar transportation reality considering that the activity going on is a student presentation. The students cannot really talk about how it is to be an airship or a motorcycle (!), which prevents an alteration of reality. Instead, one student uses his new motorcycle body to communicate non-verbally (as one typically does with a motorcycle) with another student's avatar and this is experienced as a molesting form of sociability in the student presentation reality. The cultural symbols available in the online social reality refer to a violent sociability that cannot be communicated openly and explicitly[1].

While there is a substantial body of research on avatar violence, which might be discussed in relation to the molestation of the female student, the example also illustrates another point: participants in networked communication such as the male student may have good social skills, even if they fail to show these skills in online environments. Findings from empirical studies of general Internet use suggest that users do not become more sociable because they have used the Internet. But they tend to display a higher degree of social connectivity because as a group they are better educated, better off financially, and younger than the population on average (Nie, 2001). This line of argument suggests that the young male online molesters in our example may have above average social skills and still end up in a molesting situation in the online environment. However, if we interpret the male student's behaviour as a result of inadequate designed technology, we need to be aware that the other (female) student actually experienced the event very negatively.

In summary, the examples illustrate that communicating about cultural symbols and social reality produces different sociability(ies). *Convivial sociability* is the psychological sense of a social reality associated with a communicative coherence in different ways of being, speaking, and perceiving each other, as in the example with the students accepting the strange new experience of moving collectively online. *Superficial sociability* is the psychological sense of a social reality associated with a similarity in appearance and location, but not necessarily with a shared purpose as in the example with the three gunslingers at the OK Corral and the other students. *Negative sociability* is the psychological sense of a social reality associated with technology determined, intrusive social acts. This list of different qualities of online sociability is not exhaustive. More aspects might be added and each sociability experience needs to be investigated in detail.

Solutions and Recommendations

The analysis suggests that users are active in designing their own sociability experiences, although they are not successful in all cases. Unusual forms of online social interactions emerge such as superficial sociability and convivial sociability, but also negative sociability. What can we do as designers and researchers to help users' improve their sociability experiences?

First, we must acknowledge that designers of online communities supply the cultural symbols that through computer-mediated communication form and direct participants' psychological sense of the HCI/CSCW enabled social reality—we determine the conditions for the sociability experienced by the participants. Some conditions are not optimal; it is not easy to address other people if you are a motorcycle or an airship. In the virtual world course, the students should have had the opportunity to choose wise, clever looking and listening avatars within an auditorium with a high respect for academia and with means of communication to support the students' small group presentations.

As designers, we should aim at creating cultural symbols that fit the sociability experience, which we want our users to have. However, there are no simple solutions. One approach might be to write a clear set of rules for presentations in the virtual world as suggested by the framework for online communities (de Souza & Preece, 2004), or to moderate the different phases of the community's life as suggested by research into portal management (Damsgaard, 2002) and practitioners (Kim, 2000; Powazek, 2002). However, I recommend applying the social reality theory of online sociability outlined in this chapter. Application of the social reality theory makes it possible to design and support online sociability with an emphasis on providing rich and relevant cultural symbols, and means of communication and feedback about the experienced social reality. The social reality theory of sociability also takes psychological essentialism into account. When a group is perceived as part of a social reality, people feel that the group's existence is out of their control or beyond manipulation. As designers of networked communication, we must theoretically understand what kind of group we design and support. The apparent existence of a cluster of people becomes an assumption in peoples' everyday reasoning when the group has an apparent similarity in their goal-directed activities, their characteristics such as appearance and disposition and their physical location. It becomes very hard for the group and group members to alter the group's characteristics (Kashima, 2004). For example, the three students who designed themselves as Wild West gunslingers should be aware of the consequences of their choice for the production of online sociability and social reality. The groups we design have long-lasting consequences for the members of these groups.

Second, negative sociability must be identified and treated appropriately whenever it occurs. In terms of the social reality theory, negative sociability may be caused by a lack of communication about cultural symbols and social reality. To identify negative sociability, it is therefore necessary to name it as such when it occurs. For example, in the context of the virtual world course, any violation of personal space should be addressed by the other students or the moderator (the teacher) in the (perhaps) same way as it is done in off-line classrooms. This again may require that the students are trained in social skills by following a standard behavioural program for training social skills. Such a program will teach them both the environmental social skills required to perform tasks in educational settings, such as listening to other student presentations, in addition to interactional social skills to help them start, maintain, and end all kinds of social interactions, such as making new friends in a class. Training of such social skills has been developed to facilitate cooperation in special work settings such as maritime emergencies (Clemmensen, 2001) and to help people with special difficulties in everyday social contacts (Clemmensen, Martinussen, & Skanning, 2000). These efforts may teach online community and networked communication designers to design and plan training in social skills for online users. Furthermore, it is important to add to the reasons for development of social skills provided by the general literature on social skills training. An individual may not possess an appropriate repertoire of social actions, or perhaps he or she has had insufficient opportunities to practice such actions. He or she may also suffer from emotional problems, which makes it difficult to apply the skills. As illustrated in the example on negative online sociability, all these reasons may gain a new actuality when a person moves from off-line social interaction to online social interaction. This shift in context presents new application areas and content development for social skills training and support, which may be topics for further research.

Third, superficial sociability is relevant in many situations. As humans, we often want to be like others superficially to feel at least a small sense of belonging to a group. This experience is also valid online. To support online sociability, the gestalt principles of similarity and proximity, on which the social reality theory is partly based, may be used to develop practical solutions. In virtual world courses, one solution may involve what I call "group appearance patterns", that is, a set of avatars designed to appear immediately as distinct from other avatars, but similar to each other. This will further an easy and effective administration as well as the creation of superficial sociability. Another practical solution within the same context is to provide a set of "listeners", "presenters", "opponents", and so forth—that is, provide the students with a pre-choice of relevant avatars instead of motorcycles and the like. A third solution is to provide predefined behavioural settings for different human activities such as student presentations with built-in separate locations for each student group. The main point is in online environments to develop and use our ability to design positively for similarity in appearance and for proximity in location. In off-line situations, we are already very skilled in practicing superficial sociability when we dress up for a party or try to stand physically close to the group we want to belong to, for example.

Fourth, the real positive challenge is to design in order to support convivial sociability. Our psychological sense of a social group's reality is strengthened by ongoing mutual verification of collective intentionality, that is, we constantly confirm each other in the group that we share the same target. To the extent that the participants in online communities and networked communication share a common fate, they may through extensive communication experience sociability without having to be similar in appearance or proximal in location, for example, convivial sociability. According to the social reality theory, such sociability will emerge when a number of people have an extensive communication with and about cultural symbols and social reality. These communication processes may result in the creation of new psychological perceptions in terms of new cultural models for communication acts at home (Gourna & Smoreda, 2003), for social shopping in online stores (Farnham et al., 2001), for online cantinas (Ducheneaut et al., 2004), and for customer service chat (Andrews & Haworth, 2002), and so forth.

To understand the production of convivial online sociability better, we may enhance the social reality theory by applying two current approaches to the role of communication in the construction of social reality: the articulation work theory and the sociability work theory. The articulation work theory deals with establishing conventions that are materialized in some artefact (Carla, Gloria, & Dario, 1999), such as patterns for cooperation in safety critical environments (Stanard & Wampler, 2005). If it involves the production of convivial online sociability, the articulation work requires a careful consideration of how much invisible online work can and should be made visible. On the one hand, ignoring invisible work may lead to unwanted social consequences (e.g., some participants may have to ask all the questions pertaining to where to go, what to do, and so forth, without receiving any acknowledgement for their work). On the other hand, if the work is made visible in an artefact, it also becomes objective, emotionless, and an object that can be monitored by the authorities (e.g., if group creation is supported by formal procedures to replace the often emotionally charged processes of group creation) (Star & Strauss, 1999). The sociability work theory defines sociability work as the activities involved in implementing community and charity events (Blackstone, 2004). This kind of work usually has two components: (1) sociability workers must motivate and maintain other volunteer workers by, for example, acting as role models, and (2) sociability workers must motivate and maintain donors and event participants by creating an atmosphere that will make people interested in participating (Blackstone, 2004). One important finding from the research in sociability work is that this kind of work involves costs—personal as well as financial. People involved in this kind of work (usually women) may spend many unpaid work hours and face exhaustion when they prepare for a community event. The articulation and sociability work theories are both useful additions to the social reality theory. The articulation work theory provides us with a tool for making invisible work visible, and the sociability work theory helps us analyze the communication about motivation and social atmosphere. In addition, both theories provide the analysis of online sociability with notions of power and hierarchy in social relations. However, unlike the social reality theory, the theories do not give us access to the users' psychological sense of online social reality.

Future Trends

One important emerging trend in the literature on online sociability is the prospect of a positive influence of media-life-existence on individuals off-line as well as online (Maloney-Krichmar & Preece, 2005). Despite negative expectations (Kiesler, 1998) and negative findings (Nie & Hillygus, 2002) on the impact of Internet use on people's sociability, a dedicated use of technology to support online sociability might have positive benefits. Benefits derived from sharing community knowledge (Clemmensen, 2004) and from shared comfort, humour, and support (Maloney-Krichmar & Preece, 2005) are important outcomes of online sociability. The social reality theory of online sociability should be of value to future research in terms of providing a perspective on online sociability that may encompass and relate to both psychological, sociological, and media theories while keeping a psychological perspective on sociability. For example, it is clear that future studies of the enactment of netiquette may contribute to the social reality theory of online sociability. Such research may show how inclusive and open communication processes lead to a non-discriminating online social reality and to the experience of a convivial sociability, given that available cultural symbols (such as appropriate student avatars) are used in the computer-mediated communication between participants. An important future research opportunity is to study how designers and researchers' support and design may improve users' experience of being together and having a common fate online without necessarily being similar in appearance or proximal in location, that is, the investigation of the phenomenological details of the production of convivial sociability.

Conclusion

This chapter has reviewed current approaches to online sociability and presented a psychological theory, the social reality theory, to explain online sociability as the psychological sense of social reality. Results from an analysis of a university-level virtual world course have been used to illustrate different kinds of online sociability: superficial, convivial, and negative sociability. The chapter provides solutions and recommendations to designers and researchers with a focus on online communities and networked communication.

Today, online sociability is a frequent experience for millions of people and will be for many more people across the world in the years to come. This chapter has in an implicit way focused on what is known in cognitive anthropology and cultural psychology as *cultural models*. Obviously, the experience of sociability is an outcome of complex and culture-specific structures and processes. In practice, this means that planning the sociability of both the products and the dynamic social processes in a knowledge creating context, such as a university course, only constitutes half the design for networked communications; the other half involves the understanding of how people with different cultural backgrounds actually use the processes and products. To this end, we need to understand different cultural practices in terms of cultural models for classroom performance, romance or flirt, collective movements, and so forth, both off-line and online and to design and support human forms of online sociability accordingly.

References

Al-Saggaf, Y., & Weckert, J. (2004). The effects of participation in online communities on individuals in saudi arabia. *SIGCAS Comput. Soc., 34*(1), 1.

Andrews, D. C., & Haworth, K. N. (2002). Online customer service chat: Usability and sociability issues. *Journal of Internet Marketing, 2*(1). Retrieved from http://www.arraydev.com/commerce/jim/

Avallone, F., Sinangil, H. K., & Caetano, A. (2005). *Convivence in organizations and society* (Vol. 12). Milano: Guerini Studio.

Barab, S. A., MaKinster, J. G., Moore, J. A., & Cunningham, D. J. (2001). Designing and building an on-line community: The struggle to support sociability in the inquiry learning forum. *Etr&D-Educational Technology Research and Development, 49*(4), 71-96.

Blackstone, A. M. (2004). Sociability, work, and gender. *Equal Opportunities International, 23*(3-5), 29-45.

Blum-Kulka, S. (1997). *Dinner talk – Cultural patterns of sociability and socialization in family discourse*. London: Lawrence Erlbaum.

Campbell, D. T. (1958). Common fate, similarity, and other indices of the status of aggregates of persons as social entities. *Behavioral Science, 3*, 14-25.

Carla, S., Gloria, M., & Dario, G. (1999). Interoperability as a means of articulation work. In *Proceedings of the International Joint Conference on Work Activities*

Coordination and Collaboration, San Francisco, CA, February 22-25 (pp. 39-48). New York: ACM Press.

Clemmensen, T. (2001). *Tacit social knowledge in safety critical situations (poster).* In *ECSCW – European Conference on Computer Supported Cooperative Work,* Bonn, Germany, September 16-20 (pp. 1-2). Kluwer.

Clemmensen, T. (2004). Community knowledge in an emerging online professional community: The case of sigchi.dk. *Knowledge and Process Management, 11*(2), 1-10.

Clemmensen, T., Martinussen, M., & Skanning, D. (2000). *Knowledge and skills in early psychosis: Implications for training (abstract).* Paper presented at the 13th International Symposium for the Psychological Treatments of Schizophrenia, The Stavanger Forum Conference Centre, Stavanger, Norway, June 5-9.

Constas, I., & Papadopoulos, D. (2001). Interface-me: Pursuing sociability through personal devices. *Personal Ubiquitous Computing, 5*(3), 195-200.

Damsgaard, J. (2002). Managing an Internet portal. *Communications of the Association for Information Systems, 9,* 408-420.

de Souza, C. S., & Preece, J. (2004). A framework for analyzing and understanding online communities. *Interacting with Computers, 16*(3), 579-610.

Ducheneaut, N., Moore, R. J., & Nickell, E. (2004). Designing for sociability in massively multiplayer games: An examination of the "third places" of swg, *Other Players.* IT University of Copenhagen, Denmark.

Farnham, S., Zaner, M., & Cheng, L. (2001). *Supporting sociability in a shared browser.* Paper presented at the Interact 2001, Tokyo, Japan, July 9-13.

Gourna, C. d., & Smoreda, Z. (2003). Communication technology and sociability: Between local ties and "global ghetto"? In J. E. Katz (Ed.), *Machines that become us: The social context of personal communication technology* (pp. 57-70). New Brunswick, NJ: Transaction Publishers.

Kashima, Y. (2004). Culture, communication and entitativity – A social psychological investigation of social reality. In V. Yzerbyt, C. M. Judd, & O. Corneille (Eds.), *The psychology of group perception – Perceived variability, entitativity and essentialism* (pp. 257-274). NY: Psychology Press.

Kiesler, S. (1998). An Internet paradox (panel): A social medium that may undermine sociability. In *Proceedings of the 1998 ACM Conference on Computer Supported Cooperative Work,* Seattle, Washington, November 14-18 (p. 403). New York: ACM Press.

Kim, A. J. (2000). *Community building on the Web – Secret strategies for succesful online communities.* Berkeley, CA: Peachbit Press.

Kreijns, K., Kirschner, P. A., & Jochems, W. (2002). The sociability of computer-supported collaborative learning environments. *Educational Technology & Society, 5*(1), 8-22.

Kreijns, K., Kirschner, P. A., Jochems, W., & Van Buuren, H. (2004). Determining sociability, social space, and social presence in (a)synchronous collaborative groups. *CyberPsychology & Behavior, 7*(2), 155-172.

Maloney-Krichmar, D., & Preece, J. (2005). A multilevel analysis of sociability, usability, and community dynamics in an online health community. *ACM Transactions of Computer-Human Interaction, 12*(2), 201-232.

Mantei, M. (1981). The effect of programming team structures on programming tasks. *Communications of the ACM, 24*(3), 106-113.

Nie, N. H. (2001). Sociability, interpersonal relations, and the Internet: Reconciling conflicting findings. *The American Behavioral Scientist, 45*(3), 420-435.

Nie, N. H., & Hillygus, D. S. (2002). The impact of Internet use on sociability: Time-diary findings. *IT& Society, 1*(1), 1-20.

Powazek, D. M. (2002). *Design for community – The art of connecting real people in virtual places*. Indianapolis, IN: New Riders.

Preece, J. (2000). *Online communities – Designing usability, supporting sociability*. New York: John Wiley.

Preece, J. (2001). Sociability and usability in online communities: Determining and measuring success. *Behaviour & Information Technology, 20*(5), 347 - 356.

Rutter, J., & Smith, G. W. H. (1999). Ritual aspects of CMC sociability. In *Esprit i3 Workshop on Ethnographic Studies in Real and Virtual Communities*, Queen Margaret University College, Edinburgh, January 24-26 (pp. 113-122).

Ryberg, T., & Ponti, M. (2004). *Rethinking virtual space as a place for sociability: Theory and design implications*. Paper presented at the Networked Learning Conference 2004, Lancaster University, England, UK, April 5-7.

Simmel, G., & Hughes, E. C. (1949). The sociology of sociability. *American Journal of Sociology, 55*(3), 254-261.

Stanard, T., & Wampler, J. (2005). *Work-centered user interface patterns*. Paper presented at the INTERACT 2005, Rome, Italy, September 12-16.

Star, S. L., & Strauss, A. (1999). Layers of silence, arenas of voice: The ecology of visible and invisible work. *CSCW, 8*, 9-30.

Willoughby, T. C. (1972). Staffing the MIS function. *ACM Computing Surveys, 4*(4), 241-259.

Endnote

[1]   The history of online communities show that from the very beginning molesting has occurred, see http://www.rider.edu/~suler/psycyber/palhistory.html, downloaded September 2005.

Chapter XI

Designing Control of Computer-Mediated Gifting in Sharing Networks

Jörgen Skågeby
Linköping University, Sweden

Abstract

This chapter suggests that the pro-social provision, or gifting, of goods in multiple user sharing networks is largely determined by the relationship an individual has to the larger group(s) of which he or she is a member. This relationship is often referred to as a social dilemma and can be both a conflict of interest or a pattern of cooperation reflecting a predicament in acting in self-interest versus the interest of the collective (or different groups of the collective). In this chapter, the social dilemma is modelled by the relationship model, which operates for end users on a tactical level of control and thus sets a general path of performance. Once a specific gifting act is included in such a tactic, five dimensions of control are also suggested, which operates on a situated sociotechnical level. The dynamics of sharing networks makes gifting a continuous re-negotiation between reactive actions and overall tactics. In such an environment, the relationship model is suggested to be a relatively stable determinant of types of gifting acts, while the dimensions of control are tentatively suggested to address sociotechnical control requirements of the specific gifting actions.

Introduction

An examination of end-user concerns in sharing networks can help designers understand what types of control to consider in future designs of sharing technologies. This chapter specifically acknowledges the need for understanding concerns regarding *how end users want to provide material in sharing networks*.

Computer-mediated sharing of digital goods, mostly exemplified by file sharing, has grown at a remarkable rate over the past years. More recent phenomena, such as wikis, blogs, online social networking services and collaborative bookmarking and tagging have also contributed to the overall "sharing surge". Added to this is the fact that we are seeing more and more material being released under public licenses and technology is continuously becoming more pervasive, affordable, and powerful. It seems that sharing is a fundamental human desire, and with the help of networked technology, it is claiming new arenas. However, public debate on sharing technology has been much coloured by intellectual property disputes. On a global level, numerous and anonymous relations, combined with digitalized, reproducible, and easily transferable goods have created a practice which is much contended by certain actors, while embraced by others. On a different scale, opinions on which set of values should guide cooperation online follow a similar disagreement. Put simply, there's the communitarian view—arguing that resolute community (or other administration) values should govern conduct online—or the libertarian view—which contends that individual behaviour and objectives should emerge into norms (Barnes, 2003). Although there's little agreement regarding which of these approaches is more appropriate, or even possible, in relation to design for online communities and networks, the debates themselves indicate that there may be parameters of *online* sharing that are creating a unique and different practice compared to traditional sharing.

Still, the main focus of both technical development and scientific inquiry has so far mostly been either on legal, economical, and ethical issues surrounding sharing or on how to improve accessing, downloading, and finding material (Adar & Huberman, 2000; Bhattacharjee, Gopal, & Sanders, 2003; Feldman, Lai, Stoica, & Chuang, 2004; Krishnan, Smith, Tang, & Telang, 2004). This *goods-centric* perspective has also guided much further interest and research. It seems that both popular media and scientific studies have for the most part overlooked that, for end users, sharing constitutes a *sociotechnical practice*, in which the supply of material is crucial. Put simply, without someone who provides material, there is nothing to access, retrieve, or download.

On this point, provision, or uploading, has largely been framed as a dubious practice involving copyright infringements and digital rights management. Nevertheless, previous studies have shown that the driving force for providing users is rarely as simple as to "overthrow the existing market system" or to distribute material in violation of ownership rights (McGee & Skågeby, 2004). Rather, this giving of material constitutes pro-social acts (Sproull, Conley, & Moon, 2005), which are driven by an enjoyment in the activity as such (activity-centric) or by considerations for others (relationship-centric). An interesting parallel is that there are indications that file sharing is increasingly "going social" (Kaye, 2004; Mello, 2004; Shirky, 2003), where emerging sub-communities play an increasing part in the sharing ecology; and also, that social-networking applications are increasingly including support for photo, music, and video sharing as parts of their services (Roush, 2005).

With these tendencies, *qualitative* concerns of sharing are likely to become more important to end users. Of course, much provision is performed for selfish or enforced reasons, but in order to draw a complete picture of the sharing phenomenon, we also need to consider the qualitative activity- and relationship-centred concerns regarding provision of digital goods (Skågeby, 2003).

In order to address the qualitative aspects of sharing, this chapter will use the theoretical framework of gift-giving. The reason for this is that the concept of gift-giving, or gifting, has been extensively used to examine qualitative circumstances (such as motivations, social bonding, and reciprocity) of provision in many traditional communities and networks. The potential application and existence of gifting in networked communication is consequently an interesting track to pursue.

The structure of this chapter is as follows: the background describes sharing networks as dynamic in terms of goods and relations and how a focus on gifting can address the qualitative concerns of end users of these networks. Next, the related work section presents previous efforts addressing the design of gifting, leading to the overall research question for this chapter. Then follow two sections regarding the backgrounding study as such—data collection and results. The analytical section of the chapter then presents the relationship model and five analytical dimensions by which it is possible to understand and describe how control over gifting acts are carried out (or wished to be carried out) and in what way technologies can support them. Finally, some tentative design suggestions based on the previously presented models and dimensions are presented.

Sharing Networks and Digital Gifts

What makes sharing in general, and gifting in particular, difficult to control? In the scope of this chapter, what is interesting is not so much the technical architecture, but rather the sociotechnical architecture where the digital material and the social relations are of equal general importance. Thus, gifting is an activity that is technically, structurally, and relationally embedded in computer-mediated social networks.

As seen in Figure 1, the structural setting allows resources to be distributed over the network. By acknowledging that communication networks are made up of interconnected computers *and* people, this simple figure highlights that not only computational and informational resources are important to users in the network, but also social and relational resources. All these types of resources are not discretely distributed

Figure 1. The "setting": Computers and persons are interconnected across a network

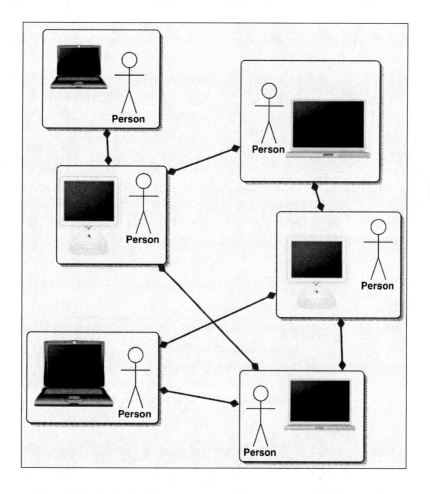

in the network but are often intertwined, reflecting that persons and computers form in this case joint systems (as does, at a different level of concreteness, the entire network). These interconnected joint systems enable the emergence of sociotechnical structures. These structures constitute an important factor in regulating how resource distribution takes place in a sharing network. Interestingly, while people are at the same time enriching the network and empowering sharing, they are also adding to the complexity of the system. Social dilemmas, free-riding, impression, and reputation management are all examples of "consequences" of human interaction that strongly influence patterns of sharing and reciprocity. Generally, sharing networks and communities are often described in terms of lacking stability and habited by overly selfish users, whose only interest consists of retrieving material at the smallest cost possible. As a consequence, many studies have taken as a starting point such problems as defectors, white-washing, resource instability, free-riding, and the tragedy of the commons (Ngan, Wallace, & Druschel, 2003; Premkumar, 2003; Ranganathan, Ripeanu, Sarin, & Foster, 2004; Sanghavi & Hajek, 2005; Shneidman & Parkes, 2003). From a control point of view, these studies describe the difficulty for end users to control the situation in terms of acquiring goods. At best, they consider the provision of goods as simple cost-benefit analyses, where the basic assumption is that "users does not want to put themselves in the risky situation of providing something to someone without getting something back".

Indeed, in public sharing milieus, the complete assurance of a guaranteed return of something specific is often hard (impossible) to control (which, in turn, suggests the applicability of a "gifting model", as we shall see), but while the efforts described earlier are certainly worthwhile, they often emerge from an understanding of "getting behaviour" (e.g., the will to retrieve and access material), and potential solutions to the problems stemming from it. In contrast, this chapter argues that the provision of goods is an under-examined practice, which bears much importance on the complete understanding of resource sharing in computer-mediated social networks. As indicated previously, theory on gift-giving has concerned itself with more qualitative concerns regarding provision of material for others. Next, we shall briefly review traditional definitions of gifts.

A Working Definition of Gifting

When discussing gifts, the literature from anthropology, sociology, and to some extent economics has concerned itself mainly with two modes of transfer: reciprocity and "pure" gift-giving (Berking, 1999; Kolm, 2000). Reciprocity involves the return of gifts, with the important distinction that there is ambiguity and uncertainty regarding what, when, and whether the return is to be completed. This vague, implicit, and non-contractual agreement is what demarcates it from exchange.

More in the line of altruism lies pure gift-giving, which is disinterested and aimed at increasing the well-being of others. There is no real consensus regarding the existence, or non-existence of pure gifts and altruism, and consequently there is a "scale of rigor" regarding the definitions of gifting in the literature. This chapter does not intend to take sides in this debate; for current purposes, it is fine to accept that there is reciprocal gifting as well as altruistic perspectives and to highlight the question of "what people expect—if anything—in return". If they expect something similar to what they give, then we are in the realm of economics and are dealing with a type of exchange. If they expect to gain in return a "better world" (by gifting their resources), explanations dealing with altruistic and unconditional motives seem more valid. We emphasize this because we believe that the stronger and more common the unconditional gifting motives, the more opportunities there are for as-yet undiscovered applications and services.

In summary, traditional gifting definitions revolve around three concepts: social bonding value, other-oriented motivations, and reciprocal ambiguity (Arrow, 1972; Bell, 1991; Godbout & Caillé, 1992; Klamer, 2003; Komter, 1996). The most generous of these definitions concerns reciprocal ambiguity, where the gift is defined as any "good", including money, that is transferred, conveyed, or transmitted from one party to another when the nature, the value, and the timing of the return of an equivalent is left undetermined" (Klamer, 2003). To further expand on the term, reciprocal ambiguity refers to situations where it is hard to calculate (in neoclassical terms) the expected returns (as is the example with many "socially reinforced" values, such as reputation)—the expectation of a return is present, but its timing, nature, and value is non-contractual (e.g., ambiguous, vague, and uncertain). The term gifting in this chapter covers both the concept of reciprocity as well as "pure" gift-giving. Furthermore, this chapter uses a pragmatic definition of gifting based on reciprocal ambiguity. This is because of the dynamics of the sociotechnical settings in which digital gifting takes place (fluent relationships, white-washing, anonymity, etc.), the inherent "scale of rigor" concerning the definitions of gifting and the exploratory approach of the studies. The basic interest lies in motivations and activities where it is *uncertain* (often to both researcher and objects of study) what,

Table 1. Properties of the two modes of gifting

Reciprocity	"Pure" Gift-giving
Interrelated two-way transfers	Independent one-way transfer
Mainly of bonding value, concerning social relationships	
Other-oriented motivations	
Vague, non-contractual, uncertain, ambiguous, implicit, serendipitous	

whether, or when someone expects or wants something in return. Naturally, social bonding value and other-orientedness were considered when these were apparent and important parts of the actual gifting situation, but as an initial "looking glass" in the search for gifting behaviour, ambiguity was primarily considered. A summary of the properties of gifting, as defined in this chapter, can be seen in Table 1.

Related Work: Designing for Sharing

To date, research on online sharing to date can be categorized by its emphasis on either getting or giving. Getting oriented research relies on studies that show that "problems of sharing" are related to an uneven balance between giving and getting (in the favour of getting) and consequently assumes that the main motivation of most users is to find and retrieve material (and thus not provide it). This problem has been described in such terms as defecting, free-riding, and tragedy of the commons. The main predicament in this research approach is that users need to be motivated or enforced to provide material for others as sharing networks and communities rely on the continuous provision of material. In other words, this body of work is in many ways interested in motivating users to share more (and in certain cases, less) (Adar & Huberman, 2000; Feldman et al., 2004; Golle, Leyton-Brown, & Mironov, 2001; Krishnan et al., 2004; LaRose, Lai, Lange, Love, & Wu, 2005; Ngan et al., 2003; Premkumar, 2003; Ranganathan et al., 2004; Sanghavi & Hajek, 2005; Shneidman & Parkes, 2003).

Another research approach focuses more on the giving minority of sharing communities and networks, and has largely been devoted to understanding motivations and general incentive structures for provision (Cooper & Harrison, 2001; Giesler & Pohlmann, 2002; Lakhani & Wolf, 2003; Zeitlyn, 2003). These range from completely selfish motivations to motivations that can appear as seemingly altruistic (although this can, of course, be debated). A variation on the giving approach is more clearly devoted to understanding the other-oriented or social parts of provision (Levine, 2001) and yet others have also tried to include design suggestions based on such an approach (Brown, Sellen, & Geelhoed, 2001; Kelly, Sung, & Farnham, 2002; Taylor & Harper, 2002; Voida, Grinter, Ducheneaut, Edwards, & Newman, 2005).

To conclude, there is surprisingly little research on designing *for* gifting (rather than against taking). Although the question of how to get users to return and contribute material has been an issue in community design for a long time, and there has been much general advice regarding designing for community participation (Godwin, 1994; Kim, 2000; Kollock, 1998a; Preece, 2000), there has been little consideration of the *specific qualitative concerns* of end users when providing material in large-scale networks.

Research Question

As the introductory section has shown, sharing end users are arguably acting in a setting with both very dynamic and vibrant aspects as well as relatively stable structures. Combined with the survey of related work, this leaves us with some important conclusions. First, superficial quantitative measures (i.e., fuelling users to share more or free-ride less) of addressing gifting may miss out on important qualitative details of the actual concerns of users. Second, research which does take gifting seriously, concentrates disproportionately on understanding motivations. A classical research question that has been used to probe the circumstances of gifts is: what is given to whom, how, and why? The previous strong emphasis on motivations leaves important questions to be answered regarding *what* is given to *whom* and *how* in online sharing venues. Not only are these questions interesting in themselves, but they might also restructure the previous understanding of motivations. This chapter will mainly address the question of *how* gifts are given and more specifically the control needs and concerns of end users. In order to approach potentially supportive design in these systems, we need to consider the end-user concerns that are predominant and what they can tell us about relevant design features. Consequently, the aim of this chapter is to address the question: in sharing networks, what concerns do end users have regarding *how* to provide material to the network and how can the systematic examination of these concerns inform the design of gifting technologies?

Data Collection

Internet use is often distributed over different techniques (such as discussion groups, instant messaging conversations, file sharing and display, member profiles, etc.) and is consequently capable of leaving many "traces". The results presented in this chapter were derived from online ethnographic studies of one sharing network. The sharing network is mainly devoted to music file sharing. The network also has an "underground spirit" (in terms of the type of music being shared) and a significant part of the shared music is made by end users participating in the network. The study was performed over a period of six months. The main data was elicited from discussion forums connected to the sharing applications. Certain complementary methods were also used to collect referential data. First, the use of the application over a long period of time (including spontaneous interviews, communication, and interaction) helped in developing a sense of what is significant to end users. Second, interviews with certain members were conducted mainly to shed more light on specific issues. Third, a deliberate return of analysis results to the network forum was conducted. Member feedback is a central process, in which the results are fed back to the community (or other target of study) in order to address the ground-ing of interpretations made. A joint goal is to instigate discussion and use this as a recurring source of data (which could challenge the analysis or be incorporated as further proof of trustworthiness). The feedback generated some debate and discus-sion that was enriching both to analysis as well as picking up on keywords and "in-vivo"-expressions. Apart from that, the feedback also had the function of meeting informants on their territory. This can help to make a more situated and grounded judgment about the appropriateness of including quotes and applying certain lines of analytical reasoning.

This method has been referred to as part of a growing body of online, Internet, or virtual methods (Bakardjieva, Feenberg, & Goldie, 2004; Hine, 2000; Johns, Chen, & Hall, 2004; Jones, 1999). Qualitative studies intended to inform applied design of technology have been part of the CSCW (computer-supported cooperative work) field for a long time. The use of ethnography as a design informant has also been suggested to expand beyond the constrained and focused area of work into other domains (Hughes, King, Rodden, & Andersen, 1994). We believe that studies of the vivid, recreational sharing (and in particular gifting) we see online today, have not only the ability to inform the design of recreational systems, but also reveal intentions and concerns that can be applicable in other, more utility-focused do-mains as well.

Regarding the "authenticity" of the data, there are many epistemological issues to expand upon. This chapter has little room to examine all of them in detail, but in summary, to simply presume that textual online communication is "less representa-tive" than, say, interviewing face-to-face, could be impetuous.

If one is simply using the Internet to expand one's reach to participants and inter-viewing them online is merely a convenience, one may want seriously to consider the extent to which people can and do express themselves well, truly or fully in text. But, if one is studying Internet contexts as cultural formations or social interaction in computer-mediated communication contexts, the inclusion of embodied ways of knowing may be unwarranted and even counterproductive. (Markham, 2004, p. 367)

In addition, as qualitative researchers of online interaction and activity, it is important to give due credit to the context in which users operate. Indeed, computer-mediated interaction facilities are the means by which users in these contexts relate and com-municate. As such, it is a very technically dependent way of interacting—identity, relationship, and social structure are most of the time emerging from textual interac-tion. This textual interaction is thus essential to include as data if we are to understand how users interact online and what concerns they have in this interaction. While the specific concerns reported in this chapter are closely connected to the studied network, they also represent instances of a class of concerns regarding provision of goods, which have been noted in many other contexts. In other words, the results are not generalizable as to what specific concerns users in other large sharing networks do actually have, but in terms of what concerns users in other large sharing networks *can* have. In this way, the study describes dimensions and variables, and the relations between them (e.g., the social significance), rather than populations and the number of specific concerns of individuals (e.g., statistical logic).

Results

The main data was obtained without "provocation" (e.g., researcher involvement/ participation/interaction). As such, data from discussion forums can be quite cluttered with nonsense messages, flaming outbursts, etc. Although these messages have been of interest to certain research on computer-mediated communication, they were only occasionally relevant to the topic of this chapter. As described in the upcoming section, the analysis used theoretical code categories, developed from backgrounding literature and the research question, as guides in the elicitation of data. As a result, the data set was, in a sense, cleaned from much irrelevant material by the way it was sampled. In total, 680 *relevant* messages were collected from the discussion forum. This data includes comments from almost 100 unique user names. Apart from this, there are also 13 informal interview logs, samples of user profiles, and sharing policies and field notes.

Controlling Digital Gifting

How can we frame end-user concerns, intentions, and efforts to control gifting? The data was, for the main part, analyzed according to the methodology described by Romano and colleagues (Romano, Donovan, Chen, & Nunamaker, 2003). This methodology allows for a selection of data according to both theoretical code categories and emergent patterns. The theoretical code categories were derived from previous theory on gifting (e.g., bonding value, other-orientedness, and reciprocity) and from the features in the sharing application. The result of this analysis (e.g., the model of relationships and the dimensions of control presented later) are, in a way, condensed "thick descriptions" from the ethnographical studies. As such, they form conceptual tools presented as an attempt to make the results useful to various groups of stakeholders interested in computer-mediated gifting. The following analysis presents the relationship model, which considers the individual's relation to the larger group(s) of which he or she is a member, and five central dimensions of control. These empirically grounded tools were developed to categorize the operational understanding of end-user concerns regarding control over how their gifting is performed. Control, in this case, refers to the sociotechnical end-user means for coordinating their concerns and thus regulate and optimize their gifting. This may be achieved either directly through interface and functional facilities, or indirectly through social interaction, or as is most often the case, sharing technologies as a co-emerging combination of both.

Recreational resource sharing is, of course, a "non-critical" domain, which does not expose users (or others) to high risks or demand high levels of compliance other than, at times, socially. Thus, it can seem that it does not matter what type of control an end user of such a system is capable of. However, although not at a critical level, computer-mediated networks have the potential of supporting intimate social relations (Hine, 2005) or bearing meaning to everyday or work activities and thus can be perceived as of being of great importance to specific users at certain times. As we shall see, it is reasonable to assume that a certain level of control is desirable. Indeed, the studies revealed that many users actively considered, argued about, and applied control over their gifting. Furthermore, they revealed that there were many occasions where users were frustrated by not being able to act at a certain level of control. These mismatches between intended control and actual outcome resulted in a pragmatic and co-evolving combination of reactive actions and overall sharing strategies.

Structural Control: The Individual and the Group

Technologies used to gift and share digital goods are good examples of everyday recreational technologies that co-emerge with values, levels of trust, identities, and social relations. Therefore, because technology-mediated gifting relies as much on a technical structure as on a social structure, we need not only to understand technical features of tools, but also define the social and structural determinants that provide background for the specific gift acts of users. In this context, users are very adaptive and innovative in coping with the "simplicity" of the social and technical means at hand. However, one structural determinant, which appears to be central, is how the individual relates to others and, specifically, the larger group(s) of which he or she is a part, usually referred to as social dilemmas (Kollock, 1998b; Orbell & Dawes, 1981).

The relation between the individual and these different levels of relationships largely regulates how specific gifting acts are performed. Thus, this model presents not only a way to structure and describe the individual and his or her relation to the larger group(s), but it also has predictive qualities in foreseeing conflicts of interest and patterns of cooperation in sharing networks. As an example of how the model can be

Table 2. Model of relationships (Skågeby & Pargman, 2005)

Level of Relation	Group Structure	Common Incentive Structures
Ego	Me, myself, and I	Self-interest, maximizing own benefit
Micro	Small group of close peers, well-known *friends*	Social, reciprocity
Meso	Small networks of peers, recognized *acquaintances*	Social, individual and general reciprocity
Macro	Large networks of sharing users, anonymous *strangers*	Ideology, Rationality of Equality, Principle of Fairness

used to analyze relationships and gifting, we shall identify two structures of gifters apparent in sharing technology use: communicators and instrumentalists.

Communicators

Some of the most interesting conflicts reflected a big divide within the sharing community at large—a conflict between what we may call communicators and instrumentalists. For the communicators, the purpose of sharing and gifting was to communicate and thereby "build on overall well-being". They emphasized the community spirit and had the intention of contributing to it by making social ties between members of the network. They argued that by creating small personal networks they would be able to direct their gifts towards those who really enjoyed them—and that this would help in establishing a more communal sharing milieu. The way they did this was by only granting gifts to users who contacted them personally and with whom they could establish a communicative relationship. That is, by setting up a social requirement for inclusion, they insisted that they made the network into more of a community and that this type of behaviour was beneficial as it strengthened the social bonds between the community members. This conduct grew into a practice undertaken by many users. The communicators' advice to potential recipients was to "just ask". By making recipients ask for material and take part in social discussions regarding the quality of material for example, communicators felt that a level of politeness and, to some extent, trust had been established. Most often, communicators acted responsively by answering recipients' requests.

Instrumentalists

The instrumentalists, on the other hand, saw the purpose of file sharing as a way to give and receive goods without restrictions, either social or technical. Their motivations were ideological in terms of information access. Anyone should be able to access anything—"Either you share files or you don't". They saw personal communication, attempts to make friends and small personal groups as a hindrance in this process. Notably, they were still generous in terms of shared goods, but did not want what some of them referred to as the "burdens of sharing". They wanted to give away goods, but they also wanted to remain undisturbed by further recommendations, requests for advice, and social small talk. One could also say that they were reluctant to expose themselves to the "transactional costs" that a gift might entail (i.e., by having to gift to all, by having to "formalize their gifting", by being unsure of the use of their effort, etc.). In terms of levels in the relationship model, *communicators* wanted to take interaction towards the micro-level, while *instrumentalists* preferred to move towards the macro-level.

As an example between these two extremes, we noted that some users were instrumentalists at heart, but communicators in practice. While communicators highlighted the value of friendly relations, there were also users who favoured the larger network over small groups of friends. Their main desire was to gift to anyone, but because this often created situations where technical and social resources were scarce, they felt they had to limit their gifting. In order to provide material to those who were really interested and at a reasonable speed, they felt they *had* to make restrictions. By restrictive and communicative features, they favoured certain strangers by turning them into acquaintances. Instead of giving to *anyone* potentially interested, they coordinated and optimized gifting by moving recipients to a closer level of relationship.

Specific Gifting Acts: Dimensions of Control

Indeed, the concerns regarding *how* to control a specific gifting act seem to relate to the relationship model, and the fact that many users differentiate between relationships. Depending on the nature of the relationship, users expressed concerns about five central dimensions of control. The following sections describe each of the five identified control dimensions in more detail:

- **Incentive:** Enforced and voluntary.
- **Limitation:** Open and restrictive.
- **Direction:** Public and private.
- **Initiative:** Active and passive.
- **Identification:** Anonymous and identified.

Although these dimensions were derived from the studies of one particular sharing network, and through the methodology are unique to that network, they also represent instances of classes of concerns that have been seen in many other services and applications. In other words, the results are not generalizable as to what specific concerns and intentions end users in large sharing networks do actually have, but in terms of what concerns and intentions users in large sharing networks *can* have.

Incentive: Enforced and Voluntary

Many systems and studies are currently operating under the assumption that gifting has to be enforced in order for a reasonable ratio between providing and free-loading to be upheld. This could be done by encouraging (or explicitly compelling) people to give or by introducing reprimands to those who do not give. An example is BitTorrent, which by design encourages uploading. There are also more "server-oriented" services, such as Direct Connect, Hotline and KDX, where hubs and servers may have strict rules about quality and amount of uploaded material and/or ratios between uploaded and downloaded content. The rationale for implementing designs, which obliges users to gift, may differ, but the most common objectives are to reduce network load or to level the differences between overall uploading and downloading (i.e., reducing free-riding). In the studies that this chapter builds on, there was no general technical enforcement of gifting, but interestingly, it was occasionally socially enforced on an individual level. The range of features in the sharing applications would allow users to manually disconnect other users who did not gift themselves. This was seen by some as an appropriate individual way to weed free-riders out of the system. The procedure was undertaken by either communicative means or by referring to the individual sharing policy. In the communicative case, a gifter would contact a recipient and ask him/her why he did not share material, and if the answer was unsatisfactory (at some level), the gifter would sever connections with the recipient. When sharing policies were used, gifters would either refer users to this policy through instant messaging or by naming shared files and folders with titles such as "check out sharing policy" or "share or be banned". An example of an explicit sharing policy can be seen in Figure 2.

Figure 2. Example of an individual sharing policy

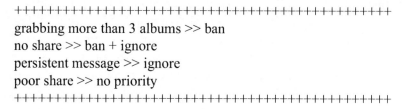

```
++++++++++++++++++++++++++++++++++++++++++++++++++++++++++++
grabbing more than 3 albums >> ban
no share >> ban + ignore
persistent message >> ignore
poor share >> no priority
++++++++++++++++++++++++++++++++++++++++++++++++++++++++++++
```

Others adopted a more liberal attitude towards free-riders and thought that gifting should not be enforced socially or technically. This demarcation illustrates the correlation between technical features and social systems. While the enforcing qualities of certain technical features allowed users to enforce gifting according to their personal ideals and norms, the non-use of them were also expressions of how users thought the overall system should operate. Naturally, not using a certain feature is not a definitive indicator of a certain intention, but nevertheless, when confronted, many users expressed that their unwillingness to use certain features was deliberate. For example, many users were reluctant to use the ban feature, since it was perceived as being very impolite and unnecessarily hard-hitting. An additional reason for analyzing digital gifting in terms of enforced and voluntary gifting is what we may call "gifting resistances". There were gifters who curbed their desire (and ability) to gift out of fear. One user referred to this as dealing with "the burdens of sharing", an expression which other users adopted. This referred to the possibility of becoming subject to follow-up questions, unwanted attempts of befriending, and requests for further recommendations and additional goods by gifting certain goods. Therefore, they were quite careful about what, when, and to whom to gift. For these users, a general technical enforcement of gifting would clearly clash with their needs and interests (unless any identification is impossible).

This dimension of control also covers mechanisms that lie in between completely voluntary and completely enforced gifting. As noted earlier, ratios are one such example. Ratios can be governed by various conditions, such as user levels (where different ratios might apply to different categories of users), publicity (whether user ratios are made public), and what type of measure is being used (amount of data, number of uploads, earned points, positive/negative reviews, etc). While ratios can be referred to as enforced, they often support the choice of *what* and *when* to return gifts to the network or specific members of it. This is more similar to the non-contractual, ambiguous, and vague nature of gift reciprocation and not so much a strict, contractual, and immediate balance that characterizes exchange. Thus, control over incentive seemed not only to effect end users, but also to constitute a measure by which they actively tried to gain increased control of their environment.

Limitation: Open and Restrictive

While all studied gifters were interested in providing material for others, there was also a distinct difference between what we may call open and restrictive gifters. Open gifters tried to keep their entire collection of material available to all without any restrictions. Their reason for this was often ideologically grounded and referred to a rationality of equality or a "principle of fairness" (see Table 2). As such, their view was that all users should be able to operate on equal terms, and no privileges or advantages should be administered. They saw the overall effects of applying restrictions as creating isolated sub-networks (or sub-communities) with various membership requirements. Open gifters saw this tendency as undesirable, since it would greatly decrease the availability, sociability, and serendipity of the networked resources.

Restrictive gifters applied different types of barring mechanisms towards different classes of receivers. The reasons for doing this, however, are still related to gifting. Restrictive gifters were still interested in providing material for other users, but saw restrictions as a way of improving gifting, both for themselves and for the intended receivers. For them, restriction has to do with resource management. Examples of technical features supporting restrictive gifting are queues and caps (download speed limits), which allow end users to manage potential recipients without necessarily excluding them completely from receiving content.

Thus, open and closed gifting does not polarize the dimension of limitation, since completely closed gifting would not be gifting at all. Increased sociability and more technically efficient transfers motivated restrictive gifters. For example, users could set up a social inclusion restriction. They would only allow downloads to users who contacted them personally. This was seen as an effective way of improving community life by introducing "social courtesy". Indeed, a common piece of advice from more experienced users, when confronted with accusations of being too restrictive (or hearing "war stories" about this phenomena), was to "just ask". That is, by being polite and social, introducing yourself rather than just beginning to download, you would generally be allowed to access the material without further restrictions.

Other restrictive users operated on a technical level of control. They noted that they had scarce technical resources (e.g., bandwidth) and as a consequence had to limit the potential number of concurrent downloaders as a way of maintaining efficiency. The rationale was that allowing some users to get complete files reasonably fast was better than allowing all interested users to receive files that would download slowly. The "other-oriented" gifting aspects of this is illustrated by one user: "I only have rules because of my consideration for everyone and my desire to share as much as possible. It sounds ironic and contradictory, but it works [...]". As noted in the description of communicators and instrumentalists, the issue of open and restrictive gifting was indeed a controversial one. On the one hand, many users were not interested in social restrictions at all and would argue that this leads to exclusive sub-populations with decreasing variations of people and goods. On the other, the same arguments were used by other users who stated that the increased similarities would result in higher degrees of appreciation and precision in terms of created network links and overall exchanged goods.

Direction: Public and Private

The question of private and public goods has, to a degree, been highlighted in the age of networked communications (Skågeby, 2006). Digital goods have often been described as public goods. Public in this case means that it is not possible or practical to limit the public access to the goods once provided to one person (non-excludable), and it is possible for several parties to use the same goods simultaneously. Digital goods in computer-mediated networks have been seen as ubiquitously transferable and reproducible without control. Furthermore, it is often suggested that online gifting is an undirected act, aimed at a large receiving network and at no particular individual. For example: "Gifts are often not given to anyone in particular. They are made public [...]" (Bergquist & Ljungberg, 2001) and "[...] actions and contributions in a virtual community are usually not of a directed nature" (Balasubramanian & Mahajan, 2001). Attempts to create digital goods without these public qualities have certainly been made, for example, by digital rights movements and copyright laws. The success of such efforts has naturally been debated. The view taken in this chapter is from an end-user perspective, and for end users, the distinctions between what is made public and what is more private is central. There are two main reasons for this: digital goods possess different characteristics in terms of their technical rivalry—some are scarce (bandwidth, hard disk space) and some are not (files); also, if we choose not just to consider the technical qualities of goods, but also the provision of them in social networks, we soon understand that the monolithic concept of digital goods as purely public needs finer distinctions. For example, including such concepts as time, effort, skill, needs, motivations, intentions, and social structures in a sociotechnical analysis is likely to reveal a more refined model of the provision of digital goods. In multiple user networks, the provision of goods shows both qualities of rivalry as well as exclusivity. For end users, this distinction comes into play when facing social dilemmas (i.e., when considering the benefits of oneself versus the larger network(s) and, more importantly, when considering gifting, between different groups of receivers). The need to direct the gifting of goods toward a specific receiving structure can be grounded in several pragmatic circumstances such as work groupings, family relations, impression management, ideologies, and so forth. Whatever the specific motivation is, the need to control who gains access to what is a central theme to gifters. This concern clearly shows how the gifting of content and the forming and maintenance of relationships co-evolve. Users find each other through gifted content, sub-communities evolve on the basis of interest in similar content, and users want to gift content to certain (groups of) relationships. Reflecting this need of controlling the "level of publicness", we can adopt the relationship model (from Table 2) to consider the gifting of content and the recipient relationship structures.

This dimension suggests that in computer-mediated social networks, the notion of digital goods as purely public goods needs to be reconsidered. Social structures

Table 3. Directions of gifts

Direction of gift	Recipient Structure
Private	Single individuals, close friends, family
Micro-public	Small group of close peers, well-known *friends*
Meso-public	Small networks of peers, recognized *acquaintances*
Public	Large networks of sharing users, anonymous *strangers*

and sociotechnical means and motivations affect the exclusivity and rivalry of the goods in a network. Certain goods are gifted strictly to other individuals (private), while others are directed towards the micro-level of relationship (micro-public), others to the meso-level (meso-public) and yet others are made available to the entire network (public). An interesting observation is that the level of publicness was occasionally used as an indicator of the (desired) proximity of the relationship. By moving specific recipients to, or toward, another level of publicness, a gifter could indicate the strength of the social tie had diminished or increased. For example, a move from a private recipient to a meso-public structure could suggest that the relationship had weakened. Notably, the column "recipient structures" describes prototypical relationships between actors at each level of the model (that of being friends, acquaintances, and strangers). That is, the *typical* relationship at the private and micro-public level is one of being friends; the *typical* relationship at the meso-level is one of being acquaintances and the *typical* relationship at the macro-level is one of being strangers. That does not mean that *every* relationship at (for example) the meso-level always has to be one of being acquaintances.

Initiative: Active and Passive

It's important to stress that these dimensions are seen mainly from the gifters' point of view, in this case the significance of gifting initiative. In the control of initiative, awareness becomes a central aspect. Much computer-mediated gifting can occur "by default", and therefore it becomes important to highlight the deliberate initiative of gifting. By active initiative, it is implied that a user acts actively to initiate a gift of goods for access or receivable by someone else deliberately. Many base technologies, such as e-mail, instant messaging, and IRC (Internet Relay Chat), support active gifting of content. On the contrary, passive gifters do not initiate gifting acts deliberately. They keep material available for access, as "gifts to be accepted" by others (e.g., shared folders). This is the most common form in peer-to-peer file sharing. Naturally, there are users who gift material without being aware of it. These situations are by definition non-deliberate and will not be expanded upon in this control dimension. Initiative control relies on the assumption that a gifting end user is aware that he or she is providing material for others, actively or passively. By highlighting the difference between active and passive gifting, we are also emphasizing trusts and types of relationship. Many users mixed active and passive gifting depending on the type of relationship (or desired type of relationship) and on the level of trust receivers had for them. Some users would actively search for material for others, or make qualified guesses about what could interest them, and in this way act "pro-actively" and upload these goods to the receiver in question. As one user states:

"[...] I often message them if I see they have a low-quality version of an album I've ripped myself in LAME APS, so they can get my better version. I've also gone out of my way on numerous occasions to help someone complete an album outside of [name omitted], either through IM [instant messaging] or email or even sometimes uploading the tracks they missed to my web site."

This also illustrates a communicative variation, which was to act actively through messaging features and provide potential receivers with information about goods of likely interest, which were then gifted actively or passively. Others were what we can call communicatively passive. Such users filled out extended user biographies and "wish lists". This information could then be used by others to find users with similar likes and dislikes and although this is obviously a getting mechanism, one of the astonishing aspects of sharing networks is the degree to which such lists result in gifting behaviours, an example being the previously-mentioned user who searched for users with (in this case) albums he or she owned and asked if they needed better encoded versions.

Another type of behaviour explained by the dimension of active and passive gifting was what we may call *responsive* gifting. This is initiated by users posting requests for files. This often generates many responses from other members willing to provide the item in question to the user "in need". The dynamics of this interaction is somewhere in-between the passive act of "only sharing a folder" and the pro-active act of foreseeing others' needs by providing potentially interesting material to them. In fact, responsive gifting is frequently observed in various sharing forums (and occasionally even part of the "guidelines" or frequently asked questions). Individuals post "requests" ("does anyone have a copy of X?") to which others may reply with either a pointer to the location of the desired item, or with the desired item "attached" to the reply itself. Similar to moving users to, or toward, a "closer" level of relationship (see the section on "Direction"), active and responsive users often wanted to boost or preserve social bonds and relationships by actively searching/finding out about potential gifts on behalf of or in response to specific others.

Identification: Anonymous and Identified

A final, central dimension of control has to do with identification. This refers to being able to create "high credibility representations" of oneself online as opposed to remaining totally anonymous and unidentifiable. Lately, many efforts have been taken to create sharing technologies which amplify anonymity (e.g., Winny, Share, Freenet, Entropy, Waste, Tor, etc.). At the same time, a lot of work is being devoted to online identity (e.g., Sxip, LID, OpenID, Passel, etc.) and ways of proving that "I am me" in networked contexts. Furthermore, the need for identification as a factor important in sustaining social interaction has been noted previously in the concept of accountability (Erickson & Kellog, 2000), where being accountable for one's actions provides social control which sustains norms, rules, and customs. As examples of in-betweens, we see pseudonymity, where users can identify each other to various degrees but rarely as more than "handles" or nicknames. Naturally, the level of identification is related to the concept of intimacy and trust and possibilities to control one's identification can have serious impacts on how one chooses to gift (and receive gifts). If I can readily identify myself as a well-known user, receivers are likely to feel more at ease and will anticipate receiving certain gifts and I, as gifter, can feel comfort in knowing that it won't be received completely without consent or entirely unwillingly. Blogs seem to support a more identified type of sharing, as do photo-sharing services such as Flickr, for example. Although these services can be supportive of anonymous relationships, there is a more distinct propensity for identified relations than for example in large-scale file sharing.

Another example of how this dimension is pragmatically embedded in networks is the structure of public attention towards identification. For example, in a file-sharing community, the *public* level of attention as to the identification of gifters and their reputation is rather low. The feedback loops are more in terms of micro- and meso-levels of relationship. To the overall network, the user is still quite anonymous. In an open-source community for example, it is often the other way round, with direction, access, and attention aimed more toward a public level. A "good" contributor to an open-source project generally receives more public attention (public in terms of the community, not society), while a "good and giving" peer in a file-sharing community gets feedback from friends and acquaintances and is rarely publicly "celebrated" as a good peer by the community or network as a whole. In this context, it is interesting to note the proliferation of mechanisms for anonymity in the file-sharing community at large. Indeed, much of the motivation behind such mechanisms and conventions is sometimes related to fears about legal action and the preservation of privacy; in other words, these mechanisms and conventions have been developed partly to ensure "safe getting". However if gifting is a strong desire, as suggested in the growing body of work, we would expect the increase of "anonymizing mechanisms" to actually allow people to express more altruistic gifting desires.

Designing Control for Digital Gifting

The domain where gifting users act is quite dynamic—socially, technically, and sociotechnically. A central concern for the users studied in this chapter was to try to *control* different aspects of their gifting, which was accomplished more or less successfully. If we are to turn computer-mediated sharing into a more collaborative and community-related activity, we need not only describe the operational "gifting side" of sharing, but also try to identify *how* these descriptions can support control of gifting. This chapter has discussed questions of the concerns of end users regarding how to provide digital material in sharing networks and how these can inform the design of gifting technologies.

In an attempt to answer these questions, this chapter has identified the relationship between the individual and the group as an indicator of how specific gifting acts are (desired to be) carried out. The subsequent specific gifting acts are categorized by five dimensions of control, which can be used to open up a discussion about gifting features in applications for multiple user sharing networks. An important conclusion is that these dimensions are best represented as continuums where specific instances may be placed on a scale. As such, they constitute conceptual ("thinking") tools for considering specific controls of computer-mediated gifting and can be considered applicable as they are to other categories of online sharing milieus. While the relationship model and the dimensions of control are derived from studies of music file sharing, they can potentially be used to analyze other sharing settings, such as open source development, meta-data sharing, and so forth. As such, it is important to understand that the dimensions of control presented in this chapter do not represent a fixed set. Optimistically, the application of them to other types of networks could help in revealing other dimensions (or nuances to dimensions) that might need consideration.

If we consider the differences in preferences of control with instrumentalists and communicators, we see that instrumentalists were open, public, passive, voluntary, and anonymous, while communicators were restrictive, passive/active/pro-active, voluntary (but at times socially enforcing) and pseudonymous (at times even identified). As noted previously, this also reflected a desire to deal mainly with relationships at a certain level in the relationship model. Instrumentalists tended to position themselves at the macro-level, and performed gifting acts accordingly and to some effect, even tried to force other users to do the same. Communicators, in contrast, tried to move relations to a more "close" level by introducing communicative "barriers" when gifting. This illustrates how the specific gifting acts, as controlled by the dimensions presented, can be linked to the relationship model.

Another important conclusion is that users are extremely innovative in combining features when attempting to improve their control. Importantly, not only technical features affect the way gifting takes place, but also emergent social objectives, structures, norms, and dilemmas are continuously affecting the domain and the activities taking place within it. In response to this, it is important to apply and consider the sociotechnical control dimensions described in this chapter, in cohort. Changes in the design of one dimension can easily have effects on other dimensions, as well as the nature of gifters' activities and overall social practices.

The social-technical design cycle also illustrates the dynamics of multiple user sharing systems, in particular where mediated human-to-human interaction and communication is a central element. In a way, these systems are always in "transition" (in particular if it is a vivid open-source project driving the artefact feature development) since social practices redefine and repurpose the use of the artefacts. At the same time, the artefacts entail barriers and facilitators that "guide" social practices. With this in mind, the intention of the control dimensions is thus to be able to characterize both specific gifting acts, as well as features of technology (as facilitators or barriers of certain types of control dimensions) or even general qualities of communities and networks (as networks where certain control dimensions govern the "spirit" or social structure of the network).

Considering an "appropriate" design of sociotechnical systems is not straightforward. The argument of this chapter has been that by helping users to control their gifting (grounded in actual user needs, objectives, and troubles), we can leverage the provision of digital goods and empower both gifters and receivers. As noted however, the process of informing design through qualitative studies is quite demanding. This is chiefly related to two difficult problems: first, how to appropriately condense qualitative results and analyses so that designers can make use of them, and second, how to address an appropriate level of concreteness (not too specific nor too general) regarding the advice as such.

Figure 3. The social-technical design cycle (O'Day, Bobrow, & Shirley, 1996)

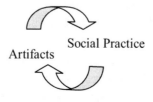

Artifacts Social Practice

This chapter has only begun to outline a central activity of networked communication but has also attempted to condense qualitative data in such a way that it can be used in the *craft* of designing for gifting, and in a larger sense, design for networked communication—if not in an immediately implementable manner, then at least as conceptual tools or prototypical design patterns that can aid in the *process* of analyzing, communicating, and developing for gifting in various domains. For designers and developers, the dimensions are intended to work as "discovery methods" to help the process of understanding which features and trade-offs will most appeal to the people who are most likely to use the system. The sociotechnical system of gifting technologies is both more complex and simpler that many other systems. The designated roles of users, for example, are not as explicit as in a more work-related setting. Users are distributed in various settings all over the world. Hardware differs and software too may differ in terms of both operating systems and (versions of) applications. Management can be explicit but it usually is not. Rules, regulations, and ways of conduct are emergent over time, as is much of the (use of) information structures (access controls, folksonomies, etc.). Support and help systems are usually embedded in the network. One thing that becomes clear from this description is that neither a solitary "getting focus" nor a simple belief in the pushing of technological frontiers as a complete solution to problems is adequate. Relationships, norms, dilemmas, needs, and joys are embedded in the collaborative use of sharing technologies and are not solely determined by it, but rather co-evolve over time.

A general problem in this domain is to balance the straightforwardness of providing material (which has arguably played a large part in popularizing sharing technologies), with a complex detail of specification for each gifting act. Although this question is beyond the scope of the present chapter, it is clear that many users had needs, objectives, and motivations regarding gifting and the control of it. A related issue is that by definition, gifting entails uncertainty, vagueness, and serendipity. Designing control to support this activity will have to actively consider these "social" characteristics and include support to leverage and empower control, not by eliminating vagueness and uncertainty, but by allowing users to control when, how, and toward whom to be vague and/or pseudonymous for example. In that sense, design of gifting technologies includes elements relating both to the libertarian approach to community design (e.g., letting cultures emerge) and the communitarian (e.g., top-down regulation), since it resembles an approach to let cultures emerge by carefully considering empowering technology features. In general, we suggest that designs should allow for readily understood end-user modifications, something that is much easier said than done. Still, a system where the control of gifting is covert or defaulted could arguably lead to ethical and social problems. Perhaps a comparison with "traditional" gifting can be made in terms of a design openness as to the control dimensions. Also, by allowing "both ends" of dimensions to co-exist, it is possible to (a larger degree) support the central values of vagueness, implicitness, and non-contractual terms that have for so long characterized non-mediated gifting.

Conclusion

The primary contribution of this research lies in a better understanding of a mediated part of human communication and interaction which is growing increasingly pervasive. The networked gifting of digital material indicates that communication that is not purely conversation-driven is important to end users, even in technology-augmented environments. The number of domains where sharing technology has been put to use is increasing: open source software development, health care, self-fulfilling leisure activities, social networking, teaching, and research are likely to be accompanied by others. This expansion of sharing technology use will need a concurrent understanding of end-user concerns and sociotechnical effects in order to take full advantage of its potential. The examination of digital gifting can, by disclosing the relational, structural, and technical embeddedness of social actions, aid in describing, analyzing, communicating, and eventually developing powerful gifting technologies. The benefits of studying and designing for gifting are several: it answers existing needs and interests with users; it is a complementary and alternative distribution model since gifting constitutes a combination of the sharing of resources and the creation of meaningful relationships; gifting practices are often central to sharing networks and an increased knowledge of these practices will aid in the effort to strengthen "community" values (since gifting supports ties, bonds, friendships, and groups based on similar interests or tastes as well as the sharing of resources) and can thus help managers in supporting sustaining communities; it provides designers and developers of services with a well-researched foundation for the design of digital gifting; it creates transferable design conclusions to be used within domains with commercial or utility-based interests; and it makes service providers able to distinguish and evolve their services.

A future research question of utmost interest is how do specific design implementations along the control dimensions affect a sharing network at large? In that perspective, it is interesting to note that gifting users combine rather simple features to create sets of functions to pinpoint and tackle specific objectives or generate desirable outcomes. At first glance, some of these features are barriers directed toward restricting access and as measures designed for preventing gifting. Undeniably, the use of barriers was often grounded in a perceived constraint regarding mostly technical capabilities, and as such, the features were considered "necessary evils". Nevertheless, users actively combined features to optimize or coordinate their gifting to acknowledge the relations considered most appropriate.

Since this chapter has suggested a complete picture of the sharing phenomena needs to include the analysis and eventually deliberate design for gifting, it is also interesting to see the increasing interest in informal networks as important parts of everyday work for many individuals (Engeström, Engeström, & Vähäaho, 1999; Henri ter Hofte & Mulder, 2004; Nardi, Whittaker, & Schwarz, 2002). An interesting next step is to identify how more instrumentally work-task-guided individuals in social networks act from a digital gifting point of view.

References

Adar, E., & Huberman, B. A. (2000). Free riding on Gnutella. *First Monday, 5*(10). Retrieved August 14, 2006, from http://www.firstmonday.org/issues/issue5_10/adar/

Arrow, K. (1972). Gifts and exchanges. *Philosophy and Public Affairs, 1*(4), 343-362.

Bakardjieva, M., Feenberg, A., & Goldie, J. (2004). User-centered Internet research: The ethical challenge. In E. A. Buchanan (Ed.), *Readings in virtual research ethics* (pp. 338-351). London: Information Science Publishers.

Balasubramanian, S., & Mahajan, V. (2001). The economic leverage of the virtual community. *International Journal of Electronic Commerce, 5*(3), 103-138.

Barnes, S. S. (2003). *Computer-mediated communication: Human-to-human communication across the Internet.* London: Pearson Education.

Bell, D. (1991). Modes of exchange: Gift and commodity. *Journal of Socio-Economics, 20*(2), 155-167.

Bergquist, M., & Ljungberg, J. (2001). The power of gifts: Organizing social relationships in open source communities. *Information Systems Journal, 11*(4), 305-320.

Berking, H. (1999). *Sociology of giving.* London: Sage.

Bhattacharjee, S., Gopal, R. D., & Sanders, G. L. (2003). Digital music and online sharing: Software piracy 2.0? *Communications of the ACM, 46*(7), 107-111.

Brown, B., Sellen, A. J., & Geelhoed, E. (2001). Music sharing as a computer supported collaborative application. In *Proceedings of the ECSCW 2001*, Bonn, Germany, September 16-20 (pp. 179-198). Dordrecht; London: Kluwer Academic Publishers.

Cooper, J., & Harrison, D. M. (2001). The social organization of audio piracy on the Internet. *Media, Culture & Society, 23*(1), 71-89.

Engeström, Y., Engeström, R., & Vähäaho, T. (1999). When the center does not hold: The importance of knotworking. In S. Chailkin, M. Hedegaard, & U. J. Jensen (Eds.), *Activity theory and social practice: Cultural-historical approaches* (pp. 345-374). Århus: Aarhus University Press.

Erickson, T., & Kellog, W. A. (2000). Social translucence: An approach to designing systems that support social processes. *ACM Transactions on Computer-Human Interaction, 7*(1), 59-83.

Feldman, M., Lai, K., Stoica, I., & Chuang, J. (2004). Robust incentive techniques for peer-to-peer networks. In *Proceedings of the EC'04,* New York, NY, May 17-20 (pp. 102-111). New York: ACM Press.

Giesler, M., & Pohlmann, M. (2003). The anthropology of file sharing: Consuming Napster as a gift. In P. A. Keller, & D. W. Rook (Eds.), *Advances in consumer research* (Vol. 30, pp. 273-279). Provo, UT: Association for Consumer Research.

Godbout, J., & Caillé, A. (1992). *The world of the gift* (D. Winkler, Trans.). Quebéc: McGill-Queen's University Press.

Godwin, M. (1994, June). *Nine principles for making virtual communities work.* Retrieved February 25, 2006, from http://www.wired.com/wired/archive/2.06/vc.principles.html

Golle, P., Leyton-Brown, K., & Mironov, I. (2001). Incentives for sharing in peer-to-peer networks. In *Proceedings of the 3rd ACM Conference on Electronic Commerce*, Tampa, Florida, USA, October 14-17 (pp. 264-267). New York: ACM Press.

Henri ter Hofte, G., & Mulder, I. (2003). Dynamic personal social networks: A new perspective for CSCW research and design. *SIGGROUP Bulletin 24*(3), 139-142.

Hine, C. (2000). *Virtual ethnography*. London: Sage.

Hine, C. (Ed.). (2005). *Virtual methods: Issues in social research on the Internet*. New York: Berg.

Hughes, J., King, V., Rodden, T., & Andersen, H. (1994). Moving out from the control room: Ethnography in system design. In *Proceedings of the ACM Conference on CSCW*, Chapel Hill, USA, October 22-26 (pp. 429-439). New York: ACM Press.

Johns, M. D., Chen, S.-L. S., & Hall, G. J. (Eds.). (2004). *Online social reseach: Methods, issues & ethics* (Vol. 7). New York: Peter Lang.

Jones, S. (Ed.). (1999). *Doing Internet research: Critical issues and methods for examining the Net*. London: Sage.

Kaye, R. (2004, May 3). *Next-generation file sharing with social networks*. Retrieved February 4, 2006, from http://www.openp2p.com/pub/a/p2p/2004/03/05/ file_share.html

Kelly, S. U., Sung, C., & Farnham, S. (2002). Designing for improved social responsibility, user participation and content in on-line communities. In *Proceedings of the CHI2002*, Minneapolis, Minnesota, USA, April 20-25 (pp. 391-398). New York: ACM Press.

Kim, A. J. (2000). *Community building on the Web: Secret strategies for successful online communities*. Berkley, CA: Peachpit Press.

Klamer, A. (2003). Gift economy. In R. Towse (Ed.), *A handbook of cultural economics* (pp. 241-247). Cheltenham, UK: Edward Elgar Publishing.

Kollock, P. (1998a). Design principles for online communities. *PC Update, 15*, 58-60.

Kollock, P. (1998b). Social dilemmas: The anatomy of cooperation. *Annual Review of Sociology, 24*, 183-214.

Kolm, S. C. (2000). Introduction: The economics of reciprocity, giving and altruism. In L. A. Gérard-Varet, S. C. Kolm, & J. M. Ythier (Eds.), *The economics of reciprocity, giving and altruism* (pp. 1-44). London: MacMillan Press.

Komter, A. E. (1996). Reciprocity as a principle of exclusion. *Sociology, 30*(2), 299-316.

Krishnan, R., Smith, M. D., Tang, Z., & Telang, R. (2004). The impact of free-riding on peer-to-peer networks. In *Proceedings of the 37th Hawaii International Conference on System Sciences,* Hawaii, January 5-8 (p. 70199c). Washington D.C.: IEEE Computer Society.

Lakhani, K. R., & Wolf, R. G. (2003). *Why hackers do what they do: Understanding motivation effort in free/open source software projects* (No. Working Paper 4425-03). MIT Sloan School of Management.

LaRose, R., Lai, Y.-J., Lange, R., Love, B., & Wu, Y. (2005). Sharing or piracy? An exploration of downloading behavior. *Journal of Computer Mediated Communication, 11*(1). Retrieved August 14, 2006, from http://jcmc.indiana.edu/vol11/issue1/larose.html

Levine, S. S. (2001). Kindness in cyberspace? The sharing of valuable goods online. In *Proceedings of the 10th Annual EICAR Conference,* Bilbao, Spain, March 3-6 (pp. 86-112). Freidberg: EICAR.

Markham, A. N. (2004). The Internet as research context. In C. Seale, J. Gubrium, G. Gobo, & D. Silverman (Eds.), *Qualitative research practice* (pp. 358-374). London: Sage.

McGee, K., & Skågeby, J. (2004). Gifting technologies. *First Monday, 9*(12). Retrieved August 14, 2006, from http://www.firstmonday.dk/Issues/issue9_12/mcgee/

Mello, J. P. (2004, Nov 16). *Wirehog P2P melds social networks and file-sharing.* Retrieved February 4, 2006, from http://www.technewsworld.com/story/38188.html

Nardi, B. A., Whittaker, S., & Schwarz, H. (2002). NetWORKers and their activity in intensional networks. *Journal of Computer Supported Cooperative Work, 11*(1-2), 205-242.

Ngan, T.-W. J., Wallace, D. S., & Druschel, P. (2003). Enforcing fair sharing of peer-to-peer resources. In *Proceedings of the IPTPS '03-2nd International Workshop on Peer-to-Peer Systems*, Berkeley, CA, February 20-21 (pp. 149-159). Berlin; New York: Springer Verlag.

O'Day, V. L., Bobrow, D. G., & Shirley, M. (1996). The socio-technical design cycle. In *Proceedings of the ACM Conference on Computer Supported Cooperative Work '96*, Cambridge, MA, USA, November 16-20 (pp. 160-169). New York: ACM Press.

Orbell, J., & Dawes, R. (1981). Social dilemmas. In G. M. Stephenson, & J. M. Davis (Eds.), *Progress in applied psychology* (Vol. 1, pp. 37-65). Chichester; New York: John Wiley & Sons.

Preece, J. (2000). *Online communities: Designing usability, supporting sociability.* West Sussex, England: John Wiley & Sons.

Premkumar, G. P. (2003). Alternate distribution strategies for digital music. *Communications of the ACM, 46*(9), 89-95.

Ranganathan, K., Ripeanu, M., Sarin, A., & Foster, I. (2004). Incentive mechanisms for large collaborative resource sharing. In *Proceedings of the CCGrid 2004 - 4th IEEE/ACM International Symposium on Cluster Computing and the Grid*, Chicago, April 19-22 (pp. 1-8). Washington D.C.: IEEE Computer Society.

Romano, N. C., Donovan, C., Chen, H., & Nunamaker, J. (2003). A methodology for analyzing Web-based qualitative data. *Journal of Management Information Systems, 19*(4), 213-246.

Roush, W. (2005, November 18). Social networking 3.0 – The third generation of social-networking technology has hit the Web, and it's about content as much as contacts. *Technology Review.* Retrieved February 4, 2006, from http://www.technologyreview.com/InfoTech-Networks/wtr_15908,258,p1.html

Sanghavi, S., & Hajek, B. (2005). A new mechanism for the free-rider problem. In *Proceedings of the 2005 ACM SIGCOMM Workshop on Economics of Peer-to-Peer Systems P2PECON '05,* Philadelphia, August 22 (pp. 122-127). New York: ACM Press.

Shirky, C. (2003, October 12). *File-sharing goes social.* Retrieved February 5, 2006, from http://www.shirky.com/writings/file-sharing_social.html

Shneidman, J., & Parkes, D. C. (2003). Rationality and self-interest in peer to peer networks. In *Proceedings of the IPTPS '03-2nd International Workshop on Peer-to-Peer Systems*, Berkeley, CA, February 20-21 (pp. 139-148). Berlin; Heidelberg: Springer Verlag.

Skågeby, J. (2003). *Sharing digital goods – The potential importance of giving* (White Paper No. SAR03-03). Linköping. Retrieved from http://www.santa-anna.se/projectbriefs/AmIGo_WhitePaper.pdf

Skågeby, J. (2006). *Public and non-public gifting on the Internet* (Licentiate Thesis, Linköping Studies in Science and Technology, Thesis No. 1244), Linköping University, Sweden.

Skågeby, J., & Pargman, D. (2005). File-sharing relationships – Conflicts of interest in online gift-giving. In *Proceedings of the 2nd International Conference on Communities and Technologies*, Milano, Italy, June 13-16 (pp. 111-127). Dordrecht; Berlin; New York: Springer Verlag.

Sproull, L., Conley, C., & Moon, J. Y. (2005). Prosocial behavior on the Net. In Y. Amichai-Hamburger (Ed.), *The social Net: Human behavior in cyberspace* (pp. 139-162). Oxford: Oxford University Press.

Taylor, A. S., & Harper, R. (2002). Age-old practices in the "new world": A study of gift-giving between teenage mobile phone users. In *Proceedings of the SIGCHI conference on Human Factors in Computing Systems: Changing our world, Changing Ourselves*, Minneapolis, Minnesota, USA, April 20-25 (pp. 439-446). New York: ACM Press.

Voida, A., Grinter, R. E., Ducheneaut, N., Edwards, W. K., & Newman, M. W. (2005). Listening in: Practices surrounding iTunes music sharing. In *Proceedings of the CHI 2005*, Portland, Oregon, USA, April 2-7 (pp. 191-200). New York: ACM Press.

Zeitlyn, D. (2003). Gift economies in the development of open source software. *Research Policy, 32*(7), 1287-1291.

Chapter XII

Mobile Networked Text Communication:
The Case of SMS and Its Influence on Social Interaction

Louise Barkhuus
University of Glasgow, UK

Abstract

This chapter introduces a qualitative study of the use of mobile text messaging (SMS) and reflects on how SMS influences social interaction. It describes how this new communication technology is used to maintain social relations and how it generally assists users in their everyday activities. Three issues are highlighted: how users use SMS to overcome shyness, how they use it for micro-grooming, and how they are able to control messages to their advantage. It is argued that SMS facilitates users in their everyday life through the ways it supports awareness and accountability. These characteristics make the communication channel a "social translucent" technology, contributing to its popularity. It is suggested that simple information and communication technologies such as SMS can provide powerful tools in new designs of information and communication technologies.

Introduction

Telephony is a communication technology that has altered our social practices in many ways, a change that has taken place over many decades (Fischer, 1992). The adoption of mobile telephony relied in many ways upon the century long diffusion of fixed line telephony. Still, researchers have been intrigued by the changing behaviour within many user groups that the mobile phone has brought about. Recent research in particular has looked at behavioural changes as people deal with being only "a phone call away" from each other (Brown, 2002; Katz & Aakhus, 2002). One of the most unlikely successes has been text messaging or SMS[1] (short message service), which, even with a limit of 160 characters, has become a very common medium of electronic communication in many parts of the world, particularly Europe and many parts of Asia. Text messaging has received considerable attention, with some researchers going so far as to argue that SMS—rather than voice calls—has been the major force in the adoption of mobile phones (Jenson, 2005). The mobile phone is not just acquired for keeping in touch with loved ones during the odd day away from home, but also for the practicalities it solves on an everyday basis, from reminders to buy milk, to arranging a birthday party for a friend. Early research on SMS use suggested that its popularity, especially among teenagers, was due to the controlled cost that SMS provides (Grinter & Eldridge, 2001). However, later research tends to differ from this, emphasizing the efficiency of the asynchronous communication model (Jenson, 2005).

Moving beyond questions of why SMS has become popular, this chapter focuses on how text messages fit into users' everyday lives and existing social practices. The chapter explores in detail how SMS is used among a group of young adults to manage the mundane activities of their lives by focusing on how text messages fit into the lives of users as well as how it both supports existing social practices and creates new ones. Instead of asking why users use "tedious" texting rather than "swift" phone calls (for example, Grinter & Eldrige, 2001; Ito & Okabe, 2005), we approach the medium with the view that mobile phones are now being bought and used as much for text messaging as for voice calls, especially in the Nordic countries where our study took place. This study provides support of how this seemingly simple communication medium is powerful enough to add new structures to users' lives without dominating their daily life. With the changing structures in users' lives, issues of design arise. Underestimating the simplicity of design within communication technologies is a threat to the potential creativity with which the user can shape the technology. Implications are therefore emphasized in relation to the design and adoption of information and communication technologies.

Background and Related Research

SMS was originally implemented into the GSM standard for mobile phone communication in the late 1980s as a replacement for pagers (Kopomaa, 2005). It was envisioned as an extra tool that business people would use on rare occasions to send messages, in a similar way as to how a pager sent a single phone number. The reasoning behind this was partly that messages were, and generally still are, limited to 160 characters and partly that the mobile phone manufactures and carriers could not imagine anyone wanting to type messages with a twelve-button keypad. However, after a slow start, SMS took off at incredible rates in the late 1990s in unison with teleoperators' subsidizing of handsets, making mobile telephones affordable for many people. In 1997, Finland, one of the earliest countries to adopt SMS, even offered it at no cost because of competition among teleoperators (Kopomaa, 2005). Figure 1 shows the increasing number of text messages sent in Denmark in the years before our study. Teenagers, in particular, represented a surprising group for the adoption of mobile telephony and, as will be elaborated upon later, much previous research has focused on this user group. A number of researchers have argued that SMS, rather than the possibility for mobile voice calls, was the main reason for teenagers' high adoption of mobile phones (Ling, 2004). Studies have looked into why teenagers have been so eager to use both mobile phones (Ling, 2004) and text messaging in Europe and Japan (Grinter & Eldridge, 2001; Ito & Okabe, 2005) as well as how they use this mobile communication technology.

Studies of Mobile Phones and SMS

Previous studies of SMS use have often been part of broader studies into the use of mobile telephony, with SMS considered as an alternative to voice communi-

Figure 1. The development of SMS traffic in relation to the number of subscriptions in Denmark between 2001 and 2005

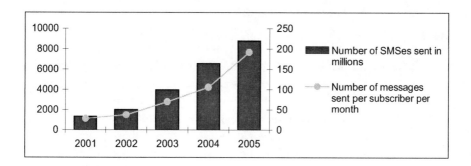

cation rather than as a medium in its own right. However, several recent studies have looked specifically at the use of "text messaging". The book, *The Inside Text* (Harper, Palen, & Taylor, 2005) collects a number of studies of SMS use as well as design issues in relation to digital text communication in a broader sense. Several studies of mobile phone use (including SMS) and only SMS use concentrate their observations on teenagers. Grinter and Eldridge (2001), for example, were among the first to explore the use of text messaging among teenagers, investigating why they have been so eager in their adoption of mobile phones and in particular text messaging. They describe how text messaging helps teenagers retain their privacy in a parent-controlled life and how they maintain social relations outside school. Alternatively, Taylor and Harper (2002) focus on the significance teenagers give to text messages themselves, comparing their communication to "gift-giving" practices. Both studies emphasize the "leisure and fun" aspects of the medium among teenage user groups, although Ling (2004) later emphasizes how (virtually) all age groups in Norway use text messages for "micro-coordination" and organizational practicalities. Ling's work is important in how it connects text messaging to broader social practices (such as arranging to meet), yet there is little discussion of the broader social contexts where text messaging takes place, such as public places.

A common finding in the literature is that text messaging increases "ad hoc" coordination (Brown, 2002; Jenson, 2005; Ling, 2004). Ling calls this micro-coordination and describes how messages are often relied upon in situations of coordinating social life, not just for teenagers (Ling, 2004). Another well-cited finding is how text messaging is a tool for users to avoid surveillance or control over their relationships (particularly parental for teenagers) (Elwood-Clayton, 2005; Grinter & Eldridge, 2001; Ito & Okabe, 2005). Since the participants in our study were not under any parental control, this issue was not a factor. However, expectations from others were found to manifest themselves within other areas of their social life, making this an issue worth exploring. Indeed, one neglected aspect of the earlier literature is how less direct social regulations such as social relationship principles also influence the use of SMS.

In relation to other communication technologies, SMS is a "lean" medium because messages are limited in length and as text only; a lean communication medium is here defined as single channel, compared to rich communication channels that contain, for example, both image and audio, or are synchronous. The limitations of texting make it difficult to compare and relate to multi-channel systems such as videoconferencing or synchronous voice communication. It appears that it would be difficult for such a lean medium to support a socially important and profound interaction of *social translucence*. Social translucence in a communication system is defined as support for coherent behaviour by making participants' activities visible and supporting communication effortlessly, for example. Erickson and Kellogg (2000) describe the advantages of a socially translucent system in that it provides the user with salient characteristics that support coherent behaviour and social activities. They mention three principles for obtaining social translucence: visibility, awareness, and accountability. A medium needs to afford visibility so that users can see the activities of each other; it needs to provide users with an awareness of the other people's presence; and finally, it needs to make users accountable for their interactions. Interestingly, two of these principles are in fact applicable to the SMS medium and thereby contribute to the medium's usefulness, particularly in social situations. Although the users' current activities are not visible to each other, as we will show in this study, messaging provides both awareness among users and accountability as the communication is instantly saved on the phone. As will be elaborated on through the present case study, SMS therefore provides, to a great extent, social translucence.

In our study, we aimed to look at the social management and general practices that govern the use of SMS by young adults in their everyday life. Young adults between 20 and 35 are an interesting group to study for two reasons. First, they have different life styles than teenagers, who live with their parents or at a dormitory in a frequently semi-controlled environment. Second, they often have fewer monetary concerns than teenagers, who most often depend on pocket money and jobs after school. Few studies of SMS include other age groups, noticeably because text messaging is used much less among people over thirty (although this is rapidly changing, as Ling (2004) points out). Moreover, studies that do include users in their early twenties often also include teenagers and thereby study a group with mixed concerns. Examples include socio-linguistic analysis of SMS messages among 12 to 25 year olds (Hård af Segerstad, 2005) and a cultural comparison between French and Japanese users where the French participants were between 15 and 28 years old (Riviere & Licoppe, 2005). The influence of text messaging on teenage culture is important to explore since new practices have been discovered although many of these practices are to be found among young adults as well. These are some of the issues that will be presented here, based on a qualitative study of text message use among young adults.

Text Messaging in the Lives of Young Adults

Methods

The first part of this study was carried out over two weeks. Twenty-one participants kept a journal every evening, describing messages received and sent that day. In addition, the journal asked participants to describe their location when messages were sent/received and the motivation for initiating messaging. Most of the participants had mobile phones that saved both outgoing and incoming messages. This enabled them to remember the messages for the diary in the evening, however, a few participants had to rely on memory in regard to outgoing messages. After two weeks, we conducted more in-depth interviews with seven of the participants, having them elaborate upon motivations and specifics of their SMS habits. These were selected from high-level users among the 21 participants and the aim was to interview a diverse subset of the group. All seven who were asked agreed to be interviewed.

The study took place in Denmark, where the rate of mobile phones was 85 phones per 100 inhabitants at the time of the study (Telecom Statistics, 2003). The participants were young adults, ranging from 21 to 36 years of age. Participants were recruited by way of e-mail lists and personal contacts (none of the participants were personally known to the author prior to the study), the main criterion being that the participants had a mobile phone.

We aimed for a diverse set of participants, not a representative set, and while this naturally limits generalization among SMS users, a purposeful selection enables insight into information rich cases, desirable in a qualitative study such as this. None of the participants had owned a mobile phone for less than two years. The participants were a mix of students (undergraduate and graduate) and young professionals. The students were mainly graduate students studying for their master's degree in subjects such as information science and political science while the professionals worked in jobs as varied as painter, waiter, and forester. A characteristic that we aimed for in recruiting participants was having an "adult life style"; this included having their own income and living either by themselves or with a partner or roommate. By studying independent adults, limitations that apply to teenage groups were minimized, and the study would provide insights into a group with a more consistent life style.

Table 1. Participant demographics

Participants	Diary study	Interviews
Number (male/female)	21 (9/12)	7 (3/4)
Age range	21-36	21-32
Students/non-students	14/8	4/3
Living with partner or room mate/living alone	9/12	3/4

General Trends of Mobile Text Communication

While the participant's diaries gave a good, if basic, impression of how SMS fits into their everyday life, the interviews provided a better understanding of motives for use. SMS was generally used for the coordination and up keep of social life, with some use of texting for work coordination. The more messages participants wrote per day, the more diverse uses text message were put to; in other words, when participants used many text messages, they communicated with a larger number of different people in different relationships such as work and family. All participants used SMS on an everyday basis. The average was four messages sent and four received per day; however the participant's level of use differed considerably. Five participants averaged only about three and a half sent and received messages per day; two participants sent and received on average 19 and 20 messages per day. Most participants sent as many messages as they received except for a few exceptions; one woman for example sent on average nine and received only four messages per day.

Relationships

The participants were asked to record to whom they sent and received messages according to relationship. The graph in Figure 2 identifies the average number of messages per day that participants reported sending and receiving, according to whether they reported having a partner or not. As shown, participants mostly communicated with friends or acquaintances and significant others. Only six of the 21 participants texted with members of their family during the two weeks, most often

Figure 2. The types of relationships SMS supported for our participants

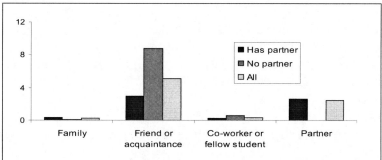

siblings and in one case the participant's mother. However, all of the participants who had a significant other, communicated with him or her almost every day.

The interviews supplied a more nuanced description of the participants' core "SMS group". For one female participant, aged 25, the group was very broad; she was the head of a political organization and often coordinated meetings over SMS. Because of this coordination with other members, she received almost three times as many text messages as she sent. She said that SMS enabled her to control her communication and that she could not imagine having to coordinate this via voice communication or e-mail. A male participant, aged 21, on the other hand, used SMS to communicate mainly with friends of both genders to coordinate evening arrangements and to meet up with friends in a casual way. Another participant used SMS on several occasions to reach his manager when the manager was out of the office or away on an international business trip.

Messaging Purpose

Text messaging was used for both social organization and professional communication. A very general taxonomy of message topics was proposed in the diary where participants were asked to characterize their messages as either coordination and practical information, social-based, or other. During analysis, this characterization was checked from the content of the messages. This showed that 55% of the messages were regarding coordination and practical information. Examples of this type of message include organization of future meetings or real-time meetings ("We are at the Mexi-Bar") and a participant coordinating gift buying with her sister. This finding is similar to what other studies report; Ling, for example, found that many users' messages mainly regard micro-coordination (Ling, 2004). Thirty-three percent of the messages were socially based and included goodnight messages and non-essential politeness ("Have a good vacation, see you soon"), and 12% were uncharacterized according to the two previously-mentioned categories.

Similarly to other communication technologies, the social context of the user influences how SMS is used. But where the context of stationary media such as PC-based e-mail or instant messaging is more predictable, mobile text messaging context is more varied. The mobile aspect in this regard facilitates a transformation in users' behaviour and attitude. One way this change was illustrated in the case study was through the messages that, according to the participants, would never have been passed on by other means if SMS had not been available. One interviewee, a 25-year old graduate student, said that she often sent little "I will be a bit late" messages, in situations where she would never have called. SMS was discrete and practical for such purposes, and the majority of participants confirmed this. SMS was used to manage participants' busy life style in relation to both work/study and social obligations.

Social Context of SMS

In other studies, the use of SMS has been found to contribute to more loose social arrangements in the social lives of users (Ling, 2004; Ito & Okabe, 2005). We found that loose social arrangements have extensive consequences to the participants' behaviour and therefore focus the analysis on user's social life and everyday practice as well. Instead of looking at SMS messages in isolation, we find it essential to describe the participants' SMS messages in relation to their social practices.

SMS supports ordinary and existing social practices in new ways. For our participants, SMS was valuable not because it was hugely different from other existing communication technologies such as voice over phone or e-mail, but rather for how it supported more *subtlety, spontaneity,* and *mobility* in their existing communication. We found three characteristics of their life style were important to the SMS users, each one relating closely to how they perceive that they have changed since SMS became available to them. First, many participants used SMS to overcome shyness; second, most of them practiced social grooming with messages that would not have taken place without SMS; and third, participants used SMS to control their communication with others. Each of these parts is elaborated upon next.

Overcoming Shyness

Shyness is part of many people's personality, and our participants were not much different. Many of them were shy about talking in public on their mobile phone, and some expressed reservations about calling people they were not very close to or perhaps wanted to become more close to. SMS provided a simple and unobtrusive method of distance communication, which enabled them to maintain spontaneous as well as frequent contact with others.

Many of our participants commented that they would send an SMS rather than calling to avoid talking in public. As one female interviewee explains: "I don't like to talk on the phone when I am outside, I actually don't like to talk on the phone at all. I just think SMS is so much easier". Although voice communication in public *was* used by the participants according to their diary and the interviews, several of our interview participants said that they tried to avoid this as much as possible by using SMS. In crowded public spaces, a spoken voice call made at least one side of the communication publicly available to others, and participants sometimes felt they were intruding on the privacy of others by talking on the bus or on the train for example. SMS messages, however, are essentially private. SMS thus offered advantages by supporting communication without attracting attention to the individual.

Another aspect of shyness concerned the actual communication content. In a number of cases, the participant found it easier to communicate invitations to acquaintances and friends by SMS rather than by phone. For example, one male participant aged 21 said that he would have found it difficult to casually call up a friend to ask if she wanted to come along to a club that night, but asking her via SMS was easy. The casualness of SMS corresponds well with the casualness of asking someone to an informal gathering among friends. The participant admitted in the latter part of the interview that he did not like phoning people at all and that he would even not see some of his friends as much if he was not able to SMS them on a regular basis. He explains:

"This girl, Linda, I would never call her, but we often SMS about where we are meeting, say, Saturday night, with the others. Sometime we also just chat, like, during the course of the day. But I don't think I would call her."

SMS enabled this participant to contact a friend where it would have been socially awkward for him to call her. In addition to other studies where SMS is found to assist the development of relationships (e.g., Elwood-Clayton, 2005; Grinter & Eldridge, 2003), SMS supports communication without the commitment and immediate reply required in a telephone call. One can send a one line SMS, or reply at leisure, without having to commit to a spoken conversation that can potentially be awkward.

In the earlier cases, SMS helped users who were shy (although most of our participants confessed to being shy in some way or another); in addition SMS allowed users to carefully manage their interactions turn by turn. This gave the users a sense of control when communicating, and they would have time to think before answering. The control that the asynchronous communication provided was essentially a "remedy" for the shyness expressed in relation to certain people.

The power of SMS is clearly illustrated in how it enables users to keep in contact with people with whom they would not keep as close contact with otherwise. However, participants may not be aware what they would do (or would have done) without SMS. Many studies have shown an increasing level of "ad hoc" arrangements with SMS due to its commonality and spread (Ling, 2004; Riviera & Licoppe, 2005), but no studies point to people being more social because of SMS. This was confirmed by our own study. One participant in the study even reflects on whether she actually *does* see her friends more often and has more "spur of the moment" meetings than she would have had without her mobile phone. First, the participant says that she feels that SMS gives her the possibility to be more spontaneous, but she then questions whether she *is* more spontaneous in regards to social activities:

"Hmmm, I don't know. I don't know if I would have called before [having the possibility to SMS]. I think we are [more spontaneous], but I am not sure if it is always

possible, because people actually do a lot of things, so it is often difficult to get it coordinated. Even if I have an hour where I can drink a cup of coffee, it is not always that my girlfriends can do that [at the same time]. So I don't know if it is actually happening that much. I think it stays with the agreement of 'lets SMS each other when we know we have ehm... some time'. And then time passes..."

Distinguishing between factors that influence users' motivation to use SMS and the consequences of it is important in this case. Where reasons for using SMS may be to better control communication (and thereby overcome shyness), the consequences for users' social life is not that the user socializes with more or different people, but merely the fact that they *experience* a more casual way of meeting up with others. By using SMS, they find that mundane communication in their everyday life is less complicated and intrusive.

Micro-Grooming

An important finding was that SMS was used to support "micro-grooming". Thirty-three percent of the messages in the diary were characterized as "social up-keeping" messages—messages that served no purpose in terms of planning or information aim, but were merely aimed at keeping up socially. Ling (2004) describes these messages as a form of social grooming. For example, the diary data contained messages such as "thank you for tonight" and a participant wishing a friend a good holiday. Because SMS is very "affordable" (both money-wise and effort-wise), our participants emphasized that these social maintenance messages would not have been expressed if they could not be sent via SMS. The "smallness" of SMS was a key aspect of the communication. In this way, these messages were more a form of micro-grooming—a wink or a small note—rather than the engaged level of interaction required by a call.

One example of this micro-grooming was a male interviewee who sent a message asking how his friend did at an exam. He explained that this was not something he would have called his friend about, but because he knew the friend had just had an important exam, he sent the SMS as part of "proper social behaviour". Another participant described in his diary how he and his friends competed to come up with the funniest movie quotes during the day:

"It is wonderful to have contact to a friend, also even if it is just gossip! It shows that they/I, during the course of the day, have thought about each other and done something about it. I got some laughs and so did my friends!"

Another example was a female participant, age 25, who sent a message to a friend living abroad and wished her a good holiday. She described that she would not have called her up or e-mailed her if SMS had not been available, but the possibility of SMS made her send an "extra message" in addition to the conversation they had had three days ago. She found messaging increased the closeness to her friend since they could communicate in an inexpensive and simple way.

These messages added to users' everyday lives and illustrate how people find it important and pleasant to stay in contact with both close and peripheral friends with "micro-grooming" messages. They are part of common politeness and have seemingly grown out of SMS technology. Comparable behaviour is one of "giving regards" to someone else; with SMS, this is being done directly rather than through someone else. It can lead to an awareness of other people's presence but also disappointment when users begin to expect these messages. Like other new communication media, SMS is still in its facilitation phase, meaning different things to different people.

Controlling the Communication

Participants' motivation for using SMS may seem straightforward; participants themselves emphasized the simplicity, discreteness, and asynchronous aspects of using SMS. However, a closer examination of our interviews revealed an additional factor: the concern that SMS senders gave to how their messages would be received, and the situation the receiver was in when they received the message. This concern, in return, resulted in meticulous composing of messages.

SMS allowed users to request a different level of attention than that of a phone call. This different level could be used to change the *meaning* of a call—for example, from a call asking why someone is late to a message notifying the recipient where they are. One female participant, for example, describes a message in her diary:

[The message was regarding] where exactly we had arranged to meet. We were actually standing at two different entrances [to the theatre]. I SMSed because I didn't want to call in case she was just a bit late. ... It was just to say where she could find me, without seeming too impatient.

This participant sent a message that from her point of view was a question asking where the other person was, but in the form of a message about where she herself was. This allowed her to avoid appearing impatient. In composing messages, users gave considerable thought to how they would be received, and this often made SMS the preferred medium for situations in which to get across important messages.

Another participant described texting her flat-mate, telling her that she was not coming home that night. She explained in her diary that she used SMS because it seemed casual and it would have been "silly to call". She thereby controlled how her friend received the information by choosing SMS rather than a voice call. While messages are used for fun and non-essential information, such as indicated by for example Grinter and Eldridge (2001), they are also incredibly valuable in how they support this subtlety of communication and respect for social relations.

One of the more cited complications with mobile telephony is the constant availability that users feel they have to live up to, especially in the initial phases of getting accustomed to mobile phones (Brown, 2002; Gant & Kiesler, 2002). In contrast, for our participants, SMS helped adjust the need for availability. By not having to answer a ringing immediately, as is the case with voice communication, participants were able to manage their communication in a controlled way. Although efficiency was the most cited reason for this need to control availability, the desire *not* to talk with a specific person was also important; one participant explained that she had sent an SMS to her mother because she just "couldn't handle the talking". In other situations, knowledge of the receiver's situation influences the choice of medium; another participant, for example, knew that her friend was in a meeting and therefore felt an SMS was more appropriate. She did not address the possibility to postpone the communication, which shows that constant availability is often taken for granted.

Returning to the three criteria for social translucence—accountability, awareness, and visibility—, these characteristics are relevant in relation to the controlling that SMS encourages. First of all, users put such great trust in messages that they hold each other accountable for receiving messages. Although some participants expressed that there were several people they could not use SMS to communicate with (most often because the recipient's lack of texting skills, less often because their lack of a mobile phone), the ones they did SMS with were trusted to always receive and answer messages. It is a stored medium, where both sender and recipient can access messages later, thereby giving it more weight and accountability. In terms of awareness, SMS provides users with, if not a direct awareness, then a perceived awareness of always being close to one another. This is naturally tied closely to the mobile phone as such, where the fact it is mobile is more important than the fact it is limited to text communication. However, the way SMS is used to keep in touch with micro-grooming messages supports the awareness factor to a great extent. The messages are often sent solely to make the recipient aware that the sender is thinking of him or her. Finally, the notion of visibility is blatantly lacking. The sender of an SMS has no idea of the visual context of the recipient, and the mobile factor means that they could be in any unusual situation. However, this also applies to voice phone calls, and we therefore argue that SMS in a sense allows for this lack of visibility by being discrete. When users are not sure what context the recipient is in, they send a message rather than risk a phone call that would be left unanswered. The SMS medium is therefore a good example of a social translucent system.

Mobile Text Communication as a New Type of Communication

As described earlier, SMS communication not only adds new behaviour to users' social life style and assists in many mundane everyday social practices, it also functions as a social medium for general up-keeping among friends and sometimes colleagues. It is argued here that SMS constitutes a new type of communication that is already an important and integrated part of the lives of young adults. Although the design and implementation of SMS were not intended for this massive use, it is important to consider the next design directions that these types of communication technologies might take. The possibility to expand text messaging with pictures and even audio or video clips has not gone unnoticed by mobile phone providers in Europe and most mobile phones released today offer multimedia services (MMS) alongside SMS capabilities. These, however, have not proven as popular as plain text messages for a multitude of reasons (such as price, complicated functionality, and lack of interest, among other reasons outside the scope of this chapter), and the consequence is that SMS use is still rapidly increasing around the world. As described in the introduction and illustrated throughout this chapter, SMS is a powerful yet simple medium that affords many types of socially based communication.

Implications for Future Information and Communication Technologies

Designing information and computing technologies (ICT) requires insight into users' everyday practices with communication and where new technologies might spur new practices. It is not necessarily from rigid design considerations that this emerges, as the example of SMS shows. Had mobile phone manufacturers and service providers been able to predict the popularity of mobile text messaging, they would have focused both design and advertising on SMS much earlier than they did. Handsets with full keyboards would have been available and promoted earlier, and marketing would have focused on pricing schemes for texting rather than voice telephony as happened in the middle and late '90s when mobile telephony took off. Because SMS has been shown to alter users' way of communicating and plan social activities, it is imperative to recognize that designers and researchers should not underestimate the power of simplicity in communication technologies. Videoconferencing may seem rich and empowering in many situations because more information is available, through both visual means as well as audio, but the complexity in interpreting more than one channel (audio and video) often results in users rejecting it (Erickson & Kellogg, 2000). This is important to remember when mobile videophones become more common. With a single channel communication medium, limitations are used to the users' advantage, as has been shown here. Design and research should therefore embrace both rich and lean types of communication but in particular the dynamics that make them work for users. For example, text messages can be defined easily by the features they do not have, such as fast text entry, long message length, tone of voice, and quick interaction. The feature of mobility, however, far outweighs the shortcomings of the medium. Therefore, it is important not to simply count the features of ICTs but rather weigh them in relation to each other.

SMS is just one example of how very simple networked communication can support users' everyday practices and social life. Other text communication such as instant messaging is another example of a communication channel that adds to the range of communication possibilities in many people's life. The synchronicity of this medium makes fluent conversations possible, which is a major difference compared to the message exchange with SMS. The advantage is a more smooth conversation, but the disadvantage in comparison to SMS is that immediate replies are required. Consequently, asynchronicity was one of the issues participants highlighted as a major benefit of SMS. All in all, the two communication media are not directly comparable in their use, but they both function as good examples of essential communication springing from simple media.

The last issue to emphasize in relation to communication technology design is therefore not to misjudge the creativity of the user. If designers assume that limited possibilities for rich communication will yield a limited amount of communication, the creativity of the user is underestimated. Users accept a technology if it supports a social or practical need and corresponds to their present life style. They have shown they are explorative and inventive in their way of using something as simple as texting.

Conclusion and Future Directions

Together with the mobile phone, SMS has been one of the more distinct innovations of ICTs in the past century. Not only has SMS altered users' behaviour, it also works as an integrated part of users' social life with few disadvantages in regards to their increased availability (as compared with mobile phones). Although many proclaim that text messages facilitate an increasing spontaneity in the lives of users, it has not been shown that SMS actually improves social settings such as increasing spontaneous meetings. Without directly comparing their behaviour to pre-SMS use (which to the author's knowledge no studies do at present), participants were likely correct in asserting that spontaneity is merely a feeling and not actual behaviour. Still, the perceived value that stems from the use of text messaging should not be disregarded. The study presented here has shown that SMS is used to both build and maintain important social relationships and by doing so, adding value to the lives of the participants.

As described in the introduction, the SMS medium provides both awareness and accountability for users. Users feel that they have a sense of awareness of their friends and acquaintances when SMS is available to them. The expectations that they are only a text message away, as well as the many "micro-grooming" messages create a sense of awareness. Users are held accountable for their communication, since they know that the message was sent to a device that the receiver carries with him/her almost everywhere; the SMS medium is mutually agreed upon to be a legitimate communication channel. The channel has in fact many aspects of being socially translucent. Even the concept of visibility was found to be relevant to the users; by sending text messages to each other and being in constant touch, the users often know where their friends are and what they are doing. In this sense, the medium also supports partial visibility.

This chapter has described three different social contexts and uses of SMS and argued why they are important in relation to future design of ICTs. The controlling of shyness that characterizes SMS use reinforces the advantages of a limited media of such short text. With limitations, the user does not have to excuse their brevity or find reasons *not* to use the potentially rich, audio or multi-channel medium to its limit; they are limited by the means of the technology. As illustrated by the findings, users do not necessarily want a rich communication medium to interact with on a daily basis. The exposure of private communication in the public sphere was to be avoided as much as possible by not talking on the phone but instead using silent text messaging.

Second, the study pointed to the concept of micro-grooming, a politeness focused type of communication that was part of the daily value that participants contributed to their use of SMS. These messages are not seen as essential for daily activities, but as essential for the maintenance of social relationships. Where users used the simplicity of text for simple but meaningful messages, it is important to realize that the power of the communication medium lies not only in its simplicity but also in its ubiquity. The mobile phone is carried everywhere, and the sender can be fairly certain that the receiver will get the message within a short time. The chance to wish an acquaintance good luck with an exam is only missed when the exam is over, so the greater time span that users have to wish good luck increases the chance that they will in fact do so by SMS.

Finally, we pointed to the controlling of the communication that the simplicity of SMS affords. Users can compose messages concisely without worrying about "accidentally" saying too much or saying the wrong thing, which they are concerned they might do in a voice conversation. They can phrase their messages to suit the situation and thereby control it more than in a synchronous conversation where speed is a factor.

In sum, SMS has shown itself to be a powerful communication technology, not only because of its mobility and simplicity but also because of the value users put into messages and the importance they attribute to this type of communication. The design considerations that arise from these findings are closely connected with the request for simple communication. ICTs might have much potential in relation to synchronous or video-based types of communication, but smaller more mobile devices become more powerful in social everyday settings, despite their communicative limitations.

Acknowledgments

The author would like to thank the participants of the study for their time. She is also grateful to Anna Vallgårda for assistance with the research. This study was funded by the Danish National Center for IT Research (CIT#313).

References

Brown, B. (2002). Studying the use of mobile technology. In B. Brown, N. Green, & R. Harper (Eds.), *Wireless world: Social and interactional aspects of the mobile age* (pp. 3-15). London; New York: Springer.

Elwood-Clayton, B. (2005). Desire and loathing in the cyber Philippines. In R. Harper, L. A. Palen, & A. Taylor (Eds.), *The inside text: Social, cultural and design perspectives on SMS* (pp. 195-218). Dordrecht: Springer.

Erickson, T., & Kellogg, W. A. (2000). Social translucence: An approach to designing systems that support social processes. *Transactions of Computer-Human Interaction, 7*(1), 59-83.

Fischer, C. S. (1992). *America calling: A social history of the telephone to 1940.* Berkeley: University of California Press.

Gant, D., & Kiesler, S. (2002). Blurring the boundaries: Cell phones, mobility, and the line between work and personal life. In B. Brown, N. Green, & R. Harper (Eds.), *Wireless world: Social and interactional aspects of the mobile age* (pp. 121-131). London; New York: Springer.

Grinter, R., & Eldridge, M. (2001). y do tngrs luv 2 txt msg. In *Proceedings of ECSCW '01,* Bonn, Germany, September 16-20 (pp. 219-238). Bonn: Kluwer Academic Publishers.

Grinter, R. E., & Eldridge, M. A. (2003). Wan2tlk? Everyday text messaging. In *Proceedings of the SIGCHI Conference on Human Factors in Computing Systems,* Ft. Lauderdale, FL, USA, April 5-10 (Vol. 441-448). New York: ACM Press.

Harper, R., Palen, L. A., & Taylor, A. (2005). *The inside text: Social, cultural and design perspectives on SMS.* Dordrecht: Springer.

Hård af Segerstad, H. (2005). Language in SMS – A socio-linguistic view. In R. Harper, L. A. Palen, & A. Taylor (Eds.), *The inside text: Social, cultural and design perspectives on SMS* (pp. 33-51). Dordrecht: Springer.

Ito, M., & Okabe, D. (2005). Intimate connections: Contextualizing Japanese youth and mobile messaging. In R. Harper, L. A. Palen, & A. Taylor (Eds.), *The inside text: Social, cultural and design perspectives on SMS* (pp. 127-143). Dordrecht: Springer.

Jenson, S. (2005). Default thinking: Why consumer products fail. In R. Harper, L. A. Palen, & A. Taylor (Eds.), *The inside text: Social, cultural and design perspectives on SMS* (pp. 305-324). Dordrecht: Springer.

Katz, J. E., & Aakhus, M. A. (2002). *Perpetual contact: Mobile communication, private talk, public performance.* Cambridge, UK; New York: Cambridge University Press.

Kopomaa, T. (2005). The breakthrough of text messaging in Finland. In R. Harper, L. A. Palen, & A. Taylor (Eds.), *The inside text: Social, cultural and design perspectives on SMS* (pp. 147-159). Dordrecht: Springer.

Ling, R. S. (2004). *The mobile connection: The cell phone's impact on society.* San Francisco, CA: Morgan Kaufmann.

Riviere, C. A., & Licoppe, C. (2005). From voice to text: Continuity and change in the user of mobile phones in France and Japan. In R. Harper, L. A. Palen, & A. Taylor (Eds.), *The inside text: Social, cultural and design perspectives on SMS* (pp. 103-126). Dordrecht: Springer.

Taylor, A. S., & Harper, R. (2002). Age-old practices in the "New World": A study of gift-giving between teenage mobile phone users. In *Proceedings of the SIGCHI Conference on Human Factors in Computing Systems: Changing Our World, Changing Ourselves,* Minneapolis, MN, USA, April 20-25 (pp. 439-446). New York: ACM Press.

Telecom Statistics (2003). *National IT and Telecom Agency Denmark*. Copenhagen: Ministry for Science, Technology and Development.

Endnote

[1] SMS will throughout this chapter be used to describe text messaging on mobile phones; this is to distinguish between that text messages over computers (instant messaging) and instant messaging services (such as AIM) available through some phones in for example the U.S.

About the Authors

Simon B. Heilesen is an associate professor in Net media and a member of the Communication Forms and Knowledge Production Research Group at the Department of Communication Studies, Roskilde University, Denmark. His principle research interests are HCI-design and communication planning for the World Wide Web, and learning and collaboration in Net environments. Since the early 1990s, he has been studying and practicing the design and evaluation of Net media products as well as Net-based/supported education and publishing, first at Copenhagen University, later at Roskilde University. He is a member of various university and national committees for the development and dissemination of information and communication technology in Higher Education. For more information, see http://www.ruc.dk/~simonhei.

Sisse Siggaard Jensen is an associate professor in Net media and a member of the Communication Forms and Knowledge Production Research Group at the Department of Communication Studies, Roskilde University, Denmark. Her recent research projects are interdisciplinary integrating research on areas such as reflective practices and designing in 3D virtual worlds; social interaction and communication in new media; knowledge sharing and management in practice, for example, in e-learning and multimedia business. She has been studying and practicing Net-based education for more than 15 years at various Danish universities and in several research projects: "Reflective Practices When Face-to-Interface", "Knowledge and Management in IT Firms", "The 3D Agora-world" EU project. A current research project is "Actors and Avatars Communicating in Virtual Worlds". Visual anthropology and video-ethnography inspires her empirical research.

*   *   *   *   *

Pieter Ballon is a programme manager at the Centre for Studies on Media, Information and Telecommunication (SMIT) of the Vrije Universiteit Brussel, which is part of the Flemish Interdisciplinary Institute for Broadband Technology (IBBT). He is also a senior consultant at TNO Information and Communication Technology (TNO-ICT). Previously, he has been head of the Network Economy and Cultural Industries research and consultancy team at TNO Strategy, Technology and Policy (TNO-STB). He specializes in new business models for mobile and fixed broadband services, on which topics he has published extensively. He has a master's degree in modern history (Catholic University of Leuven) and a degree in information and library science (University of Antwerp).

Jørgen P. Bansler is an associate professor in the Center for Information and Communication Technologies at the Technical University of Denmark. His research interests include computer-mediated communication, computer-supported collaborative work, information systems design, and organizational implementation and use of IT. His current research focuses on the use of information and communication technology in health care. Dr. Bansler holds a PhD in computer science from the University of Copenhagen, Denmark.

Louise Barkhuus is a research fellow at the University of Glasgow, Department of Computing Science. Her research focuses on ubiquitous computing and how this can be used in the real world, in particular in the context of leisure activities such as gaming and everyday communication. She received her PhD in 2004 from the IT University of Copenhagen. Her dissertation defined the context gap, a gap between context understandable for humans and context measured by technology. She plans to develop her present research to include health-related mobile computing aspects as well as home media technologies.

Keld Bødker, PhD, is an associate professor in computer science at Roskilde University, Denmark. His research interest is centred around the processes involved in the design and use of information systems in organizations. He has co-authored (with Finn Kensing and Jesper Simonsen) the book, *Participatory IT Design – Designing for Business and Workplace Realities* (MIT Press, 2004). He is currently involved in research on IT support for communication and coordination in health care.

Torkil Clemmensen has a background in psychology and holds a PhD in man-machine interaction from the Department of Psychology, University of Copenhagen. He has previously worked as a practicing social-clinical psychologist and has established a social skills training program for people diagnosed with schizophrenia. Since 1990, his research has focused on cooperation in small teams in safety critical and business domains, and on professionals' knowledge of usability. His focus is on methods and techniques for pre-investigation, analysis, design and test and evaluation of human-computer interfaces, cultural-cognitive perspectives on user representations, and online communities. He is currently an associate professor at the Copenhagen Business School.

Kathy Courtney is a senior lecturer in educational development in the Centre for Higher Education Development, Coventry University, UK. She has contributed in multiple ways to Coventry's networked learning implementation, including participation in the planning phase, supporting staff in taking up online learning, collaborating in faculty-based projects involving the use of technology, and the dissemination of examples of innovative online practice. Her research interests centre around e-learning, online accessibility, re-usable learning objects, and issues relating to the implementation of personal development portfolios.

Simon Delaere holds a Licentiate in communication sciences (VUB) and a master's degree in communications policy (University of Westminster). Following an internship at the Information Society DG of the European Commission, he joined the VUB's Centre for Studies on Media, Information and Telecommunication (SMIT) as a researcher. Within the Interdisciplinary Institute for Broadband Technology (IBBT), his research focus is on policy issues surrounding media and ICT in general, and on multi-track policies for innovation and competition in the audio-visual sector in particular. He has a specific interest in the interplay between the EU and national communication policies, and in the Public Service Broadcaster as a policy instrument.

Frances Deepwell, FSEDA, is a senior lecturer in educational development in the Centre for Higher Education Development, Coventry University, UK and currently course director for the Postgraduate Certificate in Learning and Teaching in Higher Education. Since 1998, she has worked extensively on the implementation of online learning across the university, including design and integration, administration, trouble-shooting, staff development, evaluation, and dissemination. Her research interests lie in evaluation and associated educational developments, in particular with regard to institutional change and learning technologies, and she has been involved in EU and national e-learning projects. Originally trained as a translator, she has over 10 years' experience in teaching using a wide range of evolving technologies, in community as well as university education.

Hanne Westh Nicolajsen is an assistant professor in the Center for Information and Communication Technologies at the Technical University of Denmark. Her research

interests include organizational implementation and use of IT, knowledge management, and computer-mediated communication. Her current research focus is on the
use of information and communication technology for innovation in the service
sector. Dr. Nicolajsen holds a PhD from the Technical University of Denmark.

Jo Pierson is a senior researcher at SMIT (Studies on Media, Information and
Telecommunication)—founding member of IBBT (Interdisciplinary Institute for
BroadBand Technology)—and holds a PhD in social science (communication
studies). In the past, he has worked as researcher-advisor for the Dutch knowledge
institute TNO in Delft. He now teaches bachelor's and master's courses on socio-
economic issues of the information society at the Vrije Universiteit Brussel in the
Department of Communication Studies. Dr. Pierson also holds a part-time research
position focused on applying social science research in the design and use of ICT.
His core expertise is situated in the field of innovation and strategic research on the
meaning and use of fixed and mobile media technologies at home, at work and in
public settings. In this domain, he is managing a range of projects. In addition, he
is doing research on involving users in technological development processes via
ethnographic study in test and experimentation platforms. He also publishes on the
adoption and domestication of ICT by small business (SMEs and micro-enterprises).
Other research areas include e-inclusion issues and information society policy at
European and national level.

Jens Kaaber Pors, PhD, is an ICT manager at Niels Steensens Gymnasium, Copenhagen, Denmark. His main interest is the development and employment of standard-
based information infrastructures for collaboration and other distributed activities,
such as e-learning and e-government. His PhD dissertation was entitled, "Integrating
Groupware and Distributed Work Practices" (Roskilde University, 2004).

Dan Saugstrup is a PhD student at the Center for Information and Communication
Technologies at the Technical University of Denmark. He received his BSc degree in
manufacturing engineering from the Copenhagen University College of Engineering
in 1999 and his MSc degree in information technology from the IT University of
Copenhagen in 2002. His main areas of research are within wireless technologies,
broadband developments, VoIP, mobility, and more generally techno-economic and
socio-economic aspects of information and communication technologies.

Nette Schultz is an associate professor at the Center for Information and Communication Technologies at the Technical University of Denmark. She received
her MScEE degree in 1991 and her PhD degree in 1995, both from the Technical
University, within the area of digital image analysis and applied statistics. After her

PhD, she worked for some time as a system consultant at IBM. Today she teaches and does research within the fields of human-computer interaction, application development, and artificial intelligence. She is the author of several refereed publications in journals, conference proceedings, and books covering these fields.

Jesper Simonsen, PhD, is an associate professor in computer science at Roskilde University, Denmark. His research interest is the study of work practices of users and designers for the purpose of offering theories and methods for systems design in an organizational context. He has co-authored (with Keld Bødker and Finn Kensing) the book, *Participatory IT Design – Designing for Business and Workplace Realities* (MIT Press, 2004), and he was a chapter editor of the book, *Social Thinking – Software Practice* (MIT Press, 2002). His current research, "Evidence-based IT Development", investigates how the effects of the use of a system could play a prominent role in the contractual definition of IT projects.

Jörgen Skågeby is a PhD student at the Department of Computer and Information Science the University of Linköping, Sweden. He is devoting his thesis to gift-giving behaviours in large scale online sharing networks, focusing on end-user concerns, and the ways in which systematic studies of them can inform the design of gifting technologies.

Dixi Louise Strand is an assistant professor at the IT-University of Copenhagen, working in the research group entitled Design of Organizational IT. Originally, she trained in science and technology studies (STS) and ethnography, and her research interests revolve around the analysis of distributed work practices, design and use of collaborative information systems, and more recently, IT in health care and initiatives for establishing shared care in the Danish health care sector. In her interdisciplinary research and teaching, she has also worked with user-centred development and use of ethnography in IT design.

Georg Strøm decided to become a specialist in usability and interaction design while working as a product manager in a marketing department, and he spent 15 years in various private companies before joining the Department of Computing Science (DIKU) at the University of Copenhagen as an associate professor. He has done research on mobile terminals, use of new types of written communication in software development and on how cultural differences influence the use of information technology. His other interests include fiction writing, martial arts, and his family. A selection of his articles and other information can be found at http://www.georg.dk.

Lene Sørensen is an associate professor at the Center for Information and Communication Technologies (CICT) at the Technical University of Denmark. She holds an MScEE degree from 1989 and a PhD from 1994 (both from the Technical University) in the area of applied statistics and mathematical modelling. In the years 1994-1996, she worked as a post doc at the Risø National Laboratory and was stationed at Lawrence Berkeley Laboratory, California. She has been at CICT since 1996. Her main research interests are within the fields of group decision support systems, IT strategies, and application development. She has published several refereed articles in journals and conference proceedings and is the author of a book.

Index